# ABOUT MIEKE BAL

# ABOUT MIEKE BAL

EDITED BY

DEBORAH CHERRY

WILEY-BLACKWELL
A John Wiley & Sons, Ltd., Publication

AAH
ASSOCIATION OF ART HISTORIANS

This edition first published 2008
Originally published as Volume 30, Issue 3 of *Art History*


Blackwell Publishing was acquired by John Wiley & Sons in February 2007. Blackwell's publishing program has been merged with Wiley's global Scientific, Technical, and Medical business to form Wiley-Blackwell.

*Registered Office*
John Wiley & Sons Ltd, The Atrium, Southern Gate, Chichester, West Sussex, PO19 8SQ, United Kingdom

*Editorial Offices*
350 Main Street, Malden, MA 02148-5020, USA
9600 Garsington Road, Oxford, OX4 2DQ, UK
The Atrium, Southern Gate, Chichester, West Sussex, PO19 8SQ, UK

For details of our global editorial offices, for customer services, and for information about how to apply for permission to reuse the copyright material in this book please see our website at www.wiley.com/wiley-blackwell.



A catalogue record for this book is available from the British Library.

*Library of Congress Cataloging-in-Publication Data*
About Mieke Bal/edited by Deborah Cherry.
p. cm. – (Art history special issues)
Includes bibliographical references and index.
ISBN 978-1-4051-8656-8 (pbk. : alk. paper)
1. Bal, Mieke, 1946- 2. Art criticism–Netherlands–History–20th century. 3. Art criticism–Netherlands–History–21st century. I. Cherry, Deborah.
N7483.B27A26 2008
700.92–dc22

2008030314

Set in 10/12pt SwiftEF-Regular by Macmillan India Ltd., Bangalore, India
Printed in Singapore by Markono Print Media Pte Ltd

01 2008

# CONTENTS

# NOTES ON CONTRIBUTORS

**Murat Aydemir** is Assistant Professor in Comparative Literature and Cultural Analysis at the University of Amsterdam, and research leader at the Amsterdam School for Cultural Analysis, courtesy of the Royal Netherlands Academy of Sciences. His *Images of Bliss: Ejaculation, Masculinity, Meaning* (Minnesota University Press) was published in the spring of 2007.

**Jill Bennett** is Director of the Centre for Contemporary Art and Politics at the University of New South Wales, where she is working on a number of international exhibition projects that explore intermedial and interdisciplinary practice. Her most recent book is *Empathic Vision: Affect, Trauma and Contemporary Art* (Stanford, 2005).

**Giovanni Careri** is Professor of the History and Theory of Art at the École des Hautes Études en Sciences Sociales in Paris. His scholarly interests centre on baroque art, and his publications include *Bernini: Flights of Love, the Art of Devotion* (University of Chicago Press, 1994) and *Baroques* (Princeton University, 2003). His most recent publication is *Gestes d'amour et de guerre. La Jérusalem Délivrée. Images et affects XVIe–XVIIIe siècles* (Publications de l'EHESS, Paris, 2005).

**Deborah Cherry** is Professor of Modern and Contemporary Art at the University of Amsterdam. Recent publications include *Spectacle and Display* (Oxford, 2008; co-edited with Fintan Cullen), *Location* (Oxford, 2007; co-edited with Fintan Cullen), *About Stephen Bann* (Oxford, 2006) and *Art: History: Visual: Culture* (Oxford, 2005).

**Hanneke Grootenboer** is University Lecturer in the History of Art at the University of Oxford. The author of *The Rhetoric of Perspective: Realism and Illusionism in Seventeenth-century Dutch Still-life Painting* (University of Chicago Press, 2005), she is currently preparing a book on eye miniatures and the history of vision.

**Michael Ann Holly** has been Director of the Research and Academic Program at the Clark Art Institute since 1999 and currently teaches in the graduate program of Williams College. In the recent past she has also been a Visiting Professor at M.I.T. and Northwestern University. A co-founder of the Visual and Cultural Studies Graduate Program at the University of Rochester, she was chair of the Art History Department there for thirteen years. The author or co-editor of several books on the subjects of the historiography and theory of art history – such as *Panofsky and the Foundations of Art History* (1984), *Visual Culture: Images and Inter-*

*pretations* (Wesleyan University Press, 1994), *Past Looking: Historical Imagination and the Rhetoric of Images* (Cornell University Press, 1996), *The Subjects of Art History: Historical Objects in Contemporary Perspective* (Cambridge University Press, 1998) and *Art History, Aesthetics, and Visual Studies* (Williamstown, MA, 2002) – she has received several fellowships, including a Guggenheim, a Getty Fellowship, an ACLS, a Rockefeller grant and two from the NEH. Holly has written many essays on the criticism and history of medieval and Renaissance art, and has been co-director of two NEH and two Getty summer seminars on cross-disciplinary subjects for humanities faculty.

**Sonja Neef** is Junior Professor of European Media and Culture at the Bauhaus University Weimar in Germany and author of *Kalligramme. Zur Medialität einer Schrift* (ASCA Press, Amsterdam, 2000) and a series of articles on handwriting and new media. She co-edited (with Mieke Bal) *Travelling Concepts I* (ASCA, Amsterdam, 2001), *Kulturanalyse* (Suhrkamp, Frankfurt am Main, 2002) and *Sign Here! Handwriting in the Age of New Media* (Amsterdam University Press, 2006). Her most recent book is *Abdruck und Spur. Handschrift im Zeitalter ihrer technischen Reproduzierbarkeit* (Kadmos, Berlin, 2008).

**Griselda Pollock** is Professor of Social and Critical Histories of Art and Director of the Centre for Cultural Analysis, Theory and History at the University of Leeds. She is currently working on a trilogy on trauma and representation in the wake of the Holocaust and has recently published on Eva Hesse, Agnes Martin, Amedeo Modigliani and Christine Taylor Patten. Recent edited publications include *Encountering Eva Hesse* (Prestel, 2006), *Psychoanalysis and the Image* (Blackwell, 2006) and (with Joyce Zemans) *Museums after Modernism: Strategies of Engagement* (Blackwell, 2007). New monographs include *Encounters in a Virtual Feminist Museum: Time, Space and the Archive* (Routledge, 2007) and a book on Charlotte Salomon's *Leben? oder Theater?* (Yale University Press, forthcoming).

**Kaja Silverman** is Class of 1940 Professor of Film and Rhetoric at the University of California, Berkeley. She is the author of seven books, including *The Subject of Semiotics* (Oxford University Press, 1983), *Male Subjectivity at the Margins* (Routledge, 1992) and *World Spectators* (Stanford University Press, 2000). She is currently working on two books: *Flesh of My Flesh* and *The Miracle of Analogy*.

**Ernst van Alphen** is Professor of Literary Studies at Leiden University. His publications include *Francis Bacon and the Loss of Self* (Reaktion Books, 1994), *Caught By History: Holocaust Effects in Contemporary Art, Literature, and Theory* (Stanford University Press, 1997), *Armando: Shaping Memory* (NAi Press, 2000) and *Art in Mind: How Contemporary Images Shape Thought* (University of Chicago Press, 2005).

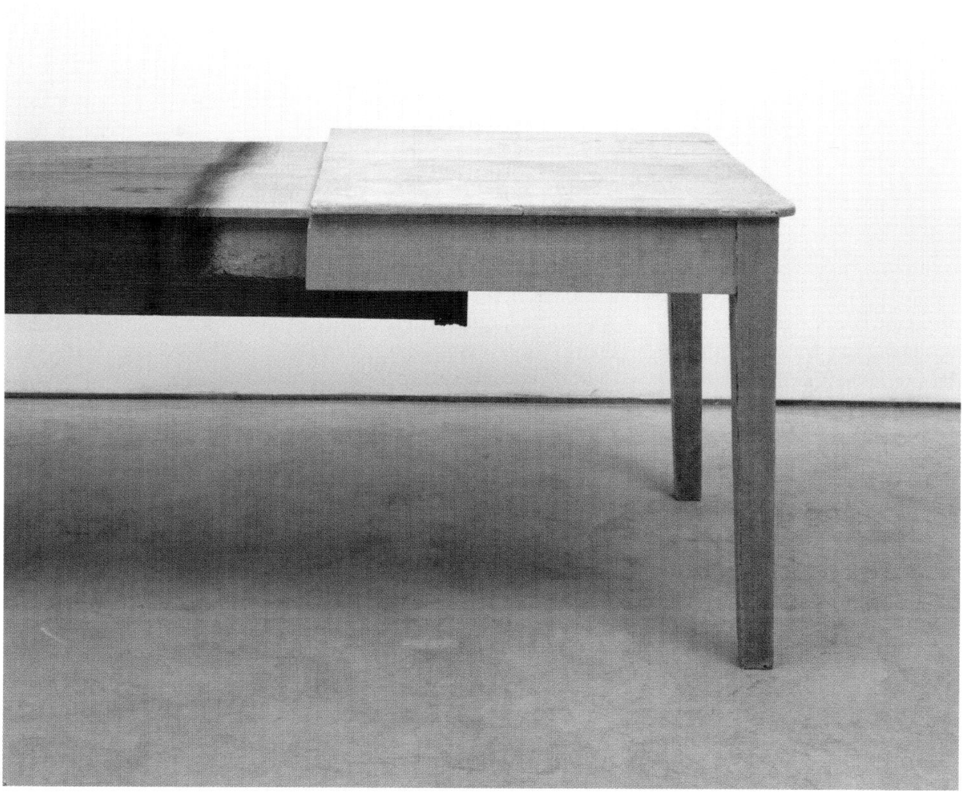

1.1 Detail of Doris Salcedo, *Unland: The Orphan's Tunic*, 1997. Photo: David Heald. Reproduced courtesy of Alexander and Bonin, New York.

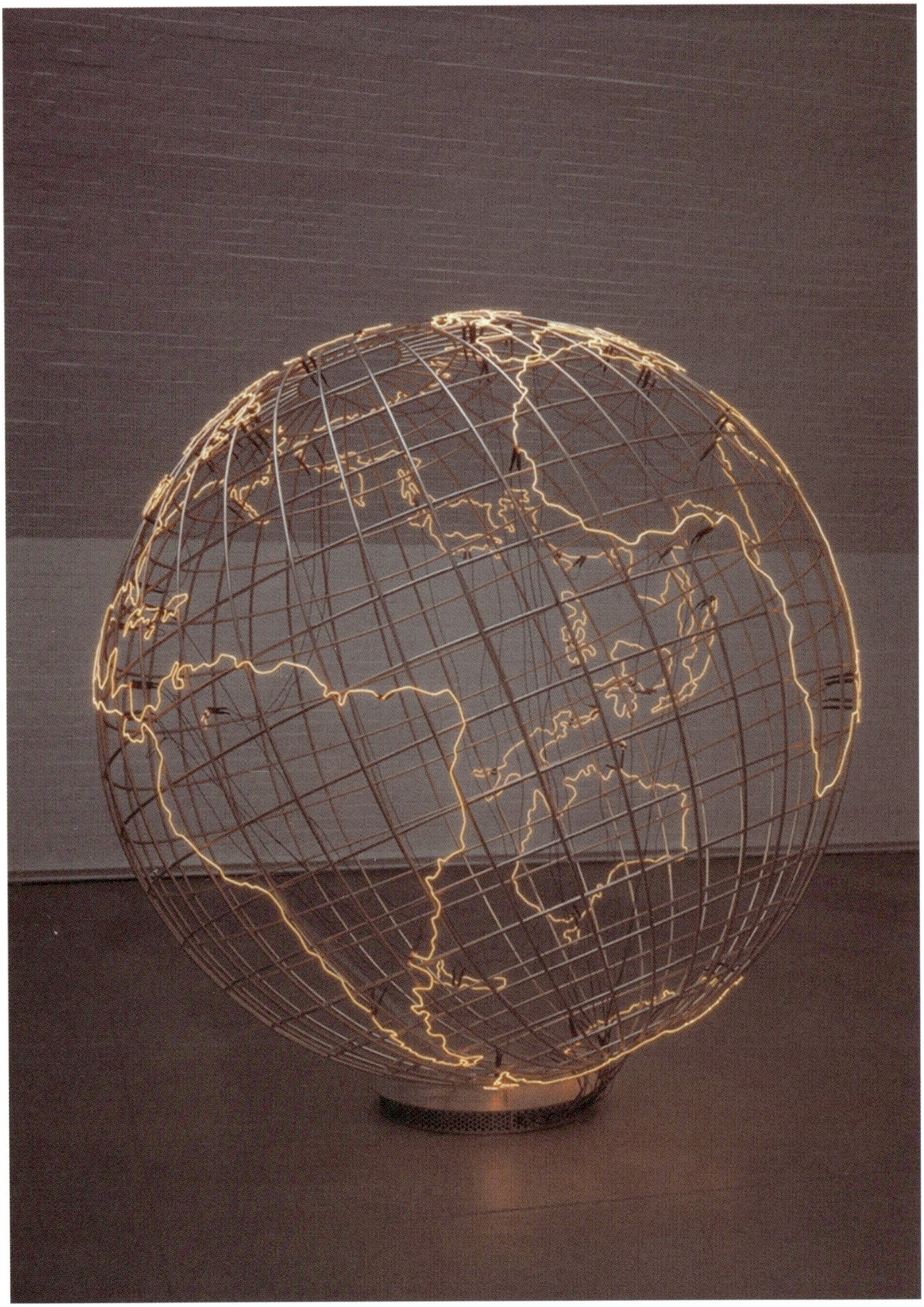

1.2 Mona Hatoum, *Hot Spot*, 2006. Stainless steel and neon tube. 230 × 223 cm. © The Artist. Photo: Jörg von Brunchhausen, Berlin. Courtesy Galerie Mx Hetzler, Berlin.

# 1

# CONVERSATION PIECES: ABOUT MIEKE BAL

DEBORAH CHERRY

*Travelling Concepts*, Mieke Bal's recent exploration of the movement and migration of concepts across and between the humanities, is, in many ways, a series of conversations, as the author engages with contemporary theories, art works and ideas, with writers, artists and philosophers. Proposed as a 'rough guide', like its travel companions *Travelling Concepts* is full of wise advice and fun to read. It is handy for consultation in emergencies – how to approach a 'difficult' text – or for quick consultation – how has a travelling concept such as hybridity moved from the sciences to critical analysis?[1] This product of deep and sustained thinking is imbued with a lively, even irrepressible wit, and it is written in a sparkling style, often in the first person. Writing and speaking from a distinctively articulated position that conjures up her own experience, history and memories, Bal addresses her readers directly, engaging us in conversation with her as well as with the objects and texts of her analysis. As she has so often indicated, encounters between the art work or visual image and the theories deployed in interpretation are reciprocal, transformative: theory, she explains, is 'not an instrument of analysis, to be "applied" to the art object'. Rather, 'it is a discourse that can be brought to bear on the object at the same time as the object can be brought to bear on *it*.'[2]

Conversation, defined as the exchange of observations and ideas, takes its form from *conversatio*, in turn derived from *conversari*, to associate with, and it is resonant with *convertare*, to convert or to turn around, suggestive of the ebbs and flows of argumentation, the changes of mind that take place in debate. And Bal's polemical style and situated stance have provoked assent and dissent in equal measure. Her writings, and equally the lectures and seminars for which she is renowned – a founder of the Amsterdam School of Cultural Analysis, she has regularly taught a seminar on critical theory – as well as those that engage with them, may thus be characterized as conversation pieces. Conversation pieces can take visual and literary form: poems with a serious subject and an informal tone, paintings of figures gathered together in convivial shared activities.

This art of conversation characterizes Bal's writings as she engages with, intervenes, interrogates, and confronts the critical and visual practices of past and present. She undertakes detailed visual and textual engagement with objects which are by no means silent witnesses but active agents in intellectual and aesthetic conversations, participants in the production of meaning and interpretation that constitutes cultural analysis. Based on her contention that 'art thinks', she has propounded the concept of 'visual thought'.[3] This empowerment of the visual image or material artefact, which counters more conventional scholarly distinctions between the subject and the object, acknowledges an inter-subjectivity between audience and interpreter, between interpreter and interpreted, in which the subject has a stake in the analysis.[4] For Bal, then, interpretation is never impartial, distanced, or objective, but engaged and situated, a recognition which has also shaped her sustained interests in Emile Benveniste's theory that the exchanges between I and you, rather than the subject/object divide, constitute the basic foundation of language. Her admissions of complicity have accompanied a profound thinking about time, a break with conventions that plot a unidirectional chronological movement, which have shaped so much art-historical endeavour, to explore how the urgencies of the here and now inform the project of scholarly analysis. In forging what Giovanni Careri calls in these pages 'a critical history of art', Bal has departed from the thorough scrutiny of archives, documents, locations, the impulse to relocate the work of art in its historical contexts; indeed she has advised time and again of the problems with 'context', favouring the concept of 'framing' as a self-reflexive undertaking established by the interpreter. This departure from historical context, archival foundation, and what have become major approaches in the recent rewritings of art's histories has certainly provoked dissent.[5] Bal has advanced interpretations of the image alive to its semantic potential, its open-ended but not unlimited profusion of meaning. And rather than returning into the past, for Bal the past is understood as part of the present, embedded in it through memory and desire. Alert to Walter Benjamin's insight that 'every image of the past that is not recognized by the present as one of its own concerns threatens to disappear irretrievably',[6] she has established that the past only appears in and through contemporary conversation with it.

Bal has called 'preposterous' that movement or reversal that 'puts what came chronologically first ("pre") as an after-effect behind ("post").[7] This reconceptualization of the relations between past and present moves beyond linear models of time. Undoing art-historical concepts of influence and artistic genealogy with their notions of direct connection and unbroken transmission, 'preposterous history' emphasizes the active engagement between the work of art and what came before (or indeed after), how and in what ways the present encounters and acts upon the past.[8] She has addressed those institutions that harbour and present to view the salvaged remains of what has gone before – the museum or the archive – and considered at length those practices of art that return to and reprise the art of the past.[9]

In investigating the relation between the historical (or perhaps more precisely, the historicized) and the contemporary, Bal has also been concerned with agency, with she or he who acts, views, interprets. *Double Exposures* offered a sustained account of the 'event' of display, the 'act of showing', examining the three-way conversations between the curator, the viewer and the object exhibited.[10] Bal's reflections on the positionality of the subject (artist, viewer, curator, scholar) are threaded through the contributions following, as is her attention to vision and viewing. And the intense focus on the work of art is matched, as in Bal's own work, by an interest in its many afterlives, its reception.[11]

The essays collected here are also conversation pieces enacting dialogues with, about and around many of Mieke Bal's most important ideas in the visual field. A point of departure is often provided by her proposition that interpretation begins with a question or an issue, a theoretical inquisitiveness. One of her major interventions in the fields of art-historical and visual studies has been her analysis of the mediation of vision, her meticulous and precise considerations of the diverse ways in which the viewer comes to vision, comes into vision, whether in her attention to the relays of the gaze, to the structures that she has identified as 'focalization', or to the many forms of looking, from the concentration of 'looking in' to more distant observation.[12] And Bal's vision is acute; it is a patient, insistent, attentive regard that in lingering on a detail elegantly elaborates an interpretation. *Reading Rembrandt* takes its readers on a journey that is as much about the paintings and prints of a canonical artist as it is about the acts and processes of investigation, of semiotic readings, of visual as well as psychoanalytic analysis. It begins with Bal's observation of the seemingly insignificant, a nail and a hole in the wall that in catching the light comes under her scrutiny. Yet her attention has

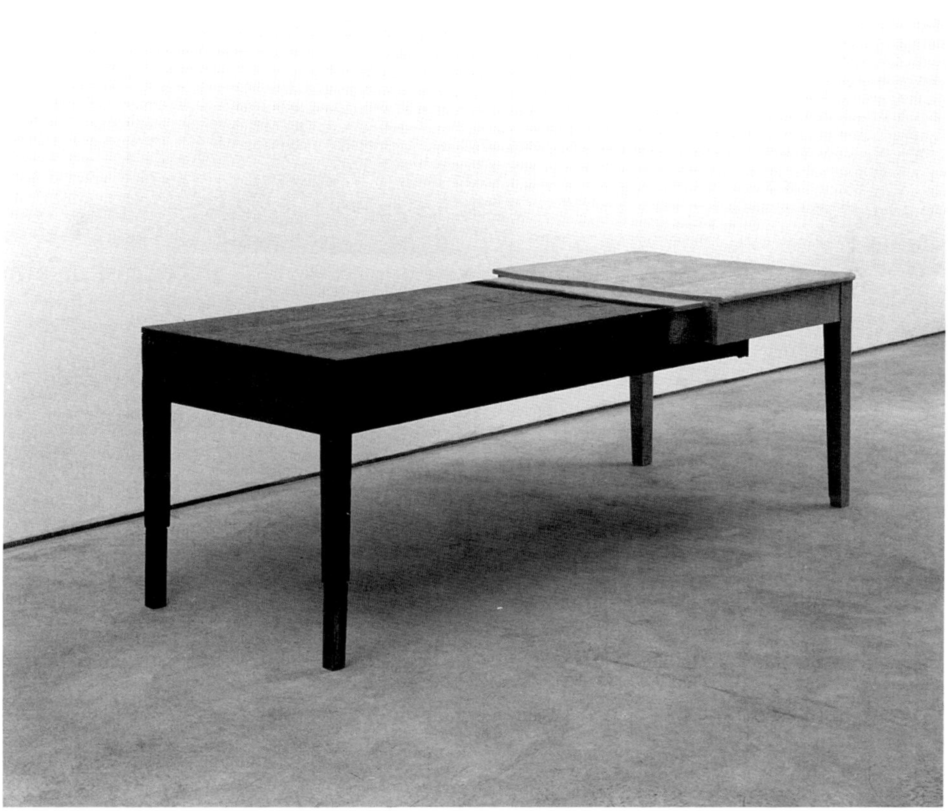

1.3 Doris Salcedo, *Unland: The Orphan's Tunic*, 1997. Wood, cloth, hair and glue, 80 × 245 × 98 cm. Collection: Barcelona: CaixaForum. Photo: David Heald. Reproduced courtesy of Alexander and Bonin, New York.

also been given to that which almost escapes from view or disappears into obscurity, whether a patch of shadow lingering in the foreground of a photograph, or a passage of painterly illegibility. And, taking as her example the intricate weavings of hair in works by Doris Salcedo, she has written hauntingly of that 'sticky image' that demands our regard, enticing the viewer to meditate on the artist's response to the political circumstances wrought into her work.[13]

The contributors of the present collection take one or more of Bal's theoretical propositions for examination, weaving her concerns with their own interests across a wide range of visual materials, from the historical art of the Sistine Chapel, altar paintings and watercolours, to more recent film, photography, graffiti, interactive immersive environments, online performance, areas of visual interest often positioned outside the pages of art history. While Bal has, unsurprisingly perhaps, become a key figure in the debates about visual culture,[14] the extraordinarily wide range of visual materials collected here speaks of her movement between the visual registers of high art and popular cultures, her resistance to clear-cut distinctions between image and text, announced decisively in the sub-title to *Reading 'Rembrandt': Beyond the Word–Image Opposition*, the first of her books to have a profound impact in art-historical studies. In her counterpart in literary studies, *The Mottled Screen: Reading Proust Visually*, Bal exposes the canonical writer's strategies of visual representation, his articulation of seeing, and his snapshots of sensations.[15]

*About Mieke Bal* is imprinted with Bal's characteristic entanglements of the intellectual, the domestic and the political. They are examined in some detail in the conversation between Bal and Michael Ann Holly at the centre of this collection. And they have been evident, too, in her films, such as *Nothing is Missing*, about mothers whose children have migrated to the West, and in this film's recent screening and installation at the Ministry of Justice in Den Haag.[16] Focusing on several of her recent films, Murat Aydemir offers a substantive discussion of cultural translation and migratory aesthetics in relation to 'minority existence in modernity'.[17] This interest in translation reappears, very differently, in Giovanni Careri's analysis of Michelangelo's Sistine Chapel interpreted through Samuel Beckett's theatre of the absurd; the author's proposition of anachronistic 'constellation' opens up an innovative analysis of the constructions of space, time and the body in the Sistina. Careri's reflections on 'preposterous history' are shared by Ernst van Alphen, whose essay focuses on the nature of the archive and the survival of a traumatic past in the present in installations by Christian Boltanski and by Ydessa Hendeles, and films by Peter Forgacs. His concern with 'Holocaust effects' resonates with Griselda Pollock's projection of an artistic moment 'before Auschwitz' in her sustained attention to Charlotte Salomon's major art work, *Leben? oder Theater?* This focus on pictorial complexity, revealed though intense and careful visual scrutiny, recurs in Hanneke Grootenboer's discussion of paintings of the Annunciation in a series, as she puts it, of 'Balian exercises', in which she demonstrates how visual analysis so often brings the invisible into visibility.

This collection has also been shaped by Bal's productive 'restlessless', her passionate interdisciplinarity.[18] Sonja Neef starts from a comparison between theories of graffiti by Mieke Bal and by Jean Baudrillard to analyse public spaces in Germany before and after the fall of the Berlin wall in 1989, developed through an engagement with one of Bal's key concepts: that culture is not object-based but performative. Jill Bennett's essay explores how new concepts emerge from an interdisciplinary nexus. Investigating the work of artists such as Gabriel Orozco and Candice Breitz, she argues for the significance of 'intermedia' as a term, not just to indicate mixed media but to signify a 'transdisciplinary sphere of operation'. Kaja Silverman considers Bal's readings of Proust (visually), revisiting Proust's 'photographic' vision and photography's early history as well as Bal's concept of 'focalization'. Reflecting on positionality in language and in the visual arts, especially through a sustained account of Chantal Akerman's film, *The Captive*, her essay explores one of the central theme of Bal's writing, one that recurs throughout this collection: the question of subjectivity.

These are essays written in the present, filled with its desires and needs for a recognition of the past, its legacies, disappearances and reappearances, whether in the 'Holocaust effects' of archival classification systems, in the recreation of a cultural moment 'before Auschwitz', in an assessment of the destruction and survivals of the Berlin wall, or in the making of a history of art that reappraises the art of the past. That they are essays written from the present is signalled by the broad engagement in these pages with contemporary theorists and philosophers, including Gilles Deleuze, Clifford Geertz, Hubert Damisch, Gayatri Chakravorty Spivak and Giorgio Agamben. Agamben's philosophical writings have provoked considerable interest in contemporary art practice and aesthetics.[19] The creation of visual and textual forms for a new empowerment of the subject alongside the visual representation of the global conditions of disposable 'bare' life remain among the most urgent issues for today.[20] Mieke Bal's writings and films have compellingly argued for an ethics and aesthetics of situated contemporary practice that comes to terms with the past, attends to 'cultural memory in the present',[21] and addresses the most demanding issues of today and tomorrow.

## Notes

This collection continues an occasional *Art History* series initiated by Adrian Rifkin's *About Michael Baxandall* (1999) and continued with *About Stephen Bann* (2006). It was first proposed in New York during a exchange between friends and colleagues early in 2003. Towards the end of its long preparation, I moved to the University of Amsterdam, where my colleagues now include Bal and other contributors.

My warmest thanks are extended to Mieke Bal, and to the scholars who have so generously and graciously contributed their work. I owe a special debt of thanks to Fintan Cullen and to the editorial board of *Art History* for their wise advice in preparing this collection. I would also like to thank Sarah Sears for her exacting copy-editing and imaginative layout, Jody Patterson for co-ordinating the essays, and Samuel Bibby for preparing the texts and for translating the text by Giovanni Careri. I am indebted to the artist and to the Artificial Eye Film Company for kind permission to reproduce stills from Chantal Akerman's *The Captive* (2000); to the artist and Alexander and Bonin, for permission to reproduce images by Doris Salcedo; and to the artist and White Cube for permission to reproduce Mona Hatoum's *Hot Spot*. I also offer special thanks to David Peters Corbett, Christine Riding, Jacqueline Scott at Wiley–Blackwell and Geoffrey Palmer for making the book version possible.

1 Mieke Bal, *Travelling Concepts in the Humanities: A Rough Guide*, Toronto, 2002.

2 Bal, *Travelling Concepts*, 61.

3 Mieke Bal, *Quoting Caravaggio, Contemporary Art, Preposterous History*, Chicago, 1999, 117.

4 Norman Bryson, introduction to *Looking In: The Art of Viewing*, London and New York, 2000.

5 On these histories, see Deborah Cherry, ed., *About Stephen Bann*, Oxford, 2006, and *Art: History: Visual: Culture*, Oxford, 2005.

6 Walter Benjamin, 'Theses on the Philosophy of History', Thesis V in *Illuminations*, ed. and with an introduction by Hannah Arendt, trans. Harry Zohn, New York, 1976, 255.

7 Bal, *Quoting Caravaggio*, 7.

8 For Bal's rethinking of influence, see Ernst van Alphen, '"Reconcentrations": Bacon reinventing his Models', in *Francis Bacon and the Tradition of Art*, eds W. Seipel, B. Steffen, C. Vitali, Vienna, 2004, 57–69. I am indebted to Jane Beckett for this reference.

9 Bal, *Quoting Caravaggio*, offers a sustained address to twentieth-century Caravaggisti artists.

10 Mieke Bal, *Double Exposures: The Subject of Cultural Analysis*, London and New York, 1996.

11 Bal's significance in reception studies has been pointed out by Elizabeth Prettejohn, 'Løve in Copenhagen', *Art History*, 29:5, 2006, 937–41.

12 Focalization is explored in detail in Bal's *Reading 'Rembrandt': Beyond the Word-Image Opposition*, New York and Cambridge, 1991, 2nd edn (paperback) 1994.

13 Mieke Bal, 'Sticky Images: the foreshortening of time in an art of duration', in *Time and the Image*, ed. Carolyn Bailey Gill, Manchester, 2000, 79–99.

14 Mieke Bal, 'Visual essentialism and the object of visual culture', *Journal of Visual Culture*, 2:1, 2003, 6, published with invited responses.

15 Mieke Bal, *The Mottled Screen: Reading Proust Visually*, Stanford, 1997.

16 Mieke Bal, *Nothing is Missing*, 2006. Multiple-screen video installation, 25–35 minutes (looped).

17 Aydemir draws on Aamir R. Mufti, 'Auerbach in Istanbul: Edward Said, Secular Criticism, and the Question of Minority Culture', *Critical Inquiry*, 25, 1998, 102.

18 The breadth of her interests is signalled in *The Mieke Bal Reader*, Chicago, 2006.

19 'What is bare life?' is one of the questions offered by the *Documenta 12* magazines project. See, for example, *Control + P : Journal of Contemporary Art*, 5, January 2007, ed. Judy Freya Sibayan, with thanks to Erika Tan for this reference. http://www.controlp-artjournal.org and http://magazines.documenta.de., accessed January 2007.

20 Giorgio Agamben, *Homo Sacer: Sovereign Power and Bare Life*, trans. Daniel Heller-Roazen, Stamford, 1996.

21 Mieke Bal co-edits, with Henk de Vries, a series of books on *Cultural Memory in the Present*, for Stanford University Press.

# 2

# PIECEMEAL TRANSLATION

MURAT AYDEMIR

The title of Mieke Bal and Shahram Entekhabi's art film and video installation *Glub (Hearts)* (2004) may initially sound barbaric in the word's etymological sense of 'unintelligible', 'rude' and 'savage'.[1] The word *glub* is the transcription in Latin script of an Arabic word. It means 'kernels', 'hearts', 'pits', or 'seeds', and connotes the everyday habit, widespread in the Near and Middle East as well as North Africa, of shelling and consuming roasted and salted sunflower, pumpkin and other seeds. Yet, the main location of Bal and Entekhabi's work on the phenomenon is Berlin, Germany's current capital and a European cultural centre. Hence, *Glub* takes the translation of a foreign habit to Western soil as its subject matter.

*Glub* comprises a thirty-minute art film and a video installation of eight monitors. The film presents casual interviews with anonymous passers-by, shopkeepers, clients, curators, artists, writers and academics, all 'talking heads' reflecting on the seeds and the habit. The interviews are combined with images of seed-eating *flâneurs* strolling through urban streets. At times, it is difficult to ascertain where exactly those streets are located: some look like Berlin, others like the Middle East. In the video installation that accompanies the film, eight monitors show various people who consume the seeds, or at least attempt to do so, without speaking (plates 2.1–2.8). The soundtrack only offers loud crackling and munching sounds. When putting on the earphones attached to each monitor, however, visitors overhear off-camera voices that recount food-related memories and stories in a variety of languages. Most faces of the non-speaking but noisy seed-eaters on the monitors belong to ethnicities other than those readily associated with the habit. Some are at ease, others seem awkwardly self-conscious, their eyes staring, their foreheads sweating, their mouths and lips struggling to handle the seeds and their shells.

Counterparts to the main film's talking heads, the monitors display '*listening* heads', people trying to listen in a language other than their own, enacting a receptive semiotic habit that is alien to them, yet desirable; as if to listen in this way, while eating the seeds, even awkwardly, enables the subjects to 'get' the recounted memories and stories far better. Caught between the talking and the listening heads, between the expressive and the receptive faces, the visitor must negotiate between two ways of responding: either just to see and hear about a habit that is probably unfamiliar, or to see and hear about a habit that is unfamiliar *while* simultaneously adopting an unfamiliar way of looking and listening. To facilitate the latter response, the installation provides baskets with ample supplies of *glub*.

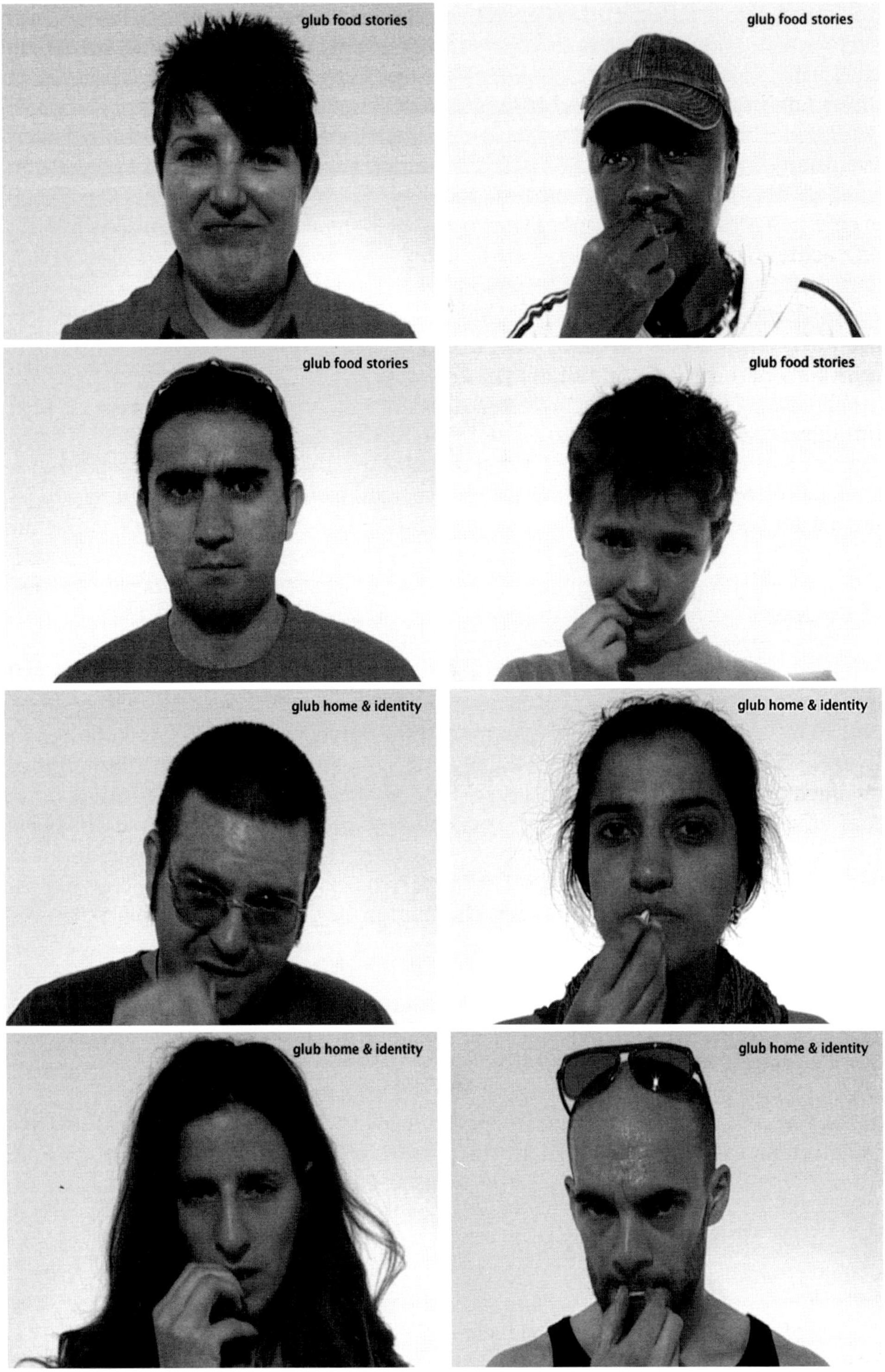


2.1–2.8 Film stills from Mieke Bal and Shahram Entekhabi, *Glub (Hearts)*, 2004. 30-minute art film and 8-channel video installation. Berlin and Amsterdam. Courtesy of the artist.

The choice that the work offers its visitors, then, is to look at and listen *to* the talking heads, or to look and listen *with* the listening heads. For English speakers, the former attitude has the distinct advantage of linguistic transparency: the film offers English subtitles. But subtitles are not available to the visitors who join the munching listeners. Nevertheless, seed by seed, bit by bit, those visitors may eventually learn more about the significance of seed-eating, gradually getting 'the hang of it, that feeling', as one of the interviewees describes the affect that accompanies the practice. Going back and forth between the two positions makes one acutely aware of how one's way of listening limits and determines what can be understood.

*Glub* can be taken to address the issue Aamir R. Mufti has summarized as 'minority existence in modernity'.[2] Present-day 'ethnic' minorities live their lives in European nation-states, inhabiting a modern condition that is founded on the divide between the West and the rest, the modern and the archaic. As a result, immigrants share the West's present in an ephemeral, ghostly way; representatives of supposedly pre-modern times and peripheral places, they do not quite partake of the modern here and now. Arguably, this ideologically induced gap is far harder to negotiate than linguistic and cultural barriers. The ways in which non-Western immigrants give form to their leisure and enjoyment – have fun, kill time, take pleasure in company – are ever at risk of registering in the aesthetic key of the 'exotic', the otherworldly.

Seducing its visitors to participate in the practice that it describes, *Glub* enforces a spatial and temporal continuum between the foreign custom and its local context: *glub* are being consumed here, now, in the present. In addition, Bal and Entekhabi's work raises the issue of how Western individuals relate affectively and perceptually to a public space that is transformed by migration, to the changed 'look' and 'feel' of the metropolis that has served as modern existence's most alluring image. For the seeds are generally consumed outside of the private sphere: in streets, squares, parks, or 'anyplace with a view', as one commentator suggests. Both aspects are crucial parts of what Bal has called a 'migratory aesthetic': an aesthetic of migration that simultaneously entails a migration of the aesthetic, its movement and change.

In what follows, I address *glub*, both the film and the phenomenon, in a number of different frames. First, I look at how the work can be situated in Bal's recent academic work, for which she has adopted the term 'cultural analysis'. Second, the film's peculiar and strategic rendering of 'street life', the ways in which it both suspends and reinforces the recognizability of the modern Western 'cityscape', will be at issue. And finally, I consider how *Glub (Hearts)*, from its title to its attempt to translate a different way of listening, engages with the possibilities and pitfalls of the cross-cultural translation of an everyday detail.

## AESTHETIC EDUCATION

Bal has termed *Glub* 'not an *object* of analysis but an *instantiation* of that activity'.[3] To analyse the work, then, is to build on the analysis that it already performs. *Glub* is part of an emerging body of video work that also includes Bal's video installation *Nothing is Missing* (2006) and the documentary *Mille et un Jours* (2003).[4] In this section, I sketch how Bal's video work can be seen as a continuation of her academic work rather than a diversion from it. Beginning by addressing *Glub* as part of Bal's latest project, migratory aesthetics, I then relate *Glub* to 'cultural analysis', the term that Bal has adopted for her critical practice in general.

In 'Food, Form, and Visibility: *Glub* and the Aesthetics of Everyday Life' (2005), Bal explains that the work grew out of an inchoate sense that some inner city streets of Berlin seemed to her simultaneously more dirty and more lively. That impression subsequently found its image in the shells of seeds lining those streets, indexing the presence of migrants from the Middle East and North Africa. The elementary visibility of the practice and the litter it produces should not be taken for granted. Indeed, having no doubt already seen the practice of eating *glub* in Berlin, where he lives, and long before in his native Iran, Entekhabi only noticed it on holiday in Turkey.[5] It took a long series of casual perceptions in Iran, Berlin and Turkey for the habit of seed-eating to emerge as a significant speck of culture in the artist's eye, for his perception to be kindled to make out its relevance as part of the everyday aesthetic of his hometown. Bal turns this unpredictable, elusive shuttle between amorphous sense and meaningful image into the stake of her understanding of the aesthetic as it has emerged from her and Entekhabi's work on *Glub*.

True to her interdisciplinary career, which took her from comparative literature to narratology to Bible studies to art history to visual culture to cultural analysis to video art, Bal takes the building blocks for that aesthetic from variegated sources. To summarize briefly, the philosopher Alan Singer conceives of the aesthetic as an attitude, a practice in which translatability and mutual recognition are important.[6] From Kaja Silverman comes an awareness that perception means to 'embed an image within a constant shifting matrix of unconscious memories, which can render a culturally insignificant object libidinally resonant, or a culturally significant object worthless'.[7] From art historians Rosalind E. Krauss and Yves Alain-Bois Bal takes the idea, introduced by Georges Bataille, of a formlessness that resists recognition and, hence, meaning.[8]

Bal assembles a political aesthetic that neither accepts the visibility of forms that are inevitably informed by ethnicizing and exoticizing stereotypes, nor submits to the invisibility of all that falls outside of sedimented cultural codes, but which 'enables us to learn to see what, by lack of recognizable form, seems invisible.'[9] This migratory aesthetic persuades one to notice with different eyes what has been seen before. From mere waste product or trace of the exotic, the empty shells lining the streets of Berlin reappear as an aesthetically resonant aspect of the imaginary of the modern Western metropolis. *Glub* practices, does, migratory aesthetics by inviting its visitors to re-appreciate the scattered shells as a formless image that deserves recognition, curiosity and wonder.

The main film apprehends its subject matter at the intersection of three domains often thought of as separate: everyday culture, creative art and reflective theory. The montage of casual interviews with anonymous passers-by, shopkeepers, clients, curators, artists, writers and academics turns the seeds and the practice of eating them into a densely textured object of culture that simultaneously participates in a lived habit, triggers aesthetic interest, and facilitates the production of knowledge. In their joint stake in the practice, the interviewed subjects do not necessarily always perform in accordance with their social or professional status: a shop owner offers crucial insights into how the habit translates to its new setting; an academic plays with the seeds, with their variegated colours, shapes and textures, as if with an artistic material; and an artist clarifies aspects of their habitual consumption. In this way, the film suggests that experience, creation and reflection continuously overlap and inflect each other; none is necessarily more or less relevant than the others. Consequently, neither seed-eaters, artists, nor academics can fully own or claim the object, or even gain the upper hand. The seeds belong to no one, so everyone has something to say about them.

Because the seeds are allowed to feature in different domains, they come alive in different ways. Initially, *glub* operates as a thing with a 'social life' that takes it from place to place, from one grouping of people to another, and takes on different functions and meanings.[10] In addition, the 'seeds' act as a verbal and visual metaphor for the implications and consequences of migration: transported by the wind or by birds, flowering in foreign soil. The seeds also acquire conceptual bearing in relation to the current theoretical term 'diaspora'. As the artist and curator Shaheen Merali explains in the documentary, 'Now it's funny talking about the idea of seeds because seeds are one way to describe the notion of diaspora because it comes from the literal term of how seeds are dispersed . . .' (i.e., the Greek *speirein*, for 'to sow, scatter'). Overdetermined as thing, metaphor and concept, the seeds can be said to acquire an agency of their own, a 'life' of sorts.

In its multiple framing of its object, making it more complex rather than less, *Glub* becomes recognizable as an instance of 'cultural analysis', the name Bal has adopted for her critical practice. Cultural analysis engages its object in relation to theoretical concepts and socio-cultural contexts without, however, reducing it to a case or illustration of either. Exceeding both conceptual knowledge, abstract and speculative, and contextual knowledge, concrete and verifiable, the object cannot be accounted for exhaustively within any singular conceptualization or contextualization. Thus, it retains its capacity to resist or 'speak back' to the analyst, as Bal often says. My own consideration of *Glub* should be seen as an analysis in precisely that vein, apprehending its object at the intersection of multiple frames, each contributing a layer of signification, while these ultimately do not add up to comprehensive description.

Cultural analysis finds one of its precursors in the anthropological work of Clifford Geertz, who uses the term as a synonym for what he calls 'thick description'. Taking minute and concrete instances of culture as its objects – Geertz characterizes them as 'specks' or 'flecks' – thick description seeks to 'ferret out the unapparent import of things' by considering the multiple frames of reference that add up to their social life, and that together give them a finely articulated texture.[11] Departing from 'exceedingly extended acquaintances with extremely small matters', the type of microscopic analysis that Geertz advocates resists 'thin', or singularly contextualized, sociological or historical description, and criticizes and nuances the yield of the capitalized master concepts of the social and cultural sciences, such as power, change, oppression, work and beauty.[12]

And, of course, diaspora. Merali's remark, connecting the seeds to the concept, further 'thickens' the film's subject matter. 'Diaspora' qualifies as one of Bal's 'travelling concepts'. In *Travelling Concepts in the Humanities: A Rough Guide* (2002), Bal proposes the reflection on the trajectories of concepts, on their movement and transformation at various levels: between literal words and concepts, between concepts and objects, between disciplines, and among concepts, rather than on their identity or definition, as a method for the interdisciplinary study of culture.[13]

In *Glub*, the seeds appear as the concrete things that inspired the metaphor – sowing, scattering – that developed into the concept 'diaspora'. In addition, 'diaspora' enacts the scattering and fracturing on which it reflects. The term has journeyed from Jewish history and religion to the contemporary post-colonial condition, dispersing into different disciplines and regions of the world, ranging from Jewish studies to American Black and ethnic studies, and British cultural studies. The definition, range of applicability and political implications of the term are all hotly contested. For instance, William Safran insists that diaspora remains wedded to its prototypical and paradigmatic 'home' in Jewish history, mainly for the long duration of Jewish exile in the absence of a nation to call home.[14] By contrast, Brent Hayes Edwards proposes a broader usage to indicate 'transnational circuits of culture and politics that are resistant or exorbitant to the frames of nations and continents'.[15]

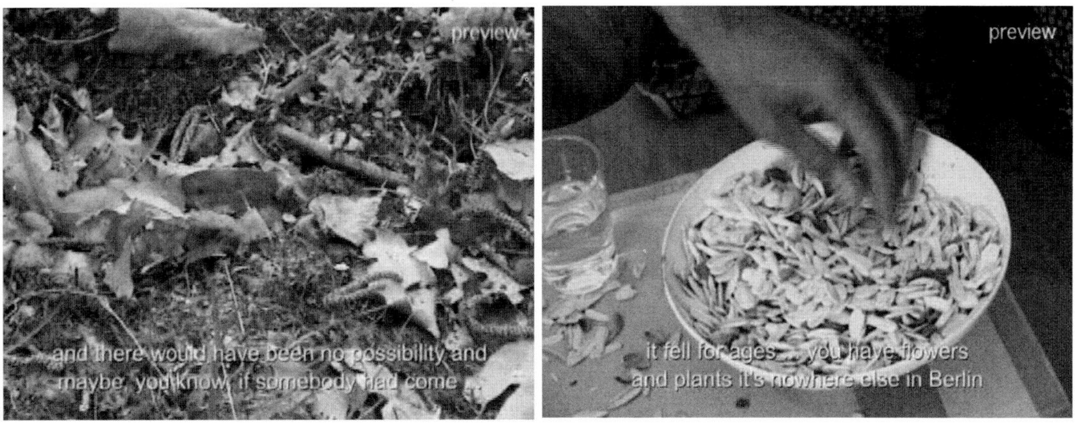


2.9–2.12 Film stills from Mieke Bal and Shahram Entekhabi, *Glub (Hearts)*, 2004. 30-minute art film and 8-channel video installation. Berlin and Amsterdam. Courtesy of the artist.

What does *Glub*'s engagement with the seeds, the social phenomenon of mass migration in modernity, and the concept of diaspora elicit? In its literalizing imagination of diaspora, the work inquires into the thing at the heart of nationalism in that it weds genealogy to territory: the seed as germinating a rooted lineage, a tree whose branches and foliage will ever relate to their shared origin. The film subverts this ideology of soil, seed, roots and tree through a series of scenes that highlight the soil's rudimentary generosity towards seeds from elsewhere; soil does not jealously guard its turf (plate 2.9).

One of the interviewees relates that on the empty grounds adjacent to Berlin's railway tracks grow flowers and plants found nowhere else in the city, their seeds and pollen inadvertently brought along by international freight trains (plate 2.10). The artist Maria Theresa Alves explains how a friend managed to grow a garden of exotic plants simply by removing parts of the fence that separated her grounds from those of a neighbour, a captain, so that the seeds of the plants that he brought from his journeys blew onto her property (plate 2.11). Another scene entangles images of flying and feeding birds with a shot of a group of Turkish-German teenagers eating *glub*, one of whom jokes: 'Yes, we like to eat them ... like little birds.' (plate 2.12)

These scenes are combined with others that attest to the ravages and losses that (neo)colonialism and global capitalism cause in migrants lives; *Glub* cannot be said to idealize migration. Nevertheless, the film's representations of the movements of seeds and people, exorbitant to national or continental borders, suggest that migration is in fact the default position of planetary life, something that, much like the weather, happens. Recontextualizing migration within the natural life of the planet, *Glub* conceives of the phenomenon in markedly other terms than those provided by contemporary European political debates in which the migrant is generally either ascribed full agency so that he or she can be condemned as a sinister usurper, or denied all agency so that she or he can be saved as a pathetic victim. Against the magnificent background of planetary life that *Glub* mobilizes, however, the lives of migrants can be allowed to move into

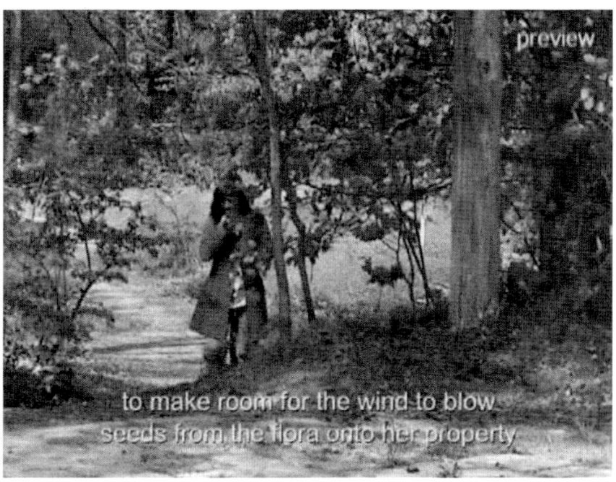


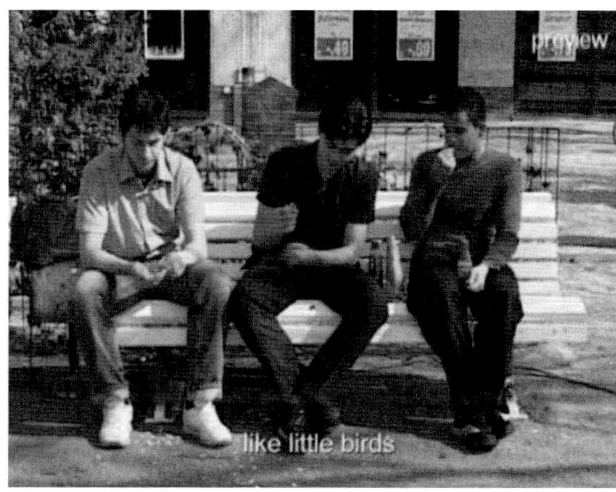


focus as enjoying a qualified – that is, restricted and conditioned by global economics and politics – yet real agency.

Gayatri Chakravorty Spivak has proposed the 'planetary' as the term to re-imagine the alterity of the Earth beyond the aggressive claims of economic globalization and elitist worldliness.[16] Connecting contemporary migration to the natural life of seeds, Bal and Entekhabi's work can be understood as re-imagining diaspora as a planetary phenomenon in Spivak's vein. *Glub* shows us migrants who suffer from economic and political exploitation. The work also features migrants as the representatives of diasporic communities that mourn their losses. But it also reminds us that migration is part and parcel of the planetary life that human beings share with birds, the wind and seeds.

## STREET LIFE

Picture this: Berlin 2004. What images come to mind? *Glub* pictures Berlin as a series of streets where people are walking, standing, crouching and sitting while eating the seeds (plates 2.13–2.20). As I have indicated above, these streets are not

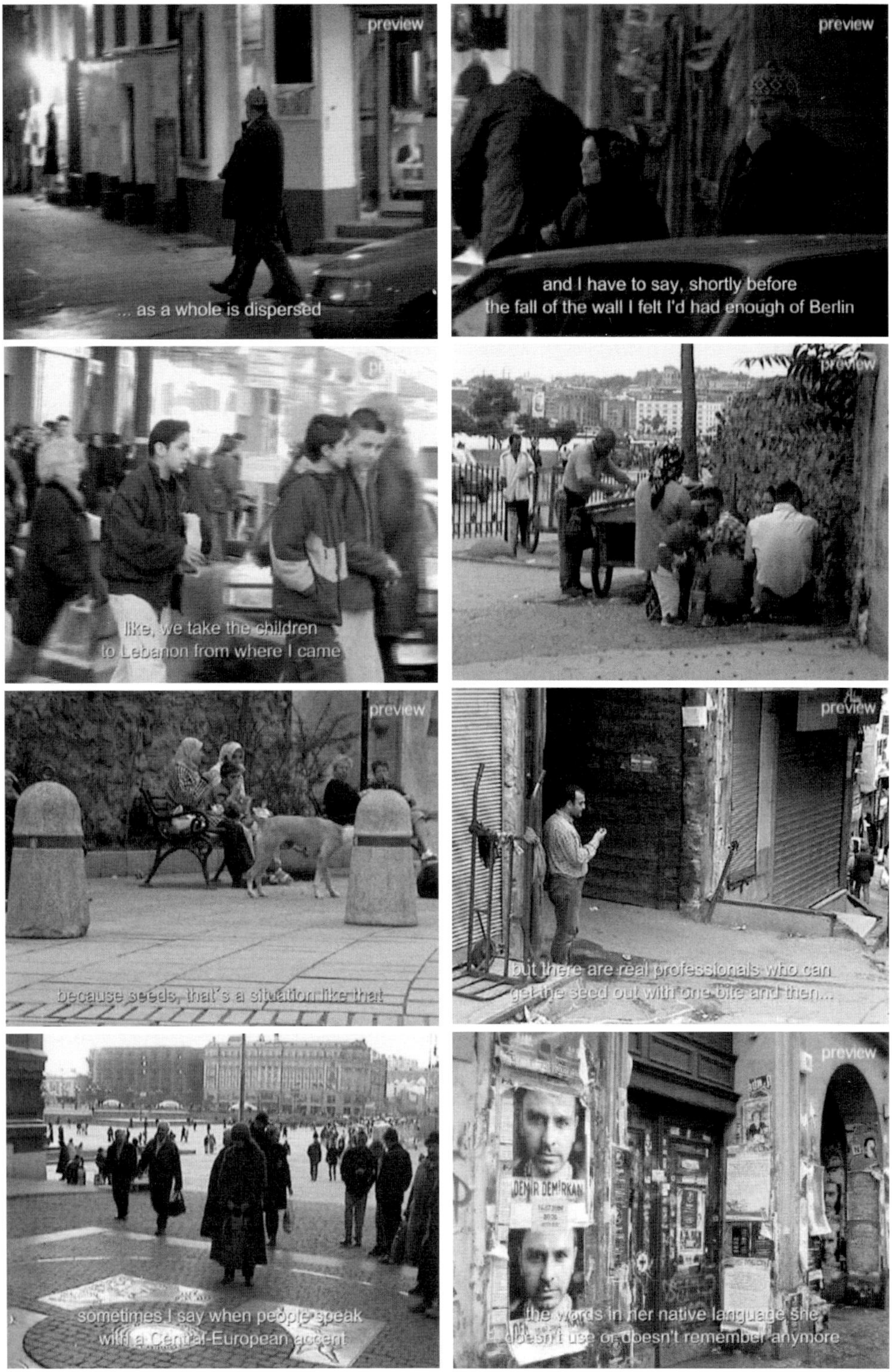


2.13–2.20 Film stills from Mieke Bal and Shahram Entekhabi, *Glub (Hearts)*, 2004. 30-minute art film and 8-channel video installation. Berlin and Amsterdam. Courtesy of the artist.

all immediately recognizable as Berlin's; some may be more easily identifiable than others. Yet by and large the film suspends the instant recognizability of its setting, dislocating its viewer's sense of place. Only at the end does it become evident that not all the streets featured in the film are located in the German city. The credits express gratitude to the inhabitants of Datca, Dortmund, Hagen, Istanbul, Moscow, Paris, Raffah and Toronto for their hospitality. Even that belated information, however, does not disclose exactly which pictured street is located in what city.

Throughout, the film omits topographical information. No on-screen captions supply place names. The soundtrack refuses to suggest local colour by offering the usual stereotypical melodies to signal location. Neither does the film indicate place by bathing Western cities in harsh and grey light, Eastern cities in soft and yellow light. *Glub* purposefully foregoes established cinematic and television conventions that work to convey location. Precisely by circumventing these conventions, however, the film re-inquires into the visibility of the inner-city streets of the West.

Centring on Berlin, the documentary imagines a continuous 'cityscape' that runs from Toronto to Raffah. Through migrants' establishments, practices, sounds and gestures, the urban streets of the West have acquired a new life and a changed appearance. In the vein of Bal's migratory aesthetics, the film's imagery of street life calls on its viewers to picture 'Berlin 2004' anew rather than to recognize a familiar form. In this section, I inquire into what may be at stake in *Glub*'s representation of a public sphere as marked by the leisure of migrants in relation to the issue that Mufti summarized as 'minority existence in modernity'. I briefly revisit the recent history that has brought large numbers of migrants to Berlin's streets. Subsequently, I connect that history to Slavoj Žižek's understanding of the racism peculiar to modern, democratic nation-states, before proposing that *Glub* ironically casts its migrant subjects in a surprisingly modern role: that of the *flâneur*, the figure through which Walter Benjamin conceptualized modern subjectivity. I offer these three aspects to contribute to the cultural and political resonance of *Glub*'s imagery of migrants inhabiting in a leisurely way the streets of the modern metropolis.

I have argued that *Glub* entices its viewers to recognize migration as part of planetary life. However, that should not be taken to preclude the acknowledgement of the phenomenon within the context of economy-driven globalization and its attendant politics. On the contrary, the planetary and the global frame both contribute to the 'thickness' or multi-facetedness of the fleck of culture that the work traces. Each is important; neither can fully contain or account for the significance of the seeds.

The modern minority at stake in *Glub* mainly consists of so-called *Gastarbeiter* (guest workers) and their descendants living in Germany. From the late 1950s the German state recruited men from Mediterranean countries; by 1973, guest workers made up twelve per cent of the workforce.[17] The policy recycled a strategy that the state had employed and perfected in the late nineteenth century when it had recruited large numbers of agricultural workers from the Slavic countries. Caught between the ideological demands of nationalism and economic expediency, Germany finessed the '*Gastarbeiter* stratagem' to permit the import of foreign workers while preventing their permanent settlement.[18] The latter aim was reached by a policy of enforced yearly rotation and deportation. The practice yielded the additional benefit of 'nationing' and pacifying German workers: the guest workers served as 'living reminder[s] to nationals of the good fortune in belonging to their nation',[19] a fortune made tangible by comparatively better pay and the enjoyment of more economic rights. In the second half of the twentieth century the rediscovered strategy similarly entrenched the ethnic hierarchization of the workforce. The state withheld citizenship and economic rights from its guests, legally facilitated easy dismissal and deportation, and enforced restrictive residency permits that had to be renewed each year, conditional on employment and good behaviour.[20]

Indexing a recent history all but forgotten in today's European culture wars, couched in terms of the alleged opposition between Western enlightenment and a 'backward' Islam, the term *Gastarbeiter* stands as a reminder of an historical policy that insisted that migrants be 'guests', their stay temporary, while the provisional hospitality extended to them remained fully conditional on their labour. Hence, guest workers were only allowed to participate in public life in their capacity as workers, while their leisure was expected to be contained within their inconsequential private lives. Consequently, the public sphere of the nation was supposed to remain relatively free of their presence, guaranteeing its cultural homogeneity.

Viewed within the context of this recent history, *Glub*'s representation of the strolling migrants becomes particularly poignant. The images of people consuming the seeds on the streets of Berlin can be seen to portray guest workers and their descendants enjoying a leisure time that they were never supposed to have in the first place, and inhabiting a public sphere in which their presence should have been temporary and ephemeral. In this sense, the seeds trace the double switch through which migrants' lives have escaped the narrow bounds of *Gastarbeiter* existence: first, from work to leisure, and then from private enjoyment to public recreation, marking the streets of Berlin and transforming their appearance, so much so, in fact, that they become nearly indistinguishable from those of Raffah or Istanbul.

To the Lacanian philosopher Slavoj Žižek, however, the contested recreation of migrants within democratic nation-states betrays a fundamental pathology at their heart, one that far exceeds the recent history of the *Gastarbeiter* policy. Žižek asks why the leisure of migrants should typically attract such disproportionate indignation and hatred:

> [W]hat gets on our nerves, what really bothers us about the 'other', is the peculiar way he organizes his enjoyment (the smell of his food, his 'noisy' songs and dances, his strange manners, his attitude to work – in the racist perspective, the 'other' is either a workaholic stealing our jobs or an idler living on our labor).[21]

According to Žižek, this type of contemporary racism reveals the larger condition of possibility for democracy as well as its ultimate failure. Liberal multiculturalism depends on the separation of the subject between its participation in a public sphere that is culturally neutral and its culturally marked private life, between public citizen and private individual. In the public realm of the state, Žižek writes, the subject of democracy functions as 'the Cartesian subject in all its abstraction, the empty punctuality we reach after subtracting all its particular contents' (163). Privately, by contrast, the subject is marked by specific desires, fantasies and enjoyments. The establishment and maintenance of the former ideally guarantees the latter's freedom to establish its own way of life. However, Žižek argues, the supposedly blank public sphere and its subjects are inevitably 'smeared' or 'smudged' by a particularity that should have been dissolved. More strongly, he claims, it is only on the condition of a shared allegiance to a particular object of desire, fantasy, or enjoyment that the levelling and abstraction necessary to constitute the subject of democracy, the blank citizen, can take effect.

That object, Žižek holds, is the nation: 'the national Cause is ultimately the way subjects of a given nation organize their collective enjoyment through national myths' (165). Because the terms of this collective enjoyment are particular and exclusive, it cannot easily be shared. Paradoxically imagined as both inaccessible to, and simultaneously threatened by, the other, the national object cannot accommodate alternative terms of gratification. Therefore, Žižek claims, the other is typically suspected of wanting 'to steal our enjoyment (by ruining "our way of life")' and/or of harbouring 'some secret, perverse enjoyment' of his or her own (165). Acknowledging the other's pleasure would require distancing ourselves from our own enjoyments and coming to terms with the 'ultimate contingency' of the fantasies and desires that shape our lives (157).

For Žižek, then, the public realm of the modern state is not so much empty or neutral, but rather exclusively occupied by the majority's collective enjoyment of the national object. Yet, here, *Glub* can be taken to nuance Žižek's stark analysis. For the work suggests that the streets of Berlin are able to host a form of enjoyment that is not part of national mythology. Furthermore, the film reveals that some native Germans, akin to the 'listening heads' on the monitors, have adopted the habit of seed-eating. Without doubt, some inhabitants of Berlin react xenophobically to the new pleasure marking the public space – the idle strollers, the munching jaws, the shells that litter the street, the new shops – that the collective enjoyment of the national object claims as its territory, as Žižek maintains. Yet, others do try to 'get the hang of it, that feeling', as one of the commentators in the film characterizes the pleasure. '[T]hat feeling', then, denotes neither the secret, perverse enjoyment of the other, nor the appropriation of the German way of life, but an affect that to some extent can be translated and shared.

Žižek's dire terms, in which to acknowledge the other's enjoyment is inevitably to lose out on one's own, seem influenced by the sheer scale and gravity of the object at stake, the nation. That object of enjoyment may indeed hardly tolerate a rival without crumbling, precisely because it is precarious and illusory. However, smaller, piecemeal 'divine details', as Žižek calls them, as small and informal as the seeds, may well circulate without being immediately perceived as existential threats. Hence, the high political stakes of Žižek's argument obfuscate the countless quiet lives of exchange that cultural details lead, one of which *Glub* brings to the fore.

*Gastarbeiter* protesting against the division of labour between hosts and guests, and minority others straddling the liberal divide between the private and the public, *Glub*'s street-walking seed-eaters invoke the figure that Walter Benjamin identified as the 'hero' of Western modernity: the *flâneur*.[22] Rather than at the apex of time, Benjamin situated the modern subject in a specific habitat, the cityscape of nineteenth-century Paris, undertaking long, passionate and aimless walks. According to Benjamin, these walks redraw the boundaries between private and public space, as well as between classes. To the *flâneur* inhabiting the streets, Benjamin suggests, the urban environment becomes both landscape and interior (417). In the crowd, he continues, members from different classes rub shoulders with one another (418); moreover, the stroller's idleness demonstrates 'against the division of labour' (427). In this vein, Bal and Entekhabi's work proposes that present-day migrants can be seen to re-enact a form of subjectivity that belongs to the West's modern history. Indeed, the film ironically implies that today's true *flâneurs*, in a West whose public spaces increasingly only accommodate the shopper, are migrants, strolling from Toronto to Raffah, enjoying their seeds, enjoying the streets.

*Glub*'s rendering of Berlin's steet life also fits the urban aesthetic that Benjamin developed. His 'M [the *Flaneur*]' advances a city aesthetic of superposition, interpenetration and simultaneity, in which times, places and classes overlap. 'We know that, in the course of the flânerie', Benjamin writes, 'far-off times and places interpenetrate the landscape and the present moment' (419). The aimless walk connects disparate temporal elements that exist side by side in the city, so that 'the most remote past is linked to the events of today' (435). The pictures of street life that Bal and Entekhabi present 'thicken' in so far as they entangle other places and other times. Spatially, the film connects Berlin with cities as diverse as Raffah and Toronto, Istanbul and Moscow; temporally, the work invokes the recent history of the *Gastarbeiter* policy as well as the nineteenth-century Paris of Benjamin's *flâneur*. From neutral or blank, public space becomes culturally and historically dense, textured.

I have interpreted *Glub*'s imagery of strolling seed-eaters as *Gastarbeiter* enjoying a leisure that their status attempted to erase, as a minority adding its alternative form of pleasure to a public sphere that is largely, though not exclusively, occupied by the majority's enjoyment of the national object, and as *flâneurs* reminding contemporary shoppers of a nearly lost delight. Neither of these contextual and conceptual frames can fully encompass the work nor the phenomenon that it takes as its subject matter. Nevertheless, they partially account for, and contribute to, the aesthetic and political significance of the street life that *Glub*, to phrase it oxymoronically, observes imaginatively. The new common sense of European nation-states increasingly insists on a politics of assimilation that would wipe clean the public realm of those signs of otherness that it regards as incommensurable. The headscarf affairs in France, the Netherlands and Great Britain are a case in point here. In the Netherlands, one politician has referred to Moroccan teenagers hanging out in the streets as 'street terrorists', calling for appropriate measures.[23] Frequently citing the need for protection of the blank neutrality of the public sphere, this type of politics demands for the national majority the monopoly of marking and inhabiting the streets, as Žižek's argument suggests. In that political climate, *Glub*'s attention to the everyday aesthetic of Europe's inner-city streets, changed and changing, does its valuable work.

## THE RELEASE OF TRANSLATION

As I have noted, *Glub* shows that the practice of seed-eating is being espoused by native Germans. In what ways, and to what extent, does *glub* translate to Berlin? To explore how *Glub* addresses the transformation of the practice in its Western appropriation, I draw on Walter Benjamin and Paul de Man's conception of translation as an occurrence, an event that changes the cultural everyday, and I specify *Glub*'s engagement with cross-cultural translation by attending to the paradoxical statement by one of the interviewees that the consumption of *glub* is 'very communicative also because you can't talk while eating the seeds'.

At one instance in the film, Parisian webmaster Tarek Mehdi notes that the seeds are 'now spreading out over other European countries'. In Berlin Davoud Changizi, at work in the Smyrna Kuruyemis seed shop, reflects:

> Muslims as well as Germans ... they are ... how to say this ... between two cultures. They discovered how we get on, enjoying sitting together, chatting and eating seeds. They got the hang of it, that feeling, and so they buy 200–300 grams and sit all night in front of the TV eating seeds. (plate 2.21)

On the one hand, Changizi's statement testifies to the successful integration of the practice of seed-eating in Berlin. Attracting a migrant as well as a native clientele, the shop manages to be commercially viable. On the other hand, the shopkeeper's words can be taken to flag the ways in which the habit transforms through its appropriation by German customers.

Prompted by the desire to mimic the migrants' way of enjoying themselves, the native clients purchase a paltry amount compared to the generous bulk normally bought by the extended households of the Near and Middle East. In addition, Changizi suggests, they typically munch on the seeds in front of the television set, detracting from the pleasurable conversation that should accompany their consumption. Hence, the Western consumers partake of the seeds in the privacy of their homes, whereas *glub* are usually consumed in public spaces: on the street, in parks, or at the seaside. Changizi implies that the habit is privatized by its Western translation. While *Glub*'s imagery of street life pictures the public import of the phenomenon, Changizi imagines his clients 'getting the hang of it' as they confine the practice to the private sphere where it does not belong. The shopkeeper envisions no crowd of *flâneurs*, but individuals consuming small amounts of seed in front of the television.

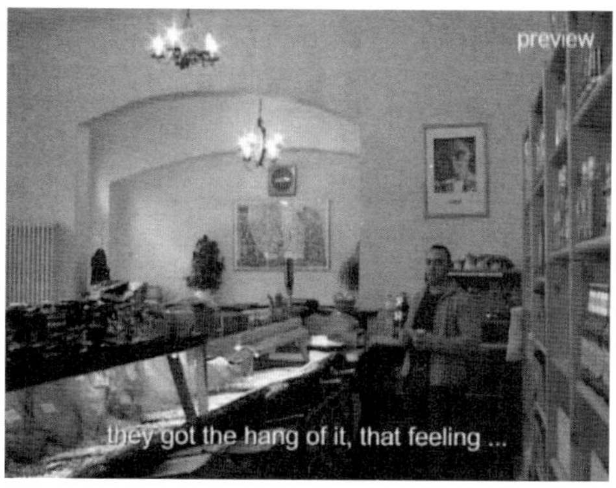


2.21 Film still from Mieke Bal and Shahram Entekhabi, *Glub (Hearts)*, 2004. 30-minute art film and 8-channel video installation. Berlin and Amsterdam. Courtesy of the artist.

Changizi's vision suggests that the discovery of a way of enjoying oneself and getting on that is alluring precisely because it is different may well end up replicating a pleasure the West already knows. As an insubstantial ethnic variety, the seeds become part of a familiar menu of television snacks that includes crisps, popcorn and peanuts. The distinct 'feeling' that to Changizi characterizes the sociable consumption of *glub* can be said to fail to translate, or to translate badly. The same arguably applies to other current appropriations of the seeds in the West as a health food rich in dietary fibre, vitamin E, foliate and zinc, and low in carbohydrates, and as a habit that can help to give up smoking, keeping hands and mouth busy.

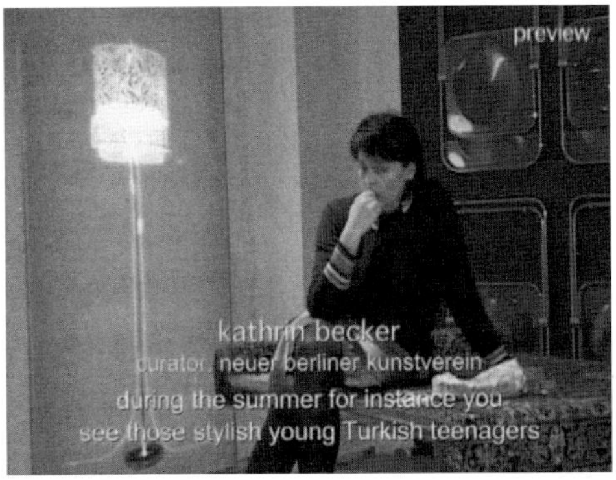


2.22 Film still from Mieke Bal and Shahram Entekhabi, *Glub (Hearts)*, 2004. 30-minute art film and 8-channel video installation. Berlin and Amsterdam. Courtesy of the artist.

In addition to Changizi's ambivalence, curator Kathrin Becker argues that the Berlinian adoption of the practice implies 'a reinterpretation of a traditional phenomenon going on now'. German youngsters take up and transform a habit observed in 'stylish' Turkish teenagers, Becker explains, and frequent the newly appearing specialized 'fancy' shops, like Smyrna Kuruyemis, rather than the Turkish supermarkets where the seeds are on sale in bulk and in unattractive packaging (plate 2.22). The Western translation of the practice not only entails its privatization and its ethnicization, it appears, but also *glub*'s up-market 'gentrification', which lends aesthetic surplus value ('stylish', 'fancy') to the migrants' unassuming habit when situated in a European capital.

What is missing in the social aesthetic, or stylized everyday behaviour, of these domesticating translations of *glub* is specified in detail by the Turkish journalist Tayfun Demiroz in his weblog on the 'Quirks of the Turks'.[24] According to Demiroz, the seeds are not about taste, nutrition, or convenience. For the Turks, the seeds are 'social and cultural accessories'. The shelling and eating of the seeds Demiroz calls an 'art form and a social event', belonging to the essential skills picked up in early childhood. Performing the social art form requires considerable skill: holding the seed between index finger and thumb, bringing it to the mouth, applying just the right amount of pressure to split the shell, using the tongue to extract the seed, and 'blow-spit' the empty shells on the pavement. 'You see', Demiroz adds,

> this is an integral part of the experience. No matter where you are, you are obliged to rid yourself of the shells immediately in any fashion you see fit. The preferred method is to blow-spit them towards the very same view you are enjoying. For this reason you will see sunflower seeds shells littering most walkways, parks, beaches and anyplace with a view.

The consumption of the seeds has to be achieved effortlessly while strolling, holding conversation with friends, and eyeing the other *flâneurs*. Demiroz has not mastered the practice; 'the coordination is just not there,' he admits. Weary of humiliating himself in public space, he is resigned to avoiding what he calls the 'seed scene'. Similarly, the Iranist Maryam Mameyhian-Prenzlov stresses that the habit not only entails the consumption of the seeds, but also 'the gesture how people do it', mimicking the spitting of the shells on the street (plate 2.23).

As Changizi and Becker suggest, the local appropriation of the seeds commodify them as stylish accessory, ethnicize them as exotic snack variety, and privatize them as individual indulgence. In that perspective, the practice fails to constitute what Demiroz describes as an 'art form and a social event' in its new context of Berlin. However, to insist on the untranslatable authenticity of *glub* in their original context runs another risk: they are easily turned into a sentimental and nostalgic reminder of what the modern West fears it has lost – communality, simplicity of life, having ample time to waste – and projects on the cultures that it conceives as archaic. That reification of the habit is decisively undercut in the film by Tarek Mehdi, who connects Changizi's 'that feeling' with unemployment, poverty, and boredom: 'you know our people have little work, so they have lots of spare time, so they buy *glub*, eat it, to pass the time' (plate 2.24). In view of the theories of translation proposed by Walter Benjamin and Paul de Man, *glub*'s eventful 'life' cannot be fully reduced to the original or the new context; translation exceeds the frames in which it takes place.

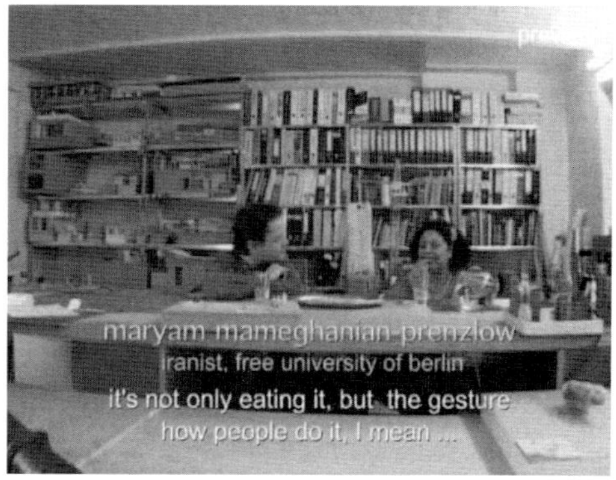


2.23 Film still from Mieke Bal and Shahram Entekhabi, *Glub (Hearts)*, 2004. 30-minute art film and 8-channel video installation. Berlin and Amsterdam. Courtesy of the artist.

Whereas the seeds and their social and affective significance, summarized by Changizi as 'that feeling', may be imagined as fitting together as tightly as 'a fruit and its skin' in their home context, their Western translations as television snack, health food, anti-smoking aid and an element of personal style loosely envelop the *glub* 'like a royal robe with ample folds'.[25] The two analogies come from Benjamin's famous essay 'The Task [*Aufgabe*] of the Translator', a title De Man has translated as suggesting 'the defeat, the giving up of the translator'.[26] For Benjamin and De Man, translation constitutes an event that cannot be reduced to either the original or the new form.

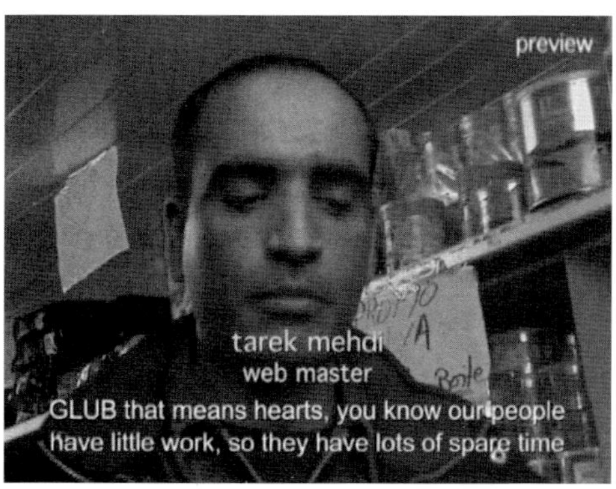


2.24 Film still from Mieke Bal and Shahram Entekhabi, *Glub (Hearts)*, 2004. 30-minute art film and 8-channel video installation. Berlin and Amsterdam. Courtesy of the artist.

Benjamin proposes a theory that looks 'for other things in a translation than reproduction of meaning'.[27] That other thing turns out to be the change that translation instigates in the languages, or broader semiotic habits, of the original as well as the translation. '[I]n its afterlife', Benjamin writes '... the original undergoes a change.'[28] Conversely, the language of the translation, in the words of Rudolf Panawitz quoted by Benjamin, is 'powerfully affected by the foreign tongue' (81). Hence, the 'afterlife' [*Überleben*] of the original in the shape of the translation does not so much imply the former's organic or spiritual continuity within a common history so that it can remain essentially the same, but rather the discontinuous, unpredictable 'outliving' of the original by the translation.[29] To be regarded with an 'entirely unmetaphorical objectivity', Benjamin argues, the 'life' of translation forges a 'history of its own', which disturbs the languages and cultures involved.[30]

In De Man's tropological interpretation of Benjamin's essay, translation does not metaphorically substitute one meaning for another on the basis of resemblance, but establishes a metonymic, hence contingent, relation between two words, 'a successive pattern, in which things follow'.[31] The effects of translation cannot remain restricted to the two words involved, because, as Benjamin writes, meaning 'is never found in relative independence, as in individual words or sentences; rather, it is in a constant state of flux.'[32]

According to De Man, translation 'de-canonizes' and 'de-authorizes' its original, because it puts in motion again what seemed to be a necessary and definitive fit between content and language, as between a piece of fruit and its skin.[33] Due to the translation, that 'skin' starts to billow around the original's content. De Man describes this renewed movement of the original as 'a wandering, an *errance*, a kind of permanent exile' (92). The translation simultaneously alienates its own language. Discussing the diverse connotations of the French *pain* and the German *Brot*, an example brought up by Benjamin, De Man argues that the metonymic relation between the two languages or semiotic habits that translation establishes transform the everyday: 'the stability of my quotidian, of my daily bread, the reassuring quotidian aspects of the word "bread," daily bread, is upset by the French word *pain*' (87). He almost seems to choke on the word. Translation, De Man stresses in conclusion, '*occurs*' (104). Hence, translation constitutes an event that transforms the actors, languages and cultures involved.

Benjamin's piece of fruit and De Man's loaf of bread situate translation in the cultural everyday. There, translation constitutes a transformative event that implicates both original and appropriation. Rather than *replacing* a foreign thing *for* a familiar thing, translation *associates* a familiar thing *with* a foreign thing, which puts *both* in a state that De Man characterized as a 'wandering' or 'exile'. To Benjamin, translation is a living force, not metaphorically so but 'objectively', which exceeds the languages and cultures involved. Within this perspective on translation, it is no longer so easy to deplore the Western afterlife of a foreign original that is fixated and reified in the process. Indeed, I have above unproblematically taken Changizi and Demiroz as my native informers, authenticating *glub*'s original and true significance. Ironically so, perhaps, because the former is, as a shop owner, economically dependent on the successful appropriation of the habit by his Western clientele, while the latter stands at some remove from the social art form even in its native context.

Associating the non-Western original and its Western appropriation without allowing the one to overrule the other requires the first half of Changizi's statement to be taken entirely seriously: in relation to *glub*, '[m]uslims *as well as* Germans [. . .] they are [. . .] how to say this [. . .] between two cultures' (my emphasis). As 'how to say this' suggests, 'between two cultures' is only an approximation, a translation, of how the migration and recontextualization of the practice resituates immigrants and Germans vis-à-vis each other. Yet, in that realm, the seeds may potentially incite what the artist Boris Mikhailov describes as 'some kind of communality', hinting at a community whose name and type cannot be easily determined. It presumably consists of natives and migrants who may not know each other very well, if at all, and who may not understand each other, but who are nevertheless bound together in 'getting the hang of it': holding the seeds between index finger and thumb, bringing them to the mouth, applying pressure to split the shells, using the tongue to extract the seeds, and spitting out the empty shells.

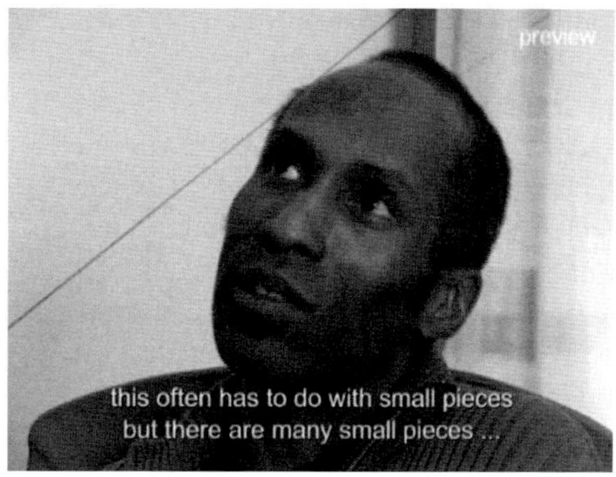


2.25 Film still from Mieke Bal and Shahram Entekhabi, *Glub (Hearts)*, 2004. 30-minute art film and 8-channel video installation. Berlin and Amsterdam. Courtesy of the artist.

The cultural translation of an everyday detail, *Glub* proposes, takes place in several ways at the same time. Changizi imagines his television-watching clients as adapting the seeds to an existing convention. The pictures of street life register the transformation of what De Man characterized as the reassuring stability of quotidian life. And the video monitors that accompany the film portray 'listening heads' who adapt themselves to the practice rather than the other way around (see plates 2.1–2.8). For them, translation is not so much about the paraphrase of the content of speech or the mimicry of a way of speaking. Rather, it is about the adoption of a way of listening. In this respect, the paradoxical statement made by one of the interviewees in the film that the consumption of *glub* is 'very communicative also because you can't talk while eating the seeds' makes perfect sense. Their mouths full of shells, like the vowels and consonants of a foreign language, the 'listening heads' on the monitors communicate, translate, by listening.

That 'translative' attitude cedes linguistic transparency. Yet, it may simultaneously garner new clarity. As the writer and translator Karl Edwards explains,

> In general, with my translations lately [. . .] this often has to do with small pieces, but there are many small pieces. I know it takes me [. . .] It's a kind of intoxication with clarity, which on the one hand is nice because it feels as if I have a power to find words I hadn't even thought of since I was ten. I had access to words. My mind becomes more like an octopus. (plate 2.25)

As Johnson speaks, the film shows the image of a shop menu advertising different varieties of seeds in Turkish as well as German (plate 2.26). Stimulated by linguistic alterity, then, *Glub* proposes, the octopus-like mind may develop multiple arms that latch on to new as well as nearly forgotten words. Quickened by cultural alterity, the mouth can grow different tongues to learn to appreciate the tastes, textures and shapes of the seeds. Words and seeds become specks of culture, there to touch and taste.

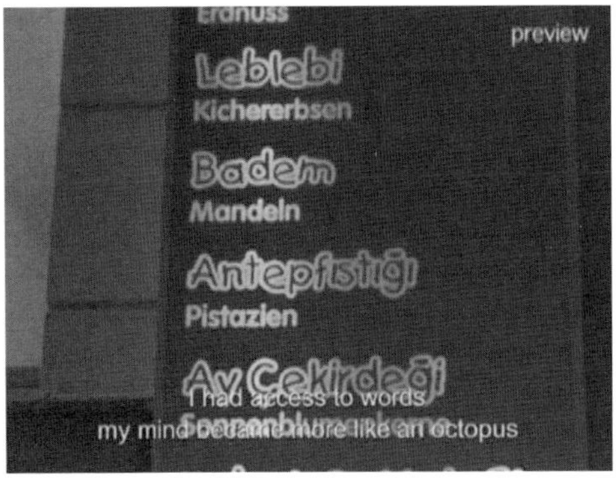


Plate 2.26 Film still from Mieke Bal and Shahram Entekhabi, *Glub (Hearts)*, 2004. 30-minute art film and 8-channel video installation. Berlin and Amsterdam. Courtesy of the artist.

In *Death of a Discipline* (2003), Spivak calls attention to what she describes as the 'restricted permeability of global culture'.[34] Satellite dishes may turn up in Nepalese villages, but the opposite scarcely happens: 'The everyday cultural detail, condition and effect of sedimented cultural idiom, does not come up into satellite country.'[35] Yet, *Glub* traces one piecemeal and qualified instance of reverse globalization, in which the translation of a cultural detail, in the spirit of Benjamin and De Man, constitutes an event that transforms the Western everyday, modifying the appearance of the metropolis, modernity's most cherished image. Bal and Entekhabi's art work shows how a minute speck of culture like *glub* can attract epistemological curiosity, aesthetic wonder and social recognition, thus allowing it to participate in the 'uncoercive rearrangement of desire' that Spivak sees as the goal of the humanities today.[36]

## Notes

I wish to extend my gratitude to the editor and anonymous reviewers of *Art History* for their incisive and helpful comments on an earlier version of this chapter.

1 The Greek *barbaros* originally referred to a person who says 'blah blah', someone stammering or speaking unintelligibly. See *The Oxford English Dictionary Online*, Oxford, 2006, available at http://dictionary.oed.com (accessed 10 November 2006).

2 Aamir R. Mufti, 'Auerbach in Istanbul: Edward Said, Secular Criticism, and the Question of Minority Culture', *Critical Inquiry*, 25, 1998, 102.

3 Mieke Bal, 'Food, Form, and Visibility: *Glub* and the Aesthetics of Everyday Life', *Postcolonial Studies*, 8:1, 2005, 58.

4 *Mille et un Jours [A Thousand-and-One Days]*, Cinema Suitcase, 43-minute social documentary on migration, 2003; *Nothing is Missing*, multiple-screen video installation, 25–35 minutes (looped), 2006. Videos are distributed by Vtape, Toronto, and roARaTorio, Paris.

5 Bal, 'Food, Form, and Visibility', 58.

6 Alan Singer, *Aesthetic Reason: Artworks and the Deliberative Ethos*, University Park, PA, 2003.

7 Kaja Silverman, *The Threshold of the Visible World*, New York, 1996, 3–4; quoted in Bal, 'Food, Form, and Visibility', 55.

8 Yves-Alain Bois and Rosalind E. Krauss, *Formless: A User's Guide*, New York, 1997.

9 Bal, 'Food, Form, and Visibility', 56.

10 The phrase refers to Arjun Appadurai, ed., *The Social Life of Things: Commodities in Cultural Perspective*, Cambridge, 1986.

11 Clifford Geertz, 'Thick Description: Towards an Interpretive Theory of Culture', *The Interpretation of Cultures: Selected Essays*, London, 1993, 71.

12 Geertz, 'Thick Description', 21.

13 Mieke Bal, *Travelling Concepts in the Humanities: A Rough Guide*, Toronto, 2002.

14 William Safran, 'The Jewish Diaspora in a Comparative and Theoretical Perspective', *Israel Studies*, 10:1, 2005, 38.

15 Brent Hayes Edwards, 'The Uses of Diaspora', *Social Text*, 19:1, 2001, 52.

16 Gayatri Chakravorty Spivak, *Death of a Discipline*, New York, 2003, 72–101.

17 Gareth Dale and Mike Cole, eds, *The European Union and Migrant Labour*, New York, 1999, 130.

18 Dale and Cole, *The European Union*, 118.

19 Dale and Cole, *The European Union*, 120.

20 Dale and Cole, *The European Union*, 130–2.

21 Slavoj Žižek, 'Formal Democracy and Its Discontents', *Looking Awry: An Introduction to Jacques Lacan through Popular Culture*, Boston, 1992, 165. Further page references are given in the text.

22 Walter Benjamin, 'M [The *Flâneur*]', *The Arcades Project*, trans. Howard Eiland and Kevin McLaughlin, Cambridge, MA, 1999, 417–55. Further page references are given in the text. For a comprehensive study, see Keith Tester, ed., *The Flâneur*, London and New York, 1994.

23 The politician at stake is called Geert Wilders. See Sanne ten Hoove, 'Wilders vreest "tsumani" moslims', *de Volkskrant*, 7 October 2006, 1.

24 Tayfun Demiroz, 'Ramblings – Seeds by the Seaside', http://www.tayfundemiroz.com/About/Quirks/seeds/htm., (accessed 21 February 2006).

25 Walter Benjamin, 'The Task of the Translator: An Introduction to the Translation of Baudelaire's *Tableaux parisiens*', *Illuminations*, ed. Hannah Arendt, trans. Harry Zorn, London, 1999, 76. Bal enlists the essay and the two analogies to account for Louise Bourgeoi's *Femme-Maison* (1983) visual 'translation' of Bernini's *Ecstacy of Saint Teresa*. See Bal, *Travelling Concepts*, 56–95.

26 Paul de Man, ' "Conclusions": Walter Benjamin's "The Task of the Translator" ', *The Resistance to Theory*, Minneapolis, 1986, 80.

27 Benjamin, 'The Task of the Translator', 78.

28 Benjamin, 'The Task of the Translator', 73. Hence, the historicity of translation is 'preposterous' in the sense that Bal has given the term as hingeing on a reversal 'which puts what came chronologically first ("pre-") as an aftereffect behind ("post-") its later recycling'. See *Quoting Caravaggio: Contemporary Art, Preposterous History*, Chicago, 1999, 7.

29 Betsy Flèche, 'The Art of Survival: The Translation of Walter Benjamin', *SubStance*, 28:2, 1999, 97.

30 Benjamin, 'The Task of the Translator', 72.

31 De Man ' "Conclusions" ', 90.

32 Benjamin, 'The Task of the Translator', 75.

33 De Man, ' "Conclusions" ', 82–3.

34 Spivak, *Death of a Discipline*, 16.

35 Spivak, *Death of a Discipline*, 16.

36 Spivak, *Death of a Discipline*, 103.

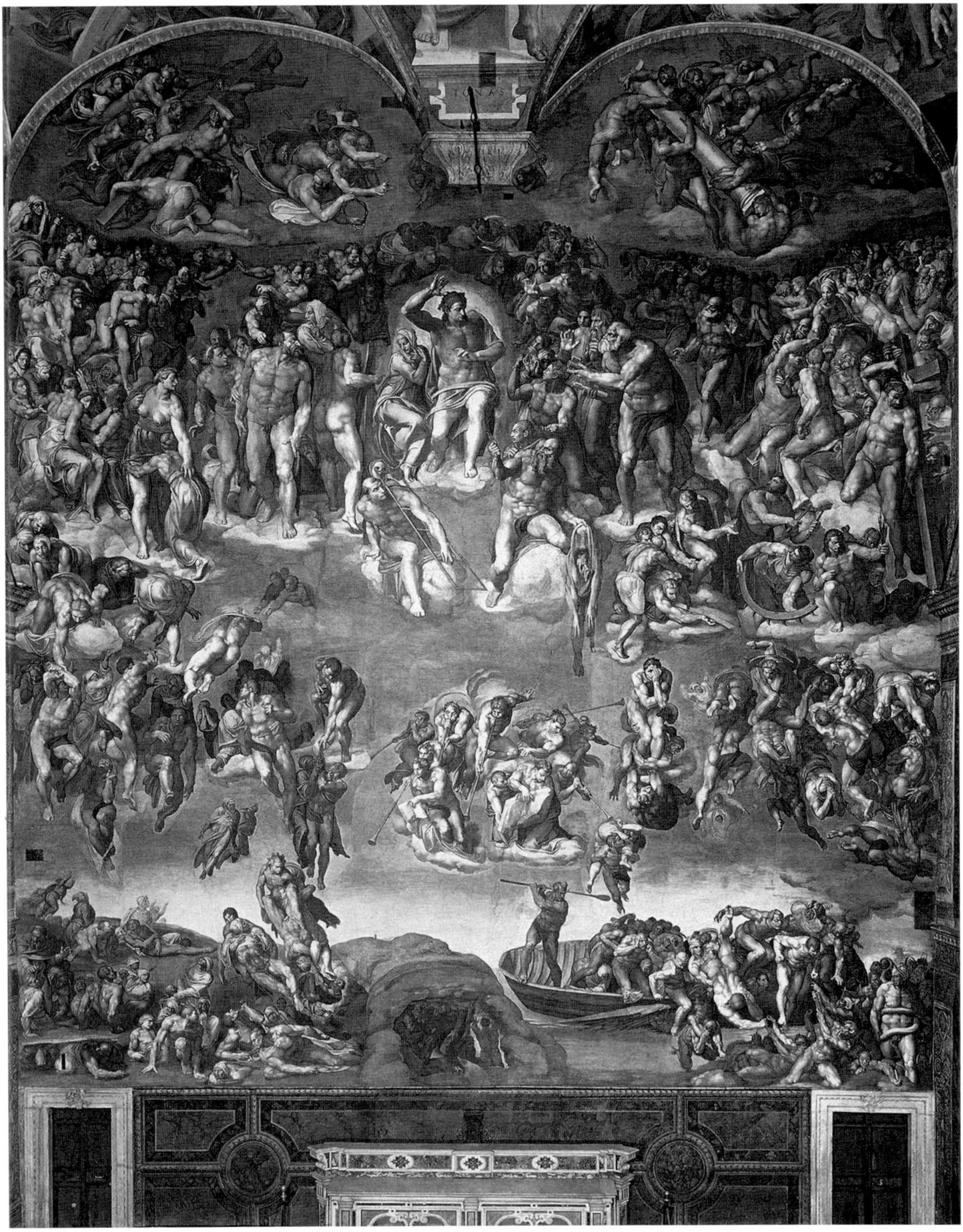

3.1 Michelangelo, *Last Judgement*, 1536–41. Fresco. Rome: Vatican Museums, Sistine Chapel.

# 3

# TIME OF HISTORY AND TIME OUT OF HISTORY: THE SISTINE CHAPEL AS 'THEORETICAL OBJECT'

GIOVANNI CARERI

> VLADIMIR: [Stooping] True. [He buttons his fly.] Never neglect the little things of life.
> ESTRAGON: What do you expect, you always wait till the last moment.
> VLADIMIR: [Musingly] The last moment . . . [He meditates.] Hope deferred maketh the something sick, who said that?
>
> Samuel Beckett, *Waiting for Godot*, 1952[1]

Why another essay on the Sistine Chapel? Because our point of view is displaced with the passing of time, setting us the Benjaminian task of addressing an 'image' of the past, liberating it from its spectral destiny. For Walter Benjamin, 'It is not that what is past casts its light on what is present, or what is present casts its light on what is past; rather, image (*Bild*) is that wherein what has been comes together in a flash with the now (*Jetzt*) to form a constellation. In other words, image is dialectics at a standstill.'[2] Mieke Bal's construction of a critical history of art has taken up Benjamin's insight that: 'every image of the past that is not recognized by the present as one of its own concerns threatens to disappear irretrievably.'[3] It is, she contends, his concept of 'translation' that allows the extension of Benjamin's philosophy to the visual arts. The act of translation – *transducere* – is a displacement that reveals what is of importance to us in the work of art of the past.[4] Bal has argued that Louise Bourgeois's *Femme-Maison* (1983) is a translation of Gian Lorenzo Bernini's *Ecstasy of Saint Teresa* (Rome: Santa Maria della Vittoria, 1647).[5] As a translation of Bernini's sculpture, Bourgeois's sculpture becomes a 'theoretical object', a term that implies a specific theoretical meaning: 'theory here is not an instrument of analysis, to be "applied" to the art object supposedly serving it but in fact subjecting it. Instead it is a discourse that can be brought to bear on the object at the same time as the object can be brought to bear on *it*.'[6] The moment of the object's return to discourse is decisive, as it defines the terrain of a specific dialogue, neither purely philosophical nor purely historical. The theoretical object, as Bal conceptualizes it, is impure and hybrid, a montage of many material and conceptual registers, often in tension with each other. Here I employ Bal's concepts of the montage of different temporalities as a theoretical model for a critical and analytical experiment conducted in dialogue with her writings. I propose that the Sistine Chapel can be seen as a 'dialectic image' suspended between the time of the beginning of Christian history and its fulfilment in the 'now' (*Jetzt*) of the *Last Judgement*. This dialectic image is open to new 'translations' if it is assembled in a constellation that permits us to recognize it 'as one of our own concerns'.

## ANACHRONISMS

My experiment proposes two forms of anachronism. The first may be understood as pertaining to the temporal machine of the Sistine Chapel since its completion in 1542; the second, by contrast, is concerned with our 'present' and is a more audacious form of anachronism defined by the relationship between Samuel Beckett's *Waiting for Godot* and the chapel. The first form of anachronism proposes that the last element of the chapel to be completed, the *Last Judgement* (1536–41), reconfigures the temporality of Christian history expressed in the ceiling (1508–12) and in the quattrocento frescoes (1480–82). In this hypothesis, the Sistine Chapel should be considered as a representation of Christian history according to the anagogical concept of St Augustine that Christian history was one of salvation.[7] Only by adopting this point of view can the temporalities of beginning (Genesis), foundation (the stories of Moses and Christ, the portrayal of popes and the Ancestors of Christ), prophecies (prophets and sibyls) and completion (the Last Judgement), be understood as correlated and interdependent. Most of the literature on the Sistine Chapel lingers on one of the three 'moments' of its production – the walls (1480–82), the ceiling (1508–12), the *Last Judgement* (1536–41) – thus foreclosing a confrontation with formally distinct works by different artists produced in diverse periods and dissimilar religious and historical settings for three papal patrons. Each of these approaches implicitly seeks to validate the style of an individual artist, the historical and artistic contexts of the work, the determining role of patronage, or, in the most interesting cases, the relationship between these elements at a precise historical moment.[8] It is my contention that the Sistine Ceiling complicates and enriches the conception of Christian history expressed in quattrocento histories, whilst the *Last Judgement* brings this concept towards a catastrophic fulfilment that transports the spatial and temporal construction of the ceiling *outside of itself.*

The underlying theoretical principle for my montage of the three parts of the chapel is the following hypothesis: the passage between the elements of the chapel defines a perceptive 'work' of cognitive and emotional 'recompostion' that is a theoretical model for the experience of the spectator. The advantage of this line of inquiry consists in showing the procedure by which the image is made to signify through the specific modalities of its enunciation.[9] The 'theoretical' spectator is, moreover, indispensable if one wants to account for the *effects* produced by montage. To avoid confusing this theoretical instance with either the historical or modern spectator (the beholder) I use the term 'viewer', which has the advantage of stressing the act of viewing, an action that links the addressee of the work to the figures depicted. This is particularly significant in the *Last Judgement*, where the act of 'looking at Christ' has specific religious meaning.

In what follows I study how the 'syntax of bodies' of the *Last Judgement* produces an inchoate temporality contracted in the present. The confrontation with this temporality produces profound reconfiguration in the structure of time of the histories of the Old and New Testaments.[10] The cycle of the *Ancestors of Christ*, situated in the lunettes and spandrels of the ceiling, is involved in this operation in a particularly interesting way: the actions of these figures are the expression of the everyday, cyclical passage of time, dedicated to the care of children, cooking, weaving and sewing, rest and sleeping.[11] The anti-heroic dimension of their actions is stressed by their melancholic postures, or, more precisely, by a torpor that relates to the iconography of the sin traditionally defined as *sloth*; in contrast to the eminently decisive actions represented in the *Last Judgement*, those of the *Ancestors* demonstrate a lassitude, a distinctly non-decisive character. Situated at the limits of a history of salvation, the position of the *Ancestors* within this anagogic construction of history opens the way for the second form of anachronism, that based on the relationship between the *Ancestors* and Beckett's *Waiting for Godot*. In order to become a 'dialectic image', this association must transform itself into a 'constellation' that presents the Sistine Chapel as an object that 'views our present'.

The *Ancestors* are usually interpreted as being either allegorical (vices and virtues) or typological (Old Testament prefigurations of the coming of Christ).[12] The anachronism suggested here leads to a more literal approach: that the Ancestors represent a misguided way of understanding the passing of time (an ignorance of the coming of Christ), a misguided way of the measuring and passing of historical time (genealogy), and a figuration of the nonsensical character of history (outside Christianity).

Bal has called 'preposterous' that movement or reversal that 'puts what came chronologically first ("pre-") as an after-effect behind ("post")'.[13] This type of theoretical operation has the advantage of provoking a shift in point of view that refocuses the questions directed to the object. For example: under what conditions can we establish a link between, on the one hand, inaction, the bearing and care of children, and on the other, the legitimizing function of the genealogy of Christ? How does the liminal figure of the Jew, condemned by the Augustinian concept of history, have a place in the overall scheme of the Sistine Chapel? Which new connections allow an understanding of the temporality of the cycle of the *Ancestors* as paradoxically belonging to three times: the time of the Old Testament, the period of Rome's Renaissance, the time of the Last Judgement?

This anachronism rests on some well-known common elements, such as the 'citation' of Dante's *Inferno* in the *Last Judgement* and in *Waiting for Godot*, and the explicit reference in both to the question of the end of time.[14] It seems, therefore, legitimate and possible to consider *Waiting for Godot* as an attempt to construct, through dramaturgy and theatrical performance, a suspended *present*, comparable to the present of the *Last Judgement*, but characterized by an inactive torpor comparable to that of the *Ancestors*.[15] Put another way, and recalling Bal's terminology, Beckett's play decentres and translates the 'dialectic image' of the history composed of the 'crystallization' of the time of the *Ancestors* and the time of the *Last Judgement*. But *Waiting for Godot* becomes, in turn, decentred by the relationship with that object of the past; its anagogic dimension is enriched, demonstrating significant similarities and differences to our 'now'.

To propose this anachronistic relation between *Waiting for Godot* and the Sistine Chapel as 'dialectic image' is to allow an understanding of the spatial and visual experience of the chapel. At the same time, it guides our understanding of the 'past'. In this new 'constellation', the figuration of the incomprehension of the meaning of (Christian) history, attributed to the Jews in the Renaissance, must be measured against the incomprehension of the meaning of history expressed in *Waiting for Godot*, in relation to the events of the 1939–45 war and the Holocaust.[16]

## THE TIME OF JUDGEMENT

The production of time in Michelangelo's *Last Judgement* is based upon the aspectualization of the actions represented (plate 3.1). Aspect, in its semiotic and linguistic origins, may be understood as a network of categories capable of describing an action's interior temporality in relation to an implied observer. Aspectualization is an enunciation device which not only characterizes linguistic expression but other forms of the figuration of the time of an action, particularly visual forms; it must be considered, therefore, as one of the mechanisms which implicate the viewer.[17]

In Christian theology, the time of the Last Judgement is that of the second coming of Christ, which closes human time. The activation of this 'last time' – the time of the *escathon* – is characterized by the simultaneity of the manifestation of the presence of Christ (his *parusia*), the resurrection of the body, and the judgement that separates the Elect from the Damned. The fresco articulates these three operations in a single regulating process: as Christ's gesture activates resurrection, the figures of the Elect and the Damned begin to manifest the results of his action. The predominating passions are surprise and suspense, situating the figures between hope and fear. And, like the figures in the fresco, the viewer waits in suspense for the completion of the action that s/he is assisting, but this accelerated waiting also closely concerns his or her judgement. The sound of the angel's trumpet is the auditory mark for the start of the action: the beginning of the end of time has the duration, speed and intensity of a breath. Even when exposed to the spectacle of time's ending, the viewer is still situated in the time of waiting, the remaining 'messianic' time between the chronological temporality of his own life and the apocalyptic *escathon* of the end.

The process of the visual configuration of the fresco is partly constructed through a group of figures whose poses are intertwined. To the left of the angel with a rosary who elevates two of the Elect is a group of seven figures, arranged very densely in a small area. The seven figures of the group 'touch' each other, if we concentrate on the fresco's surface. But their superimposition creates a stratified spatial thickness, hollowed out by the movement of the bodies on the painted surface. In the absence of any other system of reference for the measurement of space, this movement constitutes the unique device for constructing depth in the fresco. While, as I will argue in what follows, this principle of spatial articulation is linked to the pose of Christ, it should be noted here that this articulation results from a tension between the cohesive unity of the fresco's surface and a way of creating depth that is akin to the spatiality of Donatello's and Michelangelo's bas-reliefs. This production of a spatial depth that is both tense and instable (as it is defined only by the movement of bodies) corresponds to the production of a temporal depth that can also be categorized in terms of contraction and instability. The definition of space and time in the *Last Judgement* does not depend upon the articulation of figures in a pre-existing space, as in the perspectival construction of space, but rather on the production of a spatial and temporal depth in which it is impossible to separate space and time, because both are generated by the movement of bodies.[18]

The rotation and the curving forms of the figures are positioned according to the dynamic principle of the *figura serpentinata*. This formal model may be considered as one of Michelangelo's rare explicit theoretical references. The *figura serpentinata* demonstrates the dynamism of *contrapposto*. But while *contrapposto* is derived from the rhetorical notion of *antithesis* – the confrontation of opposites in a single figure – and belongs to the high language of men of letters, the *figura serpentinata* belongs to the language of artists and of Michelangelo in particular. Giovanni Paolo Lomazzo reported in his *Trattatto dell'arte della pittura, scultura e architettura* (1584):

> It is said that Michelangelo once gave this advice to the painter Marco da Siena, his disciple, that he ought always to make the pyramidal *figura serpentinata*, and multiply it by two or three. And in this precept it seems to me lies the whole secret of painting, because the greatest grace and loveliness that a figure may have is that it seems to move itself; painters call this the *furia* of the figure. And to represent this movement, no form is more suited than a flame of fire, which, as Aristotle and all the philosophers say, is the most active of the elements, and the form is the most apt of all forms of movement, because it has a cone and sharp point, with which it seems to want to rend the air, and ascend to its sphere. Thus when the figure has this form it will be most beautiful.[19]

The flame and the wave are the figures of a movement that expand to reproduce their own form and pattern. In the *Last Judgement* the *figura serpentinata* of Christ's gesture is, like the flame, a matrix of movement not only in terms of the dynamic of the creation of space by the movement of bodies but also as a postural matrix of likeness: a form that *gives its form* to other figures and thus constitutes the formal principle of their syntax.

## CONFORMATION AND DEFORMATION

I have argued that the actions represented in the *Last Judgement* are triggered by the movement of the body of Christ (plate 3.2). Giorgio Vasari describes Christ's gesture as one of anger and condemnation.[20] Ascanio Condivi, who wrote under Michelangelo's direction, remarked: 'Above the Angels of the trumpets is the sun of God in Majesty, his powerful right arm up, as an enraged man, cursing the sinners and throwing them out from his face to the eternal fire and his left stretched towards the right side as if he sweetly recovered the good ones.'[21] Christ's double gesture elevates some and casts down others. But Condivi's words, '*allontare dal volto*' ('throwing them out from his face'), are rich in theological references and they evoke in particular the letter of St Paul to the Thessalonians, in which, citing Isaiah, he describes damnation as losing the sight of Christ's face.[22] Election, by contrast, yields the sight of Christ's face, triggering a process that renders the Elect similar to Christ. This similarity is described by St Paul as a process of subjection: '. . . the Lord Jesus Christ who will change our lowly body *to be like his glorious body*, by the power which enables him even to subject all things to himself'.[23] I call this process of the assumption of likeness *conformation*, underlining how, thanks to its inherently figurative nature, this term can be used to describe the Elect of the *Last Judgement* as figures gathered in the act of assuming a form which conforms to that of Christ. In the opposite process, the denial of the sight of Christ's face to the Damned produces a likeness to the Devil. It is important not to lose sight of the visually inchoate nature of these actions and the economy of energy that links them to the action of Christ. Whereas, for Condivi, Christ's gesture is a matrix of two opposing forces, as St Paul indicates, it is force that gives form. The entire fresco may be described as a *force field* regulated

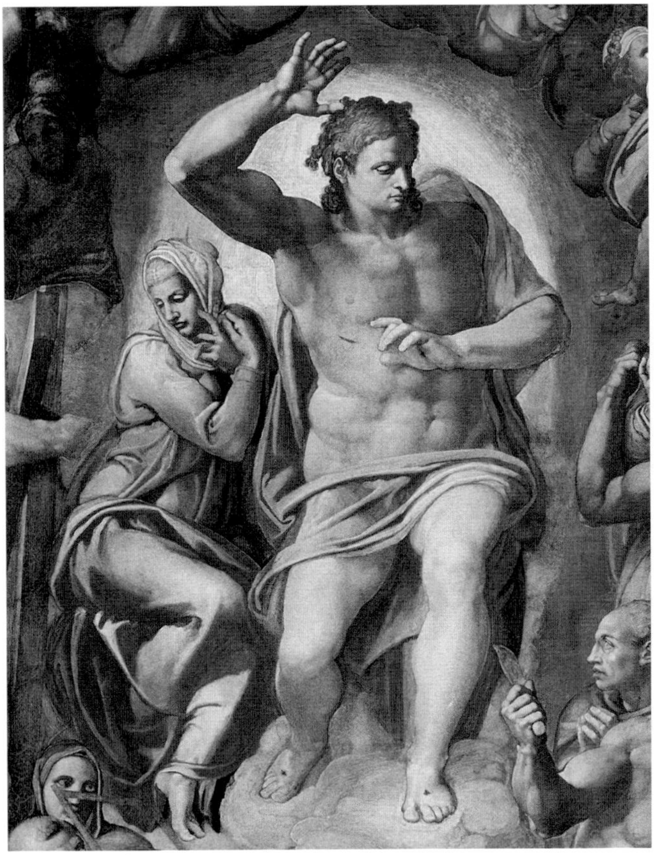

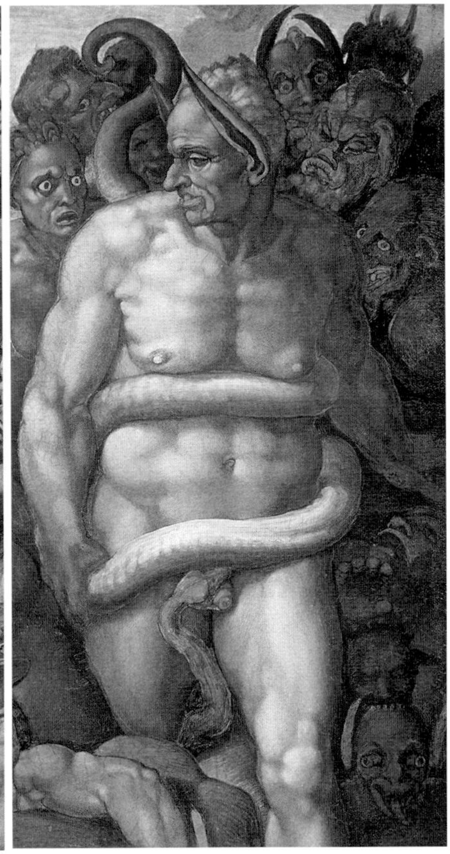

3.2 Detail of Michelangelo, *Last Judgement*, showing Christ and the Virgin Mary, 1536–41. Fresco. Rome: Vatican Museums, Sistine Chapel.
3.3 Detail of Michelangelo, *Last Judgement*, showing Minos, 1536–41. Fresco. Rome: Vatican Museums, Sistine Chapel.

by a bipolar morphological disposition: the force that elevates produces likeness while that which distances provokes dis-likeness and deformation.

In their relation to men, the angels are the principal means for the conforming and the deforming forces.[24] Their poses resemble that of Christ. And those that carry the objects of the Passion conform most, not only because of all the figures they most assume an ideal body, similar to the Apollonian body of Christ, but also because they incorporate in an extreme form, the movement of Christ's *figura serpentinata*, for which reason, it seems to me, these angels were perceived as 'dancers of the moresca', as Giovanni Andrea Gilio perceptively described them. Like the Dionysian dancers, the angel 'dancers' of the *Last Judgement* incorporate, divinity, assuming and expanding the torsion of Christ's body.[25] This movement corresponds to *agilitas*, a quality that, according to St Thomas Aquinas, defines the bodies of angels and the Elect after the Last Judgement.[26]

The figure of Mary is the first to incorporate Christ's *figura serpentinata*, becoming a privileged vehicle for the conformation of the Elect. By contrast, the serpent that coils around the heavy, awkward, animalistic form of Minos offers a caricatured *figura serpentinata* (plate 3.3). The polar opposite to Christ, Minos is the model for the Damned, for negative conformation, for the deformation of bodies and poses. This morphological interpretation of the *Last Judgement* is based on a hypothesis founded on the Pauline concept of subjection – understood as an adoption of likeness – in a formal principle of likeness of movement. However, if the general economy of form were only determined by the unfolding of the conforming power of Christ and the deforming power of Minos, there would be no space for human will. But the singularity of Michelangelo's *Last Judgement* lies in its attribution to man of a will that, however exposed and subjected to Christ's will, preserves a certain autonomy.

## SUBJECTIVATION AND SUBJECTION: THE *BOOKS OF LIFE*

Human will is paradoxically free and subject at the same time. In relation to the Last Judgement, it must be understood as within the economy of *conformation*, as defined above, and conceptualized as a condition of equilibrium produced by the encounter between an exterior force of subjection and an opposing interior force, subjectivation.[27] Subjection corresponds to the judgement of Christ, while subjectivation is the result of self-judgement.

In the fresco, two figures visually articulate these concepts: the Damned soul bitten by the serpent and the dazed Elect soul whom an angel transports towards

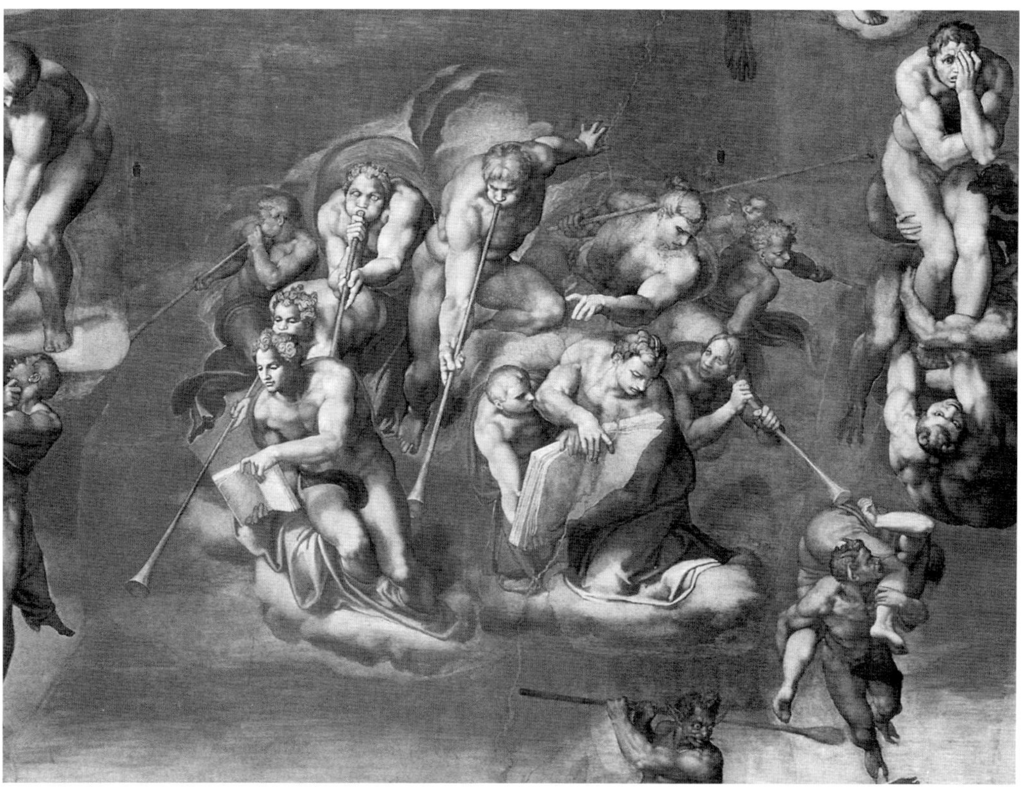

3.4 Detail of Michelangelo, *Last Judgement*, showing angels with trumpets, 1536–41. Fresco. Rome: Vatican Museums, Sistine Chapel.

heaven. Both are located at the centre of the middle ground of the fresco, which is occupied by a group of angels with trumpets, two of whom hold open books of blank pages (plate 3.4). Expanding on the brief account given by Vasari, Condivi describes this group thus:

> [. . .] in the middle of the air near the earth, are the seven angels described by Saint John in the Apocalypse. The trumpet in the hands, they call the dead to judgment from the four sides of the world, between them two bring an open book in their hands in which everyone reading and acknowledging his past life, must judge himself.[28]

This invitation to self-judgement refers to the *Books of Life*, evoked by the prophet Daniel and interpreted by Origen as conveying the image of a surface upon which everyone's deepest inner secrets become visible: 'The books about which Daniel speaks and which have to be opened to God's tribunal in order to become readable to all reasonable creatures, is the series of our thoughts and acts printed in the deepest of our hearts.'[29]

St Augustine's commentary on the *Books of Life* describes the process of inscription as the completion of an extraordinary mnemonic operation. In a passage from the *City of God* that deserves further inquiry in relation to Augustine's theory of memory and his reflections on the role of reading in the construction of self and in conversion, he writes, 'We have to admit the existence of a divine *force* under whose action the good and bad acts will be recalled to the memory of everyone, they all will be caught by a gaze of the spirit of an astonishing quickness; this knowledge will accuse or excuse the conscience, so that, at the same time, all and everybody will be judged.'[30] He adds: 'And this divine power is called a book because in it we shall see, as it were, read all that it causes to remember.'[31] The figure of the man bitten by the serpent has often been described in terms of introspective melancholy but not, to my knowledge, in terms of self-judgement (plate 3.5). This new connection allows us to perceive this desperate figure in terms of an encounter between the force of subjectivation (the result of self-analysis) and the force of subjection (of will). At the very moment that he concludes his self-accusatory examination of conscience, an external

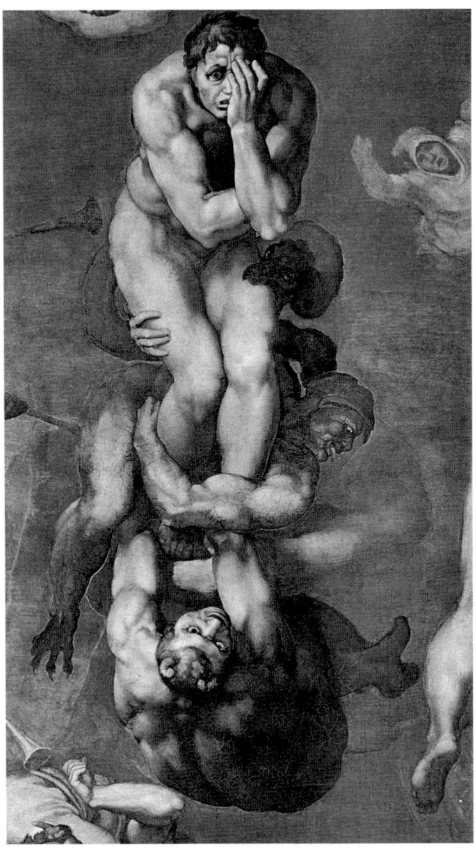

3.5 Detail of Michelangelo, *Last Judgement*, showing the Damned in despair, 1536–41. Fresco. Rome: Vatican Museums, Sistine Chapel.

force – the demons – capture him and hurl him downwards. Their body is composed of a single actor distributed into three figures: an anthropomorphic demon, a hybrid creature and a serpent. The montage of these three figures visually bears out the force that makes this desperate body resemble Minos.

In the humanist concept of punishment, as Leo Steinberg has argued, hell as a place of physical pain is replaced by the pain of a conscience troubled by remorse.[32] And it is remorse, which is derived in Italian from the verb *ri-mordere*, that allows me to return to the serpent's bite. *Ri-mordere* means to *bite again*: thus, a bite to the exterior of the body becomes a bite into the interior; self-condemnation is repeated and confirmed by divine judgement. In his *Treatise on the Immortality of the Soul* (1516), Pietro Pomponazzi qualified shame and guilt as '*pene essenziale*' or 'essential punishments', and indeed these seem to be the punishments suffered by the Damned in the *Last Judgement*.[33] The process through which punishment is interiorized, emphasized by Pomponazzi, may be recognized by the citation of the *Laocoön* (plate 3.6). This return of the antique figure is signalled by the serpent biting the figure's left thigh. The significant change introduced by the melancholic gestures of his arms imply that the tragic condition of this Christian *Laocoön* is not, however, the consequence of the inscrutable will of the gods, but an effect of the Christian interiorization of guilt.

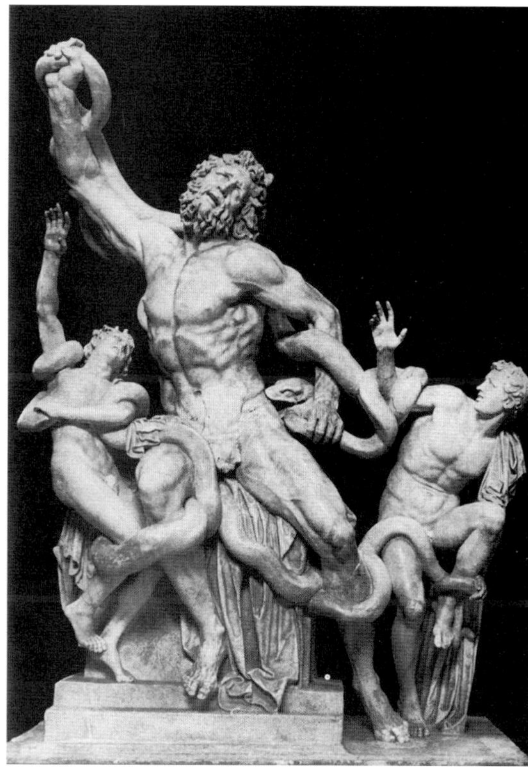

3.6 Hagesandros, Athenodoros and Polydoros of Rhodes, *Laocoön*, *c.* 175–150 BCE. Marble, height 242 cm. Rome: Vatican Museums, Museo Pio Clementino.

The Elect elevated by an angel on the left of the fresco can be considered as a pendant to this figure (plate 3.7). Self-judgement, according to Augustine, 'excuses his conscience' and destines his soul to salvation, while an external force subjects it by raising it heavenwards. The configuration of the figure of the Elect is also determined by the encounter between the forces of subjectivation and subjection. Dazed and un-coordinated, the Elect soul is placed at the centre of a group of the resurrected, whose bodies follow the conforming force that emanates from Christ's gesture and arranges them according to the *figura serpentinata*. The association allows the pinpointing of the exact moment at which the certainty of salvation or damnation appears on the threshold of conscience, an inchoate moment that from its inception encompasses ascent or descent.

Their open pages facing outwards, the *Books of Life* implicate the viewer, offering an invitation to self-judgement. They demand a double conversion – a turning of the gaze from outward to inward, and a spiritual conversion, following

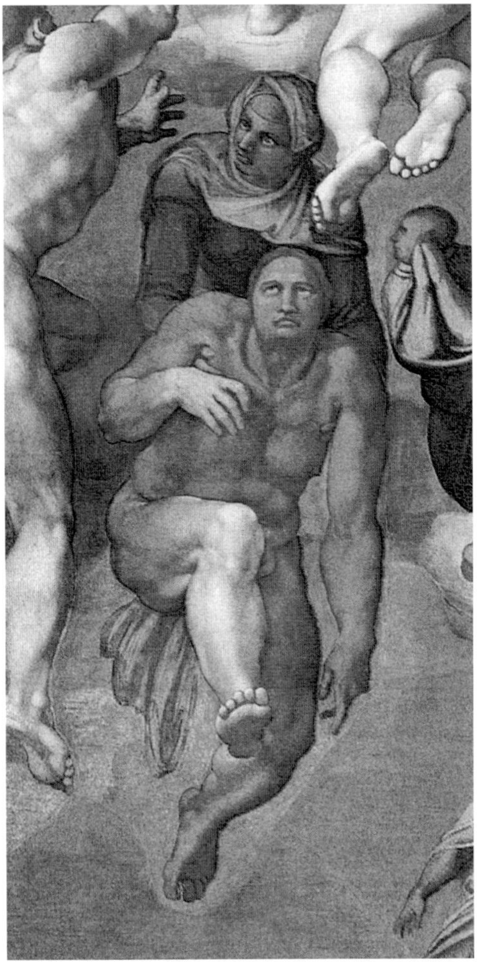

3.7 Detail of Michelangelo, *Last Judgement*, showing the dazzled Elect, 1536–41. Fresco. Rome: Vatican Museums, Sistine Chapel.

self-judgement. Everyone, inside and outside the fresco, must attempt an extraordinary feat of memory, to constitute him- or herself as a subject worthy of election or damnation. These two figures, the man bitten by the serpent and the dazed Elect soul, both of whom have started their journey to damnation or salvation, are visually situated in proximity to the viewer, just as the viewer also begins the process of self-analysis. They can be considered as two privileged thresholds giving access to participation in the process of conformation.

## THE END OF HISTORY AND THE END OF *ISTORIA*

In the aspectual organization of the *Last Judgement*, the beginning of the end of time collides with the viewer's 'now'. If the viewer's condition of waiting is intensified by this contraction of time, he is nevertheless in a different condition than that of the painted figures, a waiting made to last for an indefinite time. The fresco redefines this enduring time of waiting as messianic time, turned towards the *escathon* of the end. This procedure corresponds to the Pauline concept of Last Judgement whose temporal dimension has been underlined in Giorgio Agamben's definition of messianic time as 'the time that contracts itself and begins to end'.[34] St Paul, Agamben recalls, defines this residual time as *ho nun kairos*, the time of the 'now', or the time for self-analysis and conversion.

In the *Last Judgement* not only are many figures from different epochs united in a common present, but there are also prophets and sibyls. The identification of one sibyl,[35] situated high up on the left, is confirmed by the indicative gestures of one of the angels who carried the cross (plate 3.8). Visually, this old woman resembles more the Cumaean rather than the Erythraean sybil of the vault. But, as this sybil was credited with prophesying the Last Judgement, she seems to be a better candidate. Her unveiling is a remarkable image of revelation. Her position at the edge of the fresco associates her with the function of the 'presentation of representation', usually fulfilled by the device of the frame.[36] As a figure of the frame, she *modalizes* the gaze of the viewer, inducing a look that is informed by her gesture of the revelation of the fulfilment of the prophecy that shapes the whole of the *Last Judgement*. She links the ceiling and the space of Judgement,[37]

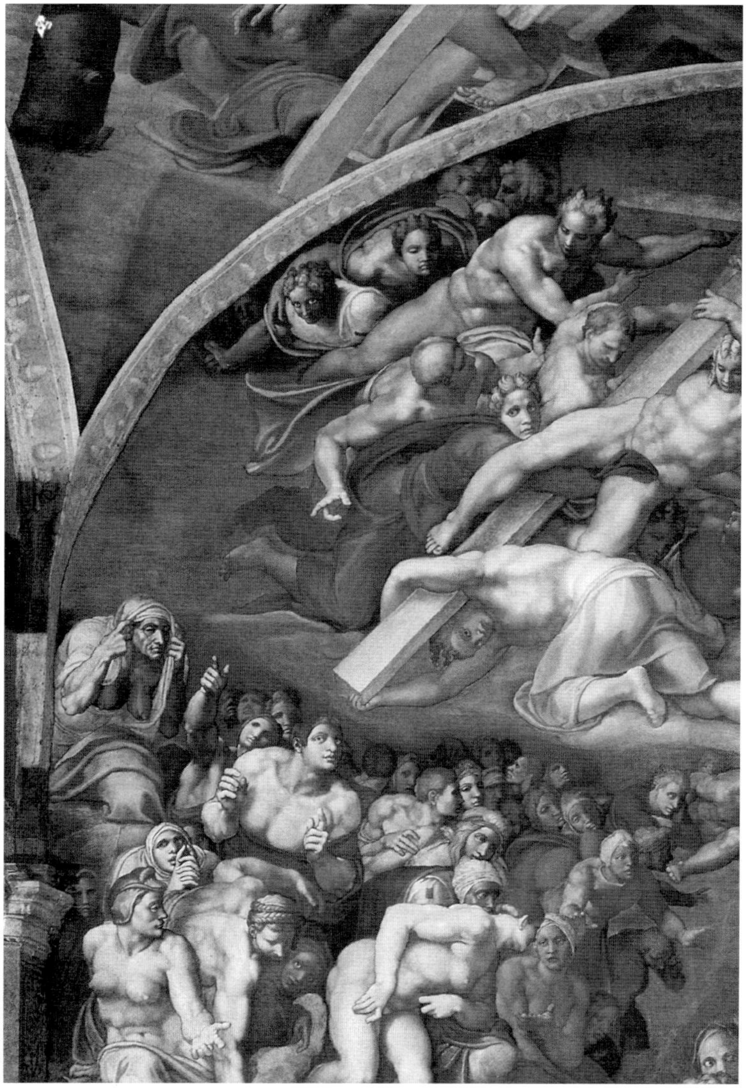

3.8 Detail of Michelangelo, *Last Judgement*, showing the Sybil, 1536–41. Fresco. Rome: Vatican Museums, Sistine Chapel.

connects the disparate times that unfold in the chapel, and links the Christian conception of historic time to messianic time, stretched towards the moment of Last Judgement. Like the viewer she beholds this sudden manifestation of Christ in the time of the present, and she witnesses here, on the edge of the fresco, the moment of apocalyptic explosion that reduces all the pasts to a single present. With the revelation of the fulfilment of the prophecy of the Last Judgement, time accelerates: the past precipitates into present, traversing historical time in a flash.

But this sense of the precipation of the past history into the present time of Judgement, marked by the sibyl, is also entrusted to the articulation of space: the Sistine Chapel may be considered as a device for constructing and regulating the Christian journey to salvation (plate 3.9). In moving from the entrance through

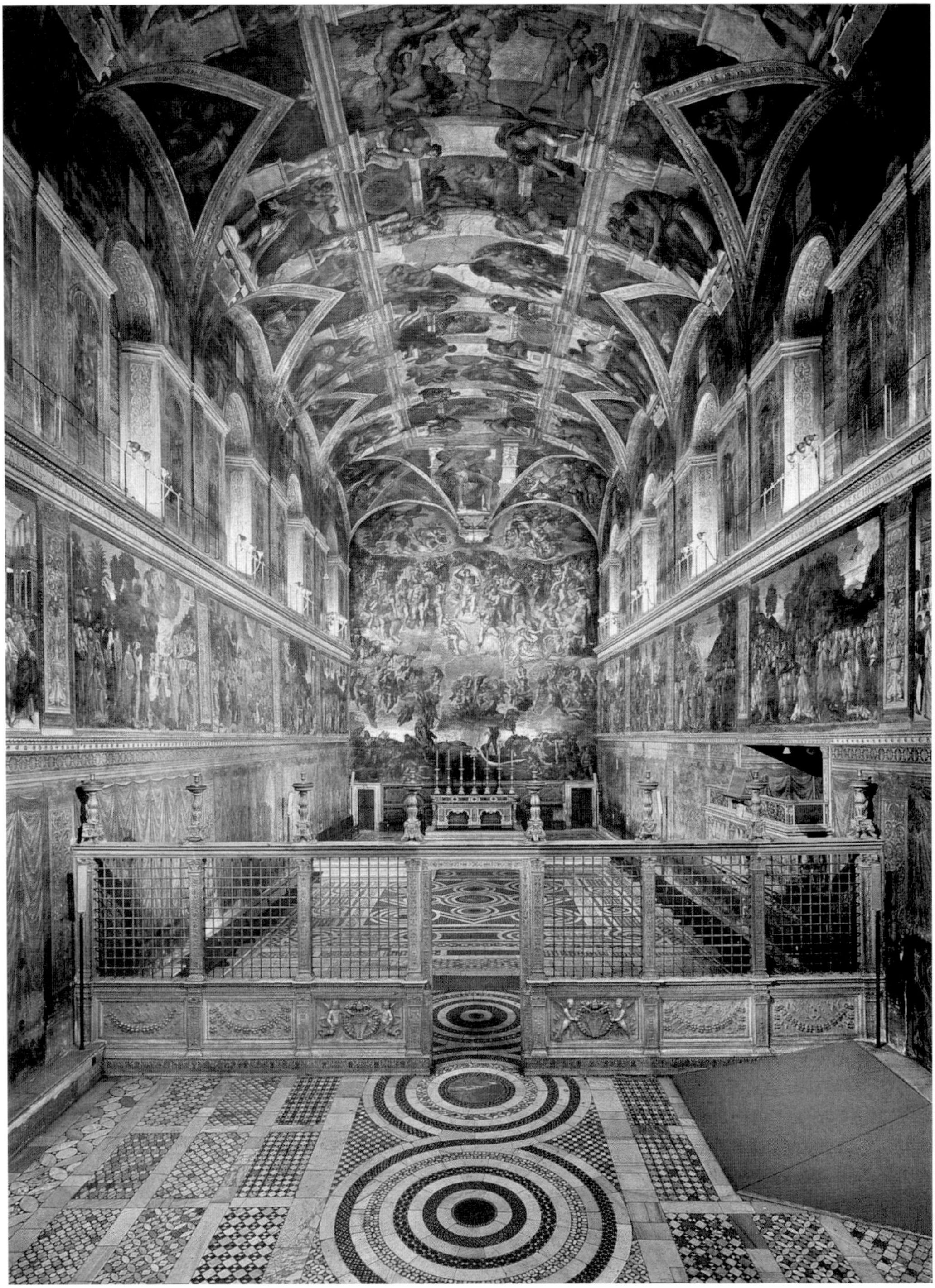

3.9 View of the Sistine Chapel. Rome: Vatican Museums.

the chapel the spectator walks through (and underneath) the figural and prophetic representation of the narrative of Christian history, to be faced with the moment of self-analysis and judgement. This is a passage from an architectonically organized zone (walls and ceiling) to a chaotic space governed by the movement of bodies. The *Last Judgement* provides neither an architectonic frame nor an internally structured geometry based on perspective that can mediate between interior and exterior space. The mobile instability of the space of the altar wall ruins the illusion of measurable and coherent space given in the walls and ceiling. The spatial and temporal elasticity of the *Last Judgement* denies the principles of intelligibility of the quattrocento *istorie*, and, to a lesser degree, the more complex spatiality of the ceiling. The organization of history is implicated in this catastrophe of space and time: the end of the time of history is figured by the 'ruination' of space, and of the time of *istoria*. The quattrocento histories are constructed to distance the viewer from the space and time represented. But the spatial and temporal structure of the *Last Judgement* (constituitively incompatible with that of an Albertian *istoria*) produces an aspectualization – inchoate, incomplete and unfinished – that renders it more intensely 'present' than perspectival illusion. The predominance of the *Last Judgement* in the Sistine Chapel certainly comes from its size, but also from its mode of confronting the viewer. For the viewer, the passage through the chapel prompts an accelerated scanning of historical time, precipitating the moment when self-judgement opens the new time of salvation or damnation.

## OUTSIDE HISTORY: THE TIME OF THE ANCESTORS OF CHRIST

Within the anagogic context of the chapel, the *Ancestors of Christ* are paradoxically placed in an 'excluding inclusion'. They establish the regal legitimacy of Christ, assigning him a decisive role in the completion of this history. But they do this by virtue of their exceeding status,[38] because they are excluded from Christian history as the history of salvation. Their state of ignorance about the coming of Christ differentiates them from the prophets or the sybils who foretell the future. Their liminal status is manifested in several forms of incongruity and by their entirely unmemorable actions.[39] David, for example, known for slaying Goliath, is here immobile with his arms crossed. This extraordinary visual representation of the Ancestors as thresholds to the time of Christian history prompts several questions about the genealogy of Christ, given in the Gospel according to St Matthew.[40] To summarize extensive debate, the list of Joseph's ancestors has to integrate Christianity into the historical design of divine origin marked by the figures of David and Abraham. At the same time, the continuity of Christian history with the genealogical history of the Jews is interrupted by the birth of Christ, who is not the biological son of Joseph and therefore eludes mortal genealogy. This break signifies the end of genealogy as a divine model of the completion of history and coincides with its opening 'to all nations' and its orientation towards the second coming of Christ on the day of Judgement. The evangelists Matthew and Luke, as Karin Friis Plum underlines, 'use the genealogical form to demonstrate that with Jesus the possibilities of genealogy have been completely exhausted. For Christianity severs the religious identity from the predominant kinship structure.'[41] The junction and the separation between the genealogical form of history (the time of the Old Testament) and the non-genealogical form of history (the time of the New Testament) hinges upon the genealogy of Christ. Given this threshold, we can expect an opposition between the aspects of the legitimating junction and the aspects of the separation, founded on the devaluing of the 'others'. The otherness of the *Ancestors* rests not only on the place of the Jews in the Christian past but also on the refusal of the Jews to recognize Christ as the messiah; here they enter the Christian story in the role of witness, or in testifying to their error by their dispersion and disgrace.[42]

Barbara Wisch has demonstrated that the dress of some of the *Ancestors* has the characteristic features of the clothing assigned to the Jewish community of Rome by the papal sumptuary laws of the sixteenth century.[43] For the viewer they are, at the same time, the Jews of the Old Testament, those of then, and the Jews of now. Aminadab wears on his left arm the *signum* that distinguished the Jew in Renaissance Rome: a yellow cloth circle sewn onto the left arm (plate 3.10).[44] Also noteworthy is the predominance of the colours of red and brilliant yellow that differentiated the Jews and signalled their special relationship with the Roman senate and with the Pope.[45] The few trades authorized to Roman Jews in the sixteenth century are represented: the retouching and sewing of used clothes (the spandrel above the lunette of Salmon, Boaz and Obed, plate 3.11) and money-lending (the lunette of Elezar and Nathan).[46] The melancholic tonality and the idle pose of the majority of the other *Ancestors* is probably connected to the condemnation of usury, shown in an anti-semitic German print of 1475

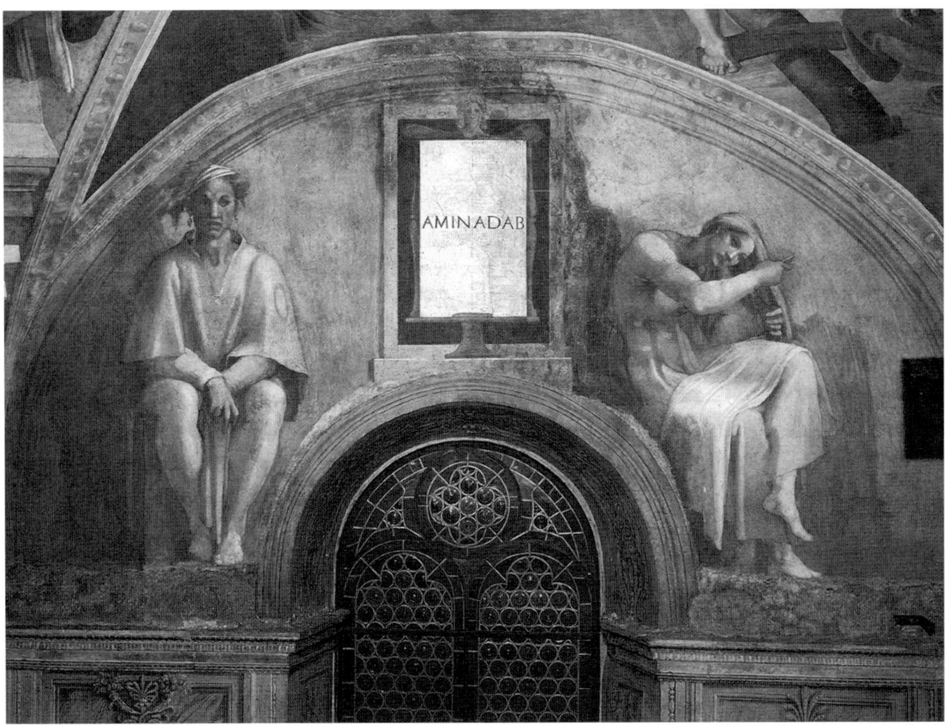


3.10 Michelangelo, *Aminadab*, c. 1508–12. Frescoed lunette. Rome: Vatican Museums, Sistine Chapel.

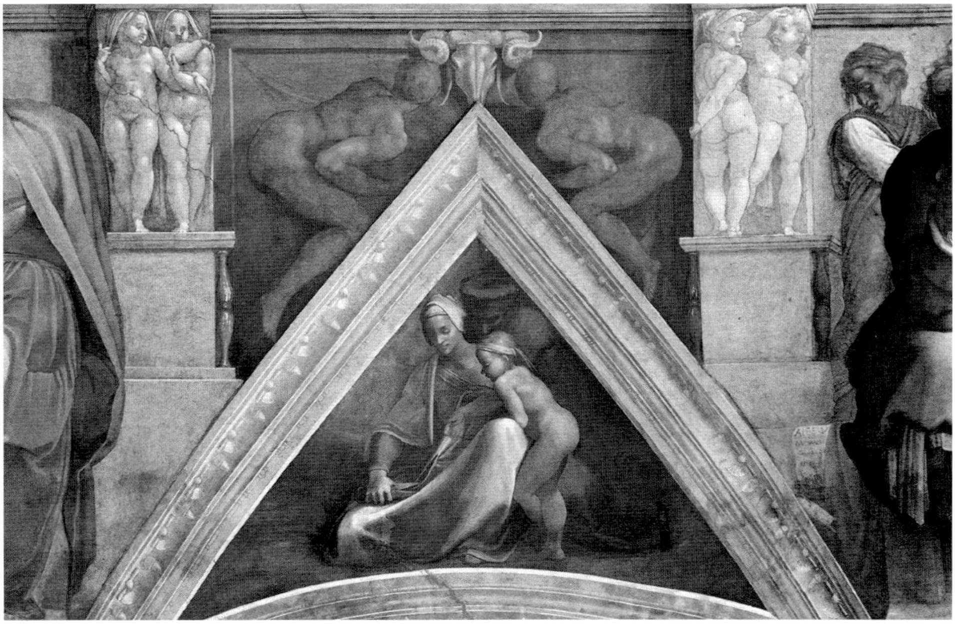

3.11 Michelangelo, spandrel above *Salmon, Boaz and Obeth* lunette, *c.* 1508–12. Fresco. Rome: Vatican Museums, Sistine Chapel.

(plate 3.12) where the usurer shows the *Talmud*, a text that legitimizes the lending of money and establishes its rules, according to some anti-semitic pamphlets, whilst the woman sleeps with her arms crossed in her lap, to indicate wealth that is not the outcome of work.[47]

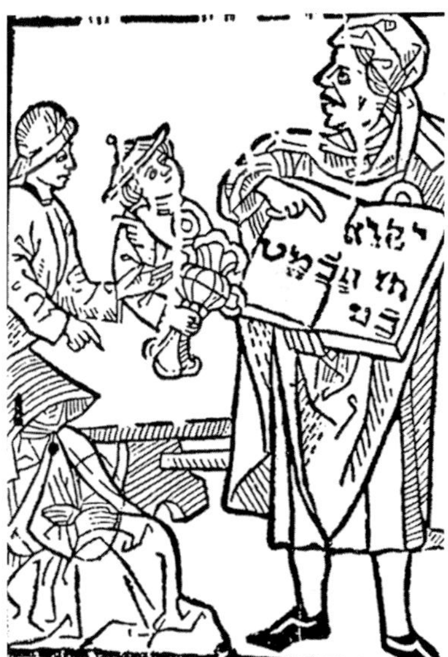

3.12 *Jewish Usurer with Family*, *c.* 1475. Woodcut. Anonymous printed broadsheet. Germany *c.* 1475. Published by George Liebe, *Das Judentum in der deutschen Vergangenheit*, Leipzig, 1903, ill. 5.

Melancholy is codified as a Saturn-like melancholic temperament in the figure of the hooded man in the lunette of Hezekiah, Manasseh and Amon, in the woman above the lunette of Roboam and Abias, and that above the lunette of Jesse, David and Solomon. Starting with an analysis of a commentary by St Augustine, Eric Zafran has convincingly elucidated the associations between the Jews and Saturn, noting that this is not the creative Saturn of Neoplatonic origin, but a late medieval Saturn who is greedy, lamenting, wandering, irrascible, fearful.[48] This figure is also the embodiment of sloth, a mortal sin because it is culpable laziness that ignores the duty to love God.[49] The torpor of the Ancestors implies condemnation, referring to the Jews' refusal to recognize Christ as the messiah.[50]

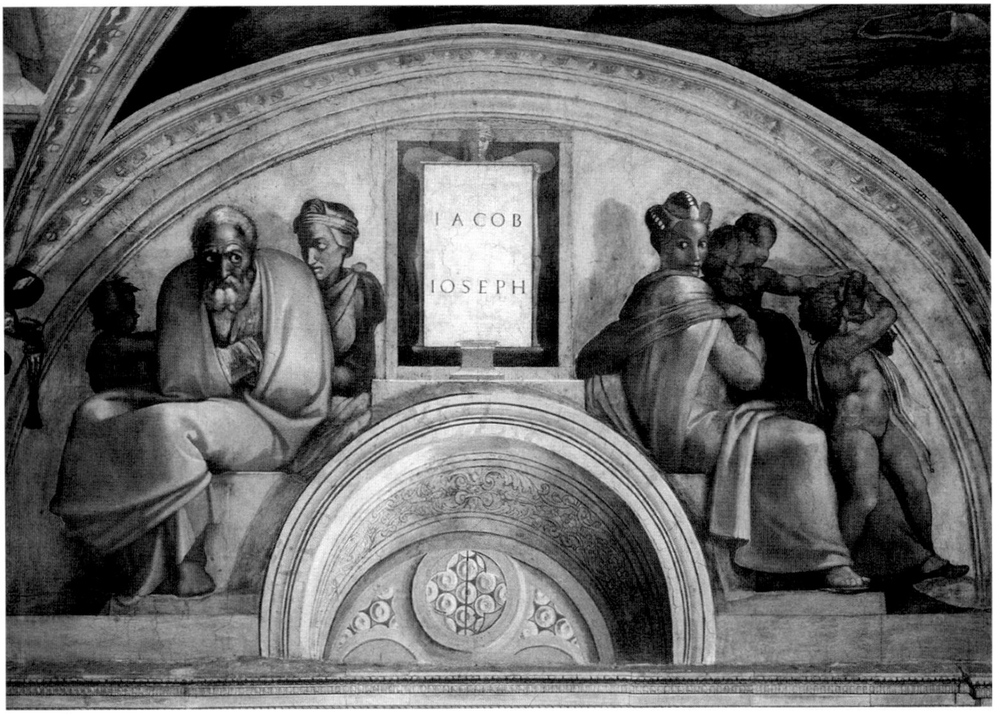


3.13 Michelangelo, *Jacob and Joseph*, *c*. 1508–12. Frescoed lunette. Rome: Vatican Museums, Sistine Chapel.

The representation of the Ancestors draws on the iconography of the Holy Family, notably in the depiction of maternity and the care of children, which culminates in the lunette with Mary, Joseph, Jesus and St John the Baptist (plate 3.13). The iconographic scheme of the Holy Family is retrospectively projected in the whole series. Adopting and transforming the Holy Family scheme, the Ancestors' families form in this way a complex nexus of *preposterous* prefiguration. In this cycle, the mothers transmit the seed of David to Joseph, reduced to the biological function of the generation of flesh (*secundum carnem*), but Mary interrupts this blood line: the Holy Family is precisely positioned between earthly genealogy and the new conception of Christian history. As the last in the genealogical series, the Holy Family has some common traits with the families of the Ancestors. But as the place in history that welcomes the birth of the Divine Child, who came in order to substitute transmission through blood with that which passes through the spirit, there are distinct characteristics of differentiation. Mary's yellow attire, which indicates that she belongs to the Jewish population, is covered by a tunic of a red more dark and rich than the clothes of the other women, and a band of blue recalls the incarnation. In the same tunic, a chromatic rainbow variation indicates the new alliance. But the most significant departure is in the torsion of the body of the little John the Baptist, a hingeing figure between the Old and New Testaments, who gives the Christ Child the bread that prefigures his sacrifice on the cross and consequently the hope of redemption 'to all nations', outside the old structures of kinship and genealogy.

Another important iconographical scheme in the Ancestors is that of the rest on the flight to Egypt. Michelangelo could have drawn on models from prints by

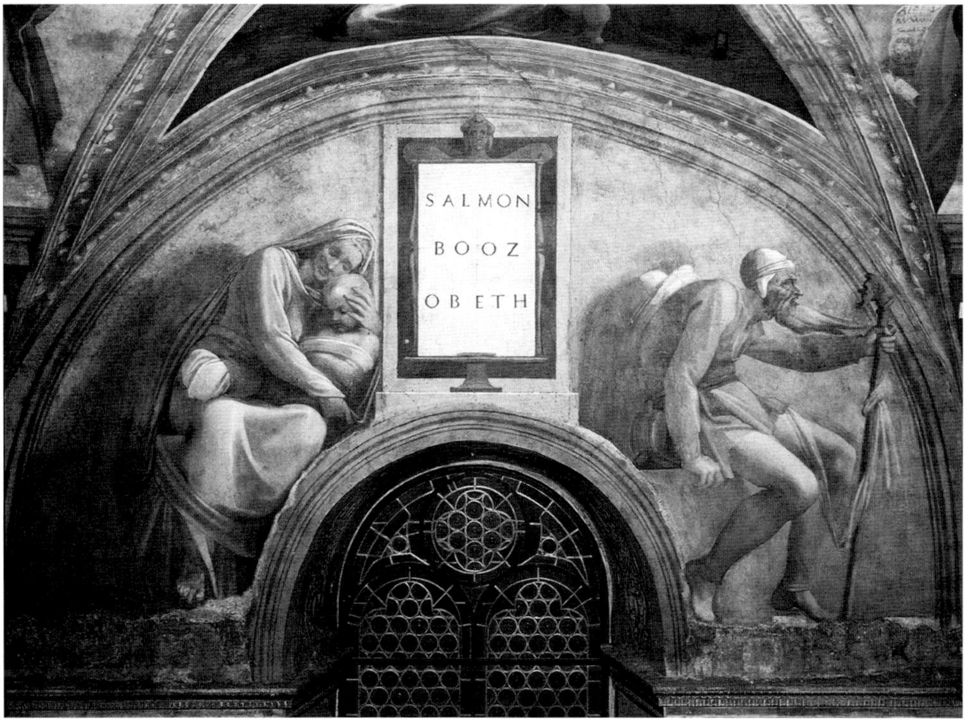


3.14 Michelangelo, *Salmon, Boaz and Obeth*, *c.* 1508–12. Frescoed lunette. Rome: Vatican Museums, Sistine Chapel.

Albrecht Dürer or paintings by Fra Bartolommeo, which situate the Holy Family in open countryside, introducing the motif of 'positive' errancy, because it was considered as an anticipation of the Universal Kingdom of Christ, as a realization of the prophecy of Josiah and as a 'repetition' of other 'flights', by Moses, Jacob and David.[51] However, it seems that the Sistine Chapel is dominated by a motif of the 'negative' errancy of the Jewish people, evidenced in the pilgrim with a stick (in the lunette of Salmon, Boaz and Obed, plate 3.14), a figure that unites traits of vagabondage and madness. The spandrels portray night and exterior, irregular ground. Associating errancy with error, this space of transit contrasts forcefully with the ideological dimension of foundation presented in the entire chapel and especially on the walls where the scenes of the life of Moses and Christ and the images of the popes legitimize the authority of the papacy and the foundation of the Church of Rome. The nomadic spatiality of the spandrels constitutes a disoriented and absurd reversal of the oriented spatiality that regulates the architecture, the pictorial structures, and architectonic structure of Christian history in the Sistine Chapel.

The plaques with the names of the Ancestors in large capital letters participate in this overall design, taking on a positive role in the genealogy of Christ to signify his legitimation in the foundation of the Church. This positive aspect can be construed as an association on the level of the semiotic registers of the chapel, one that constructs a link between texts: the names are to be associated with the titles that describe important moments of this history of foundation on the frames of the quattrocento frescoes.[52] Put otherwise: the relationship of *inclusion* rests on the name and on writing, privileged forms of foundation and authority, whilst the relationship of *exclusion* rests on the figures of the Ancestors, depositories of the marks of otherness. The Ancestors are anti-heroic in their gestures, and because they are enclosed within narrow walls on which their shadows are silhouetted, unlike the figures of the ceiling or the *Last Judgement*. Capable of projecting shadows, these Jews that err out of Christian history have carnal bodies; their extraneity to the historic construction of the chapel is inscribed in this all-too-human corporeality. Their poses express the ridiculous, litigious and slothful senselessness of a foolish expectation, waiting for the messiah who has already arrived. Their daily occupations and the biological function of generation and nursing are necessary to the sustenance of life, but they are insignificant in history.

This condition of '*bare life*' is denied by the historic and anagogic design of the Sistine Chapel.[53] But it belongs to the human condition, as Samuel Beckett revealed four centuries later in *Waiting for Godot*.[54] Two works so far apart in time can crystallize in a constellation by virtue of a preposterous history in which the work of the past contains a 'spark' of the work of the present, revealing a veiled potentiality.[55] The *Ancestors* are the concealed 'spark' in the Sistine Chapel under the mask of Jewish alterity. Excluded from history, their carnal bodies are extraneous to the ideological programme of resurrection proposed in the *Last Judgement* and to the phantasmic projection of the body in a process of rebirth that negates mortal corporeality through the processes of transformation that will conform it to the Apollonian form of Christ or the deformed body of Minos. Destined neither for election nor damnation, the bodies of the Ancestors belong to diurnal time. In the chapel's economies of time, the Ancestors represent the lack of a consciousness of any sense of history: immersed in the time of repetition and daily tasks, they are outside the economy of the contraction and acceleration of time that regulates the chapel and culminates in the *Last Judgement*. Their time is the non-sensical base on which is founded the meaning of Christian history. Their incongruous presence in the chapel highlights the ideological operation by which the flesh body and the mortal time are excluded. The Beckettian translation of the temporality of the *Ancestors* reveals the violence that in the Sistine Chapel maintains the time of the Ancestors on the other side of meaning. *Waiting for Godot* reconfigures the spatial and temporal liminality defined by the position of the *Ancestors* in the Sistine Chapel but it radically re-elaborates the components of that liminal zone: errancy, laziness, waiting, repetition. It is possible to discover in the play many of the elements that comprise the Christian historical-anagogic machine that are expressed in the Sistine Chapel. However, in *Waiting for Godot*, these elements are transported, *tradotti*, in a zone that has the characteristics of the liminality of the Ancestors. The play reverses the chapel's exclusion of the mortal body and human time. This Beckettian translation [*traduzione*], by contrast, excludes the ideal body and its metaphysical destiny. The traits of this reversal are the explicit references to the Bible and to the end of time in the context defined by the lowest occupations of life, doing up one's fly or lifting one's shoe.

In elucidating connections between the Sistine Chapel and *Waiting for Godot*, I have proposed 'constellation' rather than influence to reactivate deeper and more fundamental relations. The first 'crystallization' is the *preposterous* product of the tensions between the messianic time of the ceiling and the *Last Judgement*, and the *other* diurnal temporality of the cycle of the *Ancestors*. This tension is revitalized by the inclusion of Beckett's theatre of the absurd in this first constellation. But this second enlarged constellation offers a reversal. Whereas Michelangelo's representation of the Ancestors sought to *recharge* the messianic force of Christian history, the second 'constellation' (which includes *Waiting for Godot* ) weakens the 'messianic force' in such a way as to question any orientation of historical time in our present sense of history. This constellation so profoundly diminishes that force that it revokes any belief in the orientation or sense of history.[56] In taking a further motif from Walter Benjamin, it may be concluded that the *Ancestors* conceal the prophecy contained in the Sistine Chapel since:

> The history of art is a history of prophecies. It can only be described from the point of view of the actual, immediate, present: for each epoch possesses its own new possibility, which cannot be transmitted by legacy, to interpret the prophecies that the art of the past contains in a specific address. The most important task of art history is to decipher, in the great works of the past, the prophecies which gave them value at the time that they were made. The future, in fact, not always immediately given and never strictly definite. Moreover, nothing is more capable of transformation in the work of art, than that obscure and brewing space of the future out of which those prophecies step into the light, separating the works of art that have soul from those without interest: never a single one, but always a sequence developing, intermittently, in the course of centuries.[57]

*Translated by Samuel Bibby*

## Notes

1 Samuel Beckett, *Waiting for Godot*, 1952, in *The Complete Dramatic Works*, London, 1990, 12.

2 Walter Benjamin, *The Arcades Project*, trans. Howard Eiland and Kevin McLaughlin, Cambridge, MA, 1999, 462.

3 Walter Benjamin, 'Theses on the Philosophy of History', Thesis V in *Illuminations*, ed. and with an introduction by Hannah Arendt, trans. Harry Zohn, New York, 1976, 255.

4 Mieke Bal, *Travelling Concepts in the Humanities: A Rough Guide*, Toronto, 2002, 64ff.

5 Bal, *Travelling Concepts*, 85.

6 Bal, *Travelling Concepts*, 61. On the 'theoretical object', see Yve-Alain Bois, Denis Hollier and Rosalind Krauss, 'A Conversation with Hubert Damisch', *October*, 85, 1998, 3–17. Louis Marin, *Opacité de la peinture*, Paris, 1989, re-edited 2006. Giovanni Careri, *Bernini: Flights of Love and the Art of Devotion*, Chicago, 1995; Mieke Bal, *Quoting Caravaggio: Contemporary Art, Preposterous History*, Chicago, 1999; Mieke Bal, 'Narrative Inside Out: Louis Bourgeois's *Spider* as Theoretical Object', *Oxford Art Journal*, 22:2, 1999, 101–126.

7 On the Augustinian theory of anagogical history, see Karl Löwith, *Weltgeschichte und Heilsgeshehen: zur Kritik des Geschichtsphilosophie*, Stuttgart, 1983, chap. 6; and Esther Gordon Dotson, 'An Augustinian Interpretation of Michelangelo's Sistine Ceilings', *Art Bulletin*, 61:2, 1979, 223–56, and 405–429. On the Renaissance appropriation of Saint Augustine and the ceiling of the Sistine Chapel as the completion of his aesthetic and philosophical thought, see Meredith. F. Gill, *Augustine in the Italian Renaissance: Art and Philosophy from Petrarch to Michelangelo*, Cambridge, 2005.

8 This is not to deny the importance of the analysis of the separate parts of the chapel. Bibliography on the Sistine Chapel is immense and easily accessible; I have limited myself to citing only those texts pertinent to my discussion.

9 On the founding principles of 'visual enunciation', see Meyer Shapiro, 'On Some Problems in the Semiotics of Visual Art: Field and Vehicle in Image-Signs', *Semiotica*, 1:3, 1969, 223–42; Louis Marin, 'A propos d'un carton de Le Brun: la peinture d'histoire ou la dénégation de l'énonciation', *Revue des Sciences humaines*, 157, 1975, 40–64, reprinted in *Détruire la peinture*, Paris, 1977, 62–9, trans. Mette Hjort, in *To Destroy Painting*, Chicago, 1995.

10 The expression 'syntax of bodies' comes from Pierluigi De Vecchi, who opposes this method of the construction of space for the ceiling, 'Sintassi dei corpi e modi delle attitudini dalla

volta al giudizio', in Kathleen Weil-Garris Brandt, ed., *Michelangelo: La Cappella Sistina. Atti del Convegno Internazionale di Studi, Roma, marzo, 1990*, Novara, 1994, 201–207.

11 Dotson interprets these occupations as characteristic of inhabitants of the earthly city, 'An Augustinian Interpretation', 229.

12 My interpretation of a 'bad genealogy' contradicts received ideas about what the *Ancestors* represent: opposite groups of virtue and vices (Wind); the Biblical announcement of something related with revelation (Hartt); the figuration of the virtuous going to Heaven and the sinners destined to eternal fire (Dotson); pilgrimages of the Old Testament (Gilbert); ancestors of the popes (Pappas, Poeschel, Pon). See Edgar Wind, *The Religious Symbolism of Michelangelo: The Sistine Chapel*, ed. Elizabeth Sears, Oxford, 2000, 1–22. Frederick Hartt, 'Lignum vitae in Medio Paradisi: The Stanza d'Eliodoro and the Sistine Ceiling', *Art Bulletin*, 32:2, 1950, 115–45, 181–218. Edgar Wind, 'Typology in the Sistine Ceiling: A Critical Statement', *Art Bulletin*, 33:1, 1951, 41–7; Frederic Hartt, 'Pagnini, Vigerio, and the Sistine Ceiling: A Reply', *Art Bulletin*, 33:4, 1951, 262–73; Dotson, 'An Augustinian Interpretation', 418–21; Creighton Gilbert, *Michelangelo on and off the Sistine Chapel*, New York, 1994, 115–49; Andrea Pappas, 'Observations on the Ancestor Cycle of the Sistine Chapel Ceiling', *Source*, 11:2, 1992, 27–31; Lisa Pon, 'A Note on *the Ancestors of Christ* in the Sistine Chapel', *Journal of the Warburg and Courtauld Institutes*, 61, 1998, 254–8; Sabine Poeschel, 'Capricci straordinari e nuovi: Michelangelos 'Ahnen Christi' in der Sixtinischen Kapelle', in Michael Rolhmann, ed., *Michelangelo: Neue Beittrage*, Köln, 2000, 181–203.

13 Bal, *Quoting Caravaggio*, 7.

14 Lois A. Cuddy, 'Beckett's 'Dead Voices', in *Waiting for Godot*: New Inhabitants of Dante's *Inferno*', *Modern Language Studies*, 12:2, 1982, 48–60.

15 I thank Vincent Rafis, who first suggested to me the possibility of an anachronistic relationship between the Sistine Chapel and the theatre of the absurd during my seminar at the EHESS in 2005.

16 *Vladimir*: Where are all these corpses from?
*Estragon*: These skeletons.
*Vladimir*: Tell me that.
*Estragon*: True.
*Vladimir*: We must have thought a little.
*Estragon*: At the very beginning.
*Vladimir*: A charnel-house! A charnel-house!
*Estragon*: You don't have to look.
*Vladimir*: You can't help looking.

Beckett, *Waiting for Godot*, New York, Grove Press edn, 1954, 41. This dating of events in the second act is supported by the references to Beckett's own wartime experiences as a farm labourer in the Vaucluse. Vladimir reminds Estragon (in the French version): 'Nous avons fait les vendanges, tiens, chez un nommé Bonnelly, à Roussillon.' Daniel Stempel highlights references to the Holocaust at the beginning of the second act: 'Each in his own way is avoiding the memory of the unspoken and unspeakable horror that has taken place during the night. They talk so they will not think or hear "all the dead voices". 'History Electrified into Anagogy: A Reading of *Waiting for Godot*', *Contemporary Literature*, 17:2, 1976, 274. See also Rosette C. Lamont, 'Samuel Beckett's Wandering Jew', in *Reflections of the Holocaust in Art and Literature*, Boulder, NY, 1990, 35–53.

17 See 'Aspectualisation' in Algirdas Julien Greimas and Joseph Courtés, *Sémiotique, dictionnaire raisonné de la théorie du langage*, Paris, 1979. See also Jacques Fontanille, ed., *Le discours aspectualisé*, Limoges, Amsterdam, Philadephia, 1991; Mieke Bal, *Narratology: Introduction to the Theory of Narrative*, trans. Christine van Boheemen, Toronto, 1985; Francesco Marsciani, 'Aspetto', in Lucia Corrain, ed., *Il lessico della semiotica (Controversie)*, Bologna, 1991, 135–44.

18 This resolutely anti-perspectival solution liberates the dimensions of the figure from the principles of proportion. On the archaism of Michelangelo, see Alexander Nagel, *Michelangelo and the Reform of Art*, New York, 2000.

19 Trans. David Summers, '*Maniera* and Movement. The *Figura Serpentinata*', *Art Quarterly*, 35, 1972, 271. See also David Summers, 'Contrapposto: Style and Meaning in Renaisssance Art', *Art Bulletin*, 59:3, 1977, 336–61, and Michael Cole, 'The *Figura Sforzata*: Modelling, Power and the Mannerist Body', *Art History*, 24:4, 2001, 520–51.

20 Giorgio Vasari, *Le Vite, vita di Michelangelo Buonnaroti*, Florence, vol. 6, 70.

21 Ascanio Condivi, *Vita di Michelagelo Buonnaroti*, Florence, (1553) 1998, 50 (author's translation). On this interpretation, see Leo Steinberg, 'Michelangelo's *Last Judgement* as Merciful Heresy', *Art in America*, November–December 1975, 49–63; Marcia Hall, 'Michelangelo's *Last Judgement*: Resurrection of the Body and Predestination', *Art Bulletin*, 58, 1976, 85–92. Leo Steinberg developed his argument in relation to the theology of Juan de Valdés in 'A Corner of the *Last Judgement*', *Daedalus*, Spring 1980, 207–273.

22 *Thessalonians*, 2:9. The quotation is *Isaiah*, 2:10, 19, 21.

23 *Philippians*, 3:20–21 (author's emphasis).

24 This definition is singularly close to that proposed by Dionysius the Areopagite who describes the celestial hierarchies in terms of progressive resemblance to divinity and the action of the angels on man as a 'conforming' operation.

25 Giovanni Andrea Gilio, *Degli errori e degli abusi dei pittori circa l'istorie*, in Paola Barocchi, ed., *Scritti d'arte del cinquecento* (1564), Torino, 1978, vol. 4, 851.

26 St Thomas Aquinas, *Summa Theologica*, supplement XP, *Treatise on the Resurrection*, Question 84: 'On the Agility of the Bodies of the Blessed'.

27 This question is connected to that of justification through the effects of grace, central themes to the group of reformers frequented by Michelangelo. See Pina Ragionieri, ed., *Vittoria Colonna e Michelangelo*, Firenze, 2005, 193 ff.

28 Ascanio Condivi, *Vita di Michelangelo Buonnaroti*, 50 (author's translation).

29 Origen, *Commentarii in epistolam Romanos*, 9, 41 (author's translation). On the 'revival' of Origen in the Renaissance, see Edgar Wind, *The Eloquence of Symbols*, Oxford and New York, 1983, 42–5.

30 Augustine, *De civitate Dei*, 20, 14 (author's emphasis). On the Augustinian revival in the Renaissance, see Paul Oskar Kristeller, 'Augustine and the Early Renaissance', *Review of Religion*, 8, 1944, 355–72. See also Brian Stock, *Augustine the Reader: Meditation, Self-Knowledge and the Ethics of Interpretation*, Cambridge, MA, 1996.

31 Augustine, *De civitate Dei*, 20, 14.

32 Steinberg, 'Michelangelo's *Last Judgement*', 62, 58.

33 Pietro Pomponazzi, *Trattato sull'immortalità dell'anima* (1516), ed. Vittoria Perrone Compagni, Florence, 1999, 98. On Foucault's conception of subjectivity, see *L'herméneutique du sujet: cours au Collège de France (1981–1982)*, eds François Ewald and Alessandro Fontana, trans. Graham Burchell, Paris, 2001, *The Hermeneutics of the Subject. Lectures at the Collège de France, 1981–1982*, New York, 2005.

34 Giorgio Agamben, *The Time That Remains: A Commentary on the Letter to the Romans*, trans. Patricia Dailey, Stanford, 2005, 62.

35 Fabrizio Mancinelli briefly made a previous association with the Cumean sybil in *The Last Judgement*, vol. 1, *The Restoration*, Rome, 1999, 199. For a recent survey, see Monique Bouquet and Françoise Morzadec, *La Sybille: parole et représentation*, Rennes, 2004.

36 See Louis Marin, 'Le cadre de la représentation', *Cahiers du Musée national d'art moderne*, 1988, 62–81, re-edited in *De la représentation*, Paris, 1994 (*On Representation*, trans. Catherine Potter, Cambridge, 1994).

37 Other figures charged with linking the ceiling and *Last Judgement* include Jonah and Isaiah, who make this connection through indicative gestures; some read the books that they hold; and others perform actions that prefigure, more or less explicitly, the end of the time.

38 On the use of the notion of exception, see Giorgio Agamben, *Homo Sacer: Sovereign Power and Bare Life*, trans. Daniel Heller-Roazen, Stanford, 1998.

39 On preceeding representations of the genealogy of Christ, see Gilbert, *Michelangelo on and off the Sistine Chapel*.

40 Helen Milton, 'The Structure of the Prologue to St. Matthew's Gospel', *Journal of Biblical Literature*, 81:2, 1962, 175–81; Marshall D. Johnson, *The Purpose of the Biblical Genealogies*, 2nd edn, Cambridge, 1988; Duane L. Christensen, 'Biblical Genealogies and Eschatological Speculation', *Perspectives in Religious Studies*, 14:1, 1987, 59–65.

41 Karin Friis Plum, 'Genealogy as Theology', *Scandinavian Journal of the Old Testament*, vol. 1, 1989, 90.

42 Stephen R. Haynes, *Reluctant Witnesses: Jews and the Christian Imagination*, Louisville, 1995.

43 Barbara Wisch, 'Vested Interest: Redressing Jews on Michelangelo's Sistine Ceiling', *Artibus et Historiae*, 48, 2003, 143–72.

44 Wisch, 'Vested Interest', 161.

45 On the position of Jews in the city, see Martine Boiteux, 'Les juifs dans le Carnaval de la Rome moderne xv$^{e}$-xvii$^{e}$ siècle', *Mélanges de l'école française de Rome*, 88, 1976, 745–87.

46 Leon Poliakov, *Jewish Bankers and the Holy See from the Thirteenth to the Seventeenth Centuries*, trans. Miriam Kockan, Boston, 1977.

47 Eric Myles Zafran, 'Saturn and the Jews', *Journal of the Warburg and Courtauld Institutes*, 42, 1979, 16–27 and plate 3.6 ff; Eric Myles Zafran, *Iconography of Antisemitism*, PhD thesis, New York, 1973.

48 Zafran, 'Saturn and the Jews'; see also Hugh Michael, 'The Jewish Sabbath in the Latin Classical Writers', *American Journal of Semitic Language and Literature*, 40:2, 1924, 117–24.

49 'Sloth', writes St Thomas, 'is sorrow about spiritual good in as much as it is a divine good', *Summa Theologica*, Iia-Iia, q. xxxv, a.2. See also 'Paresse', *Dictionnaire de théologie catholique*. . ., vol. 11, Paris, 1932, 202 ff; and Siegfried Wenzel, *The Sin of Sloth: Acedia in Medieval Thought and Literature*, Chapel Hill, 1967.

50 On the theme and iconography of the Jews' refusal to acknowledge Christ as the messiah, see Zafran, 'Saturn and the Jews', 251.

51 See Dürer, *Holy Family with Three Hares* (1498, woodcut, Karlsruhe: Staatliche Kunsthalle) and *The Holy Family in Egypt* (1511, woodcut, Bruno and Sadie Adriani Collection), and Fra Bartolomeo, *The Rest on the Flight into Egypt with St John the Baptist* (c. 1509, oil on panel, John Paul Getty Museum). For a recent historical approach, see Lucette Valensi, *La fuite en Égypte. Histoire d'Orient et d'Occident*, Paris, 2002.

52 See L. D. Ettlinger, *The Sistine Chapel before Michelangelo: Religious Imagery and Papal Primacy*, Oxford, 1965; Rona Goffen, 'Friar Sixtus iv and the Sistine Chapel', *Renaissance Quarterly*, 39:2, 218–62. On the public use of the epigraphic inscription, see Armando Petrucci, *La scrittura: ideologia e rappresentazione*, Torino, 1986.

53 On the notion of 'bare life', see Agamben, *Homo sacer*.

54 See Edith Kern, 'Drama stripped for Inaction: Beckett's Godot', *Yale French Studies*, 14, 1954, 41–7. On the tensivity of the body in Beckett's characters, see Gilles Deleuze, 'L'épuisé', postfaction to Samuel Beckett, *Quad et autres pièces pour la télévision*, Paris, 1992, 57–106.

55 See Walter Benjamin, 'Paris, Capital of the Nineteenth Century', in *Selected Writings, Volume*

*3, 1935–1938*, trans. Howard Eiland, Cambridge, MA, and London, 2002, 32–49.

56 See François Hartog, *Régimes d'historicité*, Paris, 2005.

57 'Die Geschichte der Kunst ist eine Geschichte von Prophetien. Sie kann nur aus dem Standpunkt der unmittelbaren, aktuallen Gegenwart geschrieben werden; denn jede Zeit besitzt die ihr eigene neue aber unvererbbare Möglichkeit, die Prophetien zu deuten, die die Kunst von vergangen Epochen gerade auf sie enthielt. Es ist die wichtigste Aufgabe der Kunstgeschichte die der Epoche ihrer Abfassung geltenden Prophetien in den großen Kunstwerken der Vergangenheit zu entziffern. Der Zukunft – in der Tat – und nicht immer unmittelbar bevorstehenden, niemals einer durchaus bestimmten. Vielmehr gibt es nichts Wandlungsfähigeres in Kunstwerk als diesen dunklen und brauenden Raum der Zukunft, aus dem von jenen Prophetien, die die beseelten Werke von den gepfuschten scheiden, niemals eine einzig sondern stets eine Folge, wenn auch eine intermittierende, im Verlauf der Jahrhunderte an den Tag tritt.' (author's translation) Walter Benjamin, 'Paralipomena zur zweiten Fassung von *Das Kunstwerk im Zeitalter seines technischen Reproduzierbarkeit*', Benjamin-Archiv, ms 397, now in *Walter Benjamin Gesammelte Schriften*, eds Rolf Tiedemann and Hermann Schweppenhäuser, Frankfurt am Main, 1990, vol. 1, 1046.

# 4

# READING THE ANNUNCIATION

HANNEKE GROOTENBOER

## THE NAVEL OF THE PAINTING

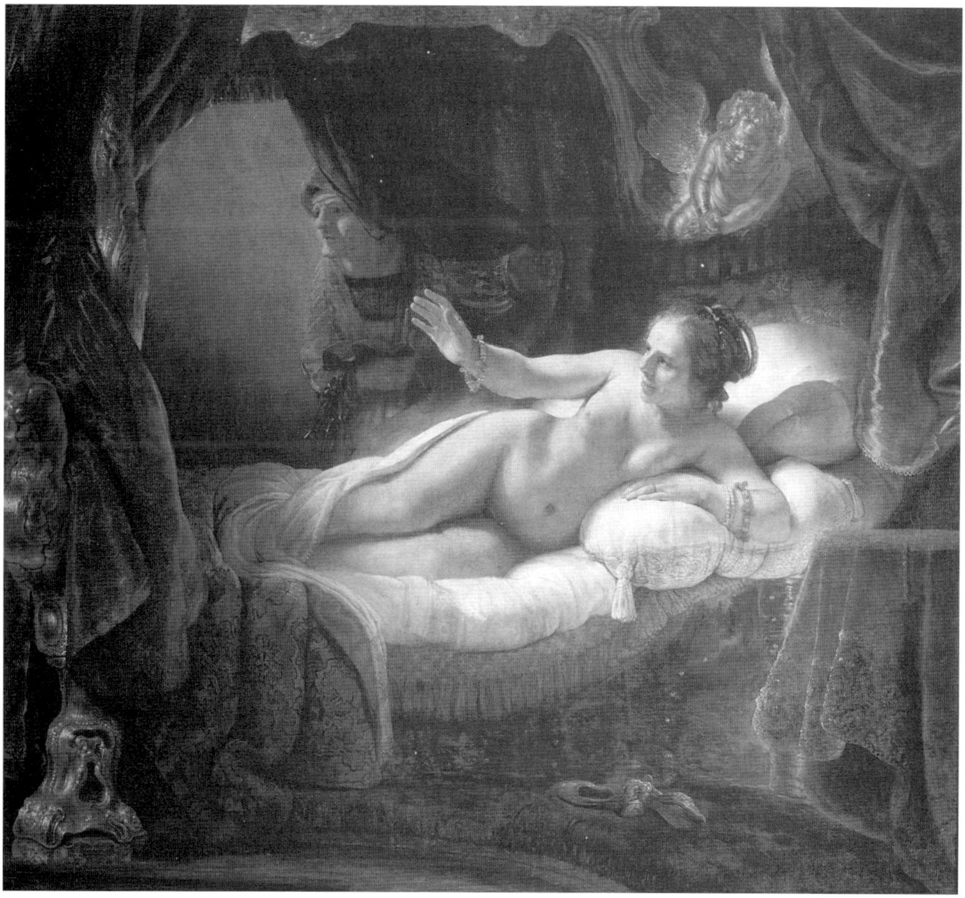

4.1 Rembrandt Harmensz van Rijn, *Danae*, 1636. Oil on canvas, 185 × 203 cm. St Petersberg: Hermitage Museum. © 1990. Photo: Scala, Florence.

In the introduction to *Reading 'Rembrandt': Beyond the Word–Image Opposition* (1991), Mieke Bal takes Rembrandt's *Danae* (plate 4.1) as a model for her mode of reading paintings.[1] Bal considers that modern viewers have accepted the common interpretation of Danae too easily, overlooking the signs of struggle with notions of gender and sexuality that frequently occur in Rembrandt's images. Disregarding the argument that this myth offered a pretext for picturing a reclining nude, she proposes that Danae's glance towards the invisible Jupiter, towards the incoming golden light, frees her from the indiscreet peeping gaze of the viewer.[2] Moreover, she continues, the obscure area of Danae's genitals is the locus where visibility and invisibility collide. This spot Bal calls the navel of the painting. No matter how closely we look, Danae's genitals seem to be vanishing in front of our eyes. That part of the painting which most lures the voyeuristic viewer is unreadable, a void, a shadowy spot left unfilled by the painting.

For Sigmund Freud the navel of the dream was a knot, an 'unplumbable' point of contact with the unknown. Bal, by contrast, sets out to unravel the visual knot, taking the potential disconnection between pictorial sign and meaning, or between her reading and more conventional iconographic interpretation, as a point of departure for her analyses.[3] In every picture by Rembrandt that she discusses, Bal searches for this knot whose cutting creates a tension between modes of interpretation, a tension that, though impossible to resolve, is fruitful in the procreative sense of the word in that it produces meaning.[4]

Bal's reading of Rembrandt's *Danae* is as much an attempt to expurgate iconography's potentially sexist readings as it is an analysis of Danae's resistance to the voyeurist gaze. Her innovative readings of Rembrandt's depictions of Lucretia, Bathshebah, Susanna, and Joseph and Potiphar's wife ultimately argue that meaning-making – always – is in some way sexual, as it is the result of a perverse desire to pry open a painting in order to reveal its most intimate, or, if you like, private, parts. We may wonder, however, why Bal argues for the bisexual metaphor of the navel – gender-specific as well as egalitarian, she asserts – by citing an example that displays (in full colour) the consummation of an (illegitimate) marriage between Jupiter's golden rain of semen and Danae's over-protected virginity. She proposes the navel as an alternative to Jacques Derrida's notion of the hymen as an analogy for the dissemination of meaning, so as to bypass 'marriage' as a metaphor for semiosis.

In this essay, I take Bal's reading of *Danae* as a starting point for an exploration of the intertwining of virginity and sexuality in the process of meaning-making in Annunciation paintings. A chaste counterpart to the Danae story, the Annunciation is an excellent site for (re-)addressing the production of meaning because it poses a particular challenge to interpretation. Figuring the infigurable mystery of the virgin conception, the Annunciation has a specific investment in virginity. To signify innocence and purity, a great variety of Marian symbols were developed in Annunciation paintings to prevent sexuality from becoming manifest. Yet, I contend, on the basis of the encounter between the Virgin and the Archangel given in the Gospels, the Annunciation tells a story of an interpretive failure. Though Gabriel's message is clearly stated, its content remains obscure: the angel fails to answer the Virgin's question as to how she is to give birth to the son of God when she has 'know[n] not a man' (Luke 1:34).[5]

In recent studies the Annunciation has been named a 'theoretical object', triggering numerous art-historical debates. Louis Marin so designated Annunciation paintings to describe the encounter between a group of works of art as historical objects and the contemporary theory of semiotics that he used to explain them.[6] Marin was among the first to point out the interpretive problems generated by the tension between Gabriel's articulation of the message and the visualization of the secret, a mystery that remains as invisible as Danae's genitals. The signalling of such problems in particular paintings often resulted in recognizing general impasses in certain methodologies for analysing painting, and correspondingly encouraged the search for alternative approaches. As a consequence, discussions about the possibilities, as well as the limits, of interpretation, and about its dangers as well as its potential, have unfolded 'around' Annunciation paintings, finding an effective starting point in Panofsky's discussion of disguised symbolism in his introduction to *Early Netherlandish Painting*, in which he employs a method largely developed through a nearly exclusive focus on Annunciation paintings.[7] Wittingly or unwittingly, later scholars have turned the Annunciation into an allegory of art-historical interpretation. Michael Baxandall discusses five different stages of depicting the Annunciation in fifteenth-century Italy to demonstrate a picture's sensitivity to various kinds of interpretive skills.[8] Michael Ann Holly drives Baxandall's point home when she takes Robert Campin's *Annunciation* of the Mérode Altar (*c.* 1425, New York: The Metropolitan Museum of Art, The Cloisters Collection) as a painted metaphor for the process of interpretation as such; the work, she claims, anticipated the various methods of decipherment applied to it.[9] Georges Didi-Huberman explains the methodological insufficiency of iconography through a study of several Annunciation paintings,[10] whereas George Steiner casts the Annunciation as a 'metaphor of passage' to illustrate the radical misconception of interpretation that he observes in present culture.[11]

This essay offers several readings of Annunciations, through a number of 'Balian' exercises upon slightly atypical Annunciations, undertaken in close connection (and here I differ from Bal) with the art-historical discourse that surrounds them. Following Marin, I demonstrate how the Annunciation's problems of interpretation result partly from its close affiliation with the discovery of perspective, a relation that has prompted Daniel Arasse to claim that the history of perspective unfolds 'in' Italian Annunciation painting. One of my aims is to make sense of Arasse's historical claim in order to show that because perspective should be considered a Marian metaphor of purity, Annunciation painting and perspective are linked historically, thematically and theoretically. Dante Alighieri had already observed the analogy between perspective and the Annunciation when he wrote in the *Convivio* that 'geometry is lily-white, unspotted by error and most certain, both in itself and in its handmaid, whose name is Perspective.'[12] Even before perspective was properly discovered, Dante had described it in terms reminiscent of the account of the Annunciation in Luke.[13] For Dante, perspective is geometry's handmaiden, as Mary was the Lord's handmaiden; its flawless system of rendering the picture plane transparent is as lilywhite and thus as immaculate as the Virgin herself. To understand better Dante's statement about perspective's virginal flawlessness, I offer some thoughts as to how the affinity, or rather, as Dante would say, complicity, between perspective – also called *costruzione legittima* – and the theme of the Annunciation has legitimized the dissemination of its meaning as an infinite unravelling of its secret. Finally, I cannot resist the temptation in this regard to return to Derrida's notion of dissemination and the hymen so as to grasp the exact nature of the connection between perspective as a method and the depiction of the Annunciation as an attempt to visualize the invisible virginal conception.

## A DEFLOWERING LILY

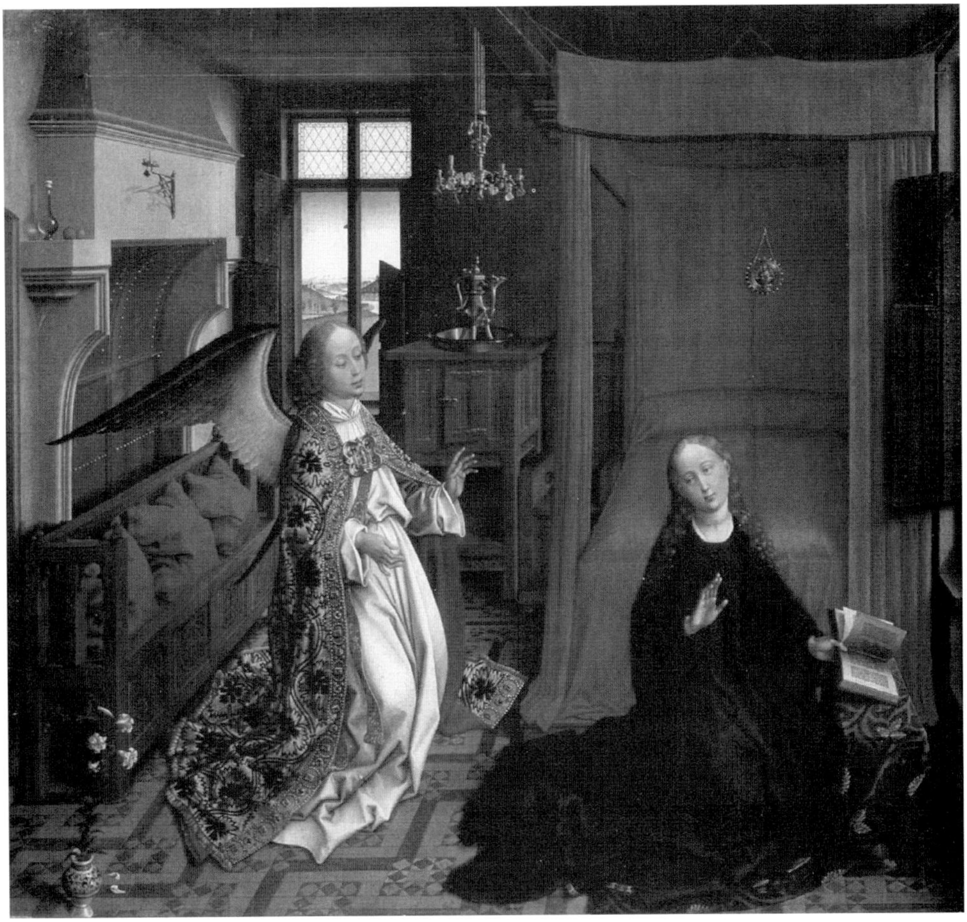

4.2 Rogier van der Weyden, *The Annunciation*, *c*. 1435. Oil on panel, 86 × 93 cm. Paris: Louvre. © 1990. Photo: Scala, Florence.

In *Early Netherlandish Painting* Panofsky formulated a dilemma: are realistically portrayed objects that enhance the realism of a scene disguised symbols or are they still-life features devoid of meaning? Panofsky observes in fifteenth-century Flemish painting a transition from pictures in which every element is recognizable as a symbol to images in which the method of disguised symbolism has been employed.[14] In Rogier van der Weyden's *Annunciation* (plate 4.2), a small yet deep fifteenth-century Flemish room with a tiled floor and open windows overlooking a fresh green landscape is depicted. The Virgin, clad in a dark blue cloak, kneels on a small bench, her left hand holding a book that has presumably fallen open to a page describing Jeremiah's prophecy, the fulfilment of which is depicted in this very scene. Her left hand is raised, indicating that she is aware of the presence of the archangel and is responding to the message he conveys. Gabriel has probably just entered through the door on the left. His posture is somewhere between kneeling and standing, a state that gives the otherwise relatively static picture a touch of 'gliding motion', Panofsky writes (254). From his gestures it can be deduced that the angel is speaking. Panofsky finds no difficulty in identifying several objects in the interior as typical Marian symbols of innocence and virginity: the water basin on the cupboard, the flask, the fireplace with its extinguished fire suggesting that Mary is protected from burning passion. Taking up nearly a third of the composition and serving as a backdrop against which the Virgin is portrayed, the bed indicates, Panofsky explains, that this room is a *thalamus*, a nuptial room, in which Mary as mother and bride of God resides.[15] I would like to add that, like many representations of the Annunciation, Van der Weyden's painting suggests that impregnation is presented as a form of communication: the Word is a kind of semen; Incarnation occurs in the interval of speech and vision when the Virgin is penetrated through the ear.

Walter Friedländer once mentioned that Van der Weyden was an inventor rather than an explorer like Jan van Eyck, a particularly apt remark in light of the subtle treatment that the artist has given the lily, a Marian metaphor *par excellence* of innocence and purity. Remarkably, Panofsky pays no attention to this detail.[16] Rather than placing a lily in the centre of the composition, as was conventional, Van der Weyden juxtaposed a vase holding a white lily with the bed in the other corner of the room. Appearing as if it were an everyday pot, it serves as a neutralizing counterpart to the obvious sexual connotations of the bed. Van der Weyden's virtuosity goes one step further, combining his skills in pictorial realism with the originality shown by his play with symbols. If we zoom in on the pot with lilies in a Balian fashion, we see that its realism is enhanced by the shadow it casts on the tile floor and the detail that two of its petals have fallen from the flowers. As superfluous information reinforcing the vase's realism they are entirely convincing as effects of the real. We could argue, with Panofsky, that the petals are free from suspicion of being a symbol, remaining mere still-life features.[17] The petals, however, appear to have fallen from the flower as if they were signs scattered on the tile floor, waiting to be interpreted. Following Bal, I suggest that we have arrived at the navel of the painting. Just as the petals are metonymically disconnected from their stem, the link between pictorial sign and meaning has been interrupted to let other meanings slip in, allowing for dissemination: here I take Derrida's term *dissemination* quite literally when I propose that the fallen petals indicate deflowering.

If disguised symbolism is a principle according to which Van der Weyden worked, as Panofsky implies, an excess of signification has never been so marvellously disguised as it is here. Camouflaging the petals as 'innocent' symbolically – as part of the lily – and pictorially – their irrelevance suggesting they are realist flourishes – a literal reading triggers a set of associations that challenges the predominant iconographic interpretation of Marian symbols as signifying innocence. Where the petals have fallen off, the stem of the flower reveals a site where fertilization occurs through pollination, without, that is, penetration.[18] Attempting to comprehend the Virgin's conception as pollination rather than impregnation, Van der Weyden has produced a pictorial instance of exegesis, rather than 'translating' a pre-existing exegesis.[19] The symbol as such has become malleable in the artist's hands, leaking information, leaving traces, slowly giving in to its meaning. Van der Weyden's picturing of deflowering carries within it the notions of contamination and of loss. Ultimately, his logic accords with other paradoxical metaphors explaining the virgin conception when he depicts the lily as an image both of deflowering and virginity, of fertilization without penetration, and of untouched innocence that is withering.

We may wonder why Panofsky overlooked these details. Perhaps he was so involved in (or blinded by, as Walter Benjamin would have it) the Romantic connotation of the symbol, that he sought meaning as the expression of coherence, determination and consistency.[20] Panofsky's well-known discussion of Robert Campin's *Mérode Altar* indicates what is at stake for him. He observes that Campin's use of the principle of disguised symbolism 'has not yet crystallized into a perfectly consistent system' because Campin's perspectival configuration had not yet been perfected either. Whereas, in the late medieval period, the symbolism of paintings was apparent, the introduction of perspective had rendered pictorial elements ambiguous: '[Campin's] reality, not as yet completely stabilised and coherent, with tables threatening to tip over, benches extended to incredible length ... could not absorb symbolic content so completely that, there remained no residue of either objectivity without significance or significance without disguise.'[21] This passage reveals that, for Panofsky, the dilemma is as much a matter of interpretation as of perspective. Equating an inconsistency of meaning with an inconsistency of perspective, he implies that Campin's lack of skill in applying perspective results in his own dilemma about where to draw the line between meaningful and meaningless elements, between symbols and their meanings. He concludes by stating that one can either suspect that objects have a deeper meaning or declare them 'innocent' of meaning as such. Panofsky does not manage to construct a unifying method of interpretation, I suggest, because he is dealing with Annunciation paintings. Paradoxically, as he has been dealing almost exclusively with Annunciation paintings, most of the objects he unmasks as symbols symbolize innocence, and, as such, are shielded from further inquiry. Therefore, the meaning he 'discovers' is an innocence of meaning, of knowledge as such, a realm where interpretation does not apply.

Moreover, what he hints at, yet fails fully to recognize, is that which Dante had posited in the *Convivio* as an analogy between perspective as instrument of representation and the Annunciation's theme. First, this connection is established on the basis of a tension between metaphors of innocence and an ambiguity of meaning entailed by pictorial realism generated from perspective. Second, the Incarnation that begins with the dialogue between Gabriel and Mary needs a locus in order somehow to *take place*, and as Marin and Arasse have explained, perspective has legitimized the existence of this place. Finally, I suggest that this affinity is founded on the similarity between the Annunciation's metaphor of the virgin conception as light falling through a window and perspective's rendering of a transparent picture as if it were a window. As I will argue, this series of metaphors of transparency can be extended by an early modern conception of seeing.

## THE SECRET OF THE MYSTERY

In *L'Annonciation italienne: Une histoire de perspective* (1999) Daniel Arasse examines what he calls the paradoxical affinity between the discovery of perspective and the theme of the Annunciation.[22] Starting from Panofsky's observation that in Ambrogio Lorenzetti's *Annunciation* (1344, Siena: Pinacoteca) the convergence of orthogonals in the centre of the panel is the first instance of a geometrically constructed vanishing point, Arasse writes the history of perspective as it unfolds in Italian paintings of the Annunciation. He follows John Spencer's claim in 1955 that a new type of Annunciation emerged in Florence around 1425 that introduced an innovative spatial iconography.[23] The modern, systematic, pictorial

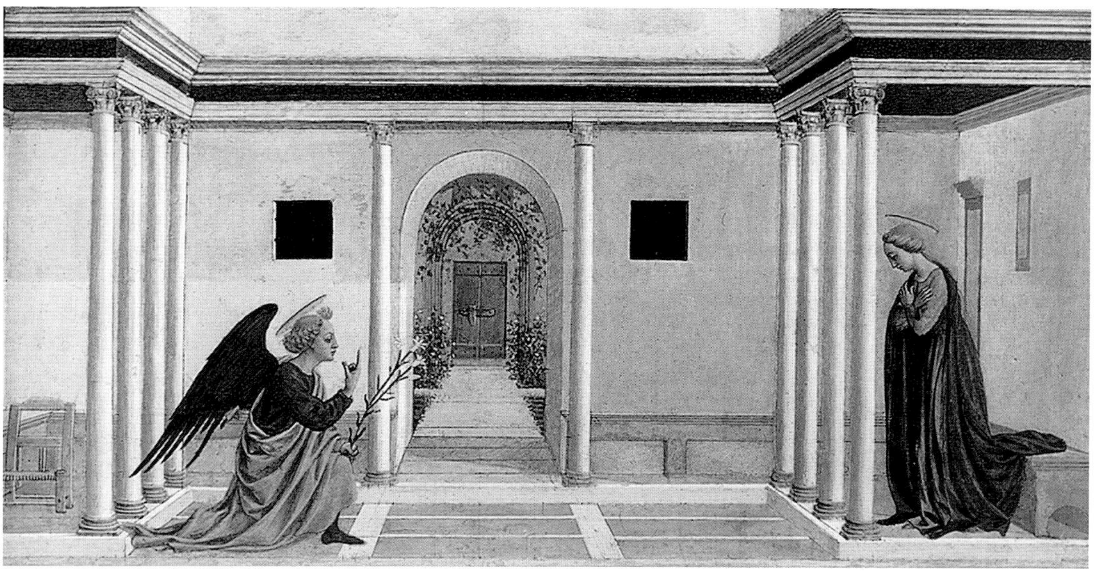

4.3 Domenico Veneziano (Domenico di Bartolomeo da Venezia), *The Annunciation*, 1442–48. Tempera on panel, 27.3 × 54 cm. Cambridge: Fitzwilliam Museum. Photo: Fitzwilliam Museum, Cambridge.

space in these novel Annunciation paintings replaced the notion of space as conceived as the total sum of occupied places. Arasse insists that the history of perspective was not a gradual development of varied experiments leading up to its invention in the early fifteenth century. Rather, he states that its discovery was a radical rupture brought about by an Annunciation painting by Masaccio (now lost but described by Giorgio Vasari). Apparently, perspective lost its prototype twice: Masaccio's painting and Brunelleschi's two-panel combination of a mirror and an image of the baptistery have both disappeared.[24]

Arasse considers the *Annunciation* by Domenico Veneziano (plate 4.3) as paradigmatic of the new kind of depiction brought about by a redistribution (rather than abandonment) of earlier elements according to the syntax of linear perspective.[25] The basic structure is formed by the in-between space that separates, as well as unites, the archangel on the left and the Virgin on the right. Even when these two figures are placed in close proximity, as in, for instance,

Sandro Botticelli's elegant rendition (plate 4.4), the Angel and the Virgin never touch; neither their outlines nor even the outlines of their garments ever overlap. When the Virgin and the Angel share the same space, as in Botticelli's painting, the composition has been carefully arranged around a strict demarcation line separating the two figures that seems to have been carved out in paint. Although the Italian Annunciation has a slightly different format to the Flemish one, both insist on this rigid separation. The bed curtain in Van der Weyden's picture is a consequence of the thirteenth- and fourteenth-century motif of the column.[26]

Like Arrase, Marin distinguishes two main axes in Veneziano's small panel as the foundation of the pictorial format of the early Renaissance Annunciation. The transversal axis of the *mise-en-scène* sets out the scene by positing the Angel on the left and the Virgin on the right, plotting ample space in between. Marin calls the axis recounting the narrative of the gospel as a message running from Angel to Mary the axis of the statement (of the uttered, *axis d'enonce*). Perpendicular to this narrative line stands the central axis of scenography leading from viewpoint to vanishing point, which is the axis of the utterance or sentence, of *énonciation*. For Marin, Veneziano created a new visualization of space where the Incarnation could *take place* in the sense of being stated in the interval between speaking and looking, on the crossing of the two axes, where the message between the two figures becomes the mystery for the painter and the viewer regarding the scene. Perspective is theologically and mystically invested at its origin.

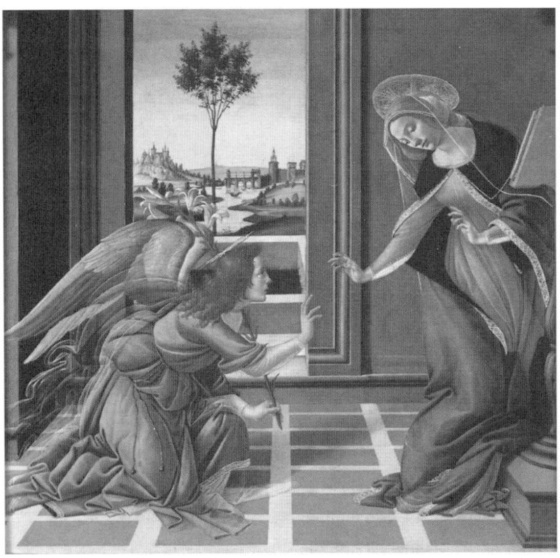

4.4 Sandro Botticelli, *The Annunciation*, *c*. 1490. Tempera on panel, 240 × 235 cm. Florence: Galleria degli Uffizi. © 1990. Photo: Scala, Florence, courtesy of the Ministero beni e att. culturali.

Veneziano's *Annunciation* and others like it demonstrate that the mystery of the Incarnation has the double logic of the secret, Marin explains. On the one hand, the mystery, profoundly incomprehensible to the human mind, is revealed to the Virgin as inaccessible mystery, yet the secret of the mystery is not that the Word of God or his invisible Image is hidden in the inscrutable Trinity, but that the unspeakable word and the infigurable figure are being revealed as hidden. The secret of the mystery, Marin writes, is the process of revelation through vision and through language, whereas the mystery of the secret is that this process retires in the figure and in speech.[27] Thus, for Marin, the configuration in Veneziano's panel does not tell a story, but rather *shows* the secret of the mystery of the Incarnation; it figures what cannot in fact be figured. As such, Veneziano's application of perspective, which became a paradigmatic format for the depiction of the Annunciation, accords with Saint Bernadino of Siena's famous articulation of the

Incarnation's mystery of as a double paradox, a unification of contradictions: 'Eternity appears in time, immensity in measurement, the Creator in the creature ... the unfigurable in the figure, the unnarratable in discourse, the inexplicable in speech, the uncircumscribable in the place, the invisible in vision, the unhearable in sound.'[28]

The proper place for figuring the infigurable mystery lies in between the two figures, that is, at the place occupied by their dialogue in which the story of redemption finds its origin. But our eye runs behind the narrative axis, plunging deep into the space as if going beyond the dialogue in an attempt to penetrate the mystery of the Incarnation taking place. In Veneziano's *Annunciation*, the vanishing point towards which our eyes are directed turns out to be purely theoretical when we realize that it is blocked by a closed door, which shows that it hides. The porch itself, though the route towards it was so easily taken, is firmly closed and bolted, prohibiting further passage of the gaze. For Marin, this combination of passage and blockage, the contrast between the opening up of pictorial space and the bolted door, shows that the infigurable is figured as hidden, the unnarratable is narrated as a secret, and the uncircumscribable is articulated as vanishing.

Therefore, perspective is theologically invested in Annunciation painting as an instrument that gives place to the mystery of the Incarnation *as a secret*. Perspective provided artists with a powerful means to create various spatial metaphors of passage that revealed the mystery as secret without disclosing its content, such as the insurmountable threshold, light falling through a glass window, open and closed doors or shutters, combinations of interior and exterior spaces, and so on. This intricate network of metaphors somehow privileged the viewer's gaze to catch glimpses of the logic of the secret. The viewer can take the veiled language and wrought metaphors for granted as a set of clues to be unravelled as secrets, because viewing from this novel, immobilized point of view, orienting our eye right to the crossing where the mystery occurs, cannot be questioned. Just how the theme of the Annunciation was invested in perspective in the sense of pictorial instrument as well as optics or vision can be found in Fra Filippo Lippi's *Annunciation*.[29]

## A CONCEPTION THROUGH THE EYE

Lippi has largely followed the paradigm set by Veneziano, but departs from it through a series of subtle variations (plate 4.5). For instance, most depictions of the Annunciation represent a hierarchy between Gabriel and the Virgin. Either a standing Angel dominates his humbly kneeling interlocutor, or alternatively the Angel respectfully bends forward as Mary raises her body in a state of surprise. Lippi has opted for parity between the two. Whereas Gabriel is kneeling and Mary is sitting on a chair, on a visual level their positions are almost identical, as if they mirror each other. Even the gestures of their hands resemble each other, as they do in Van der Weyden's *Annunciation* (Paris: Louvre). Strikingly, in Lippi's lunette, even the dove has partaken in the levelling; it hangs in mid-air right in front of Mary's stomach. To emphasize this de-hierarchization, Lippi painted Gabriel as an unusually humble young man. Eschewing even the faintest indication that he may be speaking, he lays down his right hand in the way one lays down a weapon.

Having examined Fra Roberto Lecce's 'Five Laudable Conditions of the Blessed Virgin', Baxandall states that generally most Annunciation images show the Virgin in accordance with either Fra Roberto's first category of Disquiet when the Angel salutes her ('and she was troubled') or the second condition of Reflection, when she wonders what manner of salutation this would be.[30] In the case of Lippi's painting, Fra Roberto would probably have hesitated between the fourth category of Submission, when Mary speaks the words 'Behold, the handmaid of the Lord', and the fifth and last state of Merit, which occurs after Gabriel has left. It does seem as if Lippi's Gabriel is about to retire quietly from the scene. This depiction of self-effacement results in a shifting of the painting's focus, which now lies entirely with the Virgin. In most Annunciations, the Virgin's attitude of listening to the Angel, subjecting herself to God's will, offering her body as receptacle, or letting herself be impregnated, is quite passive, like a grammatical direct object, so to speak. In Lippi's *Annunciation*, however, the narrative is

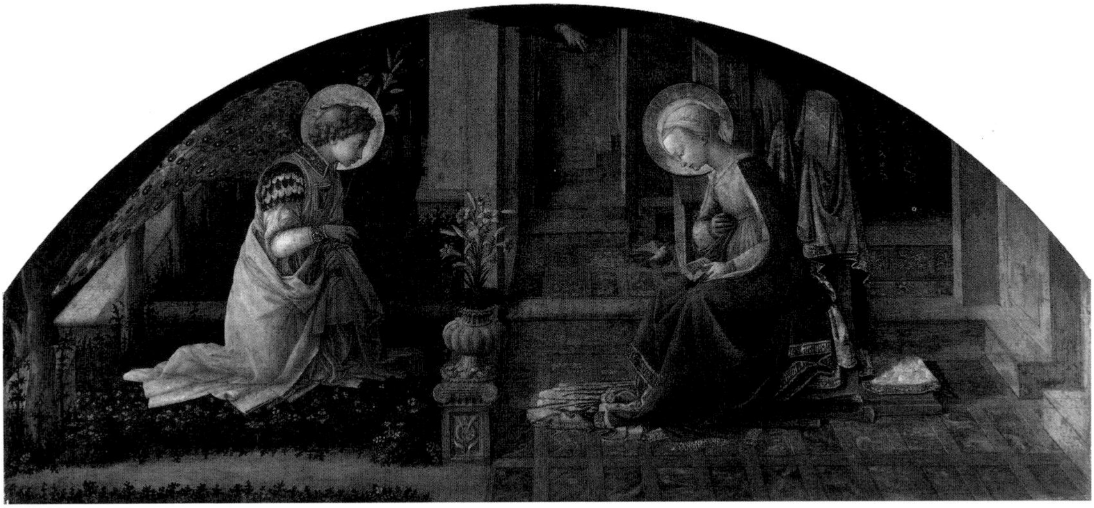

4.5 Fra Filippo Lippi, *The Annunciation*, *c*. 1450–53. Egg tempera on panel, 68.6 × 152 cm. London: National Gallery. Photo: National Gallery, London.

represented as if viewers are seeing the mysterious conception from the Virgin's point of view. To use Bal's phrase, the focalization of the biblical narrative lies entirely with Mary.[31] In full awareness of what is happening to her, Lippi's Mary looks intensely at the dove that has descended to the level of her womb propelled by golden circles of light. With her right hand, she holds up her heavenly blue cloak as if it were a curtain, to let in the golden dots that represent rays of light emanating from the dove's beak. From Mary's womb a triangular cluster of rays appear to leave her body and flow towards the bird. If this slit in Mary's dress is not a navel in Bal's sense, as a metonymical disconnection it may come close to being its opposite: we are looking with Mary and Gabriel at a unique moment, even in Annunciation painting, when conception is taking place. In contrast to other Annunciations emphasizing the interval between the figures, in Lippi's image the Virgin's body is actually touched. The conception takes place through an opening in her tunic, a cut, near her navel. A connection between the divine and the Virgin's body, the infigurable here appears as the reverse of the cutting of the umbilical cord to separate the newborn from the mother's body. With this cut-as-connection rather than as disconnection in Lippi's lunette, I contend, vision serves as metaphor for the virgin conception.

In a two-part discussion of Lippi's *Annunciation*, Leo Steinberg and Samuel Edgerton argued that by depicting the miraculous conception the artist was following the science of optics (called *perspectiva* in medieval Latin), particularly the optical model that had been developed by Roger Bacon (*c.* 1220–1292).[32] Steinberg asserts that Lippi shunned the idea that the Virgin conceived as sound penetrates the ear, the *conceptio per aurem*, and replaces this metaphor of the ear by an analogy with the eye. As Steinberg and Edgerton explain, Bacon's optics was, in fact, a synthesis of the opposed ideas of seeing through intromission and seeing through extramission. The Arab philosophers, most prominently Alhazen, claimed that seeing occurred through intromission, whereby the eye passively receives the image of an illuminated body. The opposite view, argued by Galen among others, advocated extramission, whereby light is issued from the eye, seizing the objects with its rays. In his *Perspectiva*, Bacon opts for a middle way, asserting that seeing results from the perception of a visible object at a certain distance, aided by what he calls species (light rays coming from the eye) that travel 'in the locality of the visual pyramid'.[33] According to Bacon, clear vision was thus produced by a collision of perpendicular visual rays that when entering the eye turned oblique or 'twisting'.

Steinberg and Edgerton suggest that Lippi closely followed Bacon's scientific explanations in drawing an analogy between the miraculous conception and the optical reception of images in the eye. Among the many oblique rays forming a pyramidal shape near Mary's womb, one perpendicular ray departs from her belly, or rather from the small, almond-shaped cut in her garment, the gateway to her womb. This perpendicular ray meets one that issues from the dove's beak over the book that she holds in her hand, recounting the fulfilment of Jeremiah's prophecy. The small opening in Mary's dress operates like the pupil in the eye in medieval optics, which Bacon describes as located in the forepart of the *uvea*, the second of the three membranous folds of the eye that were called 'tunics'. Edgerton explains that Lippi could have followed Bacon to the letter. The Italian and Latin words for tunic refer to membranes as well as garments. The Virgin's tunic is thus, like the *uvea* of the eye, a kind of membrane carrying an almond-shaped gaping (as in an eye seen in profile) from which a ray of light emanates and through which light is received by her body. According to Bacon, the incoming species actualize the original likeness in the *crystallinus* of each eye that would then pass through the optic nerves to the nerve in the brain where cognition of the likeness occurs.

Edgerton wonders whether Lippi would have taken his analogy so far as to theorize that God reproduced his likeness onto the Virgin's navel, from where it would pass through the umbilical cord, as if it were species passing through the optic nerves. He even ponders whether God's likeness is here imagined to pass through the Virgin's body in the way in which 'a Renaissance painter creates by applying perspective principles in a picture.' (51) Following Edgerton in this regard, I believe that Lippi's analogy between Bacon's *Perspectiva* and divine impregnation does not just hint at a possible correspondence between optics and pictorial perspective, but provides the connection between the Annunciation and perspective sought by Arasse. Lippi's reformulation of the widely applied figure of light falling through a window as an explanation for the mystery of the Incarnation in terms of Baconian optics implies that, like optics, perspective itself could be seen as a metaphor for the miraculous penetration of the Virgin's body. St Bernard compares the transition of God's likeness to the Virgin's body with the passage of sunlight through a glass window.

> Just as the brilliance of the sun fills and penetrates a glass window without damaging it, and pierces its solid form with imperceptible subtlety, neither hurting it when entering nor destroying it when emerging: thus the word of God, the splendour of the Father, entered the virgin chamber and then came forth from the closed womb.[34]

Lippi may have reasoned that if pure rays of sunlight could enter a window to emerge 'unspoiled', as St Bernard writes, such rays could also fall through the second membrane of the human eye without hurting it. Correspondingly, I would add that perspective, literally meaning 'a seeing through', has enabled the viewer's eye to plunge deep into the pictorial space without damaging the image. The viewer's eye and Lippi's ingenious conception through a slit in Mary's tunic operate according to the same principles. On the basis of Lippi's painting, we could argue that the affinity between perspective as a method assisting artists in generating a new language of form and the new networks of spatial visual metaphors it generated, as observed by Arasse, is more than mere congruity. Compared to Lippi's optical metaphor, perspective's transparency, or we may even say invisibility, enables the viewer's eye to pierce the image with 'imperceptible subtlety', as St Bernard remarks. Perspective is more than just affiliated with Annunciation paintings, as Arasse states; I would rather say, with Hubert Damisch and Dante, that perspective is their accomplice:[35] the new, perfect, geometrical space rendered by perspective conceived of as virgin territory in which the invisible becomes visible as an optical 'passage' that we do not see as we see through it. In the shape of a transparent painting window, perspective is as much a signifier of innocence as a figure of the Virgin's body (itself infigurable) as doorway through which God became human. I believe that it was this condensation of metaphors of virgin conception, optics and perspective that debarred Panofsky from devising a unifying method of interpretation.

Just like numerous other visual metaphors, perspective serves as a figure of passage even as it provides an image of the transparent hymen that obstructs such passage. Through this analogy, perspective has played a foundational role in the production of meaning in Annunciation painting, offering itself as a transparent, naturalizing, and therefore innocent medium that concealed symbols under a realistic camouflage, all the while making itself invisible. Yet it is not a mere matter of vocabulary, but also syntax.

## AN UNDECIDABLE INTERVAL

In 'Double Session' in *Dissemination* (1972), Derrida describes the hymen in its double meaning of membrane and (consummation of) marriage as a kind of medium.[36] Wedging Stephane Mallarmé's 'Mimique' (describing the poet's experience of reading a text by the mime artist Paul Margueritte) into a section taken from Plato's *Philebus* in which Socrates compares writing to painting, Derrida raises a question about *mimesis*, about what goes on 'between' literature and truth. For Derrida, the emphasis lies on the notion 'between', the polysemic, undecidable state of meaning typical of numerous signs in the work of Mallarmé. Such recurrent signs include *blanc* (white), which resonates in terms like marble, snow, or swan, as well as in the words virginity and purity, or in the white of a marked page, or the blanks in between words. Another example of a typical Mallarmian sign is *lis* (lily), pronounced indistinguishably from *lit* (bed); both are close sonic relatives of conjugations of *lire*, to read, summing up the constellation of sex, virginity and reading essential to Mallarmé's 'Mimique' (or, for that matter, to Van der Weyden's Louvre panel). The most insistent of these themes for Derrida is hymen, which means both (consummation of) marriage and membrane, the obstacle that impedes such consummation. Just as the Mime in Mallarmé's text imitates neither deed nor word, being at once page and quill, Derrida writes that the hymen confuses the two opposite meanings of consummation of marriage; membrane is the obstacle that impedes such consummation as well as that which stands *between* these opposites (198). In this state of suspense, the hymen in Mallarmé's short text produces the effect of a medium in sowing together, as it were, the confusion between opposites without giving way to either (212). The hymen is an interval, the suspense of which has been generated not by its 'lexical richness', Derrida insists, but rather through the syntax, its formal praxis. No matter which word we use to replace hymen, 'it is the "between," whether it names fusion or separation, that thus carries all the force of the operation. The hymen must be determined through the *entre* [between] and not the other way round.' (220) Derrida speaks of the irreducible excess of the syntactic over the semantic (221).

Derrida's discussion of Mallarmé sheds new light on the interpretive problems with which Annunciation paintings confront us. We may say that the double meaning of hymen on a thematic level has been firmly sown together in paintings of the Annunciation, intensifying the indecision, or rather signifying it. On a structural level, this continuous state of suspense has been generated by the paradigmatic space in between the Angel and the Virgin that Marin has called an interval between speech and vision, or between the word and its visualization. This interval enables the viewer's eye to look deep into the painting, much as it obstructs that gaze by a pot with lilies, or a threshold or a column, and on a deeper level by the closed and bolted door of the garden, as we have seen in Veneziano's picture. Oriented towards the vanishing point, the viewer's eye is arrested and suspended. This moment of undecidability, this interval, is produced by the perspectival configuration that serves as the syntax of the painting.[37] Following Mallarmé and Derrida, we may call this in-between space a syntactical blank, composing and unravelling the narrative of the Annunciation as the secret of the mystery as much as it does the mystery of the secret.

Perspective may be called a hymen in Mallarmé's and Derrida's terms, a transparent 'medium' or membrane much like Lippi's *uvea*, which allows for meaning to disseminate without ever being pierced through the multiple folds of signification. As a formal apparatus, it has sown together the notions of passage and obstacle, transparency and penetration, dissemination and purity, knowledge of sex and innocence. By letting optics and geometry, secret and mystery, and syntax and statement converge in a single point of view, the *construzione legittima* allows an infinite unravelling of the secret, on the condition that the transparency of the medium remains unquestioned. For Annunciation paintings the restraints imposed by orthodox readings can be eluded by considering perspective as a fundamental aspect of the production of meaning that is essentially void, a blank in between the visible objects. As obscure as Danae's genitals in Bal's programmatic model, as transparent and clear-cut as the knot in Annunciation painting: in both cases the knot functions as a stumbling block that arrests the gaze. It is in this void that sexuality as meaning resides, and where, as Bal has taught us, a reading into the unknown begins.

## Notes

1 Mieke Bal, *Reading 'Rembrandt': Beyond the Word–Image Opposition*, Cambridge, 1991, esp. 19–23.

2 On Danae, see Eric Jan Sluijter, 'Emulating Sensual Beauty', *Simiolus*, 27:1/2, 1999, 36–7.

3 Shoshana Felman coins 'unplumbable' and 'a knot that is cut' in her examination of Freud's use of the term in 'Postal Survival, or the Question of the Navel', *Yale French Studies*, 69, 1985, 49–72, esp. 62.

4 In addition, I suggest that in *Reading Rembrandt* Bal aims to find a confrontation between the painting as an historical object and the contemporary theory of semiotics she uses to explain the painting. See also Mieke Bal and Norman Bryson, 'Semiotics and Art History', in *Art Bulletin*, 73:2, 1991, 174–208. Her interest in this confrontation led her to coin the term 'preposterous history' in *Quoting Caravaggio: Contemporary Art, Preposterous History*, Chicago and London, 1999.

5 Recounting the story in the third century, Photius adds a line or two in which it seems that Gabriel is delicately scolding the Virgin for her inquisitiveness. 'The Holy Ghost shall come upon thee . . . it shall interpret how thou shalt conceive . . . but I am at loss to tell the manner of the conception.' Quoted in Leo Steinberg, '"How Shall This Be?" Reflections on Filippo Lippi's Annunciation in London', Part I. *Artibus et Historiae*, 8:16, 1987, 30.

6 Louis Marin, *Opacité de la peinture: Essays sur la representation au Quattrocento*, Florence, 1989, 9–12. For Hubert Damisch, perspective is a theoretical object as it is an historical object, as he explained in an interview in *The Archive of Development*, eds Annette Balkema and Henk Slager, Amsterdam, 1998. See also Stephen Bann and Damisch, *Oxford Art Journal*, 28:2, 2005, 155–83. Giovanni Careri is compiling a list of theoretical objects, among them, the detail, the fold and the threshold. Bal uses the term to refer to works of art that deploy their own artistic medium to articulate thought about art. See Bal, 'Narrative Inside Out: Louise Bourgeois's *Spider* as Theoretical Object', *Oxford Art Journal*, 22:2, 103–126, 104.

7 Erwin Panofsky, *Early Netherlandish Painting: Its Origin and Character*, New York, 1971.

8 Baxandall insists that modern viewers are no different to those of the Quattrocento in taking pleasure in exercising interpretive skills as well as enjoying the reward for our achievement when gaining insight into the painting. Michael Baxandall, *Painting and Experience in Fifteenth Century Italy: A Primer in the Social History of Pictorial Style*, Oxford, 1974, 34–5.

9 Michael Ann Holly, 'Witnessing the Annunciation', in *Past Looking: Historical Imagination and the Rhetoric of the Image*, Ithaca, 1996, 149–69.

10 Georges Didi-Huberman, *Confronting Images: Questioning the End of a Certain History of Art*, trans. John Goodman, Philadelphia, 2005.

11 George Steiner, *Real Presences: Is There Anything in What We Say?* London, 1989, 4. I thank Frans-Willem Korsten for pointing this out to me. For an analysis of Steiner's use of the metaphor of the Annunciation, see Korsten's 'Wisdom Brokers: Narrative's Interaction with Arguments in Cultural Critical Texts', dissertation, University of Amsterdam, 1998, 104–139.

12 Quoted in Baxandall, *Painting and Experience*, 124.

13 Erwin Panofsky, *Perspective as Symbolic Form*, trans. Christopher S. Wood, Cambridge, MA, 1997, 57. Hubert Damisch, *The Origin of Perspective*, trans. J. Goodman, Cambridge, MA, 1995, 80.

14 Starting in 1934, when Panofsky published his essay on Jan van Eyck's *Arnolfini Portrait* (*Burlington Magazine*, 64, 1934, 117–27), the debate about the uses and abuses of disguised symbolism has continued, especially in the field of early Netherlandish and Dutch seventeenth-century art. See Svetlana Alpers, *The Art of Describing: Dutch Art in the Seventeenth Century*, Chicago, 1983, especially the appendix; Eddy de Jongh, 'Some Notes on Interpretation', in *Art in History, History in Art: Studies in Seventeenth-Century Dutch Culture*, eds David Freedberg and Jan de Vries, Santa Monica, 1991.

15 For a collection of numerous variations on the use of the term *thalamus* as room or space in relation to the Virgin, see Don Denny, 'Some Symbols in the Arena Chapel Frescoes', *Art Bulletin*, 55:2, June 1973, 205–212, esp. 206.

16 As stated by Panofsky, *Early Netherlandish Painting*, 248.

17 There is one other example of a lily having lost some of its petals in an *Annunciation* by a follower of Rogier van der Weyden (*c.* 1465–75) in the Metropolitan Museum of Art in New York. In the German tradition of Annunciation painting, there are few examples of flowers scattered on the tiled floor, but never depicted as having fallen from the stem of a lily: for instance, Meister des Eggelsberger Altars, *Eggelsberger Retabel*, Linz, Schlossmuseum, 1481. See also Sven Lüken, *Die Verkündiging an Maria im 15. und frühen 16. Jahrhundert*, Göttingen, 2000.

18 The Church Fathers called Mary's body and her womb – as well as the interior room in which she dwells – a receptacle. Several centuries later *thalamus* was coined as the botanical term for the end of a flower stalk bearing the parts of a flower where the embryo, and later the seeds, are lodged.

19 For the notion of pictorial exegesis, see Didi-Huberman, *Confronting Images*, especially the introduction.

20 On the blind acceptance of the symbol as unifying form and content into an unbroken whole, see Walter Benjamin, *The Origin of German Tragic Drama*, trans. John Osborne, London, 1998, especially 160–1.

21 Panofsky, *Early Netherlandish Painting I*, 143.

22 Daniel Arasse, *L'Annonciation italienne: une histoire de perspective*, Paris, 1999. Following Hubert Damisch, I consider perspective as a discovery rather than an invention.

23 John R. Spencer, 'Spatial Imagery of the Annunciation in Fifteenth Century Florence', *Art Bulletin*, 37:4, December 1955, 273–80.

24 On the theoretical consequences of perspective's lost prototypes, see Damisch, *Origin of Perspective*, esp. chap. 6.

25 Arasse, *Annonciation italienne*, 122 and 164.

26 On the bed curtain, see Susan Koslow, 'The Curtain-Sack: A Newly Discovered Incarnation Motif in Rogier van der Weyden's "Columba Annunciation"', *Artibus et Historiae*, 7:13, 1986, 9–33.

27 Marin, *Opacité*, 136.

28 Quoted in Georges Didi-Huberman, *Fra Angelico: Dissemblance and Disfiguration*, trans. Jane Mary Todd, Chicago, 1995, 35. An extended fragment of the same section can be found in Marin, *Opacité*, 136.

29 Lippi's lunette in the National Gallery in London is part of a set of two, its pendant depicting a *sacra conversazione* with seven saints (London: National Gallery). It has been suggested that the lunettes were placed over doors, or used as part of the head ends of beds. Giuseppe Marchini, *Filippo Lippi*, Florence, 1975, 206–207. See also Jeffrey Ruda, *Fra Filippo Lippi : Life and Work with a Complete Catalogue*, London, 1993, 199–203.

30 Baxandall, *Painting and Experience*, 51–2.

31 Perhaps the only other Italian artist who gave the Virgin agency in a similar way is Leonardo, 1470, Florence: Galleria degli Uffizi. In *Reading Rembrandt*, Bal demonstrates how focalization, originally a literary term developed in narratology, can be a valuable tool to analyse modes of looking visualized in painting. See especially chap. 4 'Between Focalization and Voyeurism: The Representation of Vision'.

32 Leo Steinberg, 'How Shall This Be?' part 1 and Samuel Y. Edgerton, Jr., 'How Shall This Be?' part 2, *Artibus et Historiae*, 8:16, 1987, 25–44 and 45–53, respectively.

33 Quoted in Edgerton, 'How Shall This Be?', 50.

34 Millard Meiss, 'Light as Form and Symbol in Some Fifteenth-Century Paintings', *The Painter's Choice: Problems in the Interpretation of Renaissance Art*, New York, 1976, 5.

35 Arasse, *Annonciation italienne*, 9.

36 Jacques Derrida, *Dissemination*, trans. B. Johnson, Chicago, 1981. For a close analysis of figures of male sexuality in Derrida's *Dissemination*, see Murat Aydemir, *Images of Bliss: Ejaculation, Masculinity, Meaning*, Minneapolis, 2007.

37 Damisch has stated that perspective provided the painter with a formal apparatus like that of the sentence, a geometry of the sentence, through which a statement can be made. *Origin of Perspective*, esp. 446. Following Damisch, I offer a meditation on perspective as a kind of grammar in my *Rhetoric of Perspective: Realism and Illusionism in Seventeenth-Century Dutch Still-Life Painting*, Chicago, 2005.

# 5

# VISUAL ARCHIVES AS PREPOSTEROUS HISTORY

ERNST VAN ALPHEN

The archive occupies a privileged position within the cluster of genres by means of which the Holocaust is represented, taught and commemorated. This cluster consists exclusively of historical genres. The genres that are considered to be most appropriate to depict the events of the Holocaust are those that are historical par excellence, those that do not provide a fictional account of history, but that offer history in its most direct, tangible form. Testimonies, autobiographical accounts and documentaries are the forms supposed to provide the best and most responsible account of the Holocaust.

Within this group of affiliated genres, the position of the archive is emblematic as well as distinct. It is emblematic because its historical function is out of the question: it consists of leftovers, material traces of the past. But it also differs from the other historical genres because it does not represent history by means of narrative. Instead, the archive presents it directly, that is unmediated, in the form of its remains. The hierarchy within the cluster of historical genres indicates the nature of the issue: namely, that the genre considered most appropriate is the one that stays closest to the factual events.

This requirement of factuality is more than a methodological issue: it has become a moral imperative. Terrence Des Pres has formulated prescriptions for 'respectable' Holocaust studies. Appropriating the voice of God in the Commandments he dictates:

> 1. The Holocaust shall be represented, in its totality, as a unique event, as a special case and kingdom of its own, above or below or apart from history.
>
> 2. Representations of the Holocaust shall be as accurate and faithful as possible to the facts and conditions of the event, without change or manipulation for any reason – artistic reasons included.[1]

And he continues. The moral pressure exercised by these commandments specifies the available modes of representation even further. The pursuit of the barest representation of the factual events is preferred to the historian's transformation of the facts and events into an historical narrative. This preference may be unexpected for students of literature, because realism as a literary mode of representation has always used narrative plot as its most elementary and seductive device.

But when considering what it is that makes the historical mode so urgent, the inevitable conclusion is that even history-writing is not good enough for the purpose. Many historians approach even the most elementary narrative plot with suspicion. They do have a point; narrative plots are always simplifications compared to the complexity of historical reality. And the coherence and unity of traditional plots produce meaning effects that may not have been present in the past. One aspect of the realist plot, for instance, is its closure: everything comes to an end, an end that somehow satisfies. And more often than not, that end is good. If the very shaping of facts into a narrative, however truthful, is inherently unable to do justice to the facts, then the only mode of representation that might satisfy, however poorly, is the archival mode: the collecting, ordering and labelling of facts, items, pieces of evidence, testimonies.

In discussions on how best to deal with the memory of the Holocaust, given the privileged position of the archive, it is perhaps not surprising that artists, too, have become interested in the scholarly method of the archive. This raises the question of whether they do as artists, simply comply with the general pressure to adopt historical genres when dealing with the Holocaust; or whether their use of the archive, instead, complicates the issue? I discuss here three such artists. First, the French artist Christian Boltanski, most widely known for the way that he has evoked the Holocaust compellingly by means of archival installations. Often, but not always, these installations consist of found photographic portraits of Jews, plausible victims of the Holocaust. My second example is the installation made by Toronto artist, collector and curator Ydessa Hendeles, entitled *Partners (The Teddy Bear Project)*. This enormous archival installation consists of found – or rather, purchased – family-album photographs collected on the basis of a single motif: somewhere in the picture there had to be a toy teddy bear. My third example will be drawn from the work of the Hungarian film-maker and artist Peter Forgacs, whose films and installations consist exclusively of material that he finds in an archive of home movies.

These three artists not only share a common method, the archive, but also an area where the objects in their archives are situated: namely, the domestic sphere. Interestingly, then, all three artists act upon the tension between personal memory and history. For, whereas the archive is usually seen as an elementary tool for historical understanding, the portraits and snapshots from family albums and home movies belong to the realm of personal time instead of history.

The way I situate these three artists in relation to the privileged and respected position of the archival mode takes its cue from Mieke Bal's notion of preposterous history. She elaborates on this notion in her book *Quoting Caravaggio: Contemporary Art, Preposterous History* (1999). Reading contemporary art works in their relation to Caravaggio or other baroque works, she demonstrates the idea that art's engagement with what came before it involves an active reworking of the predecessor. 'Hence, the work performed by later images obliterates the older images as they were before that intervention and creates new versions of old images instead.'[2] The complex ways in which art acts upon the past – or more specifically its predecessors – and conventional motifs and modes of representation, suggests that it is the past, not the present, that is conditioned by a perpetual flux. In the light of Bal's argument, I argue that the archival practices by Boltanski, Hendeles and Forgacs are 'preposterous' in relation to the archival genre that they adopt. They do not comply with the genre and to the qualities assigned to it through the course of history, but in their practices each artist foregrounds aspects and qualities of the archival mode so far unacknowledged or repressed.

## DECONSTRUCTING THE ARCHIVE: CHRISTIAN BOLTANSKI

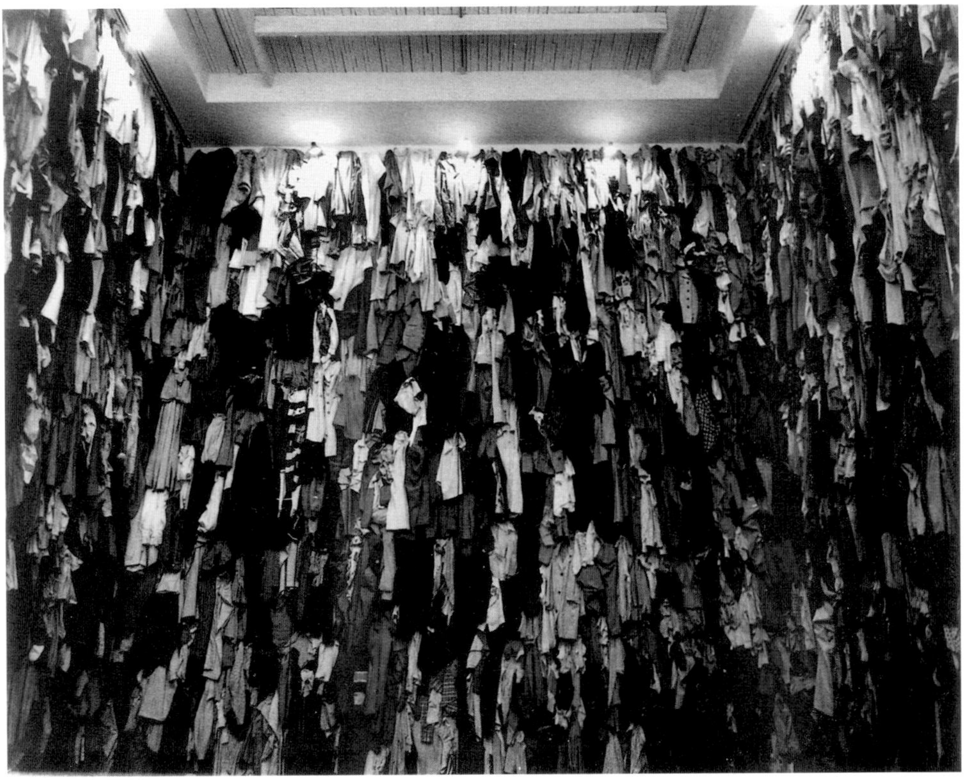

5.1 Installation view of Christian Boltanski, *Canada*, 1988. Secondhand clothing. Toronto: Ydessa Hendeles Art Foundation.

In the face of this pressure to represent the Holocaust in the mode of the historian, or even better in the mode of the archivist, it is remarkable that Christian Boltanski so consistently presents his works as the products of an archivist. He gives the impression of being the most docile artist, because he appears to be giving in to the moral imperative of the discussions about Holocaust representations. Some of his works are explicitly titled *Inventories*, or *Reserve*. And although Boltanski did not approach the subject of the Holocaust head-on until 1988 with his installations *Chases High School* (1988), *Reserves: The Purim Holiday* (1989) and *Canada* (1988), and although not all his portrayed subjects are Jewish, it can be argued that all his work deals in some degree with aspects of the Holocaust.[3] The question that arises, then, is: what does this engagement with the favourite modes of the Holocaust historian mean as an artistic practice?

The two modes of representation that produce Holocaust effects in Boltanski's work are photographic portraiture and the archive. Both modes of representing reality can be seen as emblems of realism, the representational effect that is so much favoured by Holocaust commentary. The photographic portrait and the archive seem to share an ability to represent (historical) reality in an apparently objective way. In both cases there seems to be a minimum of intrusion or 'presentness' of the subject or medium of representation in the product of representation.

Boltanski's use of the archive reveals the consequences of an archival mode for our understanding of the Holocaust. In only one series of his works is the Holocaust directly evoked by means of reference to the historical event. In 1988 he made some installations to which he gave the title *Canada* (plate 5.1). This title refers to the euphemistic name given to the warehouses in which the Nazis stored all the personal belongings of those who were killed in the gas chambers or interned in the labour camps. In the camps 'Canada' stands for the country of excess and exuberance whence one wants to emigrate, because it can offer a living to everybody. In the works entitled *Canada* Boltanski showed piles of second-hand garments. These installations not only brought to mind the warehouses in the concentration camps, but, by the sheer number of the garments, also evoked the incredible number of people who died in the camps and whose possessions were stored in 'Canada'.

Like *Chases High School* and *Monument: The Purim Holiday* (plate 5.2), *Canada* evokes the Holocaust referentially. This time it is not the used 'material' –

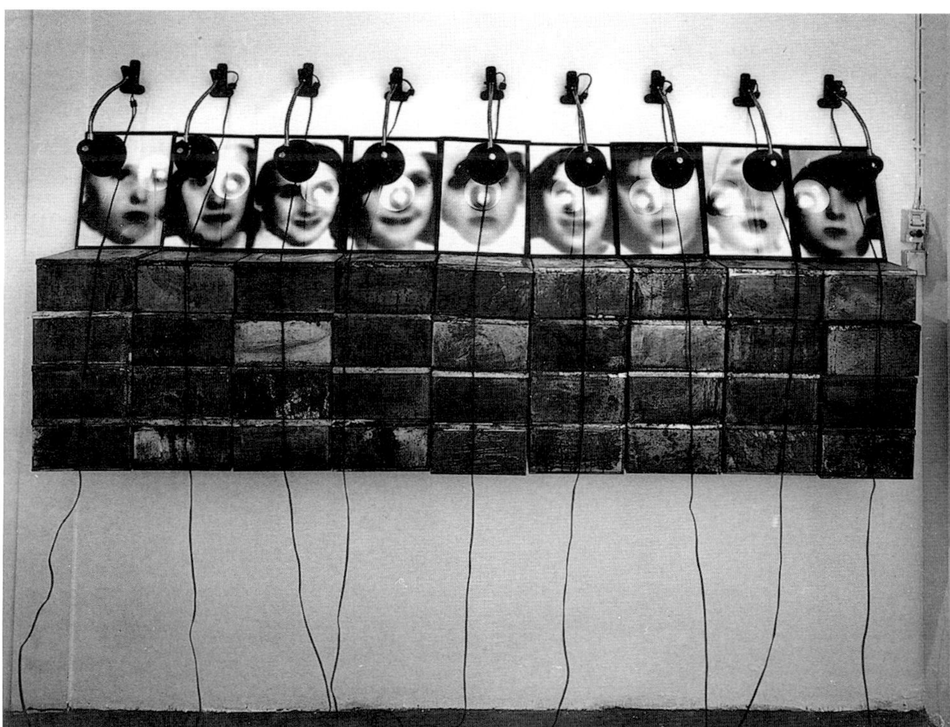

5.2 Christian Boltanski, *Monument: The Purim Holiday*, 1989. Black-and-white photographs, photomechanical prints, metal lamps, tin boxes, wire, approx. 97 × 212 × 23 cm. Basel. Museum für Gegenwartskunst.

photographs that show European Jewish children before the war, hence, targets of the Holocaust – which denote the Holocaust, but the title of the work. These garments represent a specific historical space: the warehouses in Auschwitz, because the title names the installation as such. But Boltanski's other works based on the same archival, inventory principle do not *refer* to the Holocaust by naming a specific element of it. Many of his archival installations use photographs of unknown or non-Jewish people. Nevertheless, they also have 'Holocaust effects', a term that I use in contrast to 'Holocaust representation'. In a Holocaust representation the Holocaust is referred to by means of a mediated account or representation of it. A 'Holocaust effect', on the contrary, is not brought about by means of representing the Holocaust, but by means of the re-enactment of a certain principle that defines the Holocaust. It is performatively re-enacted, producing an effect. This production of Holocaust effects explains why Boltanski's archival installations that have no referential relationship to the Holocaust and do not contain objects or representations of Jewish victims can still evoke the idea of the Holocaust.

In Boltanski's archival installations, the archivist's ambition to make history present in its remains is foregrounded as a failure. Part of the installation *Storage Area of the Children's Museum* (1989, plate 5.3), for instance, consisted of racks with

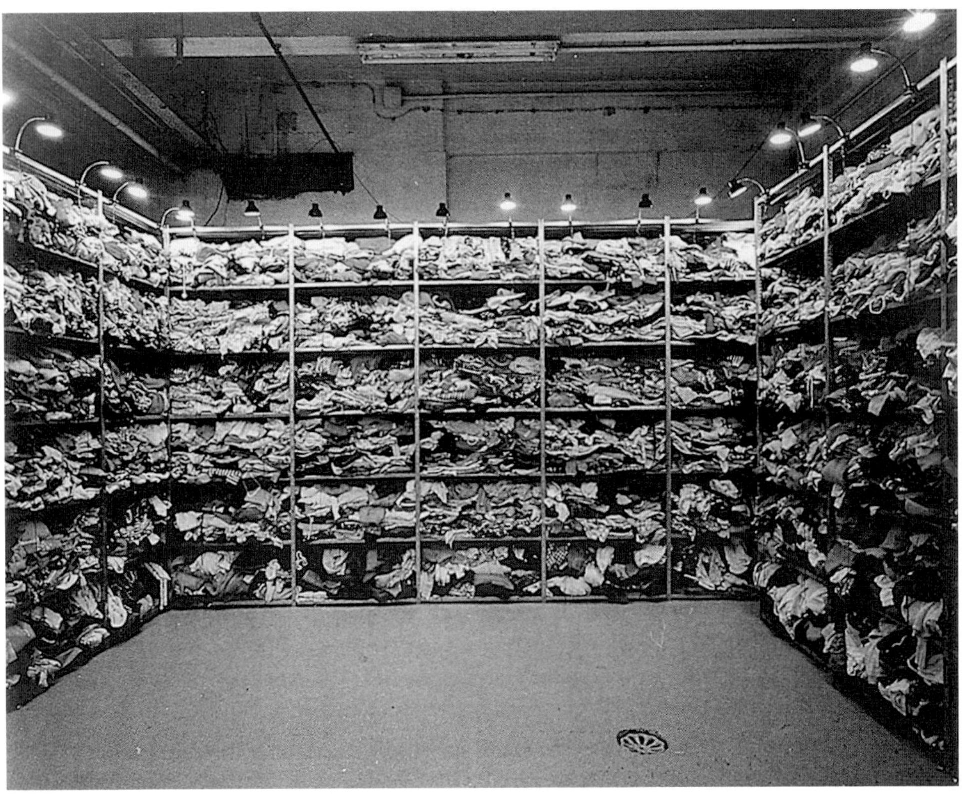

5.3 Installation view of Christian Boltanski, *Storage Area of the Children's Museum*, 1989. Children's clothing, metal shelves, lamps. Paris: Musée d'art moderne de la ville de Paris.

clothing. The piles of clothes stored on the shelves refer to the incomprehensible numbers of victims in the Holocaust. But in contrast to the series of works entitled *Canada*, these works do not refer to the Holocaust as an event; they have a Holocaust effect because they re-enact a principle that defines the Holocaust as a *method*. There the principle of deprivation of individuality was applied in the most extreme and radical way: the victims of the Holocaust were treated impersonally as specimens of a race that first had to be collected and inventoried before they could be used (in the labour camps) or destroyed (in the gas chambers). The Nazis not only inventoried the possessions of their victims; the same principles were applied to the victims themselves.

## NAZISM AND THE ARCHIVE

Boltanski reminds us provocatively of the fact that the Nazis were master archivists and that the most notorious concentration camp Auschwitz, the name of which has become synonymous with the Holocaust as such, was modelled on archival principles. Archival principles were central to the way in which the Nazis ruled most concentration camps and to their execution of the 'final solution'.

In many concentration camps the Nazis fanatically compiled lists of all the people who entered the camps, whether they went to the labour camps, or directly to the gas chambers. These lists are not unlike the catalogues that enable a visitor of an archive or museum to find out what is in the collection. It is thanks to the existence of these lists that after the liberation it was, in many cases, possible to find out if the detainees had survived the Holocaust, and if not, in which camp and on which date they had been killed.

On arrival, new detainees would have a number tattooed on their arm. They were transformed into archived objects, no longer individuals with a name, but objects with a number. Like objects in an archive or museum, the inscription classified them as traceable elements within a collection. Upon entering the camps they were also sorted into groups: men with men, women with women; children, old people and pregnant women to the gas chambers. Political prisoners, resistance fighters were not 'mixed' with Jews. Artists, musicians and architects were usually sent to camps like Theresiënstadt. Selecting and sorting on the basis of a fixed set of categories are basic archival activities.

Not only were the people who entered the camps selected and sorted, so were their belongings. It was not only the photographs of emaciated bodies that bore witness to the truth of the Holocaust, but also some of the categories used in the warehouses. Not only heaps of bodies, but also heaps of suitcases, of pairs of glasses, of shaven hair, etc. In these photographs the camps appear to be monstrous archives. This 'archiving' of belongings was primarily done so that they could be re-used by the German population. But Adolf Hitler also had other purposes in mind. After liquidating the Jewish people, he intended to build a museum of the Jewish people, the so-called 'Central Museum of The Extinguished Jewish race'.[4] For this museum, he needed objects selected from, among other places, the warehouses in the camps, a matter to which I will return.

In his artistic use of the archive, Boltanski preposterously evokes the objectifying and killing potential of the archive as exploited by Nazism. Hence, if most Holocaust scholars and students privilege archival modes of research, they seem to be unaware of the fact that their privileged medium at the same time creates

Holocaust effects. Their archival practices do not only have the Holocaust as object, they also uncannily re-enact the Holocaust's deadly objectifying technologies.

The notions of usability and uselessness are of crucial importance for an understanding of how Boltanski's archival works produce Holocaust effects. The inventories or selections performed upon entering the camps – which also returned almost daily when one had the good luck to be allowed into the labour camps – were based on the distinction between usable and unusable. The mechanisms of the Holocaust were such that ultimately everybody had to end up in the category 'useless'.

It is precisely this idea of uselessness that overwhelmed Boltanski when, like many other artists in the 1960s and the 1970s, he became interested in anthropological museums. The Musée de l'Homme in Paris made an impression on him:

> It was [. . .] the age of technological discoveries, of the Musée de l'Homme and of beauty, no longer just African art, but an entire series of everyday objects: Eskimo fishhooks, arrows from the Amazon Indians [. . .] The Musée de l'Homme was of tremendous importance to me; it was there that I saw large metal and glass vitrines in which were placed small, fragile, and insignificant objects. A yellowed photograph showing a 'savage' handling his little objects was often placed in the corner of the vitrine. Each vitrine presented a lost world: the savage in the photograph was most likely dead; the objects had become useless – anyway there's no one left who knows how to use them. The Musée de l'Homme seemed like a big morgue to me.[5]

While Boltanski expected to find 'beauty' in the museum, an expectation that seemed to be inspired by the kind of eye cubist artists had for the objects of African cultures, he found instead lost worlds in the vitrines. He sees absence instead of presence. The anthropological museum did not become a fine arts museum; it was transformed into a morgue of useless objects.

In the early 1970s Boltanski made two series of works in which he made use of the museological vitrine (*Attempt to Reconstruct Objects that Belonged to Christian Boltanski between 1948 and 1954 and Reference Vitrines*). One series of works, generically titled *Reference Vitrines* (1969–70, plate 5.4) consisted of museum-type showcases in which Boltanski displayed a sampling of the work he had made since 1969. He showed small piles of the dirt balls, some of the self-made knives and traps and some of the carved sugar cubes, pages from his books and parts of his mail-art. Each item in the glass cases had a label that usually listed the title and the date of the work. With this series of works Boltanski turned himself into the archivist of his own work. In his similar series, *Attempt to Reconstruct*, he was the archivist of his childhood.[6]

However, these 'reconstructions' fail utterly as reconstructions. They are not able to reconstruct either his childhood or his artistic career. Instead we see useless objects. The frame of the museological vitrine or the archaeological museum, in short the archival mode of representation, withdraws objects from the contexts in which they were originally present. In the vitrine, museum or archive they become subjected to principles which not only define the objects as useless, but which were defining for the Holocaust practice.

This brings us back to the Jewish museum that Hitler intended to establish after the liquidation of the Jewish people. Why was his goal not reached when all European Jews had been killed? Even after their destruction, the Jewish people could live on, not amongst the living but in memory – in living memory. The remains of Jewish people, in the form of memory, had to be dealt with effectively so that their possible continued existence in memory was also eradicated.

Boltanski helps us to understand why the museum can be such an effective tool, or perhaps I should now say weapon, in *killing memories*. Like archives, museums, especially historical museums, confront the viewer with de-contextualized objects. In this de-contextualization the objects become 'useless' and they evoke the 'absence' of the world of which they were originally part. It is in this respect that the archival museum can become a 'morgue of useless objects'. We can only speculate that Hitler's museum for the Jewish people would probably have looked like such a morgue. It would have objectified, killed and liquidated the Jewish people for a second and more definite time. Their remains would not have evoked their presence. They would not have kept their

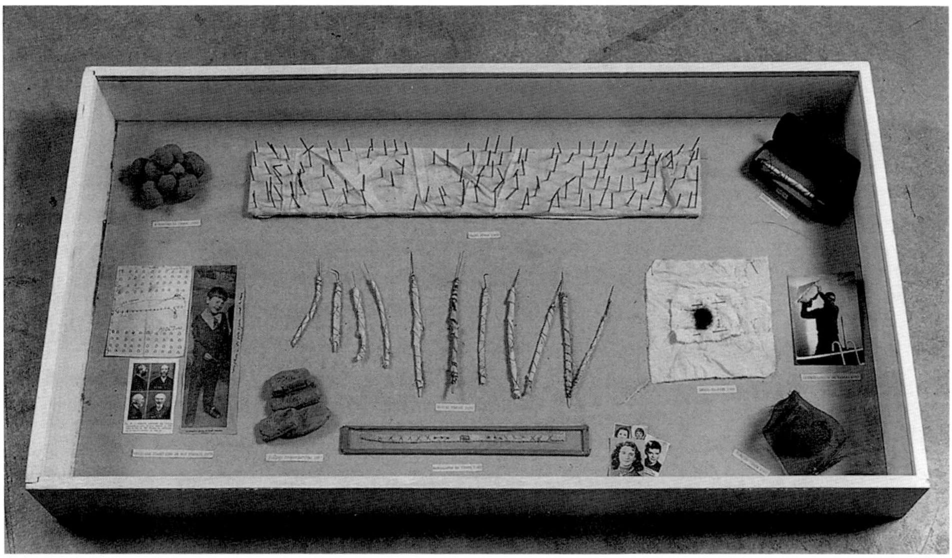

5.4 Christian Boltanski, *Reference Vitrines*, 1969–1970. Various objects in wooden vitrine with Plexiglas, 120 × 70 × 15 cm. Epinal: Musée departemental des Vosges.

memories alive. Instead, the represented objects would have penetrated the viewer with a sense of absence and lost time. Boltanski's archival art practice demonstrates the importance of preposterous history. He 'argues' something into the archival past (the categories of the sorting) that was not yet visible: the murder of memory.

## CATEGORIZATION AND OBJECTIFICATION: YDESSA HENDELES[7]

Whereas Boltanski's archival installations deconstruct the archive by showing the deadly effects of objectification, Ydessa Hendeles's installation *Partners* foregrounds another aspect of the archive's unreflected principles.[8] The thousands of snapshots, each of which include the image of a teddy bear, are arranged according to over one hundred typologies. The installation is structured like a presentation of natural history or cultural objects in a classic, traditional natural history museum. The meticulously framed snapshots completely and densely cover the walls (plate 5.5). In the middle of the space there are several antique museum display cases. Along the wall, mezzanines have been built to permit closer inspection of those photographs that hang on the upper halves of the walls (plate 5.6).

To enter the installation is to wonder what all these images have in common. It takes some time before the visitor becomes aware of the teddy bear in every photograph. The next discovery is, however, that the installation does not offer more of the same, just more pictures with teddy bears, but that the photographs have been categorized according to specific typologies. These categories are completely surprising: the installation, seemingly providing a history of the teddy bear, shows that the most different social and ethnic identities have used the teddy bear as a totem with which to identify.

When the installation was shown as part of a larger exhibition in Hitler's own former museum, the Haus der Kunst in Munich,[9] Hendeles wrote in the catalogue about the appeal of the teddy bear:

> The teddy bear has appealed not only to children as playthings and as surrogate playmates, but also to adults as props to express whimsical fantasies at parties, in the workplace, at sports events, and in sexual play. In fact, teddy bears have attended every social function in society. They have been photographed at weddings, in schools, in hospitals, on battlefields, at births, deaths, and memorials.[10]

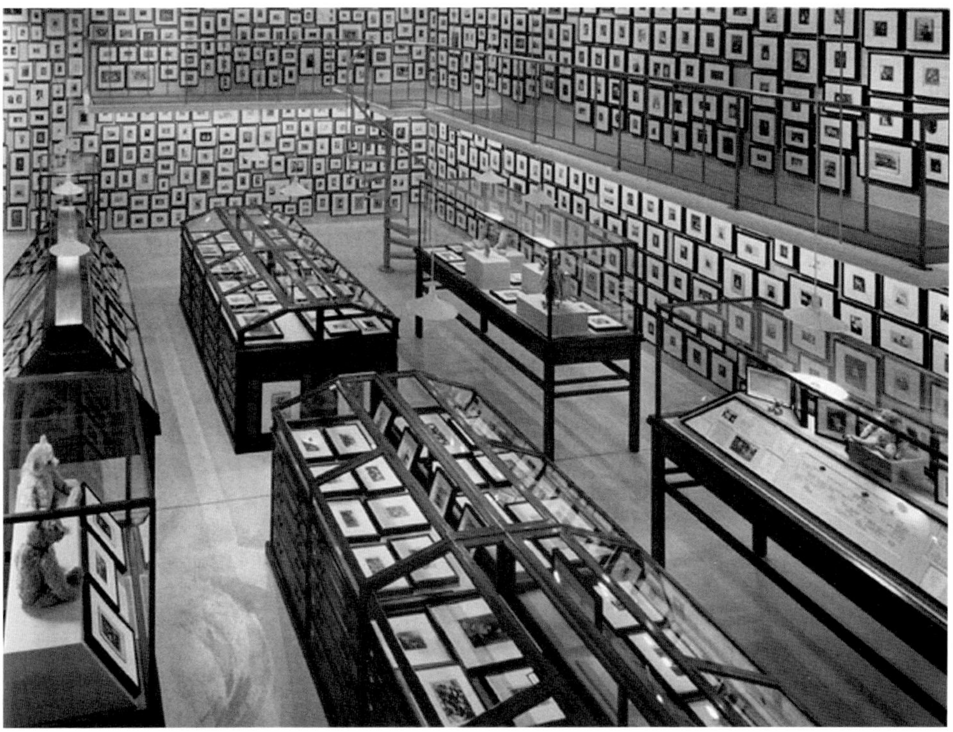

5.5 Installation view of Ydessa Hendeles, *Partners (The Teddy Bear Project)*, 2002: Teddy Bear 006. Munich: Haus der Kunst.

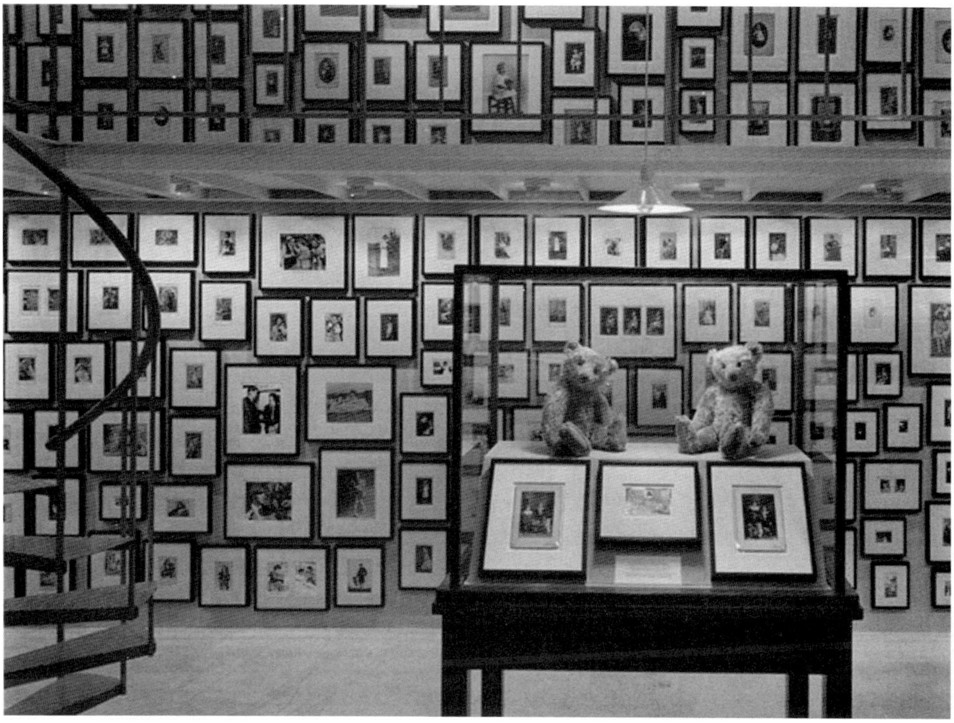

5.6 Installation view of Ydessa Hendeles, *Partners (The Teddy Bear Project)*, 2002: Teddy Bear 005. Munich: Haus der Kunst.

Her installation seems to provide evidence of this: when we start recognizing the different typologies, we suddenly see all the different groups (plates 5.7 and 5.8). Soldiers with teddy bears, students with teddy bears, prostitutes with teddy bears – there is no end to the different identities that have presented themselves with the teddy bear as their emblem and guardian.

In this respect, Hendeles's archival installation works as the opposite of those by Boltanski. Yet, I contend that her archival work is also a preposterous revisitation of the archive. Whereas, in the case of Boltanski, all individual differences dissolve within his objectifying archives, in the case of Hendeles one begins to see differences where one had not expected to see them. The thousands of teddy bear snapshots turn out to be extremely diverse. Within this corpus an endless number of individual categories can be distinguished. The pursuit of specificity and differentiation in *Partners* leads to extraordinary results.

At first sight Hendeles's 'visual thesis on the history of the teddy bear' conveys absolute trust in thorough, positivistic scholarship. She seems here to be on the site of most Holocaust scholars. But as she points out in her essay, this reassuring aura of scholarship is deceptive, 'because the use of documentary materials actually manipulates reality. Creating a world in which everyone has a teddy bear is a fantasy, as well as a commentary on traditional thematic, taxonomic curating.' Hendeles continues:

> Because of the relative rarity of photographs that include teddy bears, the resulting multitude of over three thousand pictures provides a curatorial statement that is both true and

> misleading. Viewers are inclined to trust a curator's presentation of cultural artefacts. While these systems are not necessarily objective, they can be convincing and therefore of comfort.[11]

Here Hendeles uses in a very subtle way the characteristics of the teddy bear to describe the effects of the archive. Earlier in her text she described the teddy bear in terms of a duality:

> As a mohair-covered, stuffed, jointed toy, with movable arms, legs and head, a teddy bear can be cradled and hugged like a baby. But the wild bear referenced by the toy is an animal that can be threatening to human beings. Having a ferocious guardian at one's side makes the teddy into a symbol of protective aggression, which is why, for the past hundred years, it has provided solace to frightened children and later to adults, who carry that comfort with them as a cherished memory.[12]

The duality of the teddy bear also characterizes that of the archive: comforting and aggressive at the same time. Comforting because it has the reassuring aura of objectivity and systematicity; aggressive because it subjects reality and individuality to classifications that are more pertinent to the systematic and purifying mindset than to the classified objects. It imposes the ideal of pure order on an actuality that is messier and more hybrid than the scholarly device of the archive can live with.

Ultimately, and in this it reconceptualizes the archive preposterously, *Partners* shows the utter arbitrariness of archival typologies. The excessive differentiation within the corpus of snapshots showing teddy bears produces in the viewer a feeling of being lost. The rigorous systematicity of the archive suddenly shows its Janus head of total arbitrariness. The question remains: in which sense does

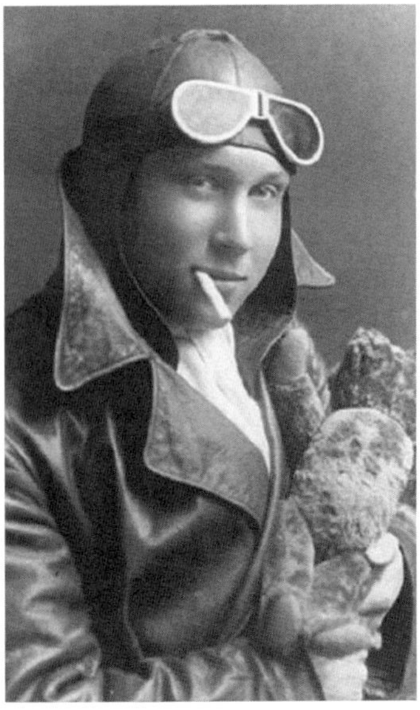

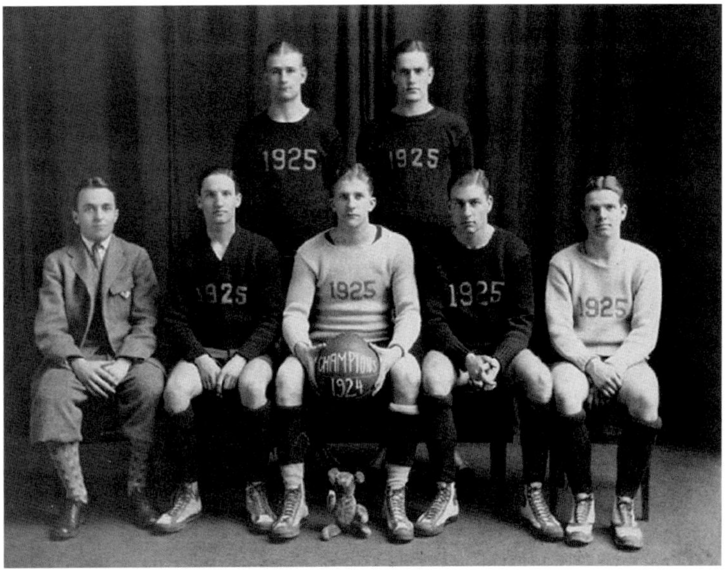


5.7 Snapshot in installation: Teddy Bear 007, from Ydessa Hendeles, *Partners (The Teddy Bear Project)*, 2002.
5.8 Snapshot in installation: Teddy Bear 010, from Ydessa Hendeles, *Partners (The Teddy Bear Project)*, 2002.

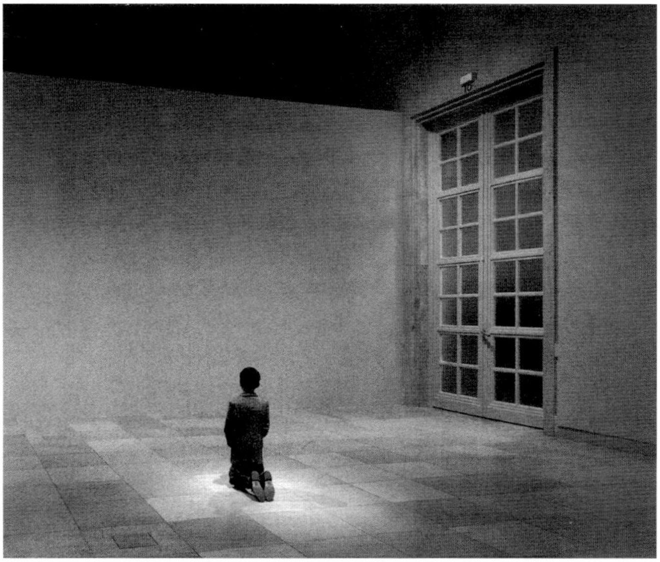

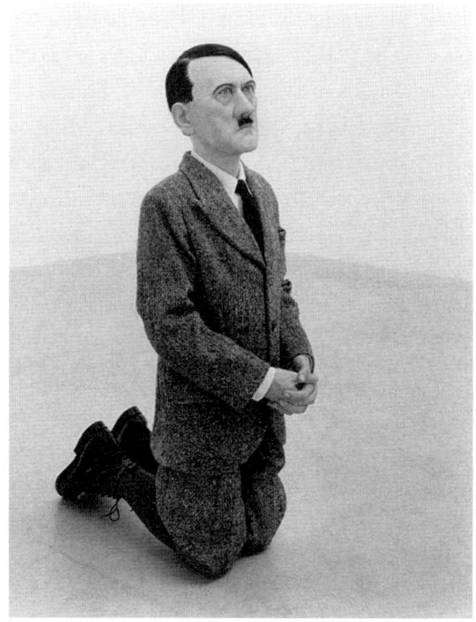

5.9 Installation view of Maurizio Cattelan, *Him*, 2001. Number two in an edition of three plus one artist's proof. Polyester resin, clothing, leather boots, human hair; 60 × 38 × 58.5 cm. Munich: Haus der Kunst.
5.10 Installation view of Maurizio Cattelan, *Him*, 2001. Number two in an edition of three plus one artist's proof. Polyester resin, clothing, leather boots, human hair; 60 × 38 × 58.5 cm. Munich: Haus der Kunst.

Hendeles's preposterous meta-commentary on the archive specifically apply to Holocaust archives, or to the Holocaust itself?

Within the endless series of typologies in this installation, the category of Jews, hence, of possible victims of the Holocaust, and of survivors of the Holocaust, forms an important category. The feeling of melancholy is immediately pervasive on entering the room. This excessive and emblematic archive shows lost worlds in the extreme. Of course, teddy bears do not belong to the past; children and other groups of people still have them and play with them. But because these snapshots are old and they are presented as part of an archive, they are automatically ascribed to the past, to a lost world. Within the metaphorical realm of 'lost worlds' the Holocaust figures as the most literal case. That is why the typology of Holocaust victims with teddy bears is central.

But Hendeles activated the frame of the Holocaust in yet other ways. Having spent some time in the teddy bear installation, the visitor entered a space that, compared to the densely packed archival installation, was almost empty, with, at the other end of the room, a sculpture of a small boy on his knees (plate 5.9). This is *Him*, a sculpture by the Italian artist Maurizio Cattelan (2001), a puppet-like figure of Hitler with the body of a small, innocent boy and his adult, moustached face (plate 5.10). The similarity between teddy bears and archives has already been suggested; now an awareness is created of the association between teddy bears and Hitler (and archives). Hitler, too, was aggressive as well as comforting. He offered a deceptive source of safety to the German people. Hendeles explains:

> The system of the teddy bear archive raises the notion of other systems created with strict stipulations, and how they can, because they appear to make sense, persuasively manipulate

> reality. The purity of race to which Hitler aspired was the application of a system of rules. Like the teddy bear, Hitler shares a duality of origin, where danger is domesticated.[13]

To frame the teddy bear archive with the figure of Hitler has particularly disenchanting consequences for the archive. Is the archive – its system and its goal – complicit in Hitler's ideal of a purity of race? Is it Hitler's modelling of the concentration camps on archival principles that makes the archive suspect, or is it suspect intrinsically? A provisional answer seems to have been given by Hendeles when she showed the teddy bear installation for the first time, as part of an exhibition at the Ydessa Hendeles Foundation, her gallery in Toronto, in an installation entitled *Same/Difference* in 2002–03. After the teddy bear installation the viewer entered a relatively narrow corridor, at the left side of which were more framed snapshots of teddy bears. At the end of the same wall was a small text panel, giving the description of an art work, the name of the artist and the date. It turns out that the viewer had missed noticing an art work. On the right side of the corridor, on a completely white wall, was a text in light grey letters. The text was by the artist Douglas Gordon, and was dated 1989:

> ROTTING FROM THE INSIDE OUT

Having read this text, the confined space of the corridor suddenly gave way to a much larger space in which Cattalan's *Him* was placed. The subtle sequentiality of art works made each function as a framing device for those that came before and after. 'Rotting From the Inside Out' became a chilling comment on the teddy bear, on Hitler, as well as on the archival genre itself.

## THE FUTURE OF THE ARCHIVE: PETER FORGACS

Boltanski's and Hendeles's use of the archive provide preposterous deconstructions of principles which underlie and define the archive. Although they foreground different aspects, in both artistic practices the archive is exposed as 'rotten from the inside out'. The unavoidable question is now whether there is still a future for the archive? . . . and, I would like to add, for related institutions such as the museum?

Since 1988 the film-maker Peter Forgacs has assembled the Private Hungary documentary series from an archival collection of home-movie stock dating back to the 1930s and up to the present. The films draw upon a film archive, established by Forgacs himself: the Private Film and Photo Archives in Budapest. It comprises more than 300 hours of home movies and an additional forty hours of interviews with the relatives of the amateur film-makers who shot the footage. For most of the films Forgacs collaborated with Hungarian minimalist composer Tibor Szemzõ. Forgacs also made some films that do not specifically focus on Hungary. One of them is the film *The Maelstrom* from 1997, which he made with the VPRO for Dutch public television. This film is also archival: it draws upon found home movies from diverse origin. For *Maelstrom* two sources are dominant. First, the larger part of the film consists of the home movies of the Dutch Jewish family Peereboom, filmed by the eldest son, Max Peereboom. These home movies cover the period from the early 1930s to 1943, when the family was transported to Auschwitz. The second important source consists of the home movies of the

Austrian Nazi Arthur Seyss-Inquart, who was appointed Reichs Commissioner of the Netherlands in 1940 as the representative of Hitler. A third source used more sparsely by Forgacs in this film is the home movies of a Dutch member of the SS. Compared to most of his other films, the overall structure of *Maelstrom* is more conventionally narrative. It begins with the oldest footage in 1933 in Amsterdam, where the father of the cameraman filmer, Max Peereboom, is editor of the *Nieuw Israelitisch Dagblad*. Max lives in Middelburg, where he works for his future father-in-law. When the chronology of the film reaches the late 1930s we get to see some of the footage of the Dutch member of the SS. The home footage of Seyss-Inquart is introduced in 1940, located mainly on his estate Clingendael, not far from The Hague, where he moved with his family after being appointed by Hitler (plate 5.11). In 1942 Max and Annie Peereboom and his family-in-law were forced to move to Amsterdam. Seyss-Inquart had ordered all Dutch Jews to move to Amsterdam in order to facilitate their deportation to Auschwitz and other camps – deportation would be much more efficient if all Jews were concentrated in one city. The film stops abruptly. When Max, the filmer of the Peereboom family, is transported and then killed (with the rest of his family and extended family), the family narrative comes to an end. The only person of this family who will survive is Max's youngest brother Simon.

It is in the structuring of narrative through home movies that Forgacs's historiography shows its preposterous hand. Home movies form a particular genre and as a genre they have specific properties in relation to memory. The genre focuses almost exclusively on the personal. The social dimension of human life only figures obliquely, if at all. We are shown anniversaries, weddings (plate 5.12), family outings, the birth and growing up of children. These personal moments in the family are restricted because they are selective: they consist of memories of happy moments. But as Forgacs pointed out in an interview, the home movie is personal in yet another way.[14] It is structured like a dream. It contains many strange ellipses and in the case of older home movies it is exclusively visual. There are no words spoken, no voice-over. Visual communication is central. Sigmund Freud's explanation of the dream work is also relevant for an understanding of home movies.[15] Although the macro-structure of *Maelstrom* is narrative, the fragments of footage which build its narrative are not so much telling as showing. Although the subtitle of *Maelstrom* is *A Family Chronicle*, the footage does not have the form of a family chronicle, but of externalized memory.

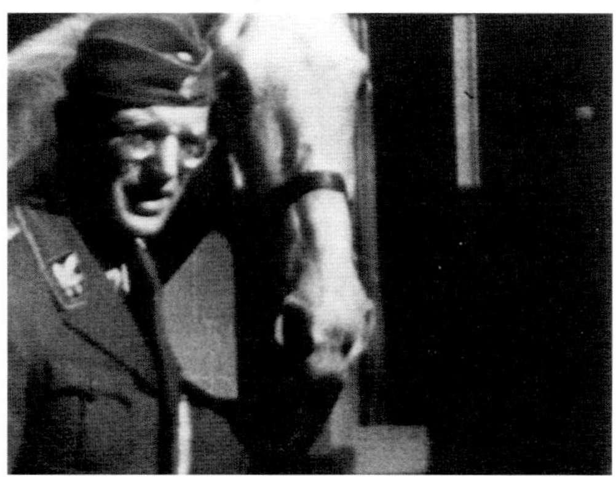

5.11 Film still from Peter Forgacs, *The Maelstrom*, 1997. 60 minutes.

Whereas home movies are almost exclusively concerned with personal time, Forgacs's montage adds public history, present in *Maelstrom*, albeit in a de-centred way. Some Peereboom footage shows a visit of Queen Wilhelmina with Princess Juliana to the town of Middelburg, or the celebration in Middelburg of the fortieth anniversary of Queen Wilhelmina. That the family filmed these events can be read as symptomatic for their assimilation into Dutch culture. But the other insertions of history are by the hand of the director. Sometimes we hear a radio broadcast, or there are titles or texts written on the screen pointing out in which historical moment the filmed family footage is embedded. At other times, the historical moment is explained by a disembodied voice. The laws, rules or articles proclaimed by Seyss-Inquart stipulating how to kill warm-blooded animals, or who is considered to be Jewish and who not, what Jews who were going to be deported were allowed to take with them, and so on, are sung by a voice in the mode of a traditional Jewish song. Whatever device to insert history Forgacs uses, it is never part of the personal time of the home footage but always superposed, *imposed* on it.

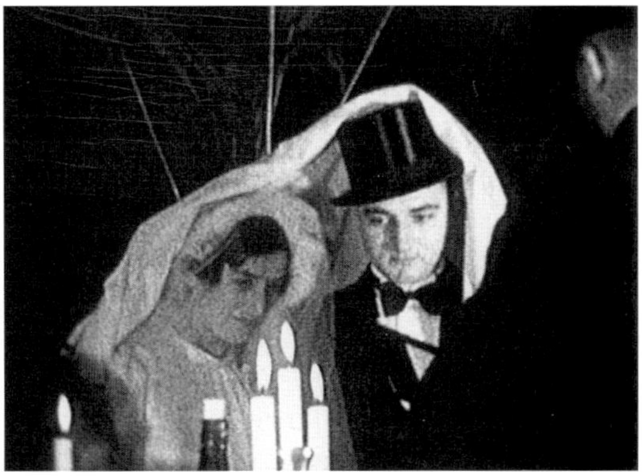

5.12 Film still from Peter Forgacs, *The Maelstrom*, 1997. 60 minutes.

The imposition of history on personal time never works smoothly. The completely different temporal dimension of the home footage again and again strikes the viewer. Personal time and historical time are in absolute tension with each other. We expect to see traces or symptoms of the dramatic history of the past in home-movie footage. But that is not the case. As the 1939–45 war and the Holocaust progress, the home movies continue to show happy family memories. Max Peereboom also filmed the moment that his family prepared for deportation to Auschwitz. It is remarkable that he decided to film this. We see his wife Annie and her stepmother around the table repairing the clothes they want to wear or take with them on deportation. They drink coffee and Max smokes a pipe (plate 5.13). What they are doing (preparing themselves for deportation) is not conveyed by the footage but told by a written text imposed on the footage. What we see is a happy – the Dutch would say cosy – family situation. Nothing of the history that will victimize them in such a horrific way is able to enter the personal realm of the home movie. The temporal dimension of the home movie does not unfold as a collective narrative, but persistently as a personal narrative.

In *Maelstrom* personal history is not represented as part of collective or 'official' history (as a synecdoche of it); it is in radical tension with it. This has important consequences for the question I raised earlier: is there a future for the archive? Or is it rotten through and through because of its objectifying mechanisms and its imposition of categories and pure order on a reality which is hybrid? As I argued in the case of Boltanski's pseudo-archives as well as the archival concentration camp, the imposition of the binary opposition, useful versus useless, seems to define the rationale of the archive. Everything that is archived seems to become subjected to this distinction. Although Holocaust archives are also seen as memorials of the Holocaust, the memories stored in it are ultimately judged on the basis of what we learn from them, that is, in how useful they are.

The Spielberg Video and Film Archive of the United States Holocaust Memorial Museum and The Fortunoff Video Archive for Holocaust Testimonies at Yale University are good examples. Geoffrey Hartman, director of the latter project, describes the function of the Fortunoff Archive first of all in terms of the process of conducting the interviews and not in terms of the products collected in the archive. To testify, he intimates, leads to a kind of re-humanization and reconstitution of subjectivity of the Holocaust victim. But the moment that the Holocaust survivor has given his testimony, the taped result becomes the object that is stored in the archive. It is almost impossible for the visitors of this kind of archive not to impose the distinction between useful versus useless on this material. The visitors are looking for something, they are usually scholars or students who want to learn something or hope that watching these tapes will be helpful in comprehending the Holocaust experience. In this respect the kind of categories used to make the archive accessible are significant. Steven Spielberg's Survivors of the Shoah Visual History Foundation indexes the archive by city and country of birth, religious identity and wartime experiences. The Fortunoff Video Archive indexes it by geographic names and topics discussed in the testimony.

Forgacs's use of the archive of home movies, however, resists the imposition of the useful/useless dichotomy. His archival films do not provide information, they do not tell history, but they show us that the experience of time in personal history cannot be integrated in or translated into collective or official history. As Kaja Silverman has argued, Forgacs's films are based on strategies of re-personalization instead of objectification or categorization.[16] His films evoke the phenomenal world; they are about vitality, enjoyment, about activities such as dancing and playing. Whereas the archival mechanisms of objectification and categorization strip images of their singularity, Forgacs's archival footage keeps insisting on the private and affective. Silverman notes that this is achieved through the many direct looks with which people face the camera (plate 5.14). This seems to be a defining feature of home movies.

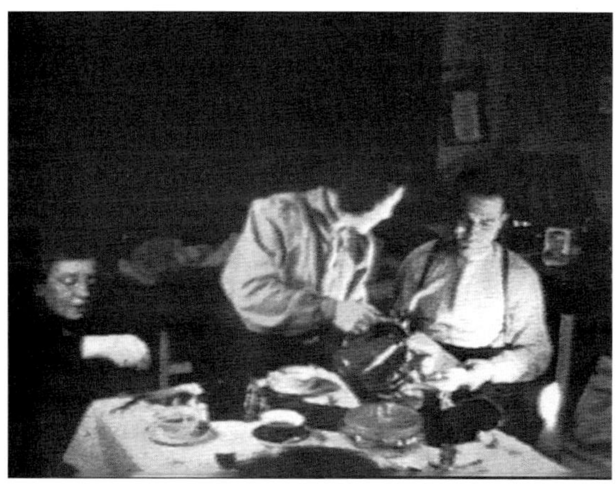

5.13 Film still from Peter Forgacs, *The Maelstrom*, 1997. 60 minutes.

When people face the camera in a fiction movie, this kind of look is self-reflexive, for a moment it short-circuits the fictionality of the film by establishing direct contact with the viewer. The film shows its constructedness. In home movies the frequent looking into the camera is of a different order, for here there is no clear distinction between the camera and the person behind the camera. *Maelstrom* has many examples of this interaction. Simon, Max's youngest brother, makes fun of the cameraman again and again, by pulling funny faces in front of the camera. He does this, not to spoil the film, but to make the cameraman laugh, or to make him angry. His funny faces function within an affective relationship between two human beings. There is another example of this in *Maelstrom*: at one of the many weddings the two- or three-year-old daughter of Max and Annie is being filmed. When she turns her face to the camera, she expects to see the face of Max her father or one of her relatives. Instead she sees a monstrous object, namely the camera. She is clearly terrified. This example shows in its negativity that people in home movies are not posing for the camera, but for the person who holds the camera. They let themselves be filmed, not to get objectified into a beautiful or interesting image, but out of love for the person who films. According to Silverman, people in home footage do not just convey Roland Barthes's idea of 'this has been' ('*ça a été*'), but 'I love you.'[17]

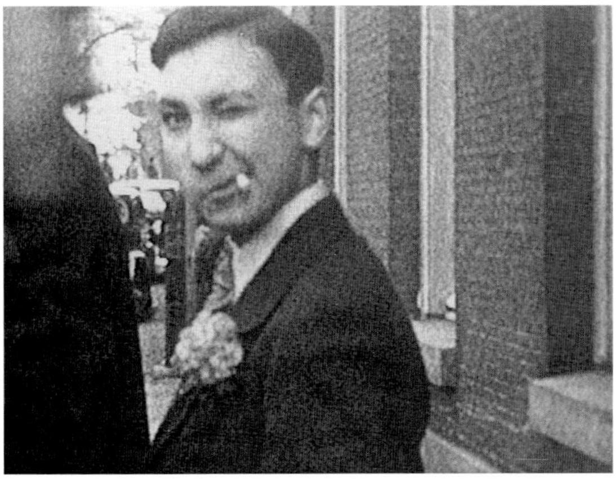

5.14 Film still from Peter Forgacs, *The Maelstrom*, 1997. 60 minutes.

As Forgacs explains in an interview, there is a fundamental difference between looking at a photograph and watching moving images. He intensifies this difference by his manipulation of film time, by slow motion or even stopping the moving image, reducing it to a film still:

> The slow-motion technique and manipulation of the film time, the movement and the rhythm, give an opposite dynamic or an opposite possibility than in the example of the photo explained in *Camera Lucida* by Roland Barthes. The frozen photographic second of the Barthes thesis is a good example why the photo is a tombstone, whereas moving image is not. [. . .] If we made right now a black-and-white photograph of ourselves, we could observe the event as already-past time: history. [. . .] But while we have moving images of the past, we always have the fluxes of life, the contrapuntal notion between Barthes's photo thesis and the movement ( = life) on film, which proves forever that we're alive. So my viewers – and you – know that they (the amateur film actors, my heroes) are physically dead, but they are still moving. They are reanimated again and again by the film.[18]

Hence, the effect of re-personalization brought about by Forgacs's films is not only the result of the specific genre of home movies, but also of his intensification of qualities of the medium of the moving image. His manipulation of moving images – the slow-downs, the movement back and forth, stopping the movement for a few seconds – creates a rhythm that makes the vitality/aliveness of the movements almost a sensorial experience. It creates a distance between real time and the time of the moving images. This de-naturalizes our reception of time and movement, as a result of which we become overwhelmed by the life embodied in these moving images.

Is this is always the case in home movies? Or does it also depend on the film-maker and the kind of family that is being filmed? In this respect, the difference between the Peereboom and the Seyss-Inquart home movies is revealing. The distinction I have used so far between personal time and historical time does not automatically apply in the same way or to the same degree in the Seyss-Inquart footage. Seyss-Inquart's position in history is radically different from that of the Peereboom family. Seyss-Inquart was appointed by Hitler, he represents him in the Netherlands. He is the representative of Hitler, of history; one could say, he *is* history, or rather, the embodiment of it. This prompts a reflection: can the embodiment of history make home movies of his family and friends? Or is the genre of the home movie disabled when history enters the realm of the personal?

Whereas the Peereboom footage is so striking because of its vitality, the behaviour of the Seyss-Inquart family is much more restrained. It seems that the Seyss-Inquart family members are constantly aware that they are regarded not only by the cameraman, but also by anonymous, abstract or, later viewers. They embody history, and later history will be judged; their role in history will be judged. When I watch the home movies of this family, I cannot avoid mobilizing the distinction useful versus useless. It is from the Seyss-Inquart footage that I get information. I become interested from an historical point of view when I notice that Reichs Führer SS Himmler visited the Seyss-Inquart couple at their Clingendael estate in the Netherlands (plate 5.15). They were not only fellow Nazi leaders, they and their wives socialized with each other and played tennis.

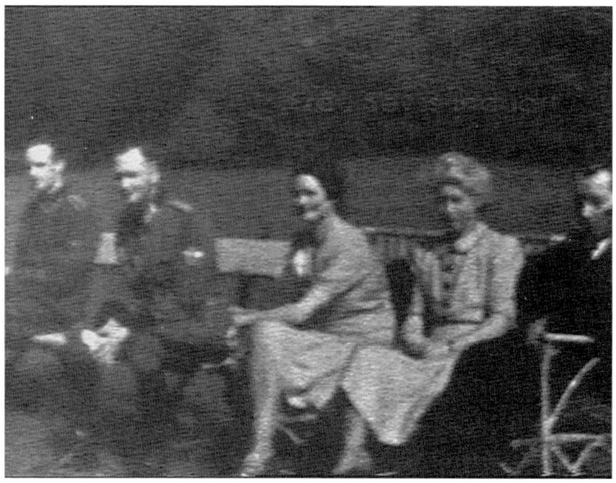

5.15 Film still from Peter Forgacs, The *Maelstrom*, 1997. 60 minutes.

The fact that Seyss-Inquart's home movies evoke a mode of looking that is usually discouraged by this genre, only foregrounds, differentially that is, the more usual mode of looking at home movies. Forgacs's combination and alternation of the Peereboom's footage with the Seyss-Inquart footage, of personal time and of a personal time that is infected by historical time, sharpens our eye for the special qualities of the Peereboom home movies.

Forgacs's archival films do not objectify or categorize. Preposterously intervening in an archival object, they transform it: they re-animate and re-personalize. Forgacs is able to do this thanks to the specific qualities of the objects collected in his archive, the nature of home movies. But in addition, he adds a rhythm to the movement of the moving image that infuses these films with reflexivity. This rhythm magnifies the nature of personal time as living, as affect, as movement and as moving. Within his artistic use of the archive the archive has a future again.

Boltanski's, Hendeles's and Forgacs's use of visual archives foreground, each in their own way, aspects of the archival mode so far unacknowledged or repressed. Their artistic practices are striking examples of what Mieke Bal has called a preposterous view of history: as she has stated, 'the work performed by later images obliterates the older images as they were before that intervention and creates new versions of old images instead.'[19] In Boltanski's use of the visual archive, the archive is deconstructed; its objectifying potential is evoked and foregrounded: the visual archive does not store memories, but murders them. Hendeles's artistic practice emphasizes the arbitrariness of the archive's categorizations. Forgacs's films activate a more positive potential of the visual archive. Avoiding the deadening suction that all archiving exerts at some point, he shows how a responsible use of visual archival material can re-animate and re-personalize the 'subject matter' contained in it.

## Notes

1 Terrence Des Pres, 'Holocaust Laughter', in *Writing and the Holocaust*, ed. Berel Lang, New York, 1998, 216–33.

2 Mieke Bal, *Quoting Caravaggio: Contemporary Art, Preposterous History*, Chicago, 1999, 1.

3 I have argued this in my book *Caught By History: Holocaust Effects in Contemporary Art, Literature, and Theory*, Stanford, 1997, chap. 4.

4 In Tsecho Slovakia the Nazis brought Jewish religious articles from 153 provincial communities to Prague for the establishment of this 'Central Museum of the Extinguished Jewish Race'. Included were 5,400 religious objects, 24,500 prayerbooks and 6,070 artefacts of historical value. After the end of the war it became the core of the Jewish Museum of Prague. See *Encyclopedia of the Holocaust*, ed. Israel Gutman, New York, 1990, 1187.

5 Delphine Renard, 'Interview with Christian Boltanski', *Boltanski*, exhib. cat., Paris, 1984, 71, quoted in Lynn Gumpert, *Christian Boltanski*, Paris, 1994, 32.

6 In his site-specific work *Missing House* (1990) in Berlin, Boltanski turned himself into the archivist of a vacant lot between other houses in a former Jewish neighbourhood. *The Missing House* consists of nameplates attached to the firewalls of houses adjacent to the empty lot, created by the destruction of a house in the 1939–45 war. The plates included the name, dates of residence and professions of the last inhabitants of the missing house. See John Czaplicka, 'History, Aesthetics, and Contemporary Commemorative Practice in Berlin', *New German Critique*, 65 1995, 155–87.

7 Ydessa Hendeles is one of the most important collectors of contemporary art and of the history of photography. She has her own museum in which she curates exhibtions out of her own collection, the Ydessa Hendeles Foundation in Toronto. For an analysis of her practice of collecting and curating, see Reesa Greenberg, 'Private Collectors, Museums and Display: A Post-Holocaust Perspective', *Jong Holland*, 1:16, 2000, 29–41.

8 The main title of the installation *Partners* refers to the intimate relationship between the owners of teddy bears and their playmate. The installation contains 3,000 family album photographs, antique teddy bears with photographs of their original owners and related ephemera, mahogany display cases, eight painted-steel mezzanines, six painted-steel spiral staircases, sixteen painted portable walls, hanging light fixtures and custom wall lighting.

9 The exhibition, which Hendeles curated for the Haus der Kunst in Munich, has the same title as her teddy bear installation *Partners*. In case of the exhibition the title has several meanings. It refers to the collaboration between a public museum and a private collector, between a German institution and a Jewish collector, between Hitler's former museum and the daughter of Holocaust survivors. For an analysis of this exhibition, see Ernst van Alphen, 'Die Ausstellung als narratives Kunstwerk/Exhibition as Narrative Work of Art' in *Partners*, eds Chris Dercon and Thomas Weski, Cologne, 2003, 143–85.

10 Ydessa Hendeles, 'Notes on the Exhibition', in *Partners*, eds Dercon and Weski, 212.

11 Ydessa Hendeles, 'Notes on the Exhibition', 211–12.

12 Ydessa Hendeles, 'Notes on the Exhibition', 211.

13 Ydessa Hendeles, 'Notes on the Exhibition', 215.

14 www.artmargins.com/content/interview/forgacs.html (1 December 2004).

15 Sigmund Freud, 'The Interpretation of Dreams', in *The Standard Edition of the Complete Psychological Works of Sigmund Freud*, vols 4–5, ed. James Strachey, London, 1973, 1–629.

16 Kaja Silverman, *Flesh of My Flesh*, Chicago, forthcoming.

17 Silverman, *Flesh of My Flesh*.

18 www.artmargins.com/content/interview/forgacs.html (1 December 2004).

19 Mieke Bal, *Quoting Caravaggio*, 1.

# 6

# WHAT DOES A WOMAN WANT? ART INVESTIGATING DEATH IN CHARLOTTE SALOMON'S *LEBEN? ODER THEATER?*

GRISELDA POLLOCK

> The place of art is for me the transport-station of trauma: a transport-station that more than a place is rather a space, that allows for certain occasions of occurrence and encounter, which will become the realization of what I call borderlinking and borderspacing in a matrixial trans-subjective space by way of experiencing with an object of a process of creation.[1]
>
> Bracha Ettinger, 2000

> Reminiscences even extensive ones, do not always amount to an autobiography. And these certainly do not ... For autobiography has to do with time, with sequence and what makes up the continuous flow of life. Here I am talking of a space, of moments, of discontinuities.[2]
>
> Walter Benjamin, 1932

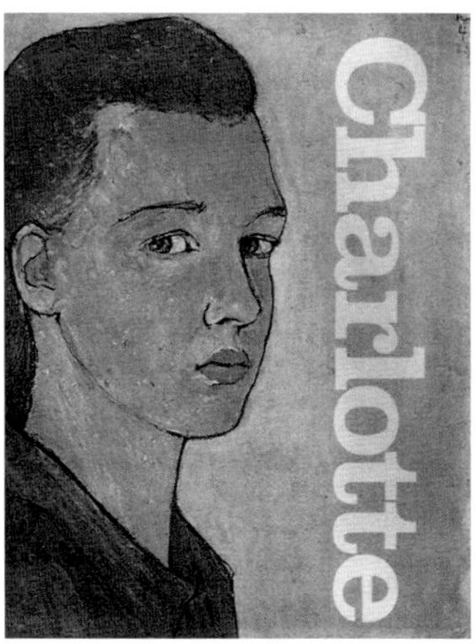


6.1 Cover of facsimile edition of *Charlotte: Life? or Theatre? An Autobiographical Play*, 1981.

A detail of a self-portrait of 1940 (plate 6.1) adorns the cover of the massive 1981 facsimile edition of *Leben? oder Theater?* (1941–2),[3] a composite art work by Charlotte Salomon (1917–43) comprising 784 gouache paintings selected from a total of 1,325 that deploy a ravishing range of visualities, textualities and musicalities. *Leben? oder Theater?* conforms to no known visual style, movement or periodization and presents a range of challenges for art-historical interpretation.[4] To what period might it belong, created by a exiled German-Jewish artist dis-emancipated by her own government, that was, even as she painted her work, encompassing genocidal annihilation of all Jewish Europeans? To what movement or style might we attribute a work that seems so promiscuously familiar with French, German, Russian modernisms, graphic modernisms, cinema, music, children's illustrated books, avant-garde theatre and popular culture? *Leben? oder Theater?* was created by Charlotte

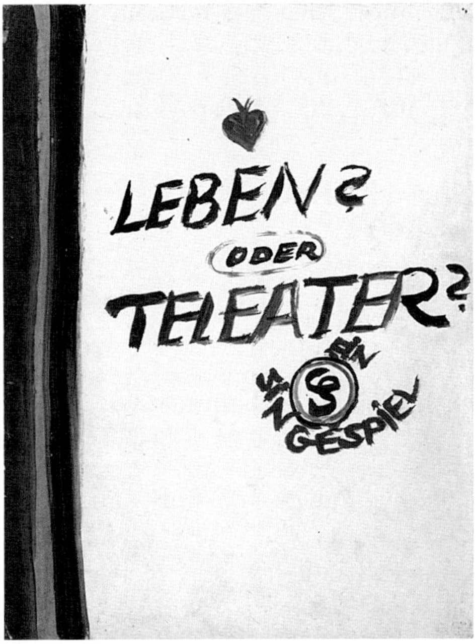


6.2 Title page of Charlotte Salomon, *Leben? oder Theater?*, 1941–42. Gouache on paper, 32.5 × 25 cm. Amsterdam: Jewish Historical Museum (JMH 4155-1). Reproduced courtesy of Stichtung Charlotte Salomon.

Salomon at a moment both traumatically shaped by and, therefore, outside of, historical time, and yet profoundly indexical of an historical moment that I have named 'before Auschwitz' (1933–42). It entered art-historical and cultural knowledge only after 1961, was donated to a public museum (the Jewish Historical Museum, Amsterdam) in 1971, and received its first comprehensive exhibition only after 1998.[5]

Charlotte Salomon was born in Berlin on 16 April 1917 and was murdered on 10 October 1943 in Auschwitz.[6] Amongst a scattered body of landscapes and portraits (now being reassembled at Yad Vashem) survives a magnum opus, *Leben? oder Theater?*, begun in the summer of 1941 and finalized by August 1942. It persists into our time by the mere chance of its being largely about a group of people who held no interest for an American woman, Ottilie Moore, to whom the project was dedicated on its second page in gratitude to her for having offered refuge to a stateless German-Jewish exile. Salvaged after the war from Moore, along with one self-portrait (see plate 6.1) by the artist's father, Professor Albert Salomon, and her stepmother, the singer Paula Lindberg, who had survived in hiding in Amsterdam, all the while imagining their daughter safely stowed away in the South of France, this strange and enigmatic volume of musically inspired paintings annotated with texts on transparent overlays or directly on the paintings and suggested melodies to which the words might be sung, has only recently begun to be considered as a modernist or avant-garde art work at all. The work has attracted growing scholarly attention in relation to studies of art and trauma, German-Jewish culture in Weimar and after the founding of the Nazi Third Reich, and specifically in relation to feminist studies in autobiography.

Clearly, the work engages with aspects of an historical biography that can be established for its maker. Members of the artist's family and circle are represented by characters ironized by Brechtian renaming. The family Salomon becomes the family Kann (is Able), the grandparents Grunwald become Mr and Mrs Knarre (Groaners), Paula Lindberg becomes the infantilized Paulinka Bimbam and so forth.[7] The autobiographical approach, however valid and theoretically elastic, closes what should be opened up: the question posed by the work. The title, *Leben? oder Theater?* (plate 6.2) contains two question marks which must invite analysis of the way that a work of art can be undertaken as an investigation. What is being interrogated? An art work that refuses the boundaries of word and image, image and music, that was made in defiance of art history's preferred models of style, movement and period, Charlotte Salomon's vast interdisciplinary project *Leben? oder Theater?* 1941–42 challenges art history but responds well to models of feminist reading of visual narrative and semiotics proposed by Mieke Bal's practice of cultural analysis and working with concepts.

The final image of *Leben? oder Theater?* (plate 6.3) involves a repetition of the two terms of the title but without interrogatives. In the painting of the young woman in her modernist bathing costume, curled up like the Copenhagen mermaid or G. F. Watts's blind figure of *Hope* (1886, London: Tate), brush poised having made the first stroke on her transparent paper as she sits beside a Raoul Dufy-inspired Mediterranean, the words 'Leben oder Theater' are painted affirmatively in bold letters on her bronzed back. But this painting was covered by a transparent overlay (plate 6.4) upon which was written the final statement of a nine-page text by the artist in painted block capital letters explaining how the work came about and concluding with three interrogatives.

> This took place in July 1940 en route from a little town in the Pyrenees to Nice.

It continues in deceptively fairy tale mode:

> One year later during which the world fell ever more apart, the spirit of this strangely twin-natured creature was ever more crushed by the proximity of her grandfather [. . .] and remained alone with her experiences and her paint brush [. . .] And she found herself facing the question of whether to commit suicide or to undertake something wildly eccentric [. . .] Thus in the presence of the scorching sun, purple sea, and luxuriant blossoms, the memory of an experience of her fervid early love came back to her. And she tried to visualise that face, that figure, And lo, she succeeded, and she noticed that this was a very interesting occupation. For she discovered that that figure [. . .] might possibly preserve her from suicide inasmuch as she remembered one of Amadeus's favourite utterances: Love, know thyself first in order to love thy neighbour. And then: one has to go into oneself – into one's childhood – to be able to go out of oneself. And he felt that the movie was the machine of modern man as a means of going out of oneself.

She then recounts how she fell asleep and dreamed the face of Amadeus, and remembered his theories of Orpheus, the artist who rivalled death.

> [. . .] And with dream-awakened eyes she saw all the beauty around for, saw the sea, felt the sun, and knew: she had to vanish for a while from the human plane and make every sacrifice in order to create her world anew out of the depths [. . .] And from that came:
> Life (Das Leben)
> or
> Theatre (Das Theater)
> ???

This use of the definite article firmly makes the final terms into nouns. Their absence in the title allows some ambivalence. Should we read it in a verb form as *to Live?* or, if we could invent such a verb, *to Theatre?* This is quite different from thinking of the work as a choice between life or theatre. The opposition life or theatre unsettles because the usual partner for life is death. Most interpreters, rightly I think, consider theatre as a reference to a kind of false self, created on the one hand by German-Jewish assimilation to German *Bildung*, a highly formalized acculturation to notions of the educated middle class, represented by, and hated in, the grandfather figure, Dr Knarre, and on the other by an over-schooled form of artistic, musical or theatrical training that is opposed to authentic creativity, a case presented by the music teacher of the text, Amadeus Daberlohn, who seeks to teach psychologically in-tune singing as opposed to trained performance.

Autobiographical interpretation responds correctly to the prompts of the narrative presentation of a work that the artist ordered in a numbered and sequential form. Yet the work is called a musical play; it has a list of characters, and is divided into a prologue, a main part and an epilogue. These in turn are divided into acts and scenes, sometimes, perplexingly, broken into chapters. The work starts with an event in 1913 and ends on the seashore of the Mediterranean in 1941. That scene (plate 6.3), however, the text overlaying it declares (plate 6.4), is the moment of the *beginning* of the very project that it, in the final sequencing, formally concludes. Thus, the temporality of the making and the temporal

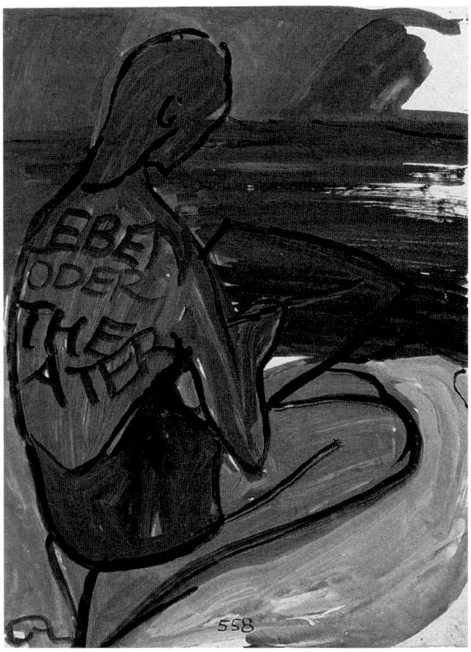

6.3 Charlotte Salomon, 'Painting by the Sea: Final Image', *Leben? oder Theater?*, 1941–42. Gouache on paper, 32.5 × 25 cm. Amsterdam: Jewish Historical Museum (JMH 4925). Reproduced courtesy of Stichtung Charlotte Salomon.

6.4 Charlotte Salomon, overlay for 'Painting by the Sea', *Leben? oder Theater?*, 1941–42. Gouache on paper, 32.5 × 25 cm. Amsterdam: Jewish Historical Museum (JMH 4925T). Reproduced courtesy of Stichtung Charlotte Salomon.

sequence of the subsequently formalized telling do not coincide (inconsistent numbering indicates that the artist made further revisions). The addressee of this work is led to this concluding image so as to understand the reasons for the investigative journey undertaken by the artist but performed by the work. The text pages preceding the final image (quoted above) tell us that in a situation of extremis, recently released from a concentrationary hell, subjected to incestuous advances by her grandfather, a rape attempt by a fellow refugee, an overwhelming knowledge of the many suicides in her own family, including her mother's, and the witness to her grandmother's, 'she', the twin-natured creature, confronted the question of suicide, or .... An alternative eccentricity involved dreaming of a lost love (giving herself over to memory and to Eros), rehearsing his aesthetic philosophy of self-analysis (studying a philosophical psychology of survivorship through an inner journey to find the sources of one's own voice), and leaving the human plane (undertaking what can only be called an imaginative Orphic journey to meet the dead) in order to *create* a world anew out of the depths, and in the face of its current historical terror. In the opening text pages that frame the work's narrative departure, the artist signs herself *Der Verfasser*, a term for author pointedly in the masculine, used for making in the sense of engineering rather than that for creativity – *Der Dichter*. In the German of the penultimate page, the phrasing works up to a crescendo of volume, marked by the size of the letters visually to 'shout' the word: *schaffen*, create. Does this suggest that creativity is the implied opposite of theatricality as death is the implied partner of life, allowing the proposition that the investigation undertaken by the work begun at the moment of the last painting was into the opposition between death and creativity? If the last painting links a woman, water and a creative act, daylight, sunshine and life, it is paired in a rhyme by the formal structure of the work's opening with the first painting linking woman, water and self-destruction, night, darkness and death (plate 6.5).

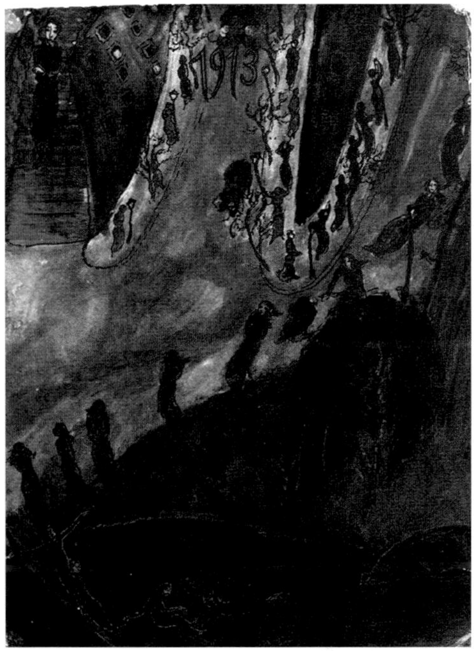


6.5 Charlotte Salomon, '1913 The Death of Charlotte Knarre' (first painting), *Leben? oder Theater?*, 1941–42. Gouache on paper, 32.5 × 25 cm. Amsterdam: Jewish Historical Museum (JMH 4156). Reproduced courtesy of Stichtung Charlotte Salomon.

Dated '1913' in gothic lettering, it is significant on many levels that this is the opening painting. Referencing, but differencing by its focus on feminine suffering rather than sexuality and commodification, the Weimar cult of city scenes and images of the city at night, the image combines many scenes on a single page: an apartment block's innards reveal a staircase that a young woman descends. Shattering into multiplying selves that both indicate psychic disintegration and the moment by moment experience of intense suffering, further signified by changing postures of the tortured body, this young woman weaves her way alone through the darkened and empty streets to a place twenty kilometres from her city-centre home, the Schlachtersee, in whose inky darkness this Ophelia drowns herself. Coded in sombre browns and greys, the dying woman is outlined in blood red as she sinks beneath the black waters of her chosen grave at the foot of the page.

A death that is never explained (is why women chose to die one of the questions of the work?) is, therefore, the beginning; the death of someone unknown to the artist who will be born four years later but whose name she will share.[8] But this is a painting. As such, it imagines and holds before our eyes the enigma of the suicide of a young woman, through a specific kind of visual device, staging the *passage* to that death, marked by the repetition of the figure of a woman in psychic pain. Bypassing the huge narrative space that intervenes between the first and last paintings, to set them side by side makes visible an almost cinematic rhyme – a repetition with a difference that bonds a durational text into a conceptual coherence – and leads into the second dimension foreclosed by a purely autobiographical reading of this work: the *work* that the art does.

Bracha Ettinger has created from her psychoanalytical reflection on her own painting practice at this borderline of trauma and representation, the concept of 'artworking', referenced in the epigraph to this chapter.[9] Artworking (*Kunstarbeit*) draws on both Freudian concepts of psychic work of analysis: *Arbeit*, work as in *Trauerarbeit,* the work of mourning, and *Durcharbeitung,* working through, both of which involve a process of internal transformation with regard to loss or neurotic resistance.[10] In what ways can art be considered a kind of psychic working, and I do not mean a therapy or a cure, but 'a transport-station for trauma', a staging of potential encounters and occurrences which allow the necessary duration for working through a psychic event and finding a means of living with it? Thus mourning is a work over time that does not remove the pain of loss or disavow the death; it enables the survivor to live in the knowledge of that which, at first, overwhelms with unprocessed shock and grief. Survivors mourn to live beside death, to reclaim the Eros, life energies necessary for a future.

Questioning the predominant interpretations of Salomon's work as a pictorial autobiography, I read *Leben? oder Theater?* as a *theatre of memory.*[11]

Produced 'before Auschwitz', *Leben? oder Theater?* looked back from its vantage point of 1941–42, when it was painted (the period of the secret implementation of the Final Solution minuted on 23 January 1942 at the meeting on the Wannsee, not far from the Schlachtersee on the outskirts of Berlin), to the period from 1913 and before, to the Wilhelmine and Weimar periods of German history. It re-wrote that history through the prism of the lives, feelings and deaths of several women. On the precipice of a real but as yet unthinkable annihilation, already traumatized by persecutory social exclusion, personal bereavement and a menaced exile, Charlotte Salomon asked the women in the generation before her, whom she summoned through her image-making and one man who had survived the trenches and slaughter of the 1914–18 war (the war that shaped this theatre of memory), whether to live or to die. And how to choose?

My process here is to explain firstly the importance of the disjuncture between the artist and her constructed others (including Charlotte Kann), which is too easily collapsed by the biographical impulse. Working back over the text, as Salomon did, a year after she made the paintings to learn for herself, and perhaps to hide by its apparently narrative form, the deeper structures embedded into the work at the level of motif and of colour, I shall work, mirroring her own secondary revision, as the text's analyst, listening for its deeper rhythms and the formal and colouristic, avant-garde and modernist carriers, or in the parlance of Aby Warburg, the *formulae* of its particular *pathos*: its aesthetically encountered, historically conditioned and brilliantly worked suffering.[12]

## WHAT'S IN A NAME?

The cover of the 1981 facsimile edition in English (see plate 6.1) bears not the title given by Salomon, *Leben? oder Theater?*, but simply a girl's given name: *Charlotte*. Feminizing, over-familiar and infantilizing, this habit erases women from cultural history. Denied acknowledgement as the artist, 'Charlotte' cannot be an Author; in the patriarchal Symbolic, authorship requires at the very least a paternal surname. The dispossession of such an expanded field for the genesis and the significance of the work is differently effected in the concurrent German-language edition by the title *Charlotte Salomons Buch* (*Charlotte Salomon's Book*)[13] (plate 6.6). I wonder about the cultural politics of ensuring the visibility of her Jewish surname in the work's introduction to her former home culture that the fascists wished to make '*Judenfrei*', free of all Jewish persons. The cover image comes from *Leben? oder Theater?*, unlike the freestanding *Self-portrait* used in the English edition.

This painting (see plate 6.6) shows an intimate scene of a mother and young daughter in bed (JHM 4175). The text overlay for this painting indicates that the mother is promising that if she goes to heaven soon (shown in a scene that repeats a tiny night-gowned figure proceeding to a Christian-looking heaven), she will return to the window of the child's room (a scene projected on the right-hand side of the drawing in pale and ghostly colours) to leave a message at the window about what heaven is like. The impossible promise will be recalled later in the painting series (plate 6.7) when this now bereaved and motherless child anxiously and repeatedly arises during sleepless nights and returns to the window. The relay of these two paintings indexes two structuring and affecting themes in *Leben? oder Theater?* as a whole: the mother/daughter intergenerational feminine bond and its rupture through maternal loss and sexual rivalry. Both themes will be

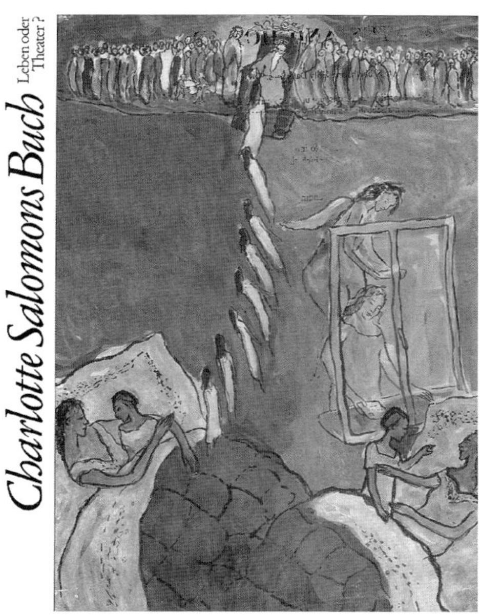


6.6 Cover of *Charlotte Salomons Buch*, 1981, showing JHM 4175.

visually staged through the window as a loaded motif, the communicating borderspace between the worlds of the living and the dead, the present and the absent, the near and the distant. The window opening onto an opaque void will become the marker of the missing mother who dissolves into the framed absence and the unfigured, colouristic support of the painter subject by being translated into a coloured, affectively charged, blue void.

These two paintings indicate Charlotte Salomon's inventive strategies as an image-maker using a single sheet to contain several narrative incidents and as a colourist deploying colour at a secondary level of symbolic substitution and affectivity. Colour, playing across and through the sequential narratives of multiple scenes, creates the possibility of inscribing a subject position, a subjectivity, that is, the 'subject' and effect of the painting practice. This creates a space for this feminine subject to be, in contrast to the evacuation of the conditions of subjective existence by Nazism's progressive assaults on Jewish subjectivity (signified by a swamping of the pictorial field and its occupants with a faecal brown).[14]

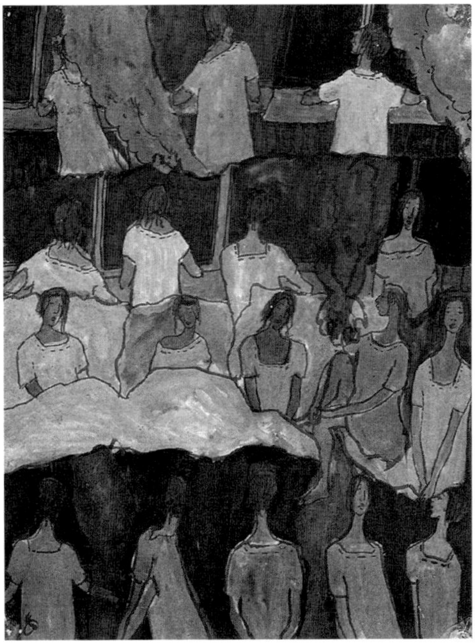

6.7 Charlotte Salomon, 'Waiting for the Message', *Leben? oder Theater?*, 1941–42. Gouache on paper, 32.5 × 25 cm. Amsterdam: Jewish Historical Museum (JHM 4188). Reproduced courtesy of Stichtung Charlotte Salomon.

Many feminist art historians have noted that artists who are women are often subjected to a reductive kind of biographical criticism.[15] The space between producer and produced, between enunciator, author, social subject and the enunciated text, is effaced to create a reflexive circle in which creative strategies by an artist who is a woman are rendered invisible. The materiality of artistic practice evaporates before what now appears as a natural correspondence between what is deemed to be the subject's psychological interior and her expressed subjectivity deposited outside, in the art work, to be read uncritically off its surface. Charlotte Salomon created her work in the name 'CS'; she invented a character called Charlotte Kann (translated from the German as 'Charlotte is Able') along with the transposition of other members of the family and friends into a Brechtian cast for what she called a *Singespiel*, a musical operetta, a *favola in musica*. Placing an alter ego and her world on stage, she re-directed a piece of cinematic theatre that was not just a work of memory, but a new creation, an other world whose inner worlds, she, author, and director, could examine using freely her accumulated knowledge of modern visualities and musicalities.

## WHAT'S IN A FACE?

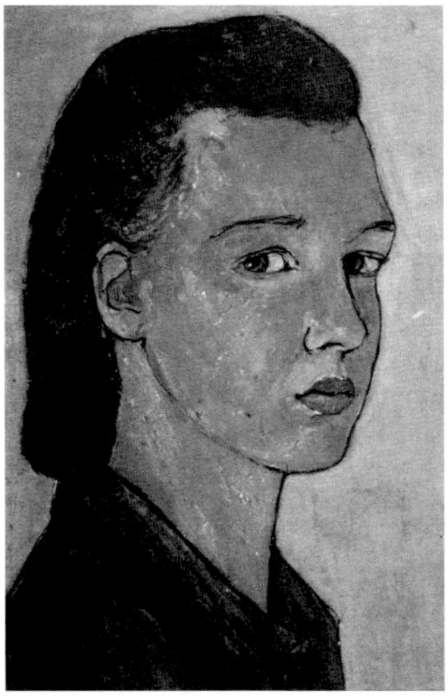

6.8 Charlotte Salomon, *Self-portrait*, signed and dated 1940. Gouache on card, 54.5 × 49 cm. Amsterdam: Jewish Historical Museum.

Charlotte Salomon's free-standing *Self-portrait* (plate 6.8, see also plate 6.1), signed 'CS' and dated to 1940, is one of the few independent works that survive beside *Leben? oder Theater?* The stern turn of the head, the careful delineation of the features, the dry but visible paint application, the acrid coloration bespeak a strong association with the art-historically enhanced persona of Vincent van Gogh: Julius Meier-Graefe's romantic biography positioned Van Gogh in the art culture of early twentieth-century Germany.[16] It serves here as a reminder, however, that in considering self-portraits, we are dealing with conventions, languages, the rhetoric of the image of the artist, especially in modernist variations and extensions of the trope. The self-portrait as a format makes a first-person statement. Its visual presentation of a direct gaze out from the surface transforms the productive confrontation with the painter's self in a mirror, when painting, into an inter-subjective address to a second person, the viewer, who takes the place of the self contemplating the self, to become an other interlocutor in an artistic dialogue: artist and viewer, self and other, I and you, I as other. The self-portrait is a painting by but also, as a result of the effect of the invention that is artistic representation, of an author marked here by the now-inscribed artistic identity 'CS'. The initials shield the artist, veiling her gender and Jewish ethnicity, reminiscent of Lee Krasner's adoption of L.K. during the 1950s.[17]

The painting uses the artistic convention of the self, scrutinized and painted, to present a self as an *artist-self*, to make a claim to be a maker of images, and here, in the feminine as well in the modernist idiom, in a perpetual present of a visual encounter that happens every time we see the painting. The painting, furthermore, does this by establishing a gaze that meets its viewer with unequivocal directness and presence.

Contrast this with a painting from *Leben? oder Theater?* embedded in the dense central section of the work (plate 6.9). In 469 paintings, the *Hauptteil* (*Main Section*) tracks the thoughts of one man, Amadeus Daberlohn, his passionate adoration of his singing pupil Paulinka Bimbam, and the sexual and emotional awakening and initiation of a seventeen-year-old girl Charlotte Kann on the edge of a complex adult love/artistic triangle. This is the first full-page representation of the character who bears the name Charlotte Kann and it is annotated on its overlay:

> Charlotte is not sure of her emotions. Is it jealousy or something else growing within her where her love is concerned?

Painted in gouache on paper, the evocation of a person caught in subjective uncertainty – is it jealousy or something else? – is signalled by the indirect gaze

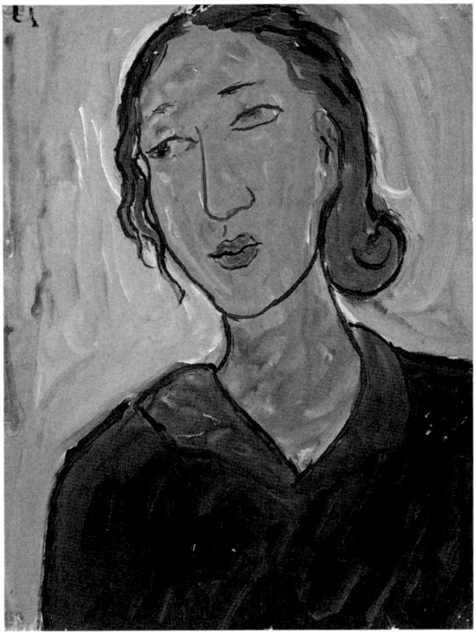

6.9 Charlotte Salomon, 'Jealous Charlotte', *Leben? oder Theater?*, 1941–42. Gouache on paper, 32.5 × 25 cm. Amsterdam: Jewish Historical Museum (JHM 4639). Reproduced courtesy of Stichtung Charlotte Salomon.

that is focused off-screen, out of the frame, in a face tilted against a lime-yellow-green wash of unspecified space. In the visual rhetoric of the work, we are looking at what can only be compared to a cinematic close-up, which usually breaks into the narrative to create a momentary visual pause for a character's inner reflection. Interiority is read by the viewer off the image because of this temporal stasis, on the one hand, and as a result of the enlargement of a face, on the other, both of which focus attention on the reflective blankness of an inexpressive yet affecting face that is the visual signifier for an internal psychological struggle. Here the painted character 'Charlotte' wears a blue shirt which is very like the one that appears in the *Self-portrait*. It might be conjectured that the second image was painted from the same model, even on the same day, although the dating suggests at least a year's gap. Yet context determines that the painting of 'jealous Charlotte' signifies a persona other than that inscribed in a signed self-portrait painted according to a different coding and artistic style. 'Jealous Charlotte' represents a young girl, 'Charlotte Kann', aged twenty, painted by 'CS', aged twenty-four/twenty-five.

It is not a self-portrait, either in intention, convention or effect. It is presented by a third person artist–narrator, framed textually by a sub-vocalized inner speech. This image represents a character who is examining conflicting emotions within herself as a result of a set of social and personal relations with others, here unseen, but active in the surrounding image-text in which this moment of close-up intervenes as a reflective interruption. Stilling the narrative that generated it, the painting zooms in on a girl's reverie and creates the visual space and sign for psychological interiority. As a painting it marks in the image the distance between the producer of the overall art work and a feminine persona/character in the work, a distance that I would argue is critical to the analysis of *Leben? oder Theater?* as a creative project/projection.

*Leben? oder Theater?* cannot be simply autobiographical, for it rarely, until its rejected final papers, uses the first person to enunciate itself.[18] Structurally, this text performs as that which linguist Emile Benvéniste distinguished as *l'histoire*, which he differentiated from *le discours*. *L'histoire* is an unmarked statement, such as 'Charlotte Salomon was born in Berlin'; *le discours* makes clear in the very structure of the statement who is speaking, and implies the situation of the enunciation.[19] In such images as 'Jealous Charlotte', the work's textuality creates a point of analysis, a telling outside the subjective focus of its narrative represented in the image by the person feeling jealousy, or something else.

Taking a cue, however, from this image and the cover of the German edition, I would like to pose *Leben? oder Theater?* as a culturally specific *fantasia on feminine subjectivity* in an historical moment that is framed with an exploration of both feminine bereavement and melancholia and, more radically, a study of the very conditions of femininity, creativity and desire. In one way, it poses what Jane Flax insists was the revolutionary question of the twentieth century articulated by Sigmund Freud in a letter to Marie Bonaparte but symptomatic of psychoanalysis as a whole in both its aspiration and its blockage: 'what does a woman want?'[20] So often treated as the sign of Freud's perplexity, Flax praises Freud for having posed so clearly the very fact of women's desire in a culture that hardly acknowledged it or sought to inquire of its nature. More radically still, this question is posed in *Leben? oder Theater? by* a feminine subject, its author, and posed *to* the lives and deaths, the art and suffering of other women that the artist recreated through her art work in order both to put the question and to track some answers at this hinge of love, death and creativity.[21] This required the creation through a singular mode of narrative visuality, textuality and musicality, of a *theatre of memory* through which to emplot a multi-charactered history within which the artist's own emergence as a gendered, sexualized and 'raced' self could be located from an outside point of view. Let me then approach *Leben? oder Theater?* through this inscription of the mother and daughter fantasy, the necessary matrix of feminine subjectivity and desire. In his essay of 1931, 'Female Sexuality', Freud poses the question 'what does the little girl require *of her mother*?' as the crucial one in feminine sexual formation.[22]

Between the what of its representation – the lives of the mother and grandmothers of the artist – and its manner of representation lies the way that painting became *Kunstarbeit*, art-working in an historical moment when socially inflicted trauma – pogrom, forced exile, imprisonment in a concentration camp, the discovery of so many women's deaths – re-opened earlier losses, themselves psychically pre-conditioned by what may be called primal loss: the loss of the mother. Yet a feminist revision of this legend of the castrated and severed subject of Freudian and Lacanian psychoanalysis might prompt reflection on whether Salomon's 'creative' work already witnesses another, not quite so phallic, economy, that plays between absence and presence, loss and disavowal. This economy seeks forms to embody its yearning for certain kinds of unconscious links and encounters, and it represents itself – the matrixial capacity for trans- and co-subjectivity – through the figure and through coloristically generated affects of shared borderspaces rather than cut edges, defined limits, confined subjectivities and absolute losses through death.[23]

## WHAT'S IN A PICTURE?

A woman in a rich blue dressing gown sits at the open window gazing out upon a lone figure in the street beyond (plate 6.10). This is but a tiny detail placed on a busy page that pictures within one frame many scenes from this bourgeois woman's daily life at home. She plays the piano and sings. She reads. She watches for, and greets, her husband returning from the war. With the fullness of her rounded form, she is awaiting the birth of a child.

The page at whose centre is seated an undoubtedly Vermeer-inspired pregnant woman in blue at the window is headed with a date: 1917. This is the year of the birth of the artist, Charlotte Salomon, who paints a scene of genesis before her own birth. In a matrixial sense, she is reclaiming her becoming-presence that is bound to the body of this musical, intellectual and loving woman. It might be argued that the painting thus represents History, the time before birth, according to Roland Barthes, in his own memorial and suicidal text *Camera Obscura*, at the heart of which lay the image as a five-year-old child of his own recently deceased mother, an image taken before he was born, and one he would never expose to any gaze but his own.[24] By starting before the lifetime of its maker, *Leben? oder Theater?* begins in History and imagines a world and others' subjectivities before the entry of the alter ego of the author, an entry into an already framed and overdetermined socio-psychic cultural space at once Jewish and feminine. This is also the space of other women's thoughts and feelings within which the as-yet-unborn subject is already a figure of becoming in fantasy, dreamed about by the woman in blue at her window.

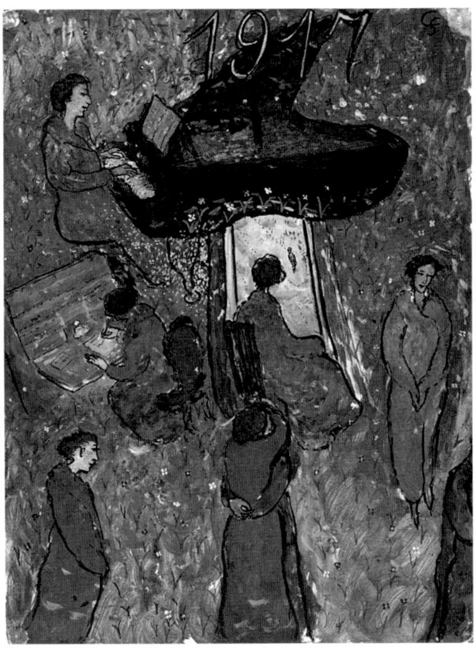


6.10 Charlotte Salomon, '1917-Waiting', *Leben? oder Theater?*, 1941–42. Gouache on paper, 32.5 × 25 cm. Amsterdam: Jewish Historical Museum (JHM 4169). Reproduced courtesy of Stichtung Charlotte Salomon.

The dating recalls that inscribed on the first painting and a retrospective connection can be established between 1917, and the birth and the naming of the child to come, with the genealogy of suicidal feminine melancholia inscribed directly in the death announcement of the first Charlotte, dying in the dark waters of the night in 1913. The work, therefore, begins with a suicide by a woman named Charlotte. It thus indirectly points to the transitivity between the two characters named across the divide of time between 1913 and 1941–42, the time span indicated in the opening pages as the period covered by this visual narrative. Indirectly, through feminine identification and dis-identification, the paintings that follow examine the question of second Charlotte's relation to life and to the possibility of suicide. But this will also be inflected by the psychological life and the death of the woman in blue at the window carrying the new Charlotte, named for her dead sister. These two dated pages set up a visual counterpoint by the contrast of the deathly, night tones tinged with red and grey-brown associated with dying versus a maternally connoted blue, which will later both signify the lost mother and become the colouristically abstract bridge to a new life with which the completed text would affirmatively end/begin.

The placing of an open window in the centre of this image punches a hole through the flat surface of the page that functions as the unifying support for all the related scenes on its surface. Almost lost and easily overlooked, this detail holds within a distractingly complex image dangerous themes that link femininity and melancholia (*Weltschmerz*) with a space beyond its frame yet deep inside this pictured world, a space of an escape that might only be achieved through passing through that opening to death. Here the window opens onto a clear, bright scene in which the tiny figure of the returning husband–soldier, father-to-be can be discerned. What does this woman want? He seems to be part of the answer.

## WHAT THE WINDOW FRAMES

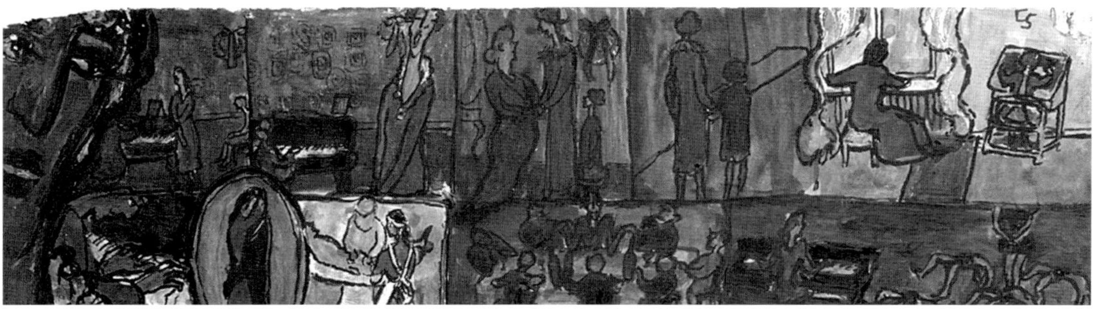

6.11 Detail of Charlotte Salomon, 'Franziska's Melancholy'. Amsterdam: Jewish Historical Museum.

From a close study of *Leben? oder Theater?*, as well as other contextual material, it can be surmised that Charlotte Salomon contemplated suicide. No evidence is so telling, as that of one of the images used to represent the life/death struggle of the pregnant woman in blue shown in this early painting, patiently watching from her window, who is known in the work as Franziska Kann. Her story is told twice in *Leben? oder Theater?*, once as *histoire*, a narrative telling, and a second time as *discours*, during the melancholic reverie of her mother Marianne Knarre. This second telling occurs inside the remembered stories of Franziska's mother's emotional life history, introducing yet a further dimension of fictive invention of memory through the artist's projection of the older woman's life and this poet's many traumatic bereavements.

The first telling of the story of the woman in blue occurs in Scene 2 of the Prologue as a simple narrative of the events preceding the birth of Charlotte Kann. Franziska Kann decides to become a nurse at the front during the 1914–18 war to relieve her grief after her sister's suicide, where she meets a field surgeon. They marry and a child is born. In images animated by the innovative modernist spatiality of Charlotte Salomon's artistic syntax, this woman bids farewell to her soldier husband and returns alone to her new home, which is shown in crane shot as if the roof had been lifted on a doll's house to show us the interior. Later in a red dirndl, she dances joyfully on holiday with her family in what is in German called '*Die Natur*' (nature), beside a blue, blue lake. This beatific sequence (the image preceding this one is plate 6.6) switches abruptly in colour and form to culminate in the suicide of Franziska Kann in tones that are reminiscent of the night death of her younger sister (see plate 6.5). In a montage of tiny images on a single

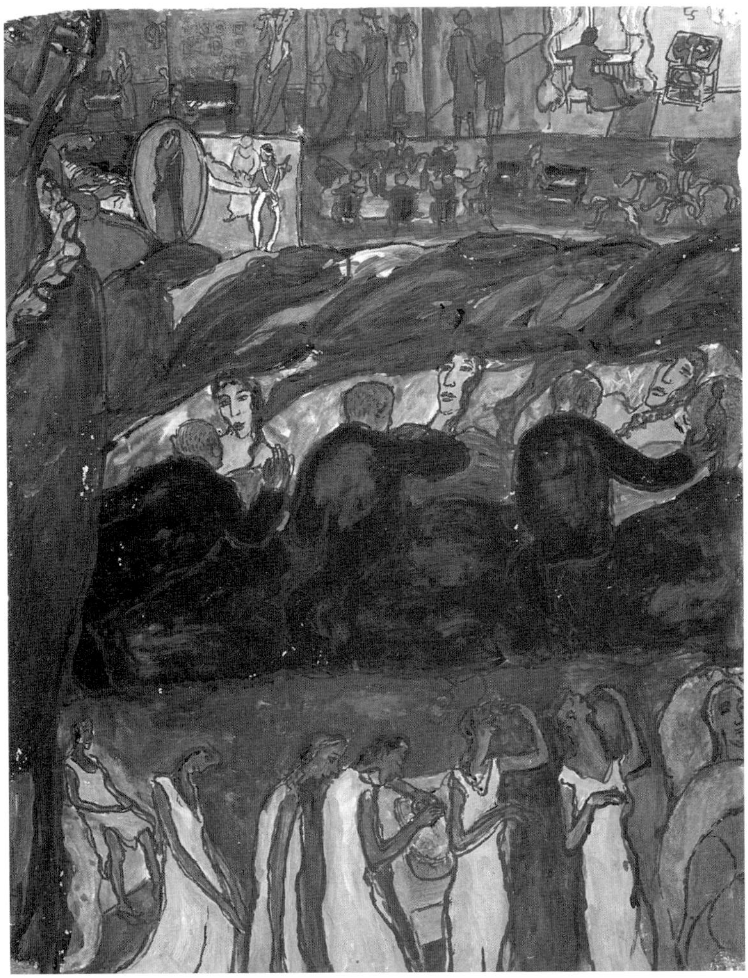

6.12 Charlotte Salomon, 'Franziska's Melancholy', *Leben? oder Theater?*, 1941–42. Gouache on paper, 32.5 × 25 cm. Amsterdam: Jewish Historical Museum (JHM 4176). Reproduced courtesy of Stichtung Charlotte Salomon.

page (plates 6.11 and 6.12), shadowed and unified by a single haunting female figure framing the left-hand side of the page and whose emanations the vignettes become, emotional breakdown is plotted by gradual discoloration and the splitting/multiplication of the figured subject. It starts with blue-toned, thus still happy, scenes of mother and child: going to the woman's singing lessons (linking music and the singing voice with the mother), the child's gym classes, greeting her husband, rounds of social visits, ending with a reprise of the woman in blue beside the open window while her little girl sits at her desk, mirroring the pose, but drawing on the rectangular page. Then below, in a coloristically charged and invented sequence, we can track the onset of melancholia and the draining of the personality from the face of this woman despite all attempts to reach out to her until, pale and colourless as a ghost, she is shown trying to poison herself. Here, again, repetition functions to signify a disintegrated state of mind and loss of

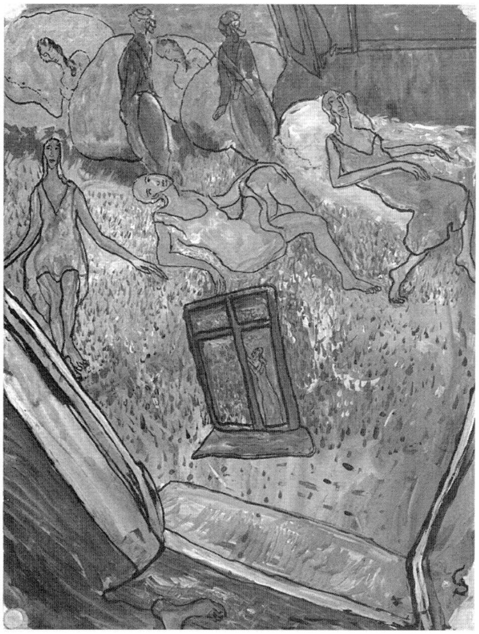

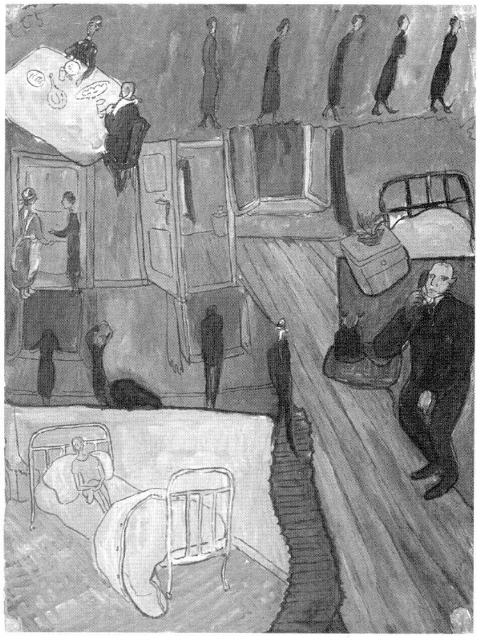

6.13 and 6.14 Charlotte Salomon, *Leben? oder Theater?*, 1941–42. (6.13 'Franziska's Suicide' and 6.14 'Franziska's Death Discovered and Reported'). Gouache on paper, 32.5 × 25 cm. Amsterdam: Jewish Historical Museum (JHM 4179 and JHM 4180). Reproduced courtesy of Stichtung Charlotte Salomon.

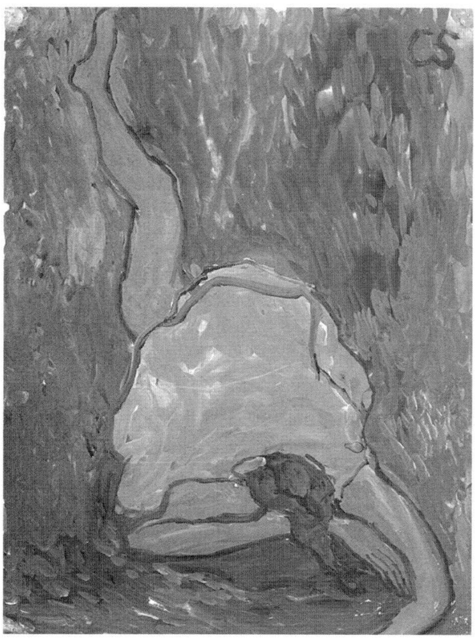

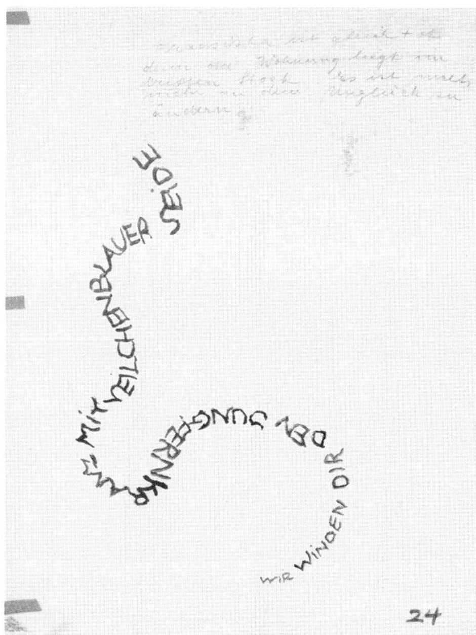


6.15 and 6.16 Charlotte Salomon, *Leben? oder Theater?*, 1941–42 (6.15 'Franziska's Body' and 6.16 overlay of 'Franziska's Body'). Gouache on paper, 32.5 × 25 cm. Amsterdam: Jewish Historical Museum (JHM 4181 and JHM 4181T). Reproduced courtesy of Stichtung Charlotte Salomon.

being. The next paintings show this woman placed under continuous nursing care. She, none the less, seizes a moment of inattention and casts herself through the open window to her death (plate 6.13).

Backtracking, the next image reveals the woman's anxious mother leaving the table to check on her depressed and suicidal daughter, only to find the room empty and the window open (plate 6.14); vignettes on the same page show the telephone communication of this event to a distraught husband and, bound within its own grey setting, the colourless solitude of the bereaved child, informed only that her absent and sickly mother had succumbed to influenza. At the centre of this image, puncturing its illustrative wholeness and its modernist flatness, there gapes the window. But instead of its usual luminous exterior world, it is now opaque. It opens only onto a dazzling blueness where the woman in her blue, blue dressing gown can no longer be figured, yet her colouristic signifier fills the entire space of otherness, and beyond.[25]

Then, brutally, and indeed shocking in its barefaced directness and graphic imagination (plate 6.15), comes a frame that positions the viewer, street-side, as witness to the mangled, disjointed body of the dead woman, her head crushed in a bloody pool. In such an image we are forced to ask: who is looking, and how or even why can such a scene, never seen by the author, have been created fifteen years later? What it is purpose, need, effect?

Such images do not, however, come before us naked and exposed. They are shielded by a semi-transparent overlay (plate 6.16) in which, in bold painted printed letters or ghostly pencil handwriting, there is a commentary, the invocation of the enunciating subject, the invisible voice that speaks from outside the images even while a representative of her past appears within the figurative scheme (in colour block-printed text following the fall of the body: 'We twine for thee the maiden's wreath with violet-coloured ribbon', from Carl Maria von Weber's opera *Der Freischutz*, and in pencil: 'Franziska died immediately, the apartment being on the fourth floor. There is nothing more to be done about the tragedy.' Over the image of the dead body of the mother was an overlay in which that crushed dead body was, as it were, caressed by a curving line of coloured words that trace and almost hold the fallen body. The curving shape is composed of the words of leitmotif associated with Franziska Kann, the bridal song from Carl Maria von Weber's opera *Der Freischütz*, whose cheerfulness now turns bitterly ironic as it becomes the lament for the dead woman. Words screen images; the written word and its invocation of the speaking voice frames the encounter with an image that is veiled, to be confronted in all its danger only after being given another image, that of words on the page, a visual poetics at once familiar to scholars of Jewish texts as well as to students of the modernist visual poetics of Andre Mallarmé's famous poem '*Coup de Dès*' ('A Throw of the Dice').

## DEATH AT THE WINDOW

Franziska's story is told a second time in this work in Scene 5, when Paulinka Bimbam, the stepmother-diva accuses grandmother Knarre of causing both her daughters' deaths by excessive attention to the Christian-German bourgeois ideals of *Bildung* and excessive self-discipline: a performed not a lived life. Seated, somewhat perplexingly, in a blue room beyond which a red-tiled roof of southern France is visible, the Berlin-based grandmother, drooping like an elegant Modigliani, is precipitated by this attack into her own melancholic narrative of her life, during which she lost a lover to a mountaineering accident (another mangled corpse), her brother to drowning, and both her daughters to suicide, while her mother daily tried to kill herself for over ten years. The narrative device of entering into this older woman's memories of love and death also punches a hole in the narrative trajectory of the work, falling through a hypertextual tunnel onto another feminine subjectivity within the narrative. This, in turn, hollows out again to track the subjectivity of her own daughter, Franziska, held in her own mother's mournful memory. This section may well have been based on incorporating into CS's work the stories of Marianne Grunwald's life, which Charlotte

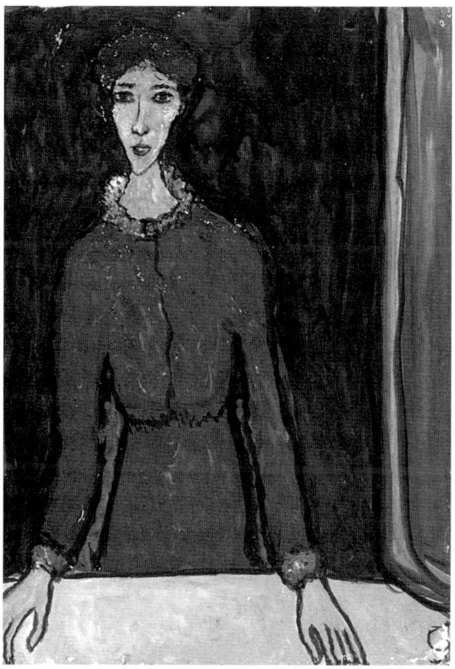

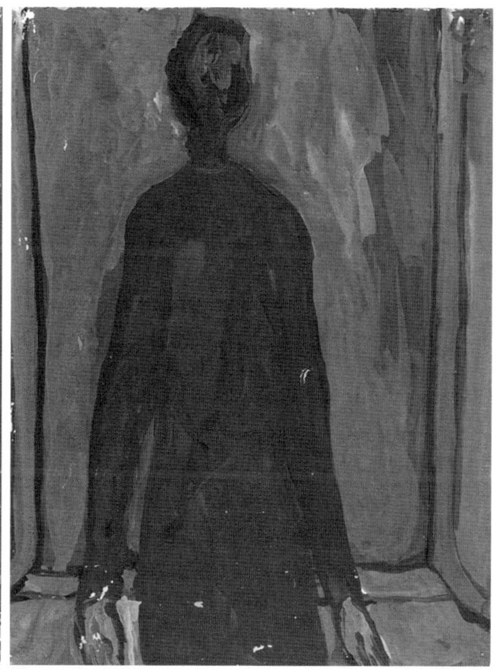

6.17 and 6.18 Charlotte Salomon, *Leben? oder Theater?*, 1941–42 (6.17 'Grandmother tells the story of Franziska's death: Franziska Dreaming at the Window' and 6.18 'Grandmother tells the story of Franziska's death: Franziska Yearning'). Gouache on paper, 32.5 × 25 cm. Amsterdam: Jewish Historical Museum (JHM 4289 and JHM 4290). Reproduced courtesy of Stichtung Charlotte Salomon.

Salomon incited her suicidal grandmother to write as part of her therapy for resisting her death wish – scenes replayed in the Epilogue that lead up to the suicide of Mrs Knarre – whose leap from a window and death on the pavement of Nice Salomon witnessed and perhaps used in her terrible imagining of her own mother's death by a similar form of suicide.[26]

The device of telling a story from another woman's point of view allows the author/artist of *Leben? oder Theater?* to image her own archaic fantasies of being with her mother by means of close-ups of the intimate embrace of the maternal gaze and mutual jouissance of the early mother and child dyad. Again blue is the field for this remembered intimacy. But this idyllic memory is amputated by the onset of melancholia, differently visualized from its first representation. Instead, the deep-blue field supports a close-up of the woman's face in an image of extreme alienation, in which the others, child and husband, within whose gaze the woman might be held and reflected, look away, leaving the agonized woman to gaze out into an abyss of abandonment and loss of inter-subjective contact. This haunting figuration of the fractured family is followed by an image sequence of the woman at the window drenched in blue.

Almost cinematically, the point of view that the image sequence produces tracks the woman to the window and the viewer encounters her from outside. Then a reverse shot positions the viewer inside, behind her blue back (plates 6.17 and 6.18). The window now opens onto a blue opacity. This combination and repetition indicates the significance of the colour and the colour field for the artist as a signifying space. Then (plate 6.19), while the viewing position remains fixed, the frame is emptied; the woman disappears. We are not taken outside to view the mangled body of death as before. Holding us there, the artist creates an image of and for absence. But this image also produces another subject, present in the image but not figured. The painting stages the effect of that absence upon an imagined viewing, but unshown, witness-subject whose viewpoint this painting now represents in the absence of the disappeared woman. That viewpoint is, in one sense, the moment of encounter with the loss by the bereaved daughter, who was left behind and has, by painting, tracked her mother to the very window sill from which she once leapt to her death, abandoning her child. But that window is also a direct reference inside this work, inside a painting that appears to be the memories of a mother of an event in Berlin in 1926, to the present of the moment of painting, and to the painter herself. What does the open window offer? The roofs beyond the frame are not those of a Berlin suburb in which the suicide being recounted took place. They are the red tiles outside the window of the room at the Hôtel Belle Aurore at St Jean de Cap Ferrat, in the south of France, where, in 1941–42, that multiply bereaved daughter sat alone, humming and painting, and looking out of this window at the intense blue Mediterranean sea.

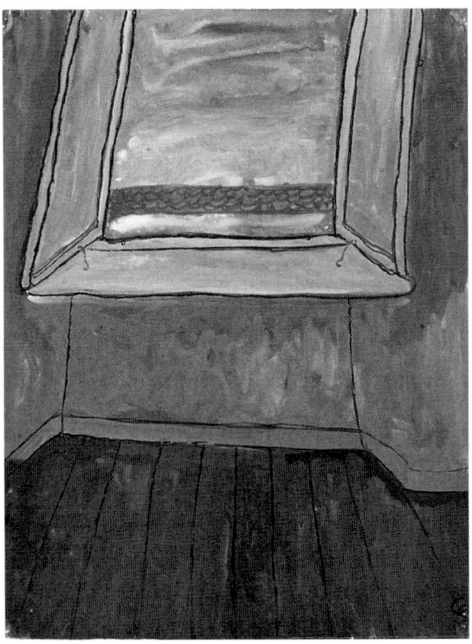

6.19 Charlotte Salomon, 'Grandmother tells the story of Franziska's death: The Empty Window', *Leben? oder Theater?*, 1941–42. Gouache on paper, 32.5 × 25 cm. Amsterdam: Jewish Historical Museum (JHM 4291). Reproduced courtesy of Stichtung Charlotte Salomon.

Words again are aggressively painted in the death – threatening red to cover this void, this window at whose frame Charlotte Salomon, the artist, stood and questioned life? or theatre? or the making of a text that would become a life-saving theatre of memory.

## WHAT'S IN A COLOUR? WHAT'S IN A SOUND?

Blue is associated with the mother, and the beyond of the lost mother and the 'transport' to her; it is a membrane of psychic connection, a thread. It is also associated, more conventionally, with music and stands in visually for an acoustic connectivity experienced by the artist, who not only hummed while she painted but tells us that the images matched what she began to sing to herself.

> The creation of the following paintings is to be imagined as follows; A person (Der Mensch) is sitting beside the sea. He is painting. A tune suddenly enters his mind. As he starts to hum it he notices that the tune exactly matches what he is trying to commit to paper. A text forms in his head and he starts to sing the tune with his own words, over and over again in a loud voice until the painting seems complete. (JHM 4155-5)

Countering the lure of those who chose death was the third key feminine figure of this work, a golden-haired (although when young she was dark-haired) singer who becomes Charlotte Kann's intensely beloved stepmother and the object of adoration by the traumatized trench survivor turned singing teacher, Amadeus Daberlohn, a penniless musical genius. Her musical *leitmotifs* are two recurring arias: '*Bist du Bei Mir*' ('If you are with me'), once attributed to Johann Sebastian Bach although now thought to be by G.H. Stölzel, a song of Christian comfort about the presence of God on the journey into death, and Orpheus's aria from Christoph Willibald von Gluck's opera of 1762, lamenting the loss of Eurydice. When Paulinka Bimbam is shown singing the achingly lovely music of '*Bist du Bei Mir*' (plate 6.20) she is either surrounded by blue or her mouth opened in song is filled with blue, an association with sound well known in modernist German culture.

> *Bist du bei mir, geh' ich mit Freuden*
> *zum Sterben und zu meiner Ruh'.*
> *Ach, wie vergnügt wär' so mein Ende,*
> *es drückten deine lieben [schönen] Hände*
> *mir die getreuen Augen zu!*[27]

Very much alive, desirable, organized, maternal and creative, Paulinka Bimbam's story is also interwoven into the text. She, too, is bereaved and mourns both father and mother. Leaving her small home town, she goes to Berlin and works as a maid before her voice is discovered and she briefly becomes an international singing star, renowned for her renditions of Bach's religious music. The counterpoint to the musical mother Franziska, who cannot survive her life and dies, Paulinka finds life in creativity and can lend her beautiful alto-soprano voice to music that performs great sadness and offers its own musical beauty as consolation.

If the feminine figures from the first Charlotte to Franziska and Marianne cannot chose life but seek death, *Thanatos*, singing Paulinka is represented as *Eros*, life, desire and creativity, which seem indissolubly linked. Marked by a golden aura in the colour semiotics of the art work, her acoustic blue-ness promises art as a transport of trauma, a place to encounter the pain of grief and the terror of loss,

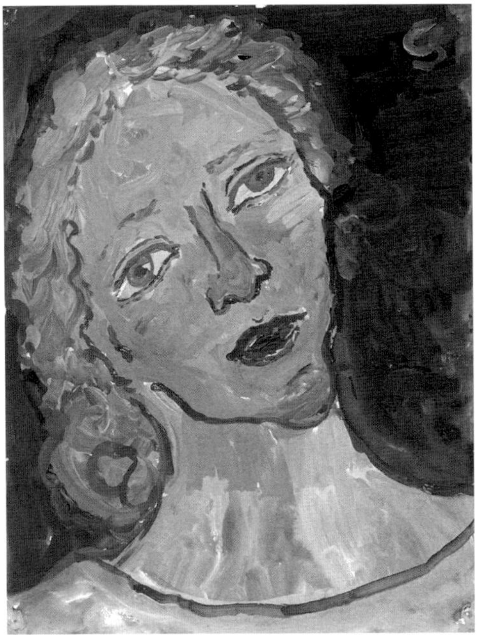

6.20 Charlotte Salomon, 'Paulinka Sings Bach', *Leben? oder Theater?*, 1941–42. Gouache on paper, 32.5 × 25 cm. Amsterdam: Jewish Historical Museum (JHM 4214). Reproduced courtesy of Stichtung Charlotte Salomon.

but to find in and through musical memory and the sonorous envelope of its form both passage and encounter. From a matrixial psychoanalytical point of view, this transposition arises through the imaginative trans-subjective dispersal of the creator's fragile, dis-assembling traumatized subjectivity into the *personae* of several generations of and conditions of adult women: mothers, grandmothers, stepmothers. One might call it a kind of aesthetically staged transference. She, the daughter, the frozen, traumatized girl asks of them, their lives and of their deaths, what woman is and what woman wants: that might be death or it could be creativity. She addresses that question to the adult woman: the nurse and musician, her mother, the poet and lover, her grandmother, her Oedipal rival and singer-stepmother, two of whom killed themselves and one who found herself as a creative and political worker through singing Bach's music under the tutelage of a war-scarred philosopher of the voice. Charlotte Kann paints and sings. She does not die.

The blueness of the woman in the blue dressing gown, the mother, however, transfers to a coloristically invoked acoustic envelope in the narrative portions of the work. In the final image, the blue as opaque colour has become a ground, associated with the Mediterranean, signifying a Schillerian vision of the cleansing and renewing natural world and the site of the French avant garde. But it is also the support for the very project of painting the theatre of memory (see plate 6.3) upon which the artist can place the frame of her drawing paper on which she is beginning to paint the dark colours for the first painting of the death of the first Charlotte in the night of 1913 (see plate 6.5).

In this artistic conclusion, the pain of bereavement has been re-imagined, re-enacted and worked through by *Artworking*. Through an unconscious signification that emerges into the visible at the level of the materials of her painting, colour, that which Bracha Ettinger theorizes as a matrixial borderspace, a co-poeïsis, is connoted coloristically as the field on which a new image of the Charlotte *persona* is painted.[28] '*Bist du bei mir*' .... Unframed and no longer glimpsed through the window or bound to the lost maternal body in her blue rooms or dressing gowns or trapped in the opened mouth of song, a pervading intense blueness becomes the very ground on which the bathing woman painter works in the sunshine of the present moment, dissolving the page into water and sky. The painter is bathed in luminous light and warmth of this joyous image and, as before, she is surrounded by blue, and contains both life and theatre.

Could this text add its own acoustic dimension you would now be listening to a surviving recording of Charlotte Salomon's stepmother, Paula Lindberg, singing '*Bist du Bei Mir*'. The words, their meaning, and the relentless but poignant structure of the music pose a question of both loss and solace in the face of dying and a promise of a 'wit(h)ness', another key Ettingerian concept of matrixial subjective capacity, which parallels the colourist resolution performed by this painting that itself leaves the site of painting open – the page is transparent.[29] The image, none the less, condenses and transforms the traces of a catastrophic journey through the theatre of memory to a point at which painting becomes the hinge between the subject and her no longer lost or abandoning feminine others, between subject and world, between a moment and time. By the strangest of effects of a loaded brush or by Salomon's artistic economy, a face, sleeping or singing, or both, seems to emerge out of the blue water and take shape on the horizon (plate 6.21).

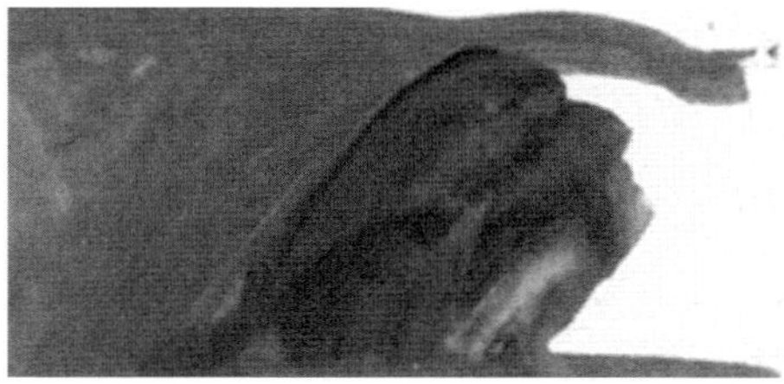

6.21 Detail of Charlotte Salomon, 'Painting by the Sea' (plate 6.3). Amsterdam: Jewish Historical Museum. Reproduced courtesy of Stichtung Charlotte Salomon.

## Notes

1 Bracha Ettinger, *Artworking 1985–1999*, Brussels and Ghent, 2000, 91.

2 Walter Benjamin, 'A Berlin Chronicle', in *One-Way Street*, trans. Edmund Jephcott and Kingsley Shorter, London, 1997, 316.

3 Charlotte Salomon, *Charlotte: Life? or Theatre? An Autobiographical Play*, ed. J. Herzberg, London, 1981.

4 This chapter is based on a paper first given at the conference on Charlotte Salomon organized by the Institute for Women and Gender at University of Michigan Ann Arbor and AHRC Centre-CATH in 2003. See also the major collection of essays on this work, Michael Steinberg and Monica Bohm-Duchen, eds, *Reading Charlotte Salomon*, Ithaca, 2006. I first used the concept of 'Theatre of Memory' in the title of my essay in that collection, 'Theatre of Memory: Trauma and Cure in Charlotte Salomon's Modernist Fairy-Tale', 34–72.

5 The full history is documented in Mary Lowenthal Felstiner, *To Paint her Life: Charlotte Salomon in the Nazi Era*, New York, 1994, 223–30.

6 See the clarification of these necessarily distinct identities in Felstiner, *To Paint her Life*; she reserves the nickname 'Lotte' for the historical subject of her biography, again performing, by acknowledged choice, the feminized familiarization [she remarks we do not speak of Pablo and Jackson] that I will not adopt, reserving the full name Charlotte Salomon for historical person and artist throughout. Felstiner rightly points out why we must distinguish between the use of characters in the work and the author herself. Charlotte Salomon wrote: 'I was all the characters in my play and thus I became myself,' (xii) Jewish Historical Museum Inventory Number (henceforth JHM), 4931.

7 Mary Felstiner tracked down surviving witnesses and some of the named personae to corroborate the accuracy of events and characters from Berlin represented in the work, binding her researched narrative to the sequence of images mostly in the Prelude and Epilogue; Felstiner, *To Paint her Life*.

8 On feminine melancholia and suicide, see Darcy Buerkle, 'Historical Effacements: Facing Charlotte Salomon', in Bohm-Duchen and Steinberg, *Reading Charlotte Salomon*, 73–87.

9 Ettinger, *Artworking 1985–1999*; the idea is developed in her essay 'Art as a Transport-Station of Trauma' in the catalogue, 91–115.

10 Sigmund Freud, 'Mourning and Melancholia', 1917, *Freud Penguin Library, Vol. 11: On Metapsychology – The Theory of Psychoanalysis*, ed. James Strachey, London, 1984, 245–69. Sigmund Freud, 'Remembering, Repeating and Working Through', 1914, *Standard Edition of the Works of Sigmund Freud*, ed. James Strachey, vol. 12, 1958, 145–56.

11 This is the title of my forthcoming monograph, *Theatre of Memory: Charlotte Salomon's* Leben? oder Theater? *1941–42*, Yale University Press.

12 Warburg's central concept *pathosformel* is never directly defined in his writings but it concerns the relation of the image as a fixing of a remembered state of intense emotion thus creating a dialectic between movement (e-motion) and fixation, between fear/feeling and defensive re-presentation. Gertrude Bing says that *pathos formulae* make visible 'not a quality of the external world like movement, distance or space, but a state of emotions'. Gertrude Bing, and 'A.M. Warburg', *Journal of the Warburg and Courtauld Institutes*, 18, 1965, 309–310. A more recent commentator formulates it thus: 'The "pathos formula", which expresses the traumatic encounter between man and the world, is a result of a visual fixation, the source of which is a process of mimicry of some unbearable (biomorphic) qualities of the threatening force that becomes petrified and fixed as an image.' Adi Efal, 'Warburg's "Pathos Formula" in Psychoanalytic and Benjaminian Contexts', *Assaph-Studies in Art History*, 5, 2000–2001, 221. For a link between *pathosformel* and symptom, see Georges Didi-Huberman, '*Dialectik des Monstrums*: Aby Warburg and the Symptom Paradigm', *Art History*, 24:5, 2001, 621–45.

13 Charlotte Salomon, *Charlotte Salomons Buch*, Cologne, 1981.

14 The possessive, *Charlotte Salomons Buch*, none the less, repeats the tendency to treat *Leben? oder Theater?* as a kind of diary or daybook which took root with the first publication of selections as Charlotte Salomon, *Charlotte: A Diary in Pictures*, New York, 1963.

15 Vanessa Corby, 'Don't Look Back: Reading for the Ellipses in the Discourse on Eva Hess(e)', *Third Text*, 57, 2001–2002, 31–42. See also Nanette Salomon, 'The Art Historical Canon: Sins of Omission', in *The Art of Art History*, ed. Donald Preziosi, Oxford, 1998, 344–55.

16 In one important painting that declares artistic allegiances, JMH 4361, the young artist Charlotte Kann is placed in the middle of the page attentively studying an array of items that reference Van Gogh, sunflowers and workmen's boots, Cézanne and Picasso; Julius Meier-Graefe, *Vincent van Gogh*, Munich, 1912.

17 Anne Wagner, 'Lee Krasner as L.K.', *Representations*, 25:Winter, 1989, 42–57.

18 There are twelve pages which were not deemed to be part of the final selection for *Leben? oder Theater?* that Mary Felstiner has named the postscript. This has been translated and analysed in Julia Watson 'Charlotte Salomon's Memory Work in the "Postscript" to *Life? Or Theater?*', and 'Charlotte Salomon's "Postscript" to *Life? Or Theater?*', trans. Julia Watson, *Signs: Gender and Cultural Memory*, 28:1, 2002, 409–429. The 'Postscript' is a very different text using the first person and lending support to the autobiographical impulse from which the text emerged. Their apparent exclusion indicates an artistic decision which demands of the reader/viewer of the final work a different orientation.

19 Emile Benvéniste, *Problèmes de linguistique générale*, Paris, 1966, chap. 19.

20 Jane Flax, 'The Scandal of Desire: Psychoanalysis and Disruptions of Gender: A Meditation on Freud's *Three Essays on Sexuality*', *Contemporary Psychoanalysis*, 40:1, 2004, 47–68.

21 Bracha Ettinger has radically extended Freud's question by arguing that the question of 'what a woman wants' for Freud implies 'from a man' whereas to become a feminine subject the girl must first address such a question to an Other-Woman. 'Fascinance and the Girl to m/Other Feminine Difference', in *Psychoanalysis and the Image*, ed. Griselda Pollock, Boston and Oxford, 2006, 60–93.

22 Sigmund Freud, 'Female Sexuality', in *Penguin Freud Library, Vol. 7: On Sexuality*, ed. James Strachey, London, 1977, 383.

23 The theory of the matrixial dimension of subjectivity shifting phallic conceptions without substituting them has been extensively developed by Bracha Ettinger. For an early statement, see 'Matrix and Metramorphosis', *Differences*, 4:3, 1992, 176–210. See also a special issue devoted to Ettinger's theoretical work in *Theory, Culture and Society*, 24:1, 2004, which includes Ettinger's 'Weaving a woman Artist with-in the Matrixial Encounter-Event', 69–94. Here I follow Mieke Bal's lead and show how the art work itself is already thinking through processes that may only later achieve theoretical formulation.

24 Roland Barthes, *La Chambre Claire*, Paris, 1980; *Camera Lucida*, New York, 1981. See also Elizabeth Bronfen, 'Death: The Navel of the Image', in *The Point of Theory*, Amsterdam, 1994, 79–89. Barthes wrote: 'That is what the time when my mother was alive *before me* is – History [. . .] No anamnesis could ever make me glimpse this starting from myself (this is the definition of anamnesis)', 65.

25 Art historians may recognize in the use of the opaque blue field of the window visual debts to Chagall, for instance. It is probable and possible that Salomon knew much work by Chagall and there can be no doubt that his work forms a support for her visual languages. But what is important is how the motif functions within the semiotics of this particular image and work, not that its work can be displaced by merely finding a source.

26 Felstiner, *To Paint her Life*, 110.

27 Be thou with me, and I'll gladly go
To death and to my repose.
Ah, how my end would bring contentment,
If, pressing with thy hands so lovely,
Thou wouldst my faithful eyes then close.

28 Bracha L. Ettinger, 'Metramorphic Borderlinks and Matrixial Borderspace', in John C. Welchman, ed., *Rethinking Borders,* Basingstoke, 1996, 125–59.

29 Bracha Ettinger, 'Traumatic Wit(h)ness-Thing and Matrixial Co/in-habit(u)ating', *parallax*, 5:1, 1999, 89–94; see also Alison Rowley, 'Introduction', in the same issue which explores the specific relation to painting as *metramorphosis*, the means by which this subjective dimension can be experienced, 83–8.

# 7

# READING, WRITING, FILMING, DREAMING, DRESSING

MICHAEL ANN HOLLY and MIEKE BAL

MH: *Let's begin by talking about 'motivation'. I would like to probe your intellectual and political 'restlessness', your persistent desire to move on to inquiries ever new.*

MB: As far as I can remember, I have always been driven by curiosity about what lies around the corner. My first chosen topics of writing were things I didn't understand, such as: why did I get bored by descriptive passages in novels, yet never skipped them? I wrote my first article about description in my favourite novel (Gustave Flaubert's *Madame Bovary*).[1] While studying French, I wanted to understand narrative in general, and while I was supposed to study structures, I tried to articulate and understand effects. Always the next question. Why would these narrative issues of the interconnection between device and effect only work in written texts, in language-based narratives?

So I turned to Rembrandt.[2] Perhaps it was no coincidence that this happened when I moved to an American university. And, to add a third around-the-corner element, that the beginning of this fascination happened when I was at Harvard [in 1985–86] under an obligation to write about the Bible. Which I did, dutifully, and often inspired, but always with Rembrandt as the promise of reward, and sometimes as the better biblical scholar.

I wanted to understand how the Rembrandt images 'spoke' – but then, speech has never been exclusively linguistic for me. It has such a strong mooring in the body, its gestures, in the face, in the interaction with the other, that it almost seemed as if visual images were more, rather than less, key to understanding speech (speech as having a component of narrative, in a very broad sense, and always considered in the situation of utterance and reception).

But, just as images made it possible to test whether whatever I had tended to attribute to language was, in fact, a more general semiotic issue, the next question, about what lies around the corner, was the delimitation of the text or image. I was trained in structuralism, a training that today I still consider precious, and so delimitation was the first thing to do. But what if ....? This brought me to *Double Exposures* – on the important contribution of presentation and combination, material such as captions, architecture and even wallpaper as contributing to the effect of art works.[3]

Of course, there are always other elements in motivation. You remember how Alexander [MH's son, then eleven years old] sent me to the American Museum of Natural History in New York instead of the eternal, and he said 'boring', Met[ropolitan Museum of Art]. This little exchange with a child had an immense impact on me. Not only the anecdotal decision to go to the Museum of Natural History that day, and subsequently to think and write about it, but also to realize how much I had always been intrigued by what was not prestigious or glamorous enough to warrant analysis. It helped me, for example, to think much more in depth about my somewhat flippant phrase, in *Reading Rembrandt*, that 'Rembrandt' is a product of popular culture.'

But these moments of motivation to cross yet another boundary are complemented with a kind of memory, or history of earlier experiences in research. I have never been able to abandon one field in favour of a newly discovered one. The temporary return to literature, when I wrote about Proust, was informed by Rembrandt more than anything, and not because Proust writes about Rembrandt. What made me go to Proust was the thought that, if Rembrandt had given rise to the analysis of so many forms of visual 'speech' or narrative, or other discursive forms, then it was likely, conversely, that a literary work would harbour forms of visuality, such as those found in description and metaphor.[4]

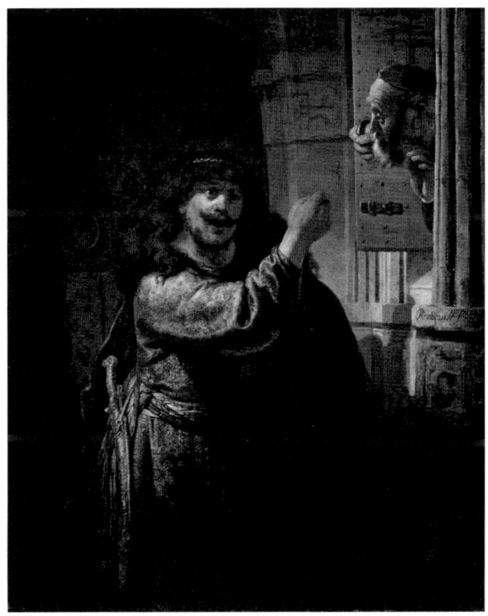

7.1 Rembrandt Harmensz van Rijn, *Samson Accusing His Father-in-Law*, 1635. Oil on canvas, 158.5 × 130.5 cm. Berlin: Gemäldegalerie, Staatliche Museen zu Berlin. Photo: Jörg P. Anders. Photo courtesy of Bildarchiv Preussischer Kulturbesitz/Art Resource, NY.

The move that seems most like a cut is the one to art-making. This, again, is more continuous with my other work than it might first seem. I have tried to perform a kind of analysis that would not be premised on earlier theoretical and scholarly notions. The ArtClips [MB's first filmic 'shorts'], for example, were an attempt to get closer to what 'really' happens when people look at art. Talking to others made it possible for the viewers that I was filming to articulate, hence, make available, what they were 'seeing' – experiencing, thinking, opining.[5] In one film I made later, I tried to avoid speech altogether, and see how far I could 'interpret' art without language, respond visually to visual images.[6]

The last move to date was from films about art to making art. This, for me, is just another step towards understanding 'from the inside'. I tried this first at a moment of great stress and then relief and joy, in the lives of very dear friends. In making *Mille et un Jours (A Thousand and One Days)* (plate 7.2) it was important to avoid constructing the story instead of facilitating their own story-telling; and

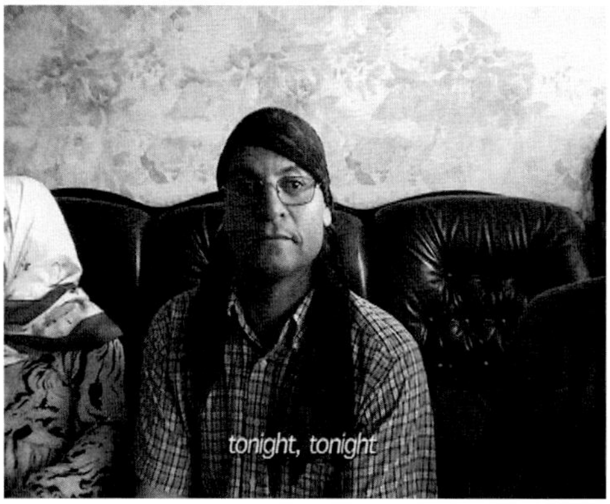


7.2 Father with headscarf on, still from Cinema Suitcase (Mieke Bal, Zen Marie, Thomas Sykora, Gary Ward, Michelle Williams), *Mille et un Jours (A Thousand and One Days)*, 2004, re-edited by Gary Ward, 2006. Photo: courtesy of the artists.

to avoid imposing an artificial chronology on an heterochronic messiness – a crossing of histories and memories with a present replete with ambivalences. I have never learned so much from an experience than I have from making this film, and no people have taught me more about cultural process, the role of traditions, and the insinuation of politics in everyday life, than the working-class immigrants who were, as they say, the 'subjects' of the film.[7]

But as in the return to literature, I have returned to academic writing with a book on migratory aesthetics and another on a story travelling between religious and secular, literary and visual cultural processes. I am sure the experience of film-making will inform both, and writing them will further inspire ideas for the film-making. This movement back and forth between fields and activities reveals a much greater coherence, or unity, in my work than is suggested by the number of fields I have worked in.

MH: *How do you identify yourself to your various audiences, to yourself? Cultural critic? Filmmaker? Art historian? Literary scholar? Feminist? And I would also like you to talk about two other personae: friend and teacher. I found it so touching that you mentioned Alexander, and it struck me how often you dedicate, or use an idea from, or refer to the work of friends and acquaintances – Alexander knew you were a sympathetic soul with whom he could share his curiosities. And your friends – like me – have gained so much from being at your side when you talk about what we are interested in and help us to clarify lines of argument, think more deeply about examples. Besides that, your teaching is legendary. No one spends more time with students than you.*

MB: Personae? There's only one. I suppose cultural critic would be the convenience term (or store). But I think of myself as someone fascinated by narrative. Everything I have done since I started to be a thinking person has had to do with narrative. I guess I read too many novels as a child (one a day, for years on end). I never get over what narratives can do: turn you into another person, make you weep for no reason, and – here it comes – manipulate you into believing, or condoning, things you would ordinarily find objectionable. That's where it all started: my sense that I could so easily be led along by narratives that it is both a wonderful and a dangerous cultural mode. The semiotic perspective is a tool of analysis, finding an angle that makes visible what matters. The feminism is a focus, a drive: something that orients my questioning, keeps me alert.

Film-making started out as a diversion, because I felt a tiny bit bored. Writing had always been a pleasure, so the minute I ceased to be excited about it, I had to take a break. But no, it's no different. My films, too, grapple with narrative and its discontents (nice title for something or other?). Making films that tell an abundance of stories but are not narrative in any classical sense, that avoid facile identification as well as aesthetic distancing, sado-pornographic display as well as indifferent reporting, is not fundamentally different from analysing narratives in literature, biblical stories, paintings. Narratives that happen between 'text' or 'work' and viewer. 'Happen' means something like 'affect', but without sentimentality; rather like getting acquainted. I'm excited about my most recent project on mothers of migrants.[8] There is a performativity in film-making that is empowering to the 'subject' (hate the word, don't know a better one). And that reflects back on the academic work: analysing is opening up, and in a sense, empowering the artefact. Letting it tell the stories, and making people interested in hearing them.

About the teaching: again, it's about empowering. I guess in my life I have felt disempowered a little, and then empowered when I realized I could nurture thought.

MH: *The other day I was reminiscing about our time together in Rochester in those heady days of the late 1980s and early 1990s, when anything seemed possible on the crest of the poststructuralist wave. I remember asking you one evening where you would like to 'end up' when all has been said and done in the academy. Your answer surprised me, but it shouldn't have, knowing you. 'In politics, in some elected or appointed office, such as the minister of cultural affairs in the Netherlands.' Is that possibility still tucked away in some corner of your mind?*

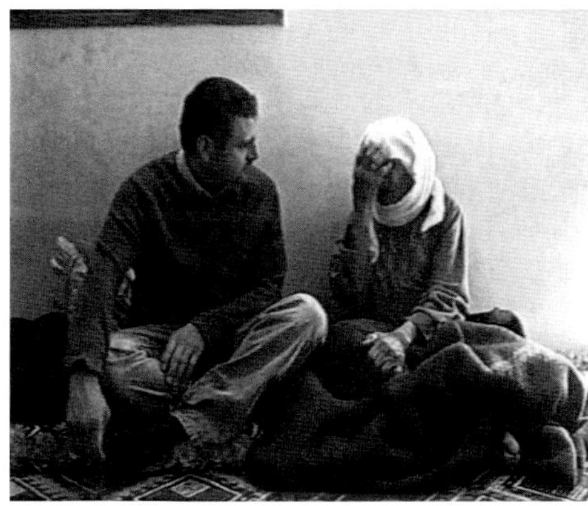

7.3 Ilhab with great-grandmother, still from Cinema Suitcase (Mieke Bal, Thomas Sykora, Gary Ward), *Access Denied*, DV colour, 2005. Photo: courtesy of the artists.

MB: I suppose I still believed politics was politics: governing a country to the best of the politicians' abilities. This was before our Prime Minister got his power on an even smaller basis than George W. Bush, but still dictates what needs to be done in all areas of Dutch public (and private!) life. But I have seen politics do too much damage to want any share in the responsibility that is always, a priori, compromised. I have no large-scale ambition, only small-scale. This is without even considering the tedium of the life in politics. Hope, though, is different from expectation. It's between illusion and expectation, and it's the place where one can at least think about what we would like to see happen. For my own country, I would hope, against all odds, that the crazy pace of the destruction of the social system that made the country humane, social, might slow down, and the movement be reversed. A country that forgets where it comes from is doomed. My hope would be that this small country can endorse the fact that there is no original great nation, that the world is the nation and that, if we have a good share of the world's riches, it's not as if this wealth belongs to 'authentic' Hollanders.

My political position is, against all odds, to promote subtle reflection where politics is grossly unsubtle; to see the good things about people where politics wants us to hate and despise. There is no party for me, only bits of some on the left. Issues I care about: social security for all (meaning not just the number of taxpayers); health care; equality in education; ecology. More and more I care about the non-assimilationist integration of migrants.

MH: *Can you explain what you mean by 'non-assimilationist integration of immigrants'?*

MB: Non-assimilationist integration: assimilation means giving up on one's own identity, making it invisible, in order to fit in. At some point the Dutch government proposed an integration examination, including eating Dutch cuisine. For a country that has the blandest cuisine of the world and is happily eating at thriving 'ethnic' restaurants, that seems a chutzpah. For me, integration means that people are at home where they live, wherever they come from, and are free to live their beliefs and cultural backgrounds openly.

Assimilation is erasure, and imposed from the side of power. Integration is connecting, and two-sided. Don't forget: in the 1930s, German Jews were assimilated, completely invisible except on Friday night at the synagogue. Then the Nazis turned them into Jews. It is always the defensiveness of a settled culture that keeps the relative newcomers at bay (even if German Jews had been in Germany for centuries). Closer to home, both spatially and temporally, last year eleven people died in a fire at the Schiphol detention centre, simply because they couldn't get out. Some were drug traffickers, others had no crime to their name other than trying to survive. And the fire would not have occurred if there hadn't been despair, and imprisonment, simply because people were considered 'illegal'. How can a *person* be illegal?

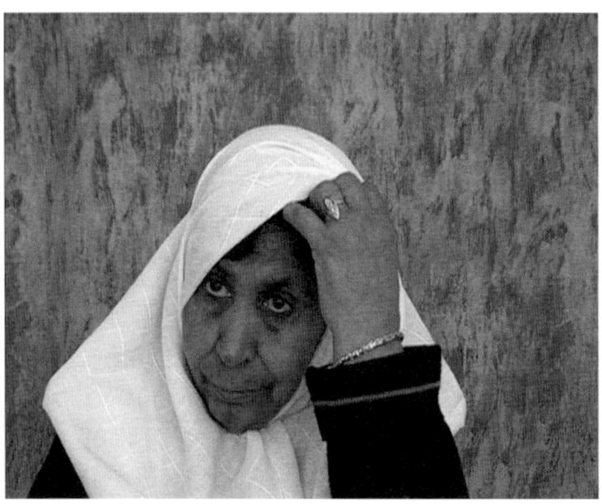

7.4 Massaouda scratching her head, still from Mieke Bal, *Nothing is Missing*, 2006. Multiple-screen video installation, 25–35 minutes (looped). Photo: courtesy of the artist.

MH: *And when you talk about the past of a place, like a country, does it mean the same thing as the past of visual art? Or of an historical period? Talking about the past always seems to me something of an oxymoron. How can we speak of something if it is authentically past? But it's Halloween here, and I guess I'm wishing for hauntings – ghosts, revenants, spectres, a presence that is here and not here simultaneously.*

MB: The past, precisely, never disappears, is never tucked away into the past, invisible; not quite. Those who cannot accept that the past is still with us keep insisting that we 'reconstruct' it, in its alterity. Walter Benjamin has that beautiful way of putting it: 'The past can be seized only as an image which flashes up at the instant when it can be recognized and is never seen again.' But then he adds: 'For every image of the past that is not recognized by the present as one of its own concerns threatens to disappear irretrievably.'[9] This corresponds more or less to my sense of the past, of history as importantly present in the present.

If we don't recognize that this so-called past concerns us, we lose it, as well as the thickness of the present. This also holds for images that, miraculously, have remained with, or returned to, us in the present. They belong with us, but, similarly to my non-assimilationist views, they should not be forced either to be identical to images just made, nor be irreducibly different, incommensurable, alien. I think it is disingenuous and even risky to repress the affective bond we feel to images from the past, and that makes us desire to understand them.

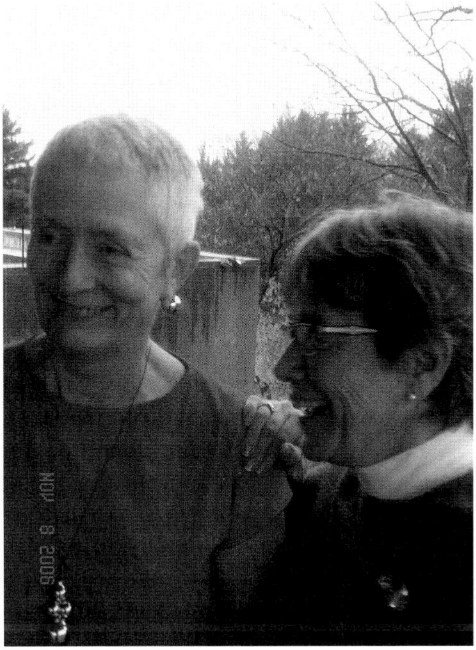


7.5 Mieke Bal and Michael Ann Holly, Williamstown, 2006. Photo: Mark Ledbury.

MH: *When were you first intrigued by all that visual art could think and do?*

MB: I vividly remember the first time I saw visual art 'think'. I was looking for a cover image, for my book on biblical narrative, and an idea for a lecture in Jerusalem. Out of courtesy I didn't want to lecture on the Bible. Looking for a cover image, I ran into Rembrandt's tiny etching on Joseph and Potiphar's wife in a book of his etchings (plate 7.6).[10] It got me thinking about the story all over again. It was as if the Rembrandt said 'yes, but ...' and listening to the image gave me entirely new ideas about the story. The imaginary register in it, the word play on house and/or as prison, the young man's dread of the female body, it all came out of that naughty little image. After that, when I was at Harvard in biblical studies, Rembrandt continued to tease, remained teasing me, and this was the year I had these illuminating experiences of literally *seeing* the meaning of texts. I think my book *Death and Dissymmetry*, the best of my 'trilogy' on the Bible, is my first book in 'visual studies', despite the fact that it is entirely on the Bible.[11] Not long after that, I went to Rochester, where I met you, Norman [Bryson], and then Kaja [Silverman]. If I hadn't met you, I don't know if I would had pursued my work so seriously in relation to art. It all fell into place.

MH: *A little while ago we were talking about the enchantments of visual art. Do you feel that works of art – in the wake of visual studies – have had their enchantments dulled? In your writing, you clearly keep some of their 'magic' very much alive. What's your secret?*

MB: For me, the enchanting quality of (some) images is not, or not primarily, or not only, their beauty, but first of all that they think and speak: interlocutors, who keep me connected to contemporary society and to the past. They heal the splits between the individual me and the people I don't even know but care about, and between me struggling with the world today and those other worlds. That enchantment has not dulled in the wake of visual studies, on the contrary.

What's my secret? I am not sure I have one. I just follow my excitement about the image, which I approach with an almost myopic attention, and then I want to show people how important it is. As a result, I end up with that integration of detailed analysis and larger framings.

MH: *So many concepts are associated with your work: 'focalization', 'narratology', 'preposterous history', and many others. What is their relevance for practising the history of art?*

MB: Concepts. Yes, this is a tricky issue. On the one hand, I have often been frustrated by the way concepts are used as labels: body, cultural memory, trauma, uncanny, whatever is next year's fad. They are often just stuck to a case as if naming a work with such terms replaces analysis, reflection, history. On the other hand, and probably because of this, I have become alert to the productivity of concepts – on the condition that they are used thoughtfully. This requires, first of all, putting on the table what an author means by them, and then using the concept as a tool for analysis. Or rather, as an interlocutor. Once you begin to think and write about what a concept means you are automatically enticed to unpack the aspects of that meaning and weave those through the art work you are looking at. It becomes a great way of resolving the problem of interdisciplinarity. The main problem in interdisciplinarity is the lack of established methods. You cannot fall back on simple iconography, or connoisseurship, or plot analysis, narratological methods and so on, when you are working in a truly interdisciplinary vein.

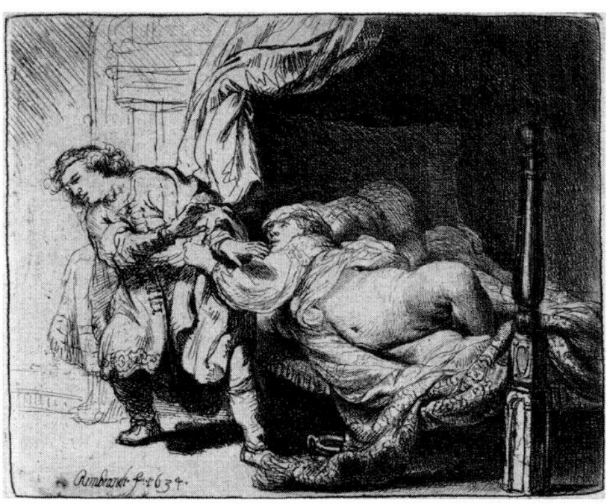

7.6 Rembrandt Harmensz van Rijn, *Joseph and Potiphar's Wife*, 1634. Etching and some drypoint, Berlin: Kupferstichkabinett, Staatliche Museen zu Berlin. Photo: Jörg P. Anders. Courtesy of Bildarchiv Preussischer Kulturbesitz/Art Resource, NY.

The concept of perspective is a good example. It means narrative situation, including focalization for some, linear perspective for others, and the two, while not entirely alien, are certainly not the same. Unpacking the differences makes the concept new again, complex and productive. Focalization, for example, is a form of orientation across the story depicted, something like a fictional mode of looking that the painter has incorporated. It is what makes a painting truly narrative, other than the insertion of a couple of elements from a known – hence, external – narrative it supposedly illustrates. You can say, for example, 'from Joseph's focalization, the woman shows her hands first.' Then you can do an iconographical analysis of those hands in terms of traditional meanings of hands as holding off, speaking, theatrical pose, what have you. But the narrative point is that Joseph sees those hands, so whatever they mean, they address to this figure. So, perspective only comes in to assess the dramatic depth of the depicted scene. Perspective moves from narrative to theatricality (not in Michael Fried's sense but in terms of theatre studies).[12] Linear perspective comes in to assess the structure of the represented space, the stage if you like, the depth, and the lack of it. When a painting has both depth and doesn't distribute the narrative, including focalization, across it 'properly', this is not clumsiness. I can't bear that word, the arrogance of it! But it might be a play with visual punning, where depth and picture plane compete, drawing attention to both and to the need to accept fictionality – the willing suspension of disbelief.

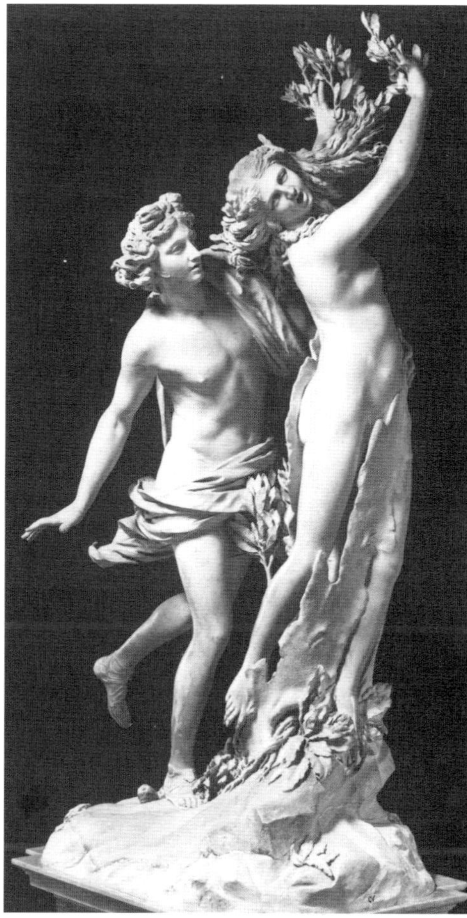

7.7 Gian Lorenzo Bernini, *Apollo and Daphne*, 1622–25. Marble, height 243 cm. Rome: Galleria Borghese. Photo: Alinari/Art Resource, NY.

Something similar can be said of preposterous history. Why study Bernini's *Apollo and Daphne* (plate 7.7)? An obscure Italian poem might have been known to the artist, but how well did he know it, and how literary was his mind? Wasn't he too busy making sculptures that cannot, ever, be 'explained' with reference to a poem? But once you say 'from a viewpoint of preposterous history', you can still bring up the poem, speculate that such metaphors from Ovid were part of popular culture in Bernini's time, possibly based on evidence but more likely not. But then, you will also be enticed to say why you, today, consider such connections important, to think about how that excitement informs your search, why look at poetry, for example. Because art ... historical method prescribes it, or your own interests in the sculpture group? Anything can come up that is totally different from a seventeenth-century fashion for Ovid's *Metamorphoses*, that has to do with certain metaphors addressing the particular appeal of Bernini's distribution of smooth and rough marble to foreground sensate looking. I am not going to 'do' preposterous history on Bernini here, but I am sure that Louise Bourgeois's *Spider*, in spite of its huge differences in theme, materials, method, meaning – in short, in spite of all of its features – has something to tell us about Bernini that is more informative for an art-historical view of Bernini's work than any amount of documentation that can be unearthed.[13]

I am currently writing about the concept of inter-facing as a tool for an intercultural aesthetics, a 'migratory aesthetics'. This evolved from *Nothing is Missing*. Here the concept came out of the practice of art-making. Thinking about and with concepts has been a great help to me. Concepts are great guides 'beyond' the tedium of methodological obedience. They don't preclude more traditional

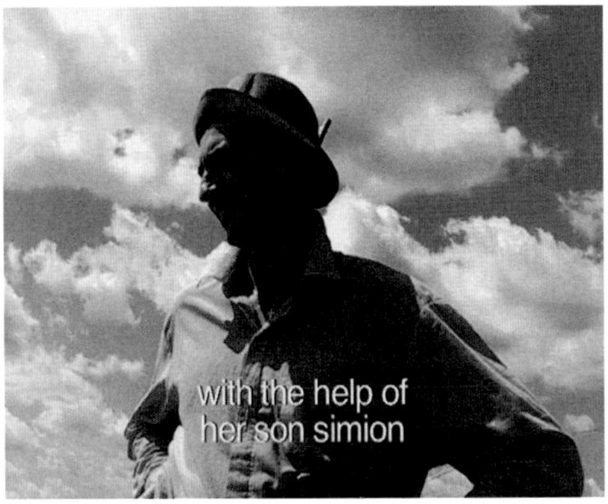


7.8 Still from Mieke Bal, *Nothing is Missing*, Simion against clouds, from Elena, 2006. Multiple-screen video installation, 25–35 minutes (looped).

methods, they just give them a frame within which they get new life. I wrote *Travelling Concepts in the Humanities* in that spirit.[14]

MH: *How do you see your place in the inevitable chain of being now that your mother has recently died?*

MB: In one or two weeks, my daughter's book came out, my son is thinking of setting up his own business, and my mother died. Not to speak of sibling problems and everything that happens in large families under the pressure of emotional turmoil. It makes me feel that I am a link in a chain. That's rather consoling. It also makes me feel utterly un-free, bogged down by worries about those people so close to me, who are so much their own persons (as they should be).

But something else occurs to me at moments such as these. This concerns subjectivity within the rippling, widening circles of social embedding. When I am worried because one of my children has problems (and whenever don't they?) I think of mothers who had to thoroughly let go of the child they raised. This thought (or should I say emotion?) inspired my recent video work, on mothers whose children left for Western Europe in hope of a better future. So far, all these mothers say the same thing: they grieved when the child left, still do; and they rejoiced that at least he or she was safe ... from hunger, domestic violence, war, revolution. This ambivalence must be terrible. For it precludes open grieving.

So, you see, even when you ask me a question about my place in history, I cannot help extending it to today. I remember an anecdote from my early days as a mother, when my daughter had nightmares for a while. I tried to soothe her by saying: 'You had a dream, didn't you? What was it about?' She was a year and a half, couldn't really speak, but she'd say one half-word, I repeated it, and together we got to the right word, and her incomprehensible murmurings riddled with anxiety amounted to something like 'When I go to sleep doesn't an owl come?' I remember the deep satisfaction in being able to communicate and reassure her, on the basis of our working out together what her fears, her fantasies were, her monsters, and to be able to make the nasty owls go away. This, in my memory, is where my interest in interpretation got a place in my personal life.

MH: *Speaking of progenitors, what thinkers, intellectuals, theorists matter most to your intellectual life?*

MB: All the books that deeply influenced me have been recent, although they discuss, analyse, make me excited about, other books, or art works, or life and thoughts from the past. Like Paul Zumthor's *La mesure du monde: Représentation de, l'espace au moyen âge.*[15] Strangely, perhaps, this book threw me into my passion for things intercultural (although my mother took us to Flamenco dance concerts long before). The idea that people in other times had a relationship to something so 'natural' as space made everything questionable. Zumthor didn't study these phenomena as if they concerned us. Instead, he made their strangeness stand out, then explained the logic. Space 'felt' different then from now. He was only able to show-and-tell this different outlook because he acknowledged his entrance from the present, then did the justice he could to the past, comparatively, as if comparing different cultures today. Tremendous.

I have been reading Henri Bergson. I love the way he makes looking strange, and perception 'unnatural'. He also wrote about issues that are current today – memory, subjectivity, matter. His careful reasoning is exemplary. I used one of his texts from *Matter and Memory* in my seminar as a model for reasoning, doing justice to objections before one even thought of them, and then answering in great detail.[16]

I read some of Leibnitz's work when I was an undergraduate student. He is one of those philosophers that I would never have touched because of his religion. I have no interest in the self-evidence of God as a figure in thought. But Deleuze picks up what matters in Leibnitz for the understanding of baroque art – its aesthetics and its thought.[17] The idea of the fold, with all its implications, demonstrates how limiting an obsession with linear perspective has been. It also shows that those obsessions that art history has incorporated so 'naturally' have a grounding in philosophy, even politics. The point of the fold is that it doesn't let the viewer feel so powerful, distant, masterly. Nor does it allow viewing to be disembodied, retinal. Leibnitz offers a grounding for a totally different view on modern and contemporary art.

Like many others, I am getting interested in Spinoza. What a crazy case ... religious but not really, just because it was the discourse of the time. A true democrat and so helpful, today, for even the most difficult political issues, such as feminism and the land claims of Australian Aborigines. I read a wonderful small book on his work by two feminist philosophers: Moira Gatens and Genevieve Lloyd.[18]

By the way, all these guys were migrants. Holland was a bit more hospitable then than now. And you see the gifts they left, the rewards for a culture that accommodated them and protected them from persecution. That free spirit of the Low Countries must not be idealized, but it did make a lot of culture possible when elsewhere it was tough. A good lesson for today.

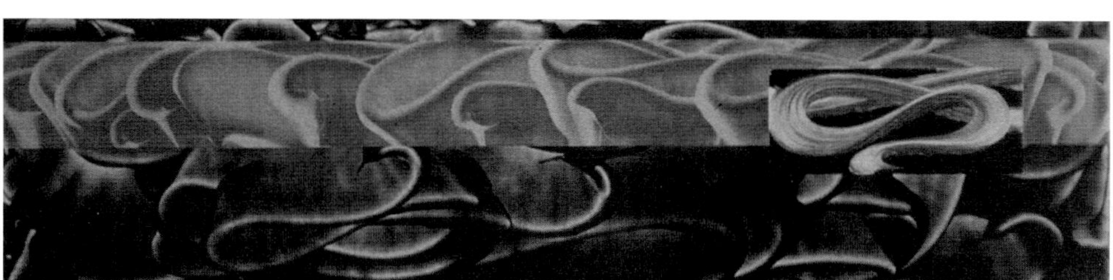

7.9 David Reed, *#275*, 1989. Oil and alkyd on linen, 66 × 259 cm. Collection of Linda and Ronald F. Daitz. Photo: courtesy of the artist.

MH: *How did you come by your love of contemporary art? Whom – or what trends and tendencies – are you currently interested in?*

MB: I was at Dartmouth College, in a Mellon seminar on 'Cultural Memory and the Present'. I was invited as senior fellow and, as happens often, I was intrigued by why they had asked me. The organizers were historians. So, the ambience was to think about memory in relation to history and to the present. Then Lisa Corrin sent me her catalogue *Going for Baroque*, – out of the blue.[19] I guess I was ready to make the leap. It got me going about some of the artists, especially David Reed, a non-figurative painter (plate 7.9). That was a great challenge. I found his work enormously appealing, attractive, and yet, there were only curves and curls. I ended up writing a twenty-five-page article about just one of those paintings.[20]

Then I started to remember art I had seen before and always considered great without feeling compelled to think more about it. Louise Bourgeois, for example (plate 7.10). I had seen some of her work in different places; always felt my heart beat; never thought more about it. After a few articles, a small book, and three films, I think I understand a little more what the attraction is.[21] And then, of course, the artists I have presented as the Caravaggisti of our time in *Quoting Caravaggio*. All for different reasons, and all very different artists, who all 'pay homage' to the human body in one way or another. Respect the body against all odds, against the tide of the violence done to it by politics and disease, and against the denial of it by established religions. The relationship that they establish between today's life culture and the culture of the past – between street violence now and public executions in Caravaggio's time – inspired me to develop a theoretical thought that would account for that relationship. If only to draw attention to the value to 'visual thinking' as an intervention in today's culture, I owed it to that art, to the works that excited and inspired me, to come up with a theoretical approach that would put them in the league/frame they deserved. Hence, preposterous history.

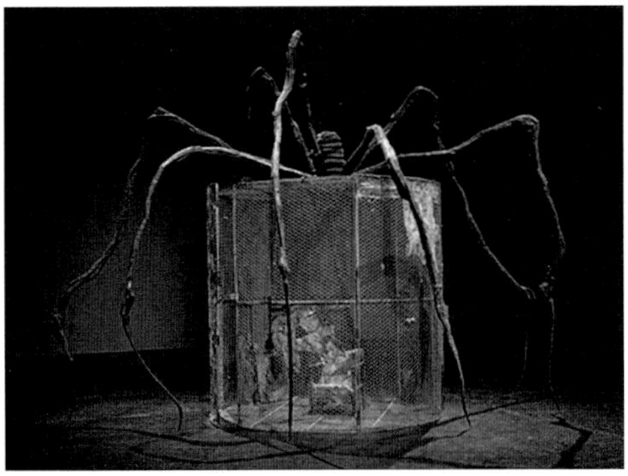

7.10 Louise Bourgeois, *Spider*, 1997. Steel, tapestry, wood, glass, fabric, rubber, silver, gold and bronze, 444.5 × 665.4 × 518.1 cm. Courtesy Cheim & Read, Galerie Karsten Greve, Galerie Hauser & Wirth. Photo: Fréderic Delpech.

MH: *And, finally, why do I always picture you in Issey Miyake?*

MB: When I was a young academic I was still surrounded by men, or a handful of honorary men: women in dress-for-success outfits. I heard back from my students how much it meant to them that I was a 'fun' woman. So, I liked the idea that I could show to the women in my classes that the profession could be fun, too, that you didn't have to choose between being a woman and being an academic, no more than between a career and motherhood. As a result, I always dress nicely for a seminar or class. Even now.

*Interview edited by Deborah Cherry*

## Notes

Mieke Bal has been my close friend for nearly twenty years, ever since we taught together and co-founded the Visual and Cultural Studies Graduate Program at Rochester. We have had many conversations, but I hope that this one, conducted by e-mail during Autumn 2005 and Winter of 2006, offers an insight into why she is a remarkable scholar, cultural theorist, teacher and friend.

1 Mieke Bal, *Narratologie. Essais sur la signification narrative dans quatre romans modernes*, Paris, 1977; reprinted Utrecht, 1984.

2 *Reading 'Rembrandt': Beyond the Word-Image Opposition*, New York and Cambridge, 1991; 2nd pbk edn 1994. Abridged and re-organized: *Verf en verderf. Lezen in 'Rembrandt'*, Amsterdam, 1990; reprinted Amsterdam, 2006.

3 *Double Exposures: The Subject of Cultural Analysis*, with Edwin Janssen, Das Gesicht an der Wand (The Stain/Face on the Wall), New York, 1996.

4 *Images littéraires, ou comment lire visuellement Proust*, Montréal and Toulouse, 1997. *The Mottled Screen: Reading Proust Visually*, trans. Anna-Louise Milne, Stanford, 1997.

5 Mieke Bal, *ArtClips*, a series of nine short films (5.5 minutes), 2002.

6 Mieke Bal and Shahram Entekhabi, *Eye Contact*, 2003.

7 Cinema Suitcase (Mieke Bal, Zen Marie, Thomas Sykora, Gary Ward, Michelle Williams), *Mille et un Jours (A Thousand and One Days)*, 2004, re-edited by Gary Ward, 2006.

8 Mieke Bal, *Nothing is Missing*, multiple-screen video installation, 25–35 minutes (looped), 2006.

9 Walter Benjamin, 'Theses on the Philosophy of History', Thesis V in *Illuminations*, ed. and with an introduction by Hannah Arendt, trans. Harry Zohn, New York, 1976, 255.

10 *Femmes imaginaires. L'Ancien Testament au risque d'une narratologie critique*, Utrecht, Montréal and Paris, 1986.

11 *Death and Dissymmetry: The Politics of Coherence in the Book of Judges*, Chicago, 1988.

12 Michael Fried, *Absorption and Theatricality: Painting and Beholder in the Age of Diderot*, Berkeley, 1980.

13 *Louise Bourgeois's* Spider: *The Architecture of Art-writing*, Chicago, 2001.

14 *Travelling Concepts in the Humanities: A Rough Guide*, Toronto, 2002.

15 Paul Zumthor, *La mésure du monde. Représentation de l'espace au moyen âge*, Paris, 1993.

16 Henri Bergson, *Matière et mémoire*, 1896, revised 1908. *Matter and Memory*, trans. Nancy Margaret Paul and W. Scott Palmer, based on French (1908), New York, 1994. Mieke Bal regularly conducts a seminar on theory at Amsterdam School for Cultural Analysis.

17 Gilles Deleuze, *The Fold: Leibnitz and the Baroque*, trans. Tom Conley, Minneapolis, 1993.

18 Moira Gatens and Genevieve Lloyd, *Collective Imaginings: Spinoza, Past and Present*, New York, 1999.

19 Lisa G. Corrin and Joaneath Spicer, eds, *Going for Baroque: 18 Contemporary Artists Fascinated with the Baroque and Rococo*, Baltimore, 1995.

20 Mieke Bal, 'Second-Person Narrative', in *Paragraph* (Special Issue 'Painting and Narrative', ed. Michael Worton) 19:3, 1996, 179–204; extended in *Quoting Caravaggio: Contemporary Art, Preposterous History*, Chicago, 1999, 2001.

21 Publications include *Louise Bourgeois's* Spider, Chicago, 2001; 'Forking Paths and Crystals in Louise Bourgeois's Philosophy of Temporality', in *Louise Bourgeois: Geometry of Desire*, ed. Jolanta Piekos, trans. Dorota Koziska, Warsaw, 2003, 253–61; 'Beckoning Bernini', in *Louise Bourgeois: Memory and Architecture*, Madrid, 2000, 75–85; 'Autotopography: Louise Bourgeois as Builder', in *Interfaces: Women, Autobiography, Image, Performance*, eds Sidonie Smith and Julia Watson, Ann Arbor, 2002, 163–85 (earlier version: 'Narrative Inside Out', *Oxford Art Journal*, 22:2, 1999, 101–126). Videos: *Favourite Spots*, 15-minute video on the exhibition *Louise Bourgeois: Geometry of Desire*, Warsaw, 2003; *Eye Contact*, with Shahram Entekhabi, 10-minute video on the exhibition *Intimate Abstractions: Louise Bourgeois*, Berlin, 2003; *Louise Bourgeois: Scuttling Around*, 6-minute video (ArtClips), 2002.

# 8

# KILLING KOOL: THE GRAFFITI MUSEUM

SONJA NEEF

In 1975 Jean Baudrillard theorized postmodern graffiti in his now legendary essay 'KOOL KILLER, or The Insurrection of Signs'. Relying on a structuralist semiotic model, he argued that 'signs don't operate on the basis of force, but on the basis of difference.' Graffiti, then, contrary to the city's 'official' semiotics, functions against this symbolic order: 'Graffiti has no content and no message: this emptiness gives it its strength.'[1]

Baudrillard's theory of graffiti as 'empty signifiers' has received considerable attention and is widely accepted in discourses on graffiti. Here, I offer an analysis which moves beyond this opposition sign/non-sign, to discuss graffiti as performative akin to a 'speech act', and as a form of handwriting which inscribes the subject and the body, drawing on Mieke Bal's understanding of the act of writing on a wall as a basic operation of culture as performative, an event rather than a predefined symbolic text. This move is enacted by exploring the inscription technologies of graffiti as a cultural practice, examined, first, on a German motorway, then in an online performance by PIPS:lab, and finally on the longest concrete canvas of the world, the Berlin Wall.

## PASSING BY

Autobahn A4, going east. For hours, the panorama consists mainly of low mountain ranges, villages with church towers nestling against hills cut by overhead cables. This is Germany, unmistakeably. Road signs functioning as position co-ordinates affirm the locations. Next exit Eisenach. A supplementary brown sign sketches the bare bones of a castle in white lines; written underneath is 'Wartburg, 5 km'. Then the famous castle where Martin Luther translated the Bible appears on the right-hand side of the road, and motorway passengers can admire it in the distance for a few minutes. Sight-seeing blends with other views: white stripes on the road pass by in *staccato*, a speed-limit sign orders 120 km per hour, after a bench Wartburg Castle is again picked up quickly, graffiti (huge silver pieces) flickers up on a bridge pier, a restriction on passing is now cancelled. The gaze keeps focusing on the castle even while the road passes an industrial area with yards and warehouses covered with graffiti in bubble style, signs blowing up the age-old forms of the Roman alphabet into an unmistakable yet illegible comic-book style. But there is no time to decipher them. Then, legible at a glance, 'McDonald's in 500 m'. And although Wartburg Castle is an unique historical site, this place could be everywhere. Keep right, you are being overtaken. The castle dissolves in a blur of speed. It materializes only for a moment as a sign pinpointing a place of which the topographic logic is determined by a movement rather than by a stable place.

Road signs become empty signifiers, those 'non-places' opposed to 'places' by Marc Augé in his postmodern ethnography: 'If a place can be identified as relational, historical and concerned with identity, then a space which cannot be defined as relational, or historical, or concerned with identity will be a non-place.'[2] Relying on Michel de Certeau's concept of 'space'[3] as a place that is experienced, moved through and thus narrated or construed, Augé sketches a 'supermodern' utopia of 'non-places' without identity, history, social or semantic urban relationships. Non-places are anonymous and temporary spaces for passage, communication and consumption: motorways seen from car interiors, petrol stations, chain restaurants, supermarkets and shopping malls as well as passenger transit lounges of airports and railway stations.

On the A4 passengers from the West may realize that Eisenach is in Thuringia. This means that, a mere five minutes ago, the road must have crossed the former border: it did so three times. At the division of Germany, this section of the historical motorway was severed by a sharp bend of the border and was reconnected only after the reunification. Only after having passed these two interfaces does one cross at the historical crossing point of Herleshausen; East and West seem to infiltrate each other, transit travellers go in and out, leaving the former American Sector without 'caution', effortless and unnoticed. There are no signs drawing attention to this stroke of pastureland bordering on a wood, an inconspicuous scar in the landscape left by the former death strip. Who (re-)minds? The Autobahn, with its specific sign system that either pinpoints places which are actually not there, or effaces places by not naming them, seems to equalize what was once strictly separated into a unitary space, turning the East's bleak greyness, to echo the famous dictum of ex-chancellor Helmut Kohl (which today seems pure sarcasm), into 'flourishing landscapes'. The graffiti along the way, ironically enough, forms an integral part of this 'unification'.

## THE INSURRECTION OF SIGNS AND THE SECULARIZATION OF CONCEPTS

Across the West and the post-communist East, graffiti is found on 'non-places': trains, subways, tunnels, bridge pillars and blind walls, all those regions extending in between identifiable, 'true' *loci*. Baudrillard stresses its nomadic urge, its taking transit areas and traffic channels for its medium. He introduces 'KOOL KILLER' with the image of a flood:

> In the spring of 1972 in New York a spate of graffiti broke out which, starting with ghetto walls and fences, finally overcame subways and buses, lorries and elevators, corridors and monuments, completely covering them in graphics ranging from the rudimentary to the sophisticated, whose content was neither political nor pornographic. These graphics consisted solely of names, surnames drawn from the underground comics such as DUKE SPIRIT SUPERKOOL KOOLKILLER ACE VIPERE SPIDER EDDIE KOLA and so on, followed by their street number – EDDIE 135 WOODIE 110 SHADOW 137, etc. – or even by a number in Roman numerals, a dynastic or filiatory index – SNAKE I SNAKE II SNAKE III, etc. – up to L (50), depending on which name, which totemic designation is taken up by these new graffitists. (76)

The graffiti wave burst from, as Baudrillard puts it, the 'ghetto' 'into the white city' (83) and quickly spread all over the industrialized world, developing a wide range of styles. Graffiti are either thrown up as quick pieces or skilfully sprayed as sophisticated painted masterpieces. On a massive scale they are tagged as cryptic nickname signatures showing up by the hundreds at different places in the city, thus installing their own grammatical order as counter-system to the official city signs. As stencils or pochoirs sprayed on mail-packet forms they are attached to electricity boxes and downspouts.[4] These styles are in no way local but part of a global network, and this nomadic dimension forms their central inscription technology.

It masks existing spatial divisions – in Baudrillard's terms, graffiti 'superimposes':

> (superimposition amounting to the abolishing of the support as a framework, just as it is abolished as frame when its limits are not respected). Its graphics resemble the child's polymorphous perversity, ignoring the boundaries between the sexes and the delimitation of erogenous zones. (82)

Graffiti has been interpreted in terms of a reclamation of identity, challenging bourgeois identity as well as the anonymity of the city. Youngsters defend their personality by tagging, bombing or throwing up their signatures on available writing surfaces, with a crowning mark on a wall or a traffic sign at neck-breaking height. The signs thus sprayed, according to Baudrillard, qualify as

> a scream, an interjection, an anti-discourse [. . .] Invincible due to their own poverty, they resist every interpretation and every connotation [. . .] In this way [. . .] they escape the principle of signification and, as *empty signifiers*, erupt into the sphere of the *full signs* of the city, dissolving it on contact. (78–9, Baudrillard's emphasis)

According to Baudrillard, graffiti operate as 'non-signs', contrary to the functioning of 'full signs'; they have, as I have already stressed, no difference but they have force; the graffito 'alone is savage, in that its message is zero' (83).

Like the graffiti discussed by Baudrillard as non-signs and their writers as anonymous non-individuals, the masses towards whom graffiti is directed can be seen as equally deprived of their semiotic possibilities as reading subjects, in whom processes of meaning production take place. Within Marc Augé's theoretical framework, graffiti's addressees can be characterized as mobile nomadic commuters without personal identity, 'non-persons' who surrender their historical selves at the onset of travel and for the duration of their journey reduced to 'no more than what he [or she] does or experiences in the role of passenger, customer or driver'.[5] And, with graffiti in mind, usually seen from the window of a car, a bus or a train, the acceleration of travelling speed stretches the syntactical flow of language to a collapse of meaning in snapshots, which, at the moment they are glimpsed, are already gone. The act of viewing is not so much forged in terms of aesthetic contemplation or intellectual engagement. Following Augé's concept of non-places and Baudrillard's analysis of graffiti as 'zero signs' generated by 'non-subjects', postsmodern graffiti is altogether an 'anti-discursive', 'anti-cultural' practice.

Indeed, Marc Augé was among the first thinkers to reconsider essentialist concepts of a relational topography for the changed circumstances of a (cybernetic) spatial order, and Jean Baudrillard was likewise the first to formulate an adequate language to describe the subversive semiotic operations of graffiti. Yet on closer examination the 'non-place', 'non-sign', 'non-subject' are based on an *ex-negativo* logic that opposes the 'non . . .' concept *against* a positive and privileged idea from which it is deduced as a secondary, intricate derivative. The idea of a 'non-sign' tacitly and implicitly assumes that of a 'sign', of the possibility of a certain unmistakable communication. My objective here is not to decide for or against these concepts, but to analyse graffiti *beyond* such binary oppositions by confronting them with some of the key insights of Mieke Bal's discussions on the 'subject of cultural analysis', and her analysis of a graffito as the epitome of the process and performance of culture.[6]

## THE GRAFFITI MUSEUM

Mieke Bal understands graffiti not as a demontage of the semiotic operations of culture, as does Baudrillard, but as a cultural act *par excellence*, or, more precisely, as an example on which she elaborates her theories of cultural analysis.[7]

A graffito, Bal argues, is an image-writing, both linguistic and visual, both allographic writing and autographic image, a doubling that problematizes the conventional dichotomy of text and image.[8] She stresses that a graffito takes the public city wall as its writing surface and, in doing so, it is 'an exhibit; it is on show; and it shows itself, shows its hand, its presence.'[9] This being public makes a graffito an exposition, and it is precisely this posture or gesture of exposition that is the key work of the museum. This specific context of the museum attains a broader meaning; the museum wall becomes a metaphor for the city wall and *vice versa*, and, along this metaphorical axis, Bal attempts to understand cultural processes as such.

The metaphor of the 'graffiti museum' is not very original; it has been used repeatedly in discourses on graffiti, notably in debates in which graffiti was defended against the reproach of being 'primitive', 'low', subversive or criminal. From the 1980s onwards several art galleries in New York became interested in 'graffiti-as-art', and moved graffiti from the 'ghettos' to the museum. Keith Haring is emblematic of this passage; he started as an anonymous painter scribbling stick men with chalk on black advertisement posters in New York's subway, but soon became the starsprayer in Toni Shafraze's gallery and, from there, an internationally acknowledged pop artist.[10] Baudrillard is critical about such 'recuperation' of 'graffiti as art', claiming that the aesthetic criterion of graffiti is 'a sign of weakness' because it gives way to a process which he labels as 'museum-culturalization' (83).

When Bal proposes the city wall as a museum, she does not imply the absorption of a free and anarchic subcultural underworld by art-marketing invasions; nor does she install any opposition between high and low, official and subversive. Rather, in Bal's theory, the museum (and the practice of graffiti) is to be understood as a conceptual metaphor for the functioning of cultural processes. For the act of exposing includes a complex discursive dimension in which diverse cultural agents are involved, agents who cannot be labelled 'non'-subjects producing 'non'-signs. In this respect, Bal's theory offers the analytical tools to secularize Baudrillard's quite mystical idea that graffiti would be 'non-discursive', being, as it is, emptied of meaning.

For Bal, the basic operation of the museum, 'showing' or 'exposing', follows the structure of a speech act, a discursive event taking place between a first person (the one speaking, 'I'), who makes a statement about a third person (the object on display, 'it') towards a second person (the addressee to whom the speech act is directed, 'you'):

> Exposing an agent, or subject, puts 'things' on display, which creates a subject/object dichotomy. This dichotomy enables the subject to make a statement about the object. The object is there to substantiate the statement. It is put there within a frame that enables the statement to come across. There is an addressee for the statement, the visitor, viewer, or reader. The discourse surrounding the exposition, or, more precisely, the discourse that *is* the exposition, *is* 'constative': informative and affirmative. [...] In expositions a 'first person,' the exposer, tells 'a second person,' the visitor, about a 'third person,' the object on display, who does not participate in the conversation. But unlike many other constative speech acts, the object, although mute, is present.[11]

The important achievement of Bal's interpretation of the act of showing as a discursive act does not only lie in its theorization of cultural agents as discursive subjects participating in acts of meaning production, but it also allows for a mobilization of the fixed position of authoritative, or 'constative', speech, thus allowing the otherwise 'mute' object to speak back. Discursive acts, as John L. Austin has pointed out in his speech act theory, not only refer to a signified meaning, they are not only 'constative', but they can also cause an effect, they are 'performative' in so far as words can also 'do what they say.'[12] The concept of exposition as a performative radically affects the debate on graffiti because it no longer insists on asking for the semiotic operativity of graffiti as (non-)sign, asking 'what does this mean?' Rather, it raises the question what graffiti *does*. In what follows the online graffiti performance by PIPS:lab and the Berlin Wall are explored to sharpen the key idea of the 'graffiti museum' as a performative.

## AEROSOL

If a graffiti museum exists, it does so on the Internet. The Internet is full of graffiti webpages used by sprayers and their sympathizers as showcases, allowing them to put their work on display under the protection of anonymity offered by the web. The visitor to http://www.pipslab.nl, like the visitor to a museum, is invited to view some lab proofs by PIPS, an Amsterdam-based group of performance artists. The Quicktime trailer opens with a black screen with a yellow dot on it. Suddenly, the dot begins to move, fluttering and twitching, then holding on for a fraction of a second, only to move on in another direction, describing stripes and loops in flashes of light. Finally, the imaginary trace left by the yellow dot of light becomes visible as an accumulation of individual stills that are gathered and now form a contiguous, sweeping line. Now, the visitor can read in very fast short shots in wild handwriting: 'Lumalive', followed by 'by PIPS:lab' (plate 8.1) Underneath this Quicktime trailer, another animated image presents a strip with other 'light writings'. When the visitor touches this strip with a roll-over, it starts scrolling from right to left, offering a menu of lab proofs selectable with a click of the mouse. Then another Quicktime track commences (plate 8.2). It shows a youngster in front of a brick wall in a dark hall, a cap hiding his eyes, his sweatshirt with the hood ready to be pulled over his head perhaps to prevent recognition. His left hand is in his trouser pocket, and in his right hand he holds an aerosol can. He is not spraying colour on the wall, though. Rather, with the aerosol he sprays looping lines, and the traces of his hand's movement are written with light instead of with ink. To become visible and legible as writing, this light performance needs the technical manipulation of what the artists call the 'PIPS (matrix) effects': using multiple cameras in a real-time multi-angle representation, the light painting takes shape as a three-dimensional letter sculpture. Thus the graffiti artist writes his name: 'OASE'.

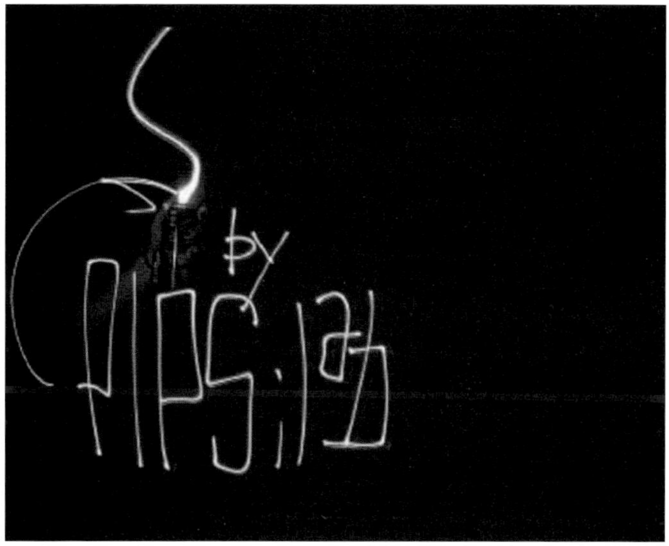

8.1 Still taken from http://www.pipslab.nl/graf/, accessed 30 September 2006.

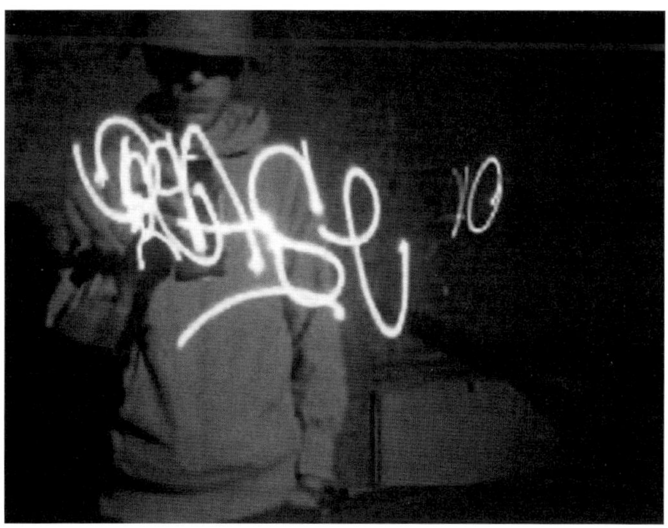

8.2 Still from the trailer 'OASE', http://www.pipslab.nl/graf/, accessed 30 September 2006.

This enactment of the graffiti tag as a light performance stresses the fact that graffiti – and this also holds for what is usually understood under post-modern urban graffiti – is an ephemeral 'live' performance rather than an eternal inscription or – as what graffiti literally means – an 'engraving' scratched (*graphit*) in a durable and resistant writing material. The surface to be written on is not a wall but rather it takes air as its medium, air in which light waves unfold and which is contrary to the durative traces of stone writing.[13] This ephemeral dimension is specific to graffiti, which is scarcely sprayed when it is already tagged over by other, competing graffitists, or removed on a regular basis. Moreover, the sweeping lines of graffiti tags refer to a writing movement that is executed quickly, in passing by, often under the cover of night, so that writing is shaped as a blind tactile gesture rather than a visual sign, a spontaneous movement rather than a careful exercise meticulously obeying the rules of the symbolic order.

The 'choreography' of the sprayer who is 'acting out' forms, I contend, a graffito's central inscription technology. The signature sprayed in aerosol becomes something of the *pneuma* of a breath; it is irreducibly bound up with the presence of the writing hand. Graffiti as handwriting emphasizes the physical presence of the writer on a historically unique moment and on an topographically exact definable 'place', a graffito also claims to connect date, place and signature into an indivisible unity; 'I was here', whether on top of the Eiffel Tower or in the bark of an age-old oak.

Much more than 'normal' writing, which functions as a durable trace to overcome time or space, graffiti follows the logic of the here and now of a choreographic act which, like ballet or theatre, takes the living body for its medium. Graffiti, and the PIPS performance shows this all the more, qualifies as performance culture, which, contrary to conventional concepts of culture as either writing or image, does not decide for a structuralist text analysis or for an iconographic image analysis. 'Performance' culture goes beyond an opposition between word and image. Epistemologically, it is studied in cultural practices such as theatre, side shows, festivities, rites, musical or dance performances, all practices that require the presence of physical bodies and thus function as singular events rather than repeatable structures.

Yet a graffito, in spite of its claim to singularity and uniqueness, like any sign must have a repeatable form for it to become meaningful.[14] The *terminus technicus* of 'choreography' precisely summarizes this double structure of a singular iterability, or an iterable singularity, because dance is in its actual performance irreducibly related to the physical body performing the '*choros*', 'dance', and yet, as a '*graphe*', the dance achieves the status of writing, not only in the sense of a *pre*-scription of dancing movements preceding the actual dance, but also and not least because it carries the structure of the possibility of repetition in it. This iterability makes graffiti a performative practice, that is, a practice that is, like dance, singular and repeatable at once.

## 'HOW CAN WE KNOW THE DANCER FROM THE DANCE'

The PIPS light performance offers ample material not only for a discussion of graffiti and the concept of culture as a performative, but also for a reflection on the status of the graffitist as a 'writer' or 'author'. In 'KOOL KILLER' Baudrillard emphasizes that 'graffiti, composed of nothing but names, effectively avoids every reference and every origin' (83). The subject of graffiti, in his revolt, 'challenges bourgeois identity and anonymity at the same time' (84). And the subject does this, he argues, by making use of 'surnames drawn from underground comics such as DUKE SPIRIT SUPERKOOL' – and this pseudonym is emblematic for the rhetoric of erasing this self – 'KOOL KILLER' (76).

'KOOL KILLER', I will argue, is not just killing the subject kool. And its reference is also not zero. After all, these names refer to the heroic figures of comics, as Baudrillard explains, and, in doing so, they have an intertextual reference, which indeed is not 'quoted' to re-install 'a bourgeois identity'. Rather, the citations take up the comic's specific inscription technology of composing text and image. This 'comic' graffiti is, as Mieke Bal stresses for the graffiti she analyses, an 'intertexual citation' and thus has an 'interdiscursive complexity' which is 'transcultural' because it repeats or translates a sign from one discursive context ('comic') to another ('city walls').[15] For a conceptualization of the subject of writing, I will add to this that this process of 'quoting' is precisely what naming does, be it the official action of inscribing a subject into the files of the registry office to establish a bourgeois identity; the age-old ritualized ceremony of baptizing; or the ephemeral light performance of a youngster naming, or 'baptizing', himself by the name of 'OASE'.

For a visual art work, the signature is traditionally written *underneath* the painting, in a corner of the canvas, and this final sealing confirms that the act of painting is completed. Likewise, a (textual) letter is first written and then signed. The PIPS artist, however, performs the art work in the very moment that he performs the signature. The signature *is* the art work. There is no art work preceding the artist's name and no art work beyond it; it emerges at the very moment, that the artist is 'spraying' his signature, and, in performing his signature, he 'invents' himself as a graffitist who is called by the name 'OASE'. Naming the subject is a discursive practice that generates what it names, and thus this speech act functions less as a constative than as a performative. Like baptizing, signing does not refer to a pre-existing subject of signing or drawing, but it 'performs' the subject.

OASE's light graffiti is not, as Baudrillard has claimed for graffiti, 'anti-discursive'. It is not a postmodern 'simulacrum' in the sense of a reproduction of an original that never existed. For the letters he uses 'repeat', or 'quote' the graphic order of an alphabet that has 'always already' been there. His signature is readable only because it is a repetition, or iteration, of letter forms that have already been used by past writers and will be readable in the future. The graffitist performs an absolutely singular sign in a live performance that is not repeatable, and yet, as a sign, it is readable only because it can be repeated, or 'quoted' with a difference. This is precisely how I would like to (re-)read Baudrillard's statement that graffiti would have 'force' rather than 'meaning'. For they have the force of a rupture, as Derrida interprets the main characteristic of a sign, which

> carries with it a *force* that *breaks* with its context, that is, with the collectivity of presences organizing the moment of its inscription. [. . .] [A] written syntagma can always be detached from the chain in which it is inserted or given without causing to lose all possibility of functioning.[16]

In baptizing himself 'OASE', the graffitist 'breaks' with the cultural context of baptizing which is normally a rite in which the name is 'given' and thus comes from the Other to 'inscribe' the subject into a social system. And yet, by reshaping the baptism as an autoreflexive system in which the subject is named by itself rather than by the Other, the act of naming is no less based on the 'rite' of baptizing; it refers to a cultural context which it repeats or iterates. '*Iter*', as Jacques Derrida has pointed out, 'probably comes from '*itera, other*' in Sanskrit' and refers to a 'logic that ties repetition to alterity'.[17] So as the signature is a repetition of the system of signing and yet is different each time it is iterated, thus the subject of (graffiti) writing is not a constative referring to a pre-existing, stable 'origin'. Rather, it invents and re-invents itself, and any act of signing or tagging offers new subject possibilities.[18]

## INSIDE OUT

Like graffiti walls, museum walls provide semiotic processes with a topographic order generating a clear distinction between the inside and the outside, and along with this, an authoritarian order structuring the positions between the one showing an object on display in the inside of the museum and a visitor coming literally from the outside. In many accounts, the modern museum is said to be born when the European sovereigns opened their private treasure houses, transgressing a border that marked the frontier between the private collection and the world outside.[19] In theorizing the museum, Mieke Bal discusses this gesture of showing in the sense of making public. For her, cultural meaning is not just 'given' to objects by a first-person connoisseur (the curator). Rather, it emerges 'at the threshold' of the museum, in a discursive interaction qualifying as performative rather than constative. In showing, the museum does not just put objects on display, but exposition is also, to quote Bal, 'always an argument. Therefore, in publicizing these views the subject objectifies, exposes her or himself as much as the object; this makes the exposition an exposure of the self.'[20] In such 'double exposures', the hierarchical positions of first, second and third person are destabilized, and the otherwise mute object on display gets the opportunity 'to speak back'.

'Speaking back', in a way, is also what graffiti does in terms of a restructuring of a spatial order which can likewise be considered as highly discursive. After all, graffiti is, as a rule, written on the *outside* of walls that constitute a private *inside* shielded against a public sphere. In writing and drawing on the wall's outside and cultivating it with symbols, graffitists literally 'wallpaper' the streets and occupy the public space as their private domains.[21] In dressing walls, they inhabit and occupy the city, turning its outer fronts into interior walls, making the public streets a private living room. Such restructuring of symbolic places is a performative, it is precisely that Archimedean point from where the museum's apparently constative speech act may unfold its performative dimension.

## THE WRITE/RIGHT SIDE OF THE WALL

The politics of a fixed distinction between an inner and an outer side, or a left and a right side, or a Western and an Eastern side, effected highly dramatic repercussions in the case of the Berlin Wall. No other wall offered such an ideal painting surface, and it became a concrete canvas of the biggest graffiti project ever.

13 August 1961. The German Democratic Republic (GDR) started building what it called its '*antifaschistischer Schutzwall*' ('antifascist protective wall'), walling-in West Berlin over a length of 164 km and turning it into an island on the mainland of 'real socialism'. Initially consisting of barbed wire and brick walls, the Wall was continuously modernized and strengthened. The wall of the first

generation, initially 30 cm thick, was made more massive, and, at street crossings, it could reach 1 m in width. From 1963 onwards, these predecessors were replaced by a wall of concrete slabs, manufactured as industrial mass products in '*Volkseigenen Betrieben*' (nationally owned companies) and held together by steel reinforcements. The Wall developed into a total-border protection system with watchtowers, electric contact fences, and a death strip with automatic spring-guns and a shoot-to-kill order. In 1974 the Wall was rebuilt with steel-reinforced concrete panels with a deeply implanted wide base and, as if following the laws of the classic column with base, pillar and capital, a split pipeline which covered the top to stabilize the Wall against forces breaking through westwards.

The Wall of the fourth generation rang in the hour of the graffitists, all the more so because the panels were now interweaving seamlessly like an endless canvas, which the GDR had even whitened. To whiten the western side of the Wall, a cage needed to be built for the painters, who were surveyed by armed border guards.[22] Through this brightening up, the government aimed at making people from both sides used to, and thus indifferent to, the Wall, counting on what Robert Musil once said, that 'nothing is so invisible as a monument.'[23]

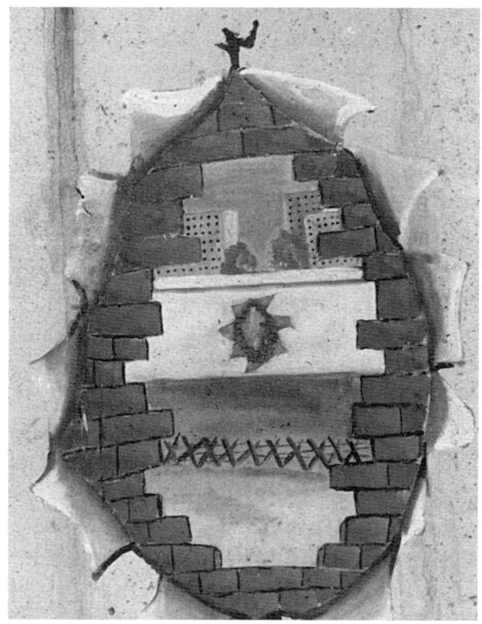

8.3 *Mis en abime* in Berlin Wedding, Bernauer Strasse, 1984 (from Kuzdas, *Berliner Mauer Kunst*, 3). With kind permission of the author.

For the monument of the Wall, however, its whiteness did make a difference, or more precisely, a *differant* in the Derridean sense of the word, because it became the almost not perceptible element that turned the invisible visible. Graffitists played with this invisibility by integrating the wall's materiality, including its political order, into their art works. Or – following Mieke Bal's proposition – to 'make the otherwise mute object speak back'.

And the Wall spoke back. Frequently used motifs included breaks, holes, doors, windows, or zips opening the illusion of a *mis en abime* into another world (plate 8.3). The graffito in plate 8.4 was made by Iranian painter Yadiga Azizy in Berlin Kreuzberg between Legien- and Leuschnerdamm in 1988. As a *trompe l'œil* it restored the torn view on a church of which the tower has been disconnected from the nave.[24] The illusionist logic of the view disempowered the Wall as a separating force, and, paradoxically enough, it did so by using the Wall as its medium. The graffito created a sutureless 'place' disrespecting the material architectonic frame, which it transgressed, or, to pick up Baudrillard's terminology, 'superimposed' or 'erogenized'. The graffito turned the Wall into an area of transit rather than of separation, at least symbolically.

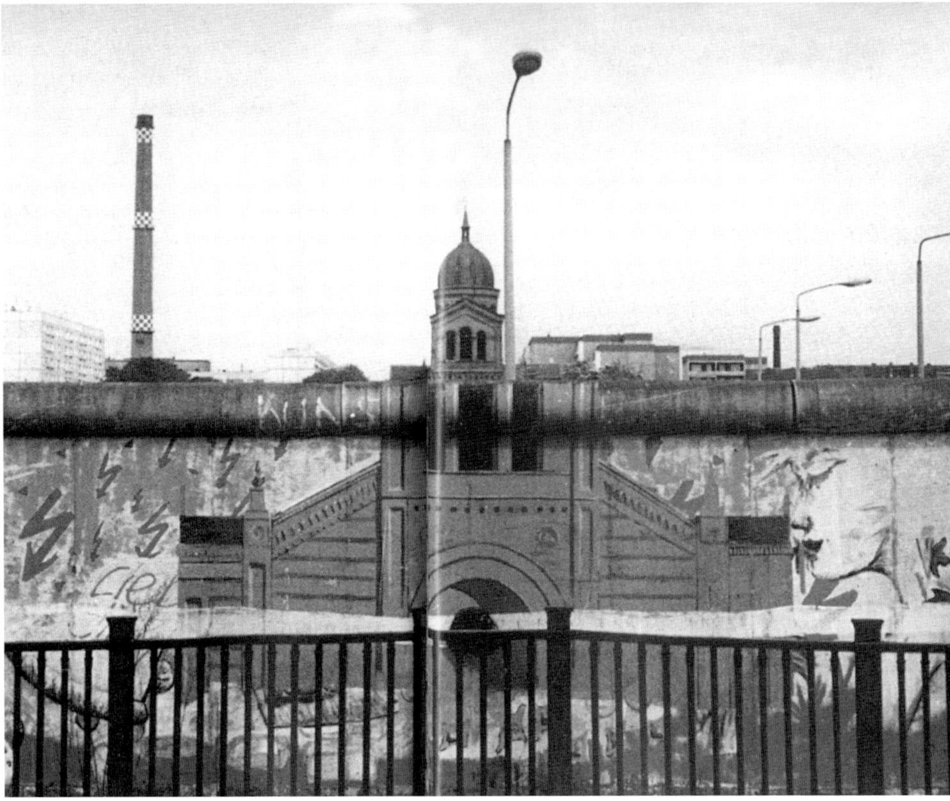

8.4 Yadiga Azizy, mural in Berlin Kreuzberg between Legien- and Leuschnerdamm, 1988 (from Kuzdas, *Berliner Mauer Kunst*, 64-5). With kind permission of the author.

## BORDER-CROSSINGS

For Michel de Certeau, such formation, displacement, or crossing of a boundary, is a discursive act, a speech act performed by a first person authorized to stipulate or constitute the border. De Certeau discusses the performative dimension of the border by the example of a rite that, in ancient Rome, was performed by priests called *fetiales* prior to any contact with a foreign people,

> such as a declaration of war, a military expedition, or an alliance. The ritual was a procession with three centrifugal stages, the first within Roman territory but near the frontier, the second on the frontier, the third in foreign territory. The ritual action was carried out before any civil or military action because it is designed to *create the field* necessary for political or military activities. It is thus also a *repetitio rerum*: both a renewal and a repetition of originary founding acts, a *recitation* and a citation of genealogies that could legitimate the new enterprise, and a *prediction* and a promise of success at the beginning of battles, contracts, or conquests. As a general repetition before the actual representation, the rite, a narration in acts, precedes the historical realization. The tour or the procession of the *fetiales* opens a space and provides a foundation for the operations of the military men, diplomats, or merchants who dare to cross the frontiers.[25]

As the *fetiales* prepared the occupation of the foreign land by first taking possession of it symbolically, the Wall's graffiti, I contend, performed a symbolic conquest of the space of the border. In 1982 artists around the world were invited to participate in a graffiti competition '*Überwindung der Mauer durch Bemalung der Mauer*' ('Overcoming the Wall by Painting the Wall'), sponsored by the Haus am Checkpoint Charlie. Christophe Bouchet and Thierry Noir painted the bright and fanciful *Red Dope on Rabbits* on Bethaniendamm/Adalberstraße in 1985 (plate 8.5); Nora Aurienne made arrows and snakes seemingly flung against the Wall; and, most famously, in October 1986 Keith Haring created a panoramic mural chaining his famous figures over a length of 100 m in the Zimmerstraße next to Checkpoint Charlie (plate 8.6). These graffiti projects all enacted the Wall's possibilities for being transgressed, and, in doing so, they turned it from an identifiable, stable and fixed 'place' into what Michel de Certeau has called a 'space' that is marked by movement rather than by stability, a concept that Marc Augé further developed into the idea of the 'non-place'. In turning the Wall from an ugly architectonic monster into a gigantic global art work of an immeasurable economic value, the art competition aimed at transforming its owner from a financially broke totalitarian regime into an art collector and dealer. Selling the art works, however, would imply breaking down the Wall.

And so it happened.

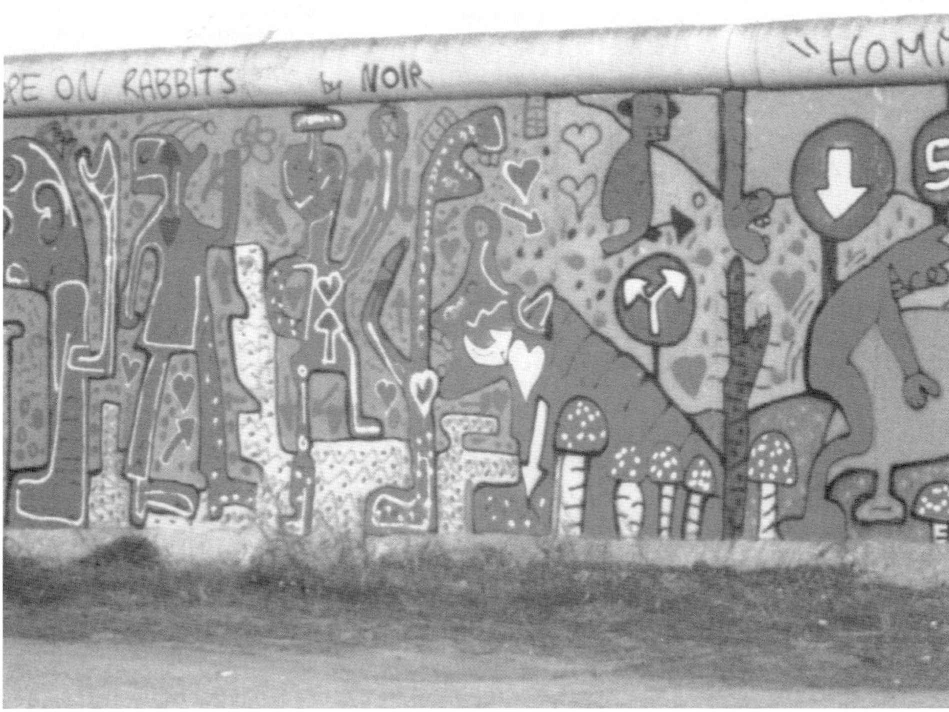


8.5 Thierry Noir, *Red Dope on Rabbits*, Berlin on Bethaniendamm/Adalberstraße, 1985 (from Kuzdas, *Berliner Mauer Kunst*, 32). With kind permission of the author.

However, the bargain was not struck by the authoritative first person that had built the Wall as a bulwark against freedom of travel, trade and expression of opinions. Rather, when the Wall came down, murals were broken out of it by souvenir hunters and other 'Wall peckers', and the best pieces were offered up for sale.[26] Even today, visitors to the Haus am Checkpoint Charlie can pick up a 5 g piece of inner German history for 20 euros. Only a few parts of the former Wall were conserved to become the official Wall memorial: namely, a section near the Berlin Parliament carrying a giant fleeing figure by Jonathan Borofsky, and another one along the Bernauer Strasse in Wedding.[27] In retrospect, it seems that it was precisely this economic drive which made the Wall come down. The symbolic forecast of a successful transgression by means of graffiti art works became true in the first place in that economic sense of a free and globalized market economy.

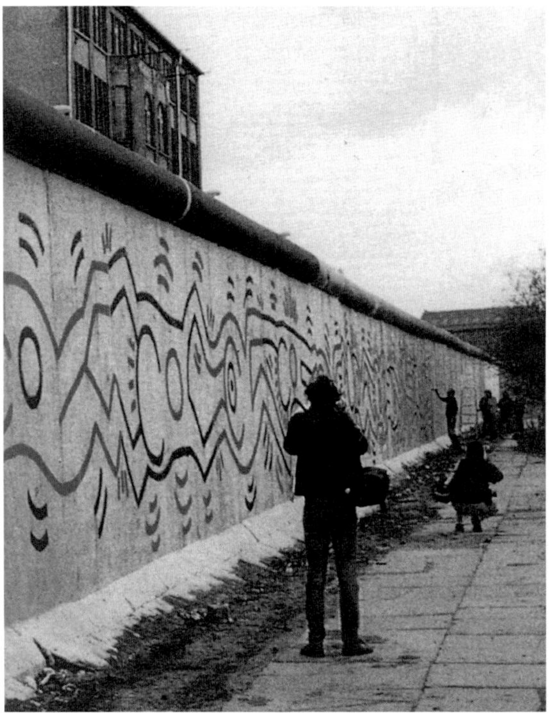

8.6 Keith Haring, Berlin Zimmerstrasse, 1986 (from Kuzdas, *Berliner Mauer Kunst*, 7). With kind permission of the author.

Such issues of ownership, along with matters of preservation, according to Mieke Bal, belong to the central interests of the museum that, as an official institution, holds the first-person position of a true 'value factory'.[28] At a time when the power legitimizing any civil, military, political or trade action across the border was exclusively reserved for the officials of the GDR, the graffiti symbolically superimposing West onto East shocked the basis of this first-person authority. Its discursive utterances (Do not cross! Stay East! Stay West!) were now answered by those otherwise mute subjects to whom they were directed or who, at least, witnessed them passively. In this shift of speech act positions, the Wall did not just expose graffiti, but it also put on display its specific mode of showing; to echo Bal once more, the double exposure of a subject *showing* an object and, in doing so, staging an exposure of the self.

The Wall, I conclude, has always been a 'double exposure' in this sense. Whereas the GDR intended it to be invisible and mute, it was, at least from the outside (the Western side), resplendent and jarring. And when its symbolic forecast was fulfilled, it destroyed its own colourful archival memory store and became invisible. It disappeared, but not without leaving a trace, taking the shape of new discourses and new 'museum's talks' on the dialectic split of the double exposures of 'in/visibilities'. Thus regarded the museum can no longer claim to function only as a constative. Its discourse also functions as a performative because it performs the subject, tagging or spraying in the same process that generates the graffiti's addressees as travellers, or, to echo Marc Augé, 'commuters between places'. In this double take, the museum *does* graffiti as a writing on the wall which has 'force' *because* it has 'meaning'.

## Notes

1 Jean Baudrillard, 'KOOL KILLER, or The Insurrection of Signs', in *Symbolic Exchange and Death*, trans. Iain Hamilton Grant, with an introduction by Mike Cane, London and New Delhi, 1975, 80.

2 Marc Augé, *Non Places – Introduction to an Anthropology of Supermodernity*, London, 1995, 77–8.

3 Michel de Certeau, *The Practice of Everyday Life*, trans. Steve Randall, Berkeley, 1984.

4 The literature on graffiti styles is substantial. See, for example, Jeff Ferrell, *Crimes of Style. Urban Graffiti and the Politics of Criminality*, New York and London, 1993; Johannes Stahl, *Graffiti: zwischen Alltag und Ästhetik*, Munich, 1990; and Beat Suter, *Graffiti: Rebellion der Zeichen*, Frankfurt am Main, 1988.

5 Augé, *Non Places*, 103.

6 Mieke Bal, 'Introduction', in *The Practice of Cultural Analysis. Exposing Interdisciplinary Interpretation*, ed. Mieke Bal with Bryan Gonzales, Stanford, CA, 1999.

7 The 'trademark' of the Amsterdam School for Cultural Analysis (ASCA), of which Mieke Bal is one of the founding directors, is a graffito, and in a detailed analysis of this graffito she characterizes the goals and methodological insights of her (inter-)discipline.

8 See, for example, Mieke Bal, *Reading 'Rembrandt': Beyond the Word–Image Opposition*, Cambridge and New York, 1991; and *The Mottled Screen: Reading Proust Visually*, trans. Anna-Louise Milne, Stanford, CA, 1997. On visual poetry, see Sonja Neef, *Kalligramme. Zur Medialität einer Schrift. Anhand von Paul van Ostaijen&apo;ss 'De feesten van angst en pijn'*, Amsterdam, 2000.

9 Bal, *The Practice of Cultural Analysis*, 4.

10 Suter, *Graffiti*, 155–61.

11 Mieke Bal, *Double Exposures. The Subject of Cultural Analysis*, New York and London, 1996, 3–4.

12 John L. Austin, *How to do Things with Words*, Cambridge, MA, 1975, 6.

13 For an analysis, of the distinction between scribing *in* and scribing *on*, see Vilém Flusser, *Die Schrift. Hat Schreiben Zukunft?* vol. 5, Göttingen, 1987, 14–25.

14 Jacques Derrida, *Signature Event Context*, in *Limited Inc.* Evanstan, IL, 1988.

15 In the case of the graffito analysed by Mieke Bal, it quotes from 'high literature', as it literally repeats the ending of a poem by Dutch poet Ellen Warmond. Mieke Bal, 'Introduction', 1999, 3.

16 Jacques Derrida, 'Signature Event Context', 9 (author's emphasis).

17 Derrida, 'Signature Event Context', 7.

18 This aspect of the performative is taken up by Judith Butler in *Bodies that Matter* to elaborate on the idea that gender identity is not an essentialist or ontological category but is generated as a performative. 'Performativity', says Butler, echoing Derrida's theory, 'is thus not a "singular" act, for it is always a reiteration of a norm or set of norms, and to the extent that it acquires an act-like status in the present, it conceals or dissimulates the conventions of which it is a repetition.' Judith Butler, *Bodies that Matter. On the Discursive Matters of 'Sex'*, New York and London, 1993, 12.

19 See, for example, Eilean Hooper-Greenhill, *Museums and the Shaping of Knowledge*, New York and London, 2001.

20 Bal, *Double Exposures*, 2.

21 I owe this idea of graffiti as wallpaper to Frank Langer.

22 Heinz J. Kuzdas, *Berliner Mauer Kunst/Berlin Wall Art*, Mit East Side Gallery, Berlin, 1998, 16–17; Rainer Hildebrandt, *Die Mauer spricht/The Wall Speaks*, Berlin, 1992, 9–17.

23 Robert Musil, 'Denkmale', in *Nachlass zu Lebzeiten*, Reinbeck bei Hamburg, 1962, 62.

24 Kuzdas, *Berliner Mauer Kunst*, 64.

25 Michel de Certeau, *The Practice of Everyday Life*, Berkeley, CA, 1984, 124 (de Certeau's emphasis).

26 See, for example, *Le mur de Berlin. Vente aux Encheres a monte-Carlo Samedi 23 Juin 1990*, Galerie Park Palace. LeLé Berlin Wall.

27 Angelika von Stocki, *Zerfall der Mauer/Fall of the Wall*, Berlin, 16; Kuzdas, *Berliner Mauer Kunst*, 32, 40, 50.

28 Bal, *Double Exposures*, 57.

# 9

# AESTHETICS OF INTERMEDIALITY

JILL BENNETT

> ... art, too, thinks; it is thought. Not the thought about it, or the thought expressed in it, but visual thought.[1]
>
> Mieke Bal, 1999

## MEDIALITY AND INTERMEDIALITY

For his series *Atomists* (1996), Mexican-born artist Gabriel Orozco over-painted and then digitally enlarged photographs clipped from the sports section of English newspapers (plates 9.1 and 9.2). In a number of these he includes the original photo credits and captions, describing the actions of footballers or other sports stars caught in the frame:

> Asprilla, the Newcastle United substitute, attempts an overhead kick despite the close attention of Calderwood at St James' Park yesterday.

> Ferdinand powers his header past a helpless Ehiogu and Bosnich to clinch a vital victory for Newcastle at St James' Park yesterday.

> Blindside run: Les Ferdinand fails to connect with his head but Darren Anderton ghosts in to open for England.

Orozco captures these moments in the game as a molecular abstract pattern, over-painting a grid of circular and elliptical forms, keyed to the dominant colours of the underlying photograph. This atomistic translation of the image of dynamism, speed and the body in motion conjures an array of art-historical associations (from the geometrics of Russian constructivism to Robert Delaunay's *The Cardiff Team* begun in 1912, as well as the tradition of 'motion study' in photography). Yet these are clearly not scientific inquiries into bio-mechanics, nor do they orient specifically towards painterly or art-historical concerns. Rather than simply rendering the images of athletes in paint, Orozco elaborates the found photographic image, overlaying one form of media with another to trace lines of tension and energetic flows within the image. In doing so he creates cells that serve to frame various details: gestures, points of contact, facial expressions.

The image of the athlete in effect *becomes gestural* in this convergence of media. Bodies engaged in the purposive action of a game are broken into their component parts by the segments and spheres that reframe particular aspects of

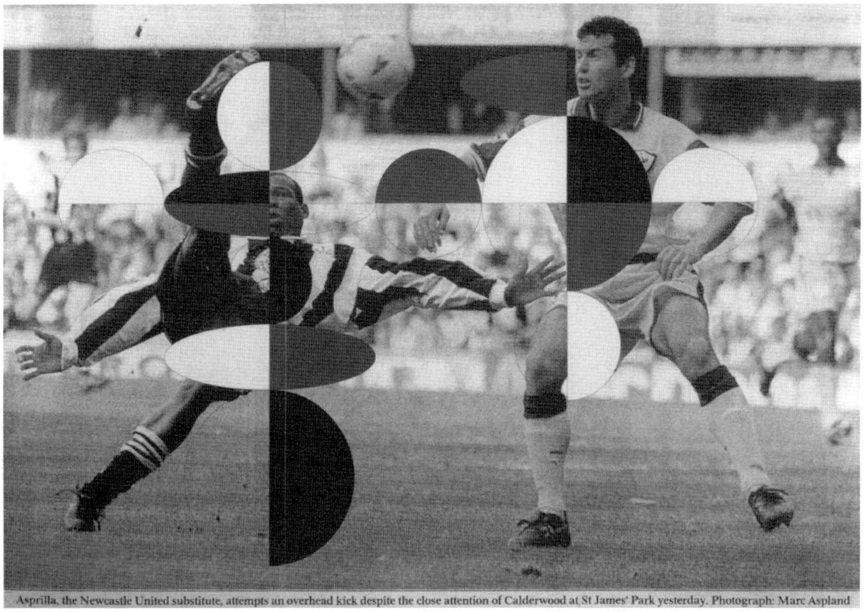


9.1 Gabriel Orozco, *Atomists: Asprilla*, 1996. Two-part computer print, 198.7 × 292.1 cm. Courtesy Marian Goodman Gallery, New York. Photo: Cathy Carver, New York.

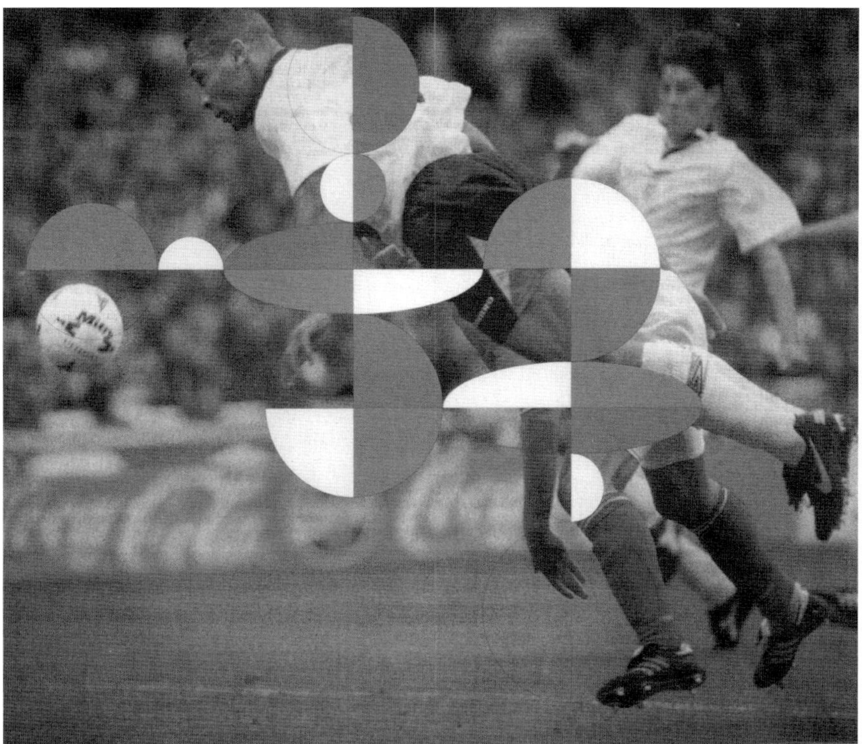


9.2 Gabriel Orozco, *Atomists: Blindside Run*, 1996. Two-part computer print, 198.7 × 292.1 cm. Courtesy Marian Goodman Gallery, New York. Photo: Cathy Carver, New York.

the action as gestures or expressive movements. To highlight the gestural character of action in this way is to view it not as goal-directed but as activity that is inhabited or 'supported', in the sense proposed by Georgio Agamben.[2] For Agamben, an activity that is commonly regarded as a means to an end – he cites porn acting but competitive sport is another example – may be reconfigured in a way that does not deny its function as a means but focuses on 'being-in-a-means'. Gesture is the key figure for this, particularly when it reveals the slippage between an action performed or spoken and the 'inner' sense of this activity, thereby embodying a dialectic between the communicative (externally directed) and the solitary (inwardly felt).[3] In this sense, the incidental gesture that manifests self-consciousness may be seen as a direct expression of its own being-in-a-medium, and thus as a means of deriving a portrait from an action image.

In a more general sense, gesture reveals what Agamben terms 'the media character of corporeal movements'.[4] In doing so, it constitutes corporeal actions – or bodies – as interfaces, engaged in a relational dynamic, whether with an 'interiority', with media proper (film, video, image) or with the larger action that encompasses it (the game, the sex in a porn film). This interface is manifested when gesture is isolated within the image of an action, originally configured as a means; in other words, through an intervention within media.

In this regard, the convergence of media that characterizes the *Atomists* must be understood not simply as a translation of an image into paint, but as an intervention (through painting and digital reproduction) into a wider knowledge nexus. If the *Atomists* evoke bodies and actions as 'medial' in a conceptual sense, the works embody, in the broadest sense, a tendency in contemporary practice to operate *between* media (and between all kinds of semiotic codes). The old descriptors of 'mixed media' and 'appropriation' are inadequate in the characterization of such practice, which is more readily captured by the concept of 'intermedia' – a term which implies more than the internal differentiation or mixing of media that occurs within art itself. Realized as the intersection of different practices, technologies, languages and sign systems, intermediality posits a broad transdisciplinary sphere of operation, open to – but not restricted to – interventions in aesthetic form.

Intermediality, then, is not just an issue of medium; nor can it be confined to semiotic or iconographic operations. One of Orozco's *Atomists*, with the title *Ascention*, plays on an iconographic correspondence, relating a photograph of a rugby union line-out (a formation in which players are held aloft by team members) to the image of the Christ's Ascension into heaven. The joke arising from transposition is a familiar trope of contemporary art. British artist Simon Patterson (best known for his revision of the London Underground map, which he populates with the names of famous people) also conflates football and religion in a wall-drawing of 1990 snappily titled, *The Last Supper Arranged According to the Sweeper Formation (Jesus Christ in Goal)*. Such work clearly plays on the significance attached to the organizational schema. The *Atomists*, however, are concerned less with significations or the associations of particular sign systems, than with the staging of intermedial relationships, and thus with the creation of an 'intermedial aesthetic' per se.

The possibility of an intermedial aesthetic remains a blind-spot for art history, which misses the concept when it reduces the image of the athletes in action to the 'subject matter' of the painter, or when it confines formal analysis to the identification of an artistic lineage. Paradoxically, however, the *Atomists* provide more than ample scope for an art-historical criticism of this nature. Benjamin Buchloh locates the *Atomists* in relation to a rich history of art focused on kinetic movement and the representation of athletic skill, citing orphism, futurism, constructivism and the early modern fascination with athletic performance.[5] Buchloh's account is exemplary and informative art history, well attuned to Orozco's manifest interest in the historical avant garde, but it confines the issue of intermedia to the parameters of fine arts (specifically, to the interrelationship of sculpture–painting–photography), leaving aside the question of how the *Atomists* configure art media within a contemporary cultural formation. Yet amidst the layering of art histories, the *Atomists* register a relationship between quite diverse practices and technologies, orchestrating a biomechanics in painting around sport and print media. The geometric grids painted onto the sporting scenes seem to float somewhere between the underlying photograph and the surface of the image, itself generated through a process of digital remediation, so that painting is, as it were, suspended within the image itself.

A further medium in play in this dynamic is text: the words subtitling the photograph, about which Buchloh is silent. The journalistic captions no doubt resonate more deeply with the sports fan. A Newcastle United supporter (unlike a regular art historian) would derive particular enjoyment from the framing of 'a helpless Ehiogu and Bosnich' or 'the close attention of Calderwood' in a manner informed by – though not reducible to – their earlier viewing of the game, or reading of the sports pages. But the issue here is not whether the art historian's reading should prevail over the popular cultural reading; notwithstanding one's orientation towards either art or football, the inclusion of a caption locates the aesthetic operation not just with one supervening discourse but somewhere within the triangulation of painting, sporting image and text. *Asprilla* presents movements, gestures and affects combining in the event of the overhead kick. The caption keys us to the portrait of 'close attention', much as the word 'concentration' resonates with the image of a snooker player in an *Atomist* captioned 'Griffiths, who now needs spectacles, gives a testing shot complete concentration.' These images are not 'about' attention or concentration, any more than they are about sport; rather, these words, clipped and quoted in such a way as to bracket their discursive or idiomatic status, are linguistic elements in play, bouncing off the segmented visual components (Griffiths's one bespectacled eye; Calderwood's relaxed hand in its circular frame; Bosnich's 'helpless' startled face watching the ball head into the goal).

The wit of the *Atomists* derives in part from the extent to which the serviceable text of the sub-editor is drawn into an interactive poetics with the image above. The segmentation of pictorial elements in the frozen tableau has the effect of amplifying certain descriptors in the text, so that captions, economically penned to capture the action in its entirety, give rise to abstractions; conceptualizations of elusive actions or expressions such as 'failing to connect' and 'ghosting in'.

Words, then, are operative elements in the generation of a conception of movement, dynamism and interaction, though it is the medial rather than signifying function of signs that is highlighted. The *Atomists* do not decontextualize signs; rather, elements or details of the image are transformed as they are framed within – and in relationship to – media. In other words, the *Atomists* do not complete an intersemiotic translation – a movement from one sign system to another, such that signs are now open to a reading within another organized structure (the protagonists of the Last Supper, turned footballers, in the 'sweeper' formation). Instead, movements, gestures and words are, in the terminology of Agamben, 'suspended in and by their own mediality'.[6]

The exploration of mediality in this sense implies more than – the opposite of – a focus on medium or mediation, since it reveals the condition of being-in-a-medium, or of inhabiting actions that are generally viewed as a means, like the (literally) goal-directed activity of a football match. For Agamben (as for Orozco), gesture constitutes the exhibition of a mediality. It is neither the means of addressing an end, nor an end in itself (a purely aesthetic form) but 'the process of making a means visible'.[7] Hence, Asprilla's attempt at the overhead kick is not shown as the means of gaining possession of the ball, and is set against, rather than transformed into, an abstract pattern. Through the convergence of the gridded molecular patterns, action photograph and caption, the action of and around the kick is presented as a matrix of gesture, expression and affect. The effect of such a capture is to refigure the sign to reveal, in the first order, its medial dynamics, and the media character of corporeal movements, rather than its signifying or instrumental function. It is to ask, in Agamben's formulation, not what is being produced or acted but 'in what way is an action endured and supported?'[8] It is in this particular sense that I invoke the term [inter]mediality to describe not just the literal intersection of media but the inquiry focused on – and conducted through – medial relationships or mediality itself.

## CULTURAL STUDIES WITHOUT WORDS

The *Atomists* effect a 'visual cultural' study without words. Operating at the intersection of different discourses, practices and aesthetics, these images constitute an intermedial space through which new ways of seeing and new terms for analysis can emerge. In this regard, the *Atomists* are emblematic of a mode of contemporary art practice that, by its very interdisciplinary constitution, sits within a visual cultural paradigm. That is to say, the work's theoretical counterpart may be understood as an art theory that formulates itself within the expanded field of cultural studies.

In spite of the emergence of visual culture studies as a multifarious practice, operating beyond the boundaries of art history, leading voices allied with both visual culture (Mieke Bal) and the broader field of cultural theory (Brian Massumi) continue to argue that cultural studies has missed expression (Massumi) in critical ways, too readily confining itself to a bounded domain of popular culture that effectively excludes art and analysis of its particular modes of operation (Bal).[9] In this sense it does not take up the challenge of describing an intermedial aesthetic as this is embodied in contemporary art practice. In this essay I situate these theorists and others in relation to both current trends in practice and a mode of art analysis undertaken in a broader interdisciplinary field, going back to Aby Warburg.

I am not interested here in the turf war between art history and visual culture, for, as Bal has shown, the discussion of disciplinary demarcation is a futile diversion; methodology is the substantive issue. Thus, I seek to account for the elements of a visual cultural method that is equal to the task of extending an aesthetics of intermediality. These elements may be distinguished in terms of three interlocking concepts: 'whole-field analysis', 'co-production' and 'differential', through which a fourth, 'visual thought' – conceived by Bal as a constitutive feature of art – may be extended.

## WHOLE-FIELD ANALYSIS

The concept of a 'whole-field' operation emerges in Brian Massumi's critique of cultural studies as a defining feature of a practice that cuts across disciplinary boundaries and divisions between 'high' and popular culture.[10] In contrast to the discipline that defines its parameters in terms of a specific group of either objects or subjects, an interdisciplinary cultural studies engages what Massumi calls 'whole-field modulation'. The 'whole field' in this sense is not a substantive concept that lays claim to a particular terrain, but a description of the potentially unlimited arena of a practice that relinquishes the need to predetermine its object domain.

Nevertheless, Massumi argues, this cultural studies does not exist, except as a potentiality. The reason for this is that cultural studies, in its current institutional formation, has missed two key concepts: process and expression. It clings to the notion that 'expression is of a particularity'; in other words, it treats expression as an attribute or property of a predefined group of persons (a culture, a sub-culture, a gender, a minority).[11] In doing so, it fails to actualize in its own more radical terms, veering back towards sociology or social policy studies. Rather than practising intervention within an expanded field, it turns to regulation and reform. On this basis, *visual* cultural studies may be readily aligned to the study of popular culture, and art (and its formal analysis) ceded to art history. Art may be embraced by visual culture studies by virtue of its content, context of production or the cultural identity of its producers. But aesthetics – the dynamics of form – is not prima facie the business of visual culture studies, if and when it exhibits the limitations ascribed by Massumi to cultural studies.

The concepts of process and expression to which Massumi alludes are methodologically allied to whole-field modulation in as much as they describe the dynamics of cultural forms, insisting on a focus on movement and transition (the behaviour of aesthetic entities) rather than on their classification (the definition and qualification of an object as art or popular culture). What, then, might a visual cultural analysis in these terms look like? And how can art figure in an analysis that traces process lines running through a range of disciplines and practices? If analysis is not circumscribed by classifications of discipline, genre or iconography, how is the 'line through' characterized?

Aby Warburg stands out as a pioneer of whole-field analysis, exemplifying the methodological embodiment of the concepts of both visual thought and co-production. Warburg's key work in this regard is *Mnemosyne*, the atlas, compiled between 1924 and 1929.[12] The atlas was, for Warburg, a means of doing art history without words – performing image analysis through montage and recombination. *Mnemosyne* is constituted from the large panels, stretched with black cloth, on which Warburg arranged images from disparate sources: photographs of classical statuary, news clippings, magazine advertisements, maps and amateur snaps, which were then rephotographed. Like Orozco, Warburg finds formal resonances linking certain sporting images to painterly and sculptural compositions (on one panel two images of golfers in mid-swing are juxtaposed with an image of Judith holding the head of Holofernes, as well as several advertising images and classical seals).[13] But *Mnemosyne* is not an art work, nor even a finished object. Having been subject to continual modification by Warburg, it is best understood as the embodiment of a method: a means of studying the internal dynamics of imagery, and the ways in which formulas emerged in different contexts and periods in history.

Central to Warburg's method was the idea that pictorial forces were at work across a wide-open field. Thus he insisted that the analysis of art – of aesthetic form in a given medium – could not be undertaken without exceeding the borders of art history; that it must entail a kind of geography of a vast field of visual imagery. The atlas was in this regard 'an instrument of orientation', tracking the emergence of figures at different points in a history of representation and tracing their migration into different cultural domains, areas of knowledge, genres and media.[14]

For Warburg, *Mnemosyne* was a psychological study, rather than one that is art-historical in the pure sense; it might now be routinely classified under the rubric of visual culture studies, but for the fact that its inquiry is closely focused on aesthetic principles. Those who persist in defining visual culture as art history's other, as the study of culture excluded by the 'high art' cannon, might find *Mnemosyne* disappointingly orthodox in its disproportionate focus on classicism. Yet, its radical nature lies precisely in the fact that it constitutes its domain as the whole field of culture. Thus, it cannot be defined through delineation of a group of material objects. It enshrines a practice that is no longer the study of art per se, but the study of dynamic principles within imagery.

The precise terms of analysis emerge in the execution as sets of relations cohere around the dynamics of gesture, and affect. These terms arise from the recombination and reframing of pictorial elements, not by virtue of their iconographic significance, but through the dynamics of interaction. Warburg, as Georges Didi-Huberman notes, did not strive to 'create a structure out of iconographic detail':

> Instead he would discern suddenly a formal line of tension, a sort of symmetry in movement line, sinuous or broken with the alternately slackening or coiling body. Dancing or explosive, yet ever present in the very crux of the gestural chaos distributed by each part of its ungraspable geometry.[15]

His method entailed the identification of 'formal pivots' (in Didi-Huberman's term) – the hinges around which the internal dynamics of an image are organized. Orozco's *Atomists* work in similar fashion; geometry, introduced as a distinctive and separate semiotic code, is not a 'graspable' totalizing schema, but a visual method for identifying pivots. If the *Atomists* transform the sports image into a study of gesture and expression, then expression and gesture are not merely semantic or iconographic categories, nor individual properties, but revealed as formal components in a pictorial dynamic. This dynamic has both a critical and cultural dimension in so far as gesture is understood as exposing action as it is inhabited in a given site. For the same reason, Agamben notes that *Mnemosyne* was 'historical' precisely through its capacity for transforming the image:

> Because of the fact that this research was conducted through the medium of images, it was believed that the image was also its object. Warburg instead transformed the image into a decisively historical and dynamic element.[16]

Hence, *Mnemosyne* is in part a study of the elements of portraiture as they emerge at a particular historical or cultural juncture. One panel of the atlas features a fifteenth-century Florentine altarpiece by Domenico Ghirlandaio, from which the figures of the patron Franceso Sassetti and his circle are clipped and included as separate details (plate 9.3). This extraction has the effect of highlighting the entry of the contemporary portrait into the religious scene, and the means by which figures are characterized and rendered expressive. 'Attentiveness' becomes a focus in its own right as a feature of the supplicant figures. Like some of Orozco's *Atomists* that highlight the expression – or what certain psychologists classify as the affect[17] – of interest (concentration, attention), this reframing of elements from a larger pictorial structure functions to suspend gesture (and its dimensions of expression and movement) within the context of the medium. This is the mode of analysis that Agamben identifies as operating through the reduction of works to the sphere of gesture, a sphere which lies 'beyond interpretation'; in other words, a level of analysis that cuts across signification or iconographic meaning, while at the same time tracing the emergence of cultural forms, the dynamics of which are constituted within the image.[18]

That a contemporary artist like Orozco would turn his attention to the sports photograph is not surprising in an era where the technical imagining of the athlete in motion has become so advanced as to constitute a mode of portraiture in itself. Interactive television now allows us to select a point of view on a football match, or a player on which to focus, and replays in *super slow-mo* reveal the muscle contractions generating specific movments. In 2006 video artists Philippe Parreno and Douglas Gordon premiered *Zidane: a Portrait of the Twenty-First Century* at Cannes, described as 'a portrait on film, in action and in real time, of one of the greatest players in the history of soccer, Zinédine Zidane' (plate 9.4). Filmed with seventeen synchronized cameras, each focusing (almost exclusively) on Zidane throughout the entire course of a Spanish premier league match, the film is presented as 'a unique endeavor midway between the work of a portrait artist and a high action movie for a broad viewing public'.[19] The elements of a portrait (gesture, expression, affect) are, in other words, found within the very space of sport (the stadium in the real-time of a game), bracketed as a study in concentration and movement.

For the full ninety minutes of the game the cameras follow the trajectory of the body in motion, breaking into details: the soles of Zidane's feet crunching

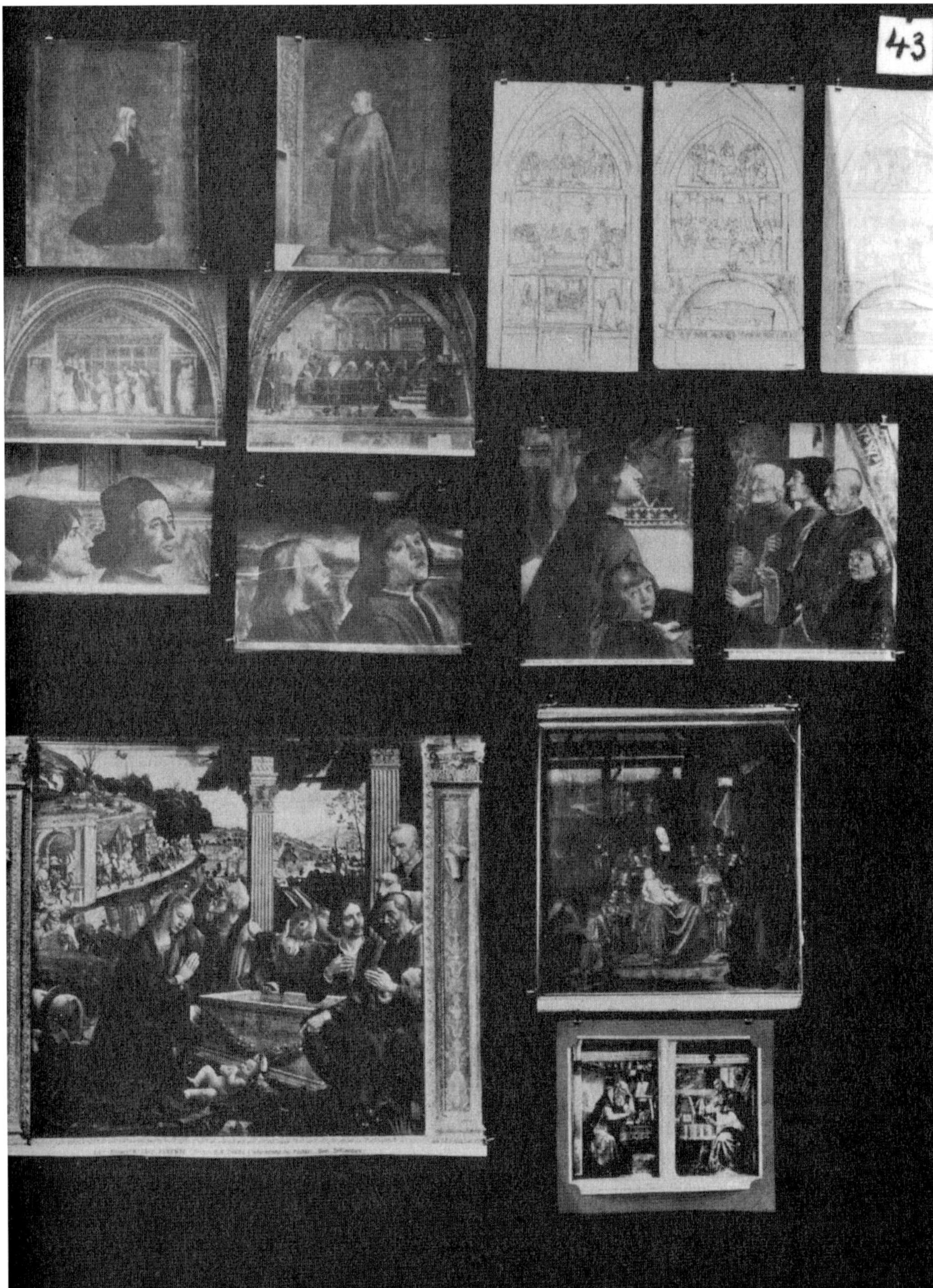


9.3 Aby Warburg, *Mnemosyne*, (panel 43: the Sassetti Chapel) 1924–29. Photograph courtesy the Warburg Institute, London.

the grass, his relaxed arm and straight back as he runs, his attentive eyes, his smile. Zidane watches the game incessantly as the viewer watches him. As critics have noted, by means of this intense focus on a single player, the film offers a study of a 'man at work', an *ouvrier*.[20] Work, however, is described through interaction and response, registered in movement, gesture, affect and expression. The absence of the whole narrative and whole-game perspective transforms Zidane into the image of the hyper-responsive figure. Every action – from intense concentration and scrutiny to explosive intervention – is keyed to the game, and to largely off-screen action.

The exclusive focus on the single player functions as a constraint, which in turn dictates a pace and rhythm determined by Zidane himself as he moves through phases of relaxed concentration, coiled energy and explosive bursts of activity, and occasionally of emotion. If (as Agamben suggests) gesture registers a tension or dialectic between the solitary and the communicative,[21] such that it expresses precisely the experience of 'being in' an interaction – rather than simply the articulated communication – then *Zidane* is poised exactly at this interface. Rather than constructing an external (or completely internal) perspective onto the spectacle of the game, or presenting movement and expression as a means to an end, it simply follows the single strand weaving through a game, registering various points of connection and contact along the way.

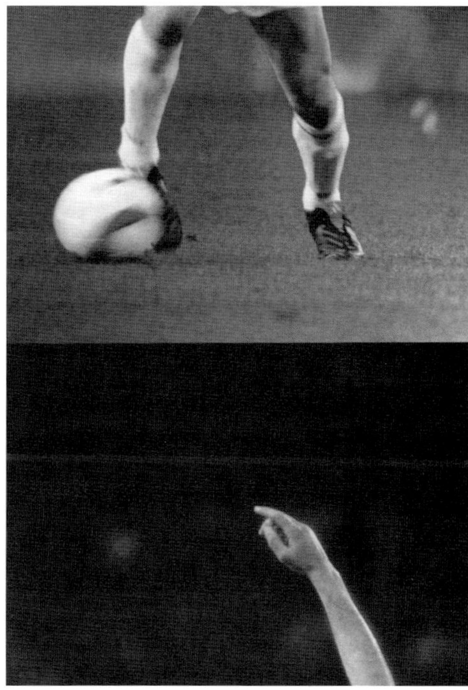

9.4 Douglas Gordon and Philippe Parreno, *Zidane: a Portrait of the Twenty-First Century*, 2006. Stills from 90-minute video. Courtesy Artificial Eye Film Company.

A similar logic, and effect, is pursued even more starkly by South African-born video artist Candice Breitz, in whose *Soliloquy Trilogy* protagonists of three well-known Hollywood movies are cut away from the scenes that make the narrative legible (plate 9.5). Dropping in a monochrome black screen (the digital filmic version of the atlas panel screens), Breitz recompiles clips of these characters speaking, though now without evidence of others present in conversations, with the effect that every word, sound and gesture acquires a prominence and intensity. With no context to absorb or make sense of a (corporeal or verbal) gesture, the soliloquy intensifies into a spiralling word flow. As Marcella Baccaria has noted, language loses not just its external context but its 'transcendental angst and inner necessity', taking on an almost psychotic quality as it degenerates into solipsistic babble.[22] No longer psychological, spoken language becomes (as Beccaria puts it) 'solidified matter' (much as the captions of

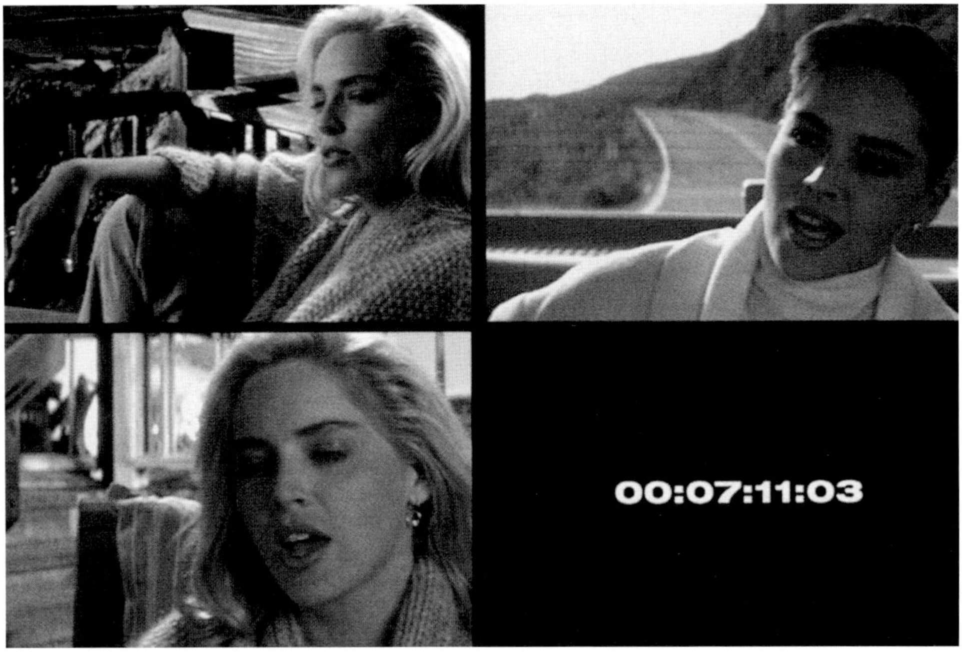


9.5 Detail of Candice Breitz, *Soliloquy (Sharon)*, 1992–2000. Film on DVD. Courtesy White Cube, London and Francesca Kaufmann, Milan.

the *Atomists* acquire a material dimension). Speech runs on relentlessly, unable to flow through the normal communication channels that articulate it into conversation and feedback. It registers as pure intensity: affect characterized by urgency and lack of attachment, disarticulated from motives or drives. In this sense its performance is literally captured in its own mediality.

Overtly, *Zidane* is a study of the dynamics of movement and gesture, though in this instance – as in *Mnemosyne* – gesture is conceived less as subject matter than as method. As has been widely reported, on the morning of the shoot/match Gordon and Parreno took their film crew (whose combined experience ranged from Martin Scorsese films to National Football League events) to the Prado to look at the portraits of Goya and Velazquez. If these were to serve as models for the creation of the portrait of the twenty-first century, it is not in the manner of direct reference but in the mode of visual thought that Bal characterizes in the book, which, more than any other, identifies this form of transhistorical relationship, *Quoting Caravaggio*. Put another way, they served as a way of identifying – seeing, understanding, modulating – the gestural components of a portrait, conceived in terms of its emergence in the modern arena, forged from a conflation of representational codes, and designed and executed by the subject in collusion with the film-makers.

## THE CO-PRODUCTION OF ANALYSIS

At the heart of this intermedial constitution of a portrait, as in Warburg's study of the Renaissance portrait, is a conception of co-production, operating at a number of levels: between artist and subject (both with a particular relationship to the medium); between artist and art theorist; between the art work and the interdisciplinary knowledge nexus in which it is created. This notion describes, but is not reducible to, intersubjective relations, but it emerges from the very logic of cultural studies, conceived as true interdisciplinarity. Hence, Bal concludes her methodological argument in these terms:

> Neither the boundary between 'high' and 'popular' culture can be maintained, nor that between visual production and its study. If the object co-performs the analysis [...] then creating and policing boundaries of any sort seems the most futile of all futilities that academic work can engage in.[23]

In the absence of a consensus about what constitutes the object domain of visual culture, we are, Bal infers, in the realm of the interdisciplinary. The error, then, is 'to persist in [the separatist project of] defining'. The challenge is to negotiate the apparently contradictory demands of a field that cannot be defined in terms of a unified object domain but at the same time derives its ideas, methods and concepts from its objects. If the aesthetic can no longer be located through the classification of an object domain, it must be traced through the distinctive operations of images inhabiting the interdisciplinary field. Its object is, to borrow Philippe-Alain Michaud's description of Warburg's proposition, the 'image in motion'.[24]

Co-performance, in Bal's sense, can be conceived as the co-production of an object of study. As Bal reminds us, Roland Barthes distinguished interdisciplinary practice from multidisciplinarity on the basis that it is no longer a question of lots of people from different disciplinary perspectives looking at the same objects, but rather the creation of a new object.[25] The object that emerges from the interdisciplinary nexus is, of course, not simply a material object but a conceptual one: an object of knowledge that comes into being through the enmeshed practice of philosophy, art, literature, cultural studies, anthropology and so on. This is the hybrid object described by Bruno Latour as calling for a new methodology in the philosophy of knowledge.[26]

Interdisciplinarity is, for Latour, axiomatic since knowledge can no longer be considered the product of a pure science. Typically, he argues, a newspaper article on the ozone layer will feature the voices and concepts of industrialists, chemists, politicians, ecologists, perhaps not fully commensurable but somehow caught up in the same story, linked by a single thread. Newspapers are full of 'hybrid articles that sketch out imbroglios of science, politics, economy, law, religion, technology, fiction',[27] churning up all of culture and all of nature so that even the most fundamental distinctions in the philosophy of knowledge (like nature – culture) are compromised. If ideas come from amalgams, philosophers must attend to the crossings and meetings between disciplines or languages, and to the way that a knowledge matrix works. This, Latour argues, is best understood in terms of a network: 'more supple than the notion of a system, more historical than the notion of structure, more empirical than the notion of complexity, the idea of network is the Ariadne's thread of these interwoven stories.'[28] Since discussions of scientific phenomena can no longer be assimilated in specific disciplines, the analytic methods of a single discipline are inadequate in isolation; the philosopher must follow the imbroglios wherever they lead, shuttling back and forth within a network of ideas.

The 'object' of knowledge in this sense is not the pre-given object of the discipline of philosophy of science, since it is necessarily the emergent or 'becoming' object of interdisciplinary production: the amalgam, hybrid, or Bal's 'travelling concept',[29] made up of the threads of distinct practices and modes of understanding, which can only be expressed in terms of their connectivity or symbiosis. These interweaving threads may be distinguished as differently behaving components of an amalgam but not as separable disciplinary perspectives on an object. Thus, visual thought (a particular behaviour) is located within cultural studies only when symbiosis is articulated in its full aesthetic dimension.

## DIFFERENTIAL

> One process line cannot judge another. Process lines can interfere with each other. They can modulate each other. They can capture each other's effects and convert them into more of their own. But they cannot judge each other because they are immersed in the empirical field, not 'reflections' of it.[30]

The intersection of art and other discourse may be conceived as a production born of the slippages that occur when different practices encounter one another and start to 'speak' from the same field of operation. The field, constituted through intermedial relationships, is contingent and unnamed; it is the space of the differential. The term differential has a currency in media studies where it describes (in Andrew Murphie's definition) 'cultures and technologies that are based upon the in-between, that is, difference in itself'.[31] Difference in this sense is a constitutive force functioning to create intermedial environments in a context where media are no longer bound forms (film, television) or genres (television drama, news or sports coverage), but constantly differentiate themselves.[32]

Agamben tellingly refers to Warburg's project as the 'discipline that exists but has no name'.[33] This 'nameless science' was variously described by Warburg in terms that convey the sweep of cultural studies: a 'history of the psyche', a 'history or culture'; and in more precise methodological or processual terms as an 'iconology of the intervals', evoking not so much an object of study as the relational space between that comes into being in the collage of the atlas, and the means by which the object of knowledge is created.

*Mnemosyne* is itself an active production instantiating an intermedial or transdisciplinary arena. As Michaud emphasizes, it

> does not limit itself to describing the migrations of images through the history of representations; it reproduces them. In this sense, it is based on a cinematic mode of thought [the reproductions of paintings and sculpture that comprise *Mnemosyne* are treated as film stills, argues Agamben], one that aims not at articulating means but at producing effects.[34]

This, then, is both a thinking cinematically or thinking visually, and a co-production in which Warburg uses ('abductively', as Bal might say)[35] imagery to create a new effect.

Warburg is by practice a co-producer, an art historian deriving a conception of history from found images and reproductions. As Kurt Forster first noted, Warburg's sense of the production of art was profoundly collaborative, in so far as he regarded the emergence of secular portraiture not as an artistic phenomenon but as the result of the relationship between artist and patron, and hence as linked to broader cultural shifts.[36] Indeed, Latour's imagery of the network spun from threads (which are traced rather than disentangled by the cultural analyst) finds resonance in Forster's metaphorics when he describes Warburg's own written analysis of Domenico Ghirlandaio's portraits:

> Warburg inlays the threads of an essentially pre-photographic, verbal replication of the paintings with the strong yarn of his own concerns. He works them into an interpretation that entangles conflicts [...] But he unites the weave and the inlay by transforming the ostensibly self-sufficient, purely aesthetic character of the work of art – as caught in the web of his own enchanting description – into 'something quite different'. And this 'something quite different', which transcends the purely visual substance of the work, is not of the artist's devising, or of the beholder's, but derives solely from the effort of understanding that Warburg demands of his cultural studies. What is quite different is the recognition that works of art are 'documents' that bear a special charge.[37]

Cultural analysis thus engages the 'thought' inherent in aesthetic production. The 'effort of understanding' is itself an aesthetic (rather than interpretive) operation in the first instance, grounded in the double action of the reduction to gesture and the constitution of the interval as a space for the re-emergence and activation of pictorial forces. It is through the interval, conceived as differential, that Warburg generates an understanding of the gesture/image within an historical dynamic. For him, the differential is a space of return, the site at which a latent cultural memory resurfaces in a gestural dynamics. The gesture is itself 'intended as a crystal of historical memory',[38] so that its irruptions, plotted in the differential spaces of the atlas, act as coordinates for the tracing of process lines along a continuum or 'vectors of exchange between heterogeneous spaces and times'.[39] Warburg's 'cultural studies' is, then, the expression of the process line – of an historical and cultural dynamic – as visual thought.

This line, characterized by symbiosis, does not, of course, plot the re-emergence of an unchanged form. The concept of gesture as always embodying a differential leads towards the notion of media as an interface, folding out into new relationships.

## THE EFFORT OF THINKING VISUALLY

Thus, gesture (or 'gestural criticism') is a means of investigating media itself. Media art opens up such a critical engagement when it promotes looking *through,* rather than looking at gesture. The *T-Visionarium* project is archetypical in this regard, furnishing an apparatus for a co-produced criticism (plate 9.6). *T-Visionarium* is a differential structure without predetermined content, an interactive immersive environment that allows viewers to navigate spatially a vast televisual database. Produced by a team of artists, critics and programmers, under the auspices of iCinema, this apparatus functions as an instrument of orientation: an atlas of the digital televisual domain.[40]

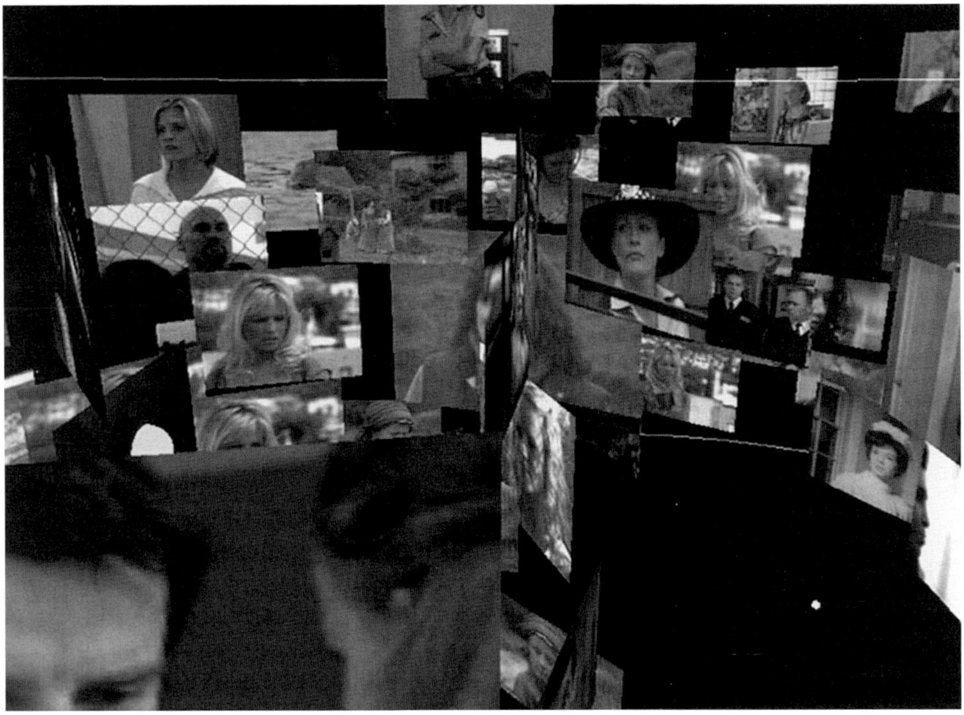

9.6 iCinema, *T-Visionarium*, 2006. Interactive immersive environment. Courtesy iCinema.

*T-Visionarium* engenders both art and criticism, though resists classification in either category. As a result, viewers and critics may have problems conceptualizing their role in the *T-Visionarium* environment. It is certainly 'user-friendly' – spectacular and quite easy to navigate – but the constitution of the virtual atlas is the viewer's prerogative; aesthetic selections must be continually re-made. It is, in essence, a project without an object that forces users to address it as mediality, and to think and do co-production.

The second phase of *T-Visionarium*, premiered in 2006, comprises sixty-four separate video recordings, viewed on 'windows' (rectangular surfaces) positioned in three-dimensional space. The viewer wanders freely in the darkness of the room, experiencing the spectacle in three dimensions of two hundred floating windows, each playing footage recorded from network television. Equipped with a remote control, the viewer may click on any single image to trigger a sort of all sixty-four windows according to type. Each of the (22,636) segments making up the footage has been tagged according to the degree that it exhibits various kinds of emotion, expressive behaviour, physical behaviour, or spatial and structural characteristics, and also whether it contains male or female characters. The values assigned to each shot are used as the basis for the distribution, along with automatically detected similarities of colour and movement. Thus, if a viewer selects a close-up of a woman speaking on the phone in the bluish light of a television morgue, a flood of images with similar colour values and formal or dynamic properties fly across to the area around the chosen image. The most dissimilar images move to the spaces furthest away – so that all the images facing the viewer will likely be of women, and those on the opposite wall of men. Whereas some of the images in the cluster will be of people holding phones, in others the gesture may correspond in a looser way to that of the figure with the telephone (holding a cup to the mouth, for example), or may exhibit only colour or movement similarities. Footage is broken into segments, averaging four seconds long, which loop continually until a further selection is made. The viewer may double-click on a chosen screen to elect to play the footage on that screen in full (for around thirty minutes). When such a selection is made the remaining windows freeze into silent stills, catching the resonant gestures and movements in midstream.

The experience of these images is both visual and auditory and part of the interest emerges from the mismatch or crossover of soundtracks. While words are often emphatic elements, their syntax and dialogic context are rarely, if ever, preserved in these brief clips. Dialogues are transformed into fragmentary monologues, sounds and gestures, stripped of their communicative function. The viewer cannot 'interpret' these gestures, other than in reference to the correlative movements that surround them. *T-Visionarium* is, thus, radically synchronic. Fragments of conversation are re-absorbed immediately into the synchronic arrangement, configured in a variety of new relationships based in shared movements and affects, rather than in the logic of dialogue. This process of recombination tends to mitigate any sense that these are truncated or incomplete actions in need of extension or a response. Seen in this format, corporeal and verbal gestures no longer appear as the tools of interpersonal communication or as properties of the individual, because the overriding impression is one of gestural echo, or of the migration of affect and gesture across the medium.

Again, this effect is crystallized by Breitz. In the companion works *Mother* and *Father* six Hollywood stars perform motherhood, and a further six fatherhood in a separate ensemble (plate 9.7). Extracted from their respective movies and re-assembled twitching and fidgeting against a black backdrop, the actors' incidental gestures of distress, betrayal, self-pity and loss of esteem are transformed

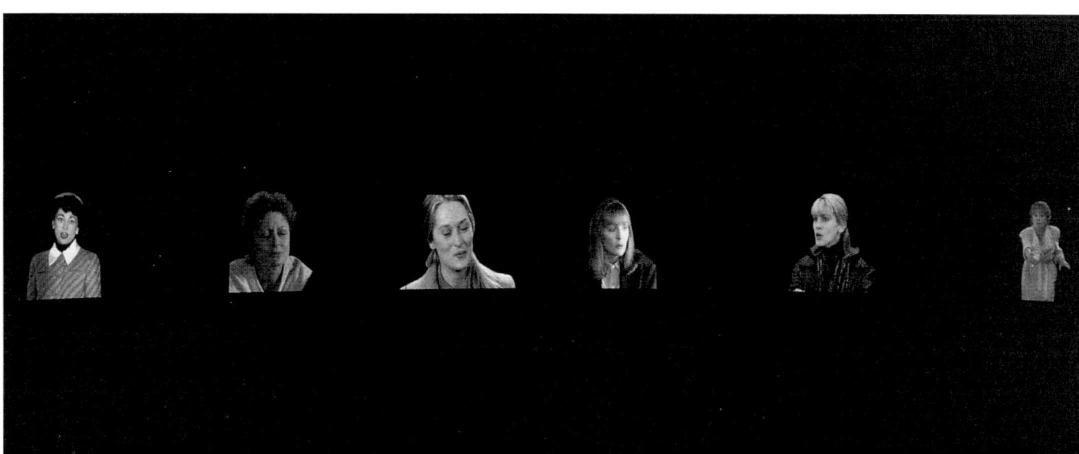

9.7 Candice Breitz, *Mother*, 2005. Video Installation. Courtesy White Cube, London and Francesca Kaufmann, Milan.

from 'meaningful' expressions into displaced symptoms. Julia Roberts's eye roll, stripped of context, and repeated with a digital twitch, looks hysterical, and when orchestrated with gestural sequences, performed in similar isolation on the other five screens, appears contagious. Breitz's characters do not converse or interact but perform gestures directed outward, towards the viewer; for want of a reverse-shot, the logic of conversation operates at the level of gestural echo, across a horizontal plane.

In turning this methodology over to the spectator, *T-Visionarium* reveals, simultaneously, how homogenous, yet radically impure and hybrid television is. *T-Visionarium* combines the full range of free-to-air television screened over an eleven-day period in the peak-hour evening slots (which includes news and current affairs and the odd feature film), within which there is a marked prevalence of drama, principally US crime drama: *Law and Order, CSI, Cold Case, Without a Trace*. As a mediascape it is marked by the economy of gesture and movement that characterizes such drama. Headshots and dialogue prevail. There are very few panoramic shots (except in occasional frames from feature films or news footage) or full-body gestures.

There are few silences. Characters seem to talk most of the time, or, failing this, to generate some form of noise (breathing, panting, sighing). An occasional musical score will waft across from one window to another, impressing itself onto the conversation, much as the diegetic sound of *Zidane* (featuring sounds of the game and the stadium) fuses with the soundtrack provided by the band Mogwai. This impure, transient, intermedial space thus seems always to exist already in media – not just in a specific but a general sense. Every mix is already envisaged by the medium.

*T-Visionarium* is not about television in the same way that *Mnemosyne* is not about art objects – though it uncovers a televisual vocabulary of gesture. Agamben argues that in the early modern period gesture migrated from everyday life into the domain of cinema. Hence, much like Warburg's atlas, early cinema has its centre in gesture and not in the image. Television, ostensibly, has its centre not in the grandiloquent full-body gestures of early silent movies, but in the restrictive close-up (which registers facial affect and micro gestures), and in the performance of dialogue. Its gestural dimension is reclaimed from dialogue once the medium is reconfigured – through a new technological aesthetics – and made to display its own media character in a changing set of relationships.

Similarly, if the portrait has now migrated to the cinematic domain of sport, where technology reconstitutes it (via Goya, Velázquez and the action movie) through the expansive full-body spectacle, what enables this is the possibility of registering the body within media in its gestural dimension. Hence, Zidane is not a narrative portrait but a genuinely cinematic – or more accurately, intermedial – one.

## TRANSITIVE VERBS: INCOMPLETE CONVERSATIONS

The striking feature of Candice Breitz's aesthetic, as well as of *T-Visionarium* and *Zidane*, is the degree to which the truncating of a conversation or an action focused on another does not register as a loss. Gestural activity without an object is rapidly redistributed across new sets of relations.

Orozco's frozen action gestures and expressions are suspended in a way that brackets them from their objects (which are still visible in the larger frame but no longer figured as the end point of activity). They are like transitive verbs that remain incomplete for want of a direct object (a footballer 'attends . . .'). Zidane, in Gordon and Parreno's film, is often performing in relation to an absent or off-screen focus. Yet in these instances, the whole body in its multiple relationships is the site of expression; technologies converge to frame each aspect of movement and engagement, so that it becomes gestural rather than communicative or directed towards an end.

In a sense, the portrait – the close-up, registering the detail of expression – is written onto the body of the performing athlete in the intermedial space. Yet, it is not configured as a face or an identity. In *Zidane* it is constituted as a continuum, a dynamic trajectory in space and time, subject to interconnection and modes of contact that engage different aspects of the body, at points along the way. The body is fragmented into multiple frames, multiple gestures (as in the *Atomists*); gesture is itself intermedial.

Breitz's movie stars and the athletes of the *Atomists* and *Zidane* should not be reduced to studies of the iconic celebrity forms of the times, and they are certainly not critiques of 'media constructions'. They create a zone between the celebrity 'bio-pic' and a tradition of semiotic media analysis in which technologies can claim the portrait in the form of the image in motion: the full-body performance of concentration, attention, engagement, interaction. Here the corporeal body's media character is neither denied nor presented as its determining feature; it is, however, inhabited. The contemporary portrait, in this sense, can only emerge in the dimension of 'being-in-a-medium'. The portrait is the effect of showing how a body endures an activity, broken into gestural components, which exhibit the interface between body and action. This is not, of course, to argue that the subjectivity of the one who sustains the gesture is at stake; rather that media should be understood through its interfaces, and the slippages that characterize intersections. Gesture, as 'the process of making a means visible' – and as the indication of a body–media dialectic or interface – is the manifestation of slippage.

As Bal has long argued, to fetishize popular cultural content (rather than to treat it as part of an expressive continuum) under the rubric of visual culture studies is to reduce the field to its most banal constitution. It is to 'miss process' and to miss the forms of expression that characterize the whole field of contemporary culture and intermedia – and that ultimately reveal how media relations operate. I have indicated here that it is a mistake to reduce method to content. Gesture is an operative concept: a mode of criticism or thinking visually that is fundamentally relational and intermedial. Rather than carving up the object domain, we might simply allow that the media character of a given object is revealed, as it moves, in slippages and interactions. For this reason we need to follow it wherever it leads.

## Notes

1 Mieke Bal, *Quoting Caravaggio*, Chicago, 1999, 117.

2 Georgio Agamben, 'Notes on Gesture', *Means Without End*, trans. Vincenzo Binetti and Cesare Casarino, Minneapolis, 2000, 49–59.

3 For an explication of the 'dialectic of gesture', see Georgio Agamben, 'Kommerell, or On Gesture', *Potentialities*, trans. Daniel Heller-Roazen, Stanford, 1999, 77–85; also Jill Bennett,

'A Feeling of Insincerity: Politics, Ventriloquy and the Dialectics of Gesture', in *The Rhetoric of Sincerity*, eds. Ernst Van Alphen, Mieke Bal and Carel Smith, Stanford, forthcoming.

4 Agamben, 'Notes on Gesture', 49–59, 58.

5 Benjamin Buchloh, 'Cosmic Reification: Gabriel Orozco's Photographs', in *Gabriel Orozco*, London and Cologne, 2004, 75–96.

6 Agamben, 'Notes on Gesture', 58.

7 Agamben, 'Notes on Gesture', 58.

8 Agamben, 'Notes on Gesture', 57.

9 Brian Massumi, *Parables for the Virtual: Movement, Affect, Sensation*, Durham and London, 2002; Mieke Bal, 'Visual Essentialism and the Object of Visual Culture', *Journal of Visual Culture*, 2:1, 2003, 5–32.

10 Massumi, *Parables*, 253–4.

11 Massumi, *Parables*, 253.

12 Archive of the Warburg Institute, London. For a recent edition, see Aby Warburg, *Mnemosyne: l'Atlante delle immagini*, ed. Martin Warnke, Turin, 2002.

13 See Philippe-Alain Michaud, *Aby Warburg and the Image in Motion*, trans. Sophie Hawkes, New York, 2004, 263.

14 Michaud, *Aby Warburg*, 277.

15 Georges Didi-Huberman, 'Dialektik des Monstrums: Aby Warburg and the symptom paradigm', *Art History*, 24:5, 2001, 621–45, 637.

16 Agamben, 'Notes on Gesture'. 54.

17 See Silvan S. Tomkins, *Affect Imagery Consciousness, Vol 1: The Positive Affects*, New York, 2004.

18 Agamben, 'Kommerell', 80.

19 http://www.festival-cannes.fr/films/fiche_film.php?langue=6002&id_film=4359365 (accessed 3 September 2006).

20 See Michael Fried and Tim Griffin, 'Douglas Gordon and Philippe Parreno's *Zidane: a Portrait of the Twenty-First Century*', *Artforum*, 45:1, 2006, 332–9.

21 See Agamben, 'Kommerell'.

22 Marcella Beccaria, 'Process and Meaning in the Art of Candice Breitz', in *Candice Breitz*, Turin, 2005, 19–81, 43.

23 Bal, 'Visual Essentialism', 25.

24 Michaud, *Aby Warburg*.

25 Bal, 'Visual Essentialism', 7.

26 Bruno Latour, *We Have Never Been Modern*, trans. Catherine Porter, Cambridge, MA, 1993.

27 Latour, *We Have Never Been Modern*, 2.

28 Latour, *We Have Never Been Modern*, 3.

29 Mieke Bal, *Travelling Concepts in the Humanities: A Rough Guide*, Toronto, 2002.

30 Massumi, *Parables*, 246.

31 Andrew Murphie, 'Electronicas: Differential Media and Proliferating, Transient Worlds', *fineart forum*, 17:8, 2003, 8. http://www.fineartforum.org/Backissues/Vol_17/faf_v17_n09/reviews/murphie.html and http://hypertext.rmit.edu.au/dac/papers/Murphie.pdf.

32 See also, Andrew Murphie, 'The Mutation of "Cognition" and the Fracturing of Modernity: Cognitive Technics, Extended Mind and Cultural Crisis', *Scan journal of Media Arts Culture*, http://scan.net.au/scan/journal/display.php?journal_id=58.

33 Georgio Agamben, 'Aby Warburg and the Nameless Science', in *Potentialities*, trans. Daniel Heller-Roazen, Stanford, 1999, 89–103.

34 Michaud, *Aby Warburg*, 278; Agamben, 'Notes on Gesture', 54.

35 Bal, *Quoting Caravaggio*.

36 Kurt Forster, 'Introduction', in Aby Warburg, *The Renewal of Pagan Antiquity*, trans. David Britt, Los Angeles, 1999 [1932], 1–75.

37 Forster, *Aby Warburg/The Renewal of Pagan Antiquity*, 56; see also Michaud, *Aby Warburg*, 102.

38 Agamben, 'Notes on Gesture', 54.

39 Didi-Huberman, 'Dialektik des Monstrums', 641.

40 *T-Visionarium* is a project of iCinema (the Centre for Interactive Cinema), led by Dennis Del Favero, Neil Brown, Jeffrey Shaw, Peter Weibel (lead software engineer: Matt McGinity). The first phase was premiered in Lille in 2003, the second in Sydney in 2006.

# 10

# JE VOUS

KAJA SILVERMAN

Much has been made of the gap separating the 'I think' from the 'I am' in Descartes's *Sixth Meditation*. However, the first-person pronoun is not the only word that splits us in two: the 'I' has no effectivity unless it is addressed to, and acknowledged by, a 'you', and the relationship between these two pronouns is infinitely reversible. And not only can we never fully know the one to whom we say it, but the other that we are for him or her is also permanently unavailable to us. Because of this, Mieke Bal writes in an essay of 1991, the second-person pronoun 'constitutes the scandal, the stumbling block, of orthodox epistemology.'[1]

In the essay from which I have just quoted, 'First Person, Second Person, Same Person: Narrative as Epistemology', Bal discusses two books that attempt to make room within their discursive organization for the second-person pronoun: Johannes Fabian's *Power and Performance*,[2] and Hubert Damisch's *The Origin of Perspective*.[3] She argues that both authors fail to accomplish what they set out to do, because the 'I' reasserts its primacy through the stories they recount. Narrative is also a 'telling', she writes in the concluding sentence of this essay – an address from a speaker to a listener or reader (318). Bal also helps us to see that the first-person pronoun is not the only way to 'tell', because whenever there is a 'focalizer', there is also a teller. The focalizer is 'the implied "subject" who colors the story' (308), and this subject can be the narrator or a fictional character.

Although Bal devised the concept of 'focalization' to account for narratological effects, it is an implicitly visual concept, and in her book *Reading 'Rembrandt': Beyond the Word–Image Opposition* (1991), she uses it to analyse the discursive aspects of Rembrandt's paintings.[4] In the years that followed, she wrote about a wide range of other artists and visual practices. She also began exploring the visual aspects of literary focalization, and the technologies that structure how we see. In *The Mottled Screen: Reading Proust Visually* (1997), Bal shows that Proust's *magnum opus* is focalized not just through the narrator's look, but also through the lens of a camera, and that this has important formal consequences. 'The photographic mechanism can be seen at work in the cutting out of details, in the conflictual dialectic between the near and the far, and in certain "zoom" effects', she writes there, 'it can also be seen in the effects of contrast, which prevent or enable the under- or overexposed image to be seen. It appears in the focusing, when the image oscillates between clarity and indistinction.'[5]

The first-person pronoun figures prominently in Marcel Proust's *À la recherche du temps perdu* (*In Search of Lost Time*),[6] so much so that it has been called an 'egophany'.[7] The camera often functions not merely as an extension of this pronoun, but also as the means by which it triumphs over others. In one of the passages discussed by Bal,[8] Saint-Loup offers to take a photograph of Marcel's grandmother. Since she knows that she will soon die, she sees this as a way of providing her grandson with a lasting image of herself. She therefore accepts his offer 'with a joyful air', and searches for a flattering hat and her 'nicest dress'.[9] Marcel is extremely irritated by his grandmother's 'vanity', but rather than accepting her offer to forego the photograph, he encourages her to have it taken, and then ruins it with a few 'sarcastic and wounding words' (501).

As Bal notes, this story resurfaces a number of times, and constitutes one of the most important entry points into the novel.[10] On one of the occasions when Marcel returns to it, he acknowledges that what really angered him was not his grandmother's vanity, but rather the fact that she had oriented herself towards someone else's look – a look to which he had no access. To make matters worse, the unknowable person she was on her way to becoming would be authenticated and immortalized by the camera – and this would prove that his grandmother was not 'created solely' for him.[11] Unlike Marcel's mother, who is only intermittently available to him during his childhood, and who largely disappears after the 'Combray' section of *Du côté de chez Swann* (*Swann's Way*), his grandmother remains at his beck and call until the moment of her death, and he views her as the prolongation of himself. 'I knew [. . .] that everything that was mine, my cares, my wishes, would be buttressed, in my grandmother, by a desire to preserve and enhance my life,' he tells us in the second volume of the novel, 'and my thoughts were continued and extended in her without undergoing the slightest deflection, since they passed from my mind to hers without any change of atmosphere or of personality.'[12] Since Marcel is also 'as gluttonous' as 'a babe at the breast', he is unwilling to grant his grandmother even a modicum of independence, so he wrests control of the camera away from Saint-Loup. With his wounding words, he engineers the production of a different kind of photograph: one that has *him* as its ocular referent.

As Bal also notes,[13] this story is closely linked to the scene in which Marcel enters the drawing room, and sees his grandmother absorbed in thoughts that she has never allowed him to 'see'. For a moment, he becomes a 'spectator to [his] own absence'; he realizes that she continues to exist when he is not there, and that even when he is with her, he is not seeing all of her. This alarming thought leads to the bizarre fantasy that a stranger has just entered the room, and is photographing his grandmother as she would appear if he were not there to protect her. What this imaginary camera sees is a 'heavy', 'vulgar' and 'red-faced' woman sitting on a sofa, letting her '"slightly" crazed eyes wander over a book'.[14] Although Marcel spends most of the rest of the paragraph insisting upon the objectivity of this image, his look was clearly the apparatus with which it was 'taken'.

Given all of this, one would expect Bal to offer a highly critical account of Proustian focalization, but she defies this expectation. She argues that the narrator's imaginary camera ultimately works *against* him rather than *for* him, because the photographs through which he attempts to master the world prevent him from knowing it. Every time he tries to approach Albertine, he bumps his head against the wall of a two-dimensional representation. The novel also places a similar barrier between *us* and Albertine, because rather than presenting Marcel's perceptual 'snapshots' as a temporal sequence, it spatializes them – because it treats them like a contact sheet, instead of a strip of film. 'In this spreading-out', Bal writes near the end of her book, 'the subject comes up against the partition that no ethnographic attempt at dialogical, communicative epistemology has managed to break down' (244).

Because Marcel cannot penetrate the mental photographs separating him from Albertine, he subjects their surfaces to a relentless scrutiny. But these 'zooms', 'close-ups' and 'magnifications' not only heighten the unreality of the images, but also render them internally heterogeneous; 'stretch' their space; and create breast-like 'mounds' or 'swellings'. At key moments in the novel, Marcel stops trying to know Albertine, and 'presses against' these 'mounds'. This activity blurs the opposition between the subject and the object. It also 'lesbianizes' his desire.[15] Bal links the scenes in which Marcel presses against the impenetrable surface of his perceptual photographs to those in which he presses against Albertine's body, and interprets both activities through an important passage from *Sodome et Gomorrhe* (*Sodom and Gomorrah*). In this passage, Marcel and Cottard watch Albertine waltzing with Andrée, and Cottard says: 'I've left my glasses behind and I can't see very well, but they are certainly keenly roused. It's not sufficiently known that women derive most of their excitement through their breasts. And theirs, as you see, are touching completely.' Marcel confirms that the 'contact' between the two women's breasts was 'constant', and then adds: 'Albertine appeared to be conveying, to be making Andrée share, some secret and voluptuous thrill.'[16] At the moments when he stops trying to know Albertine, and presses against her body or the images he has produced of her, he – too – experiences this thrill.

I have been reading Proust for as long as I can remember, but it did not occur to me to think about *In Search of Lost Time* in photographic terms until 1997, when I first read *The Mottled Screen*. Now the entire novel seems to me to be 'about' photography. I have, of course, my own ideas about the medium, and will also provide a somewhat different reading of *In Search of Lost Time*. But as the following pages will demonstrate, the concept through which Bal theorizes Proust's treatment of this medium – focalization – has profoundly shaped my way of thinking about it. I will also return at the end of this essay to the notion of a second-person narrative, through a work that 'rhymes' with *The Mottled Screen*: Chantal Akerman's film *The Captive* (France, 2000).

There are in my opinion *two* focalizers in *In Search of Lost Time*, both of whom use the first-person pronoun, have the same name, and are closely related to the author: the Marcel who used to go to bed early, and the one who reflects upon this phenomenon from a subsequent moment in time. One of these Marcels springs into existence at the moment of his birth, but the other does not emerge until he is a middle-aged man. He is conjured, like so many other things, out of the famous cup of tea.[17] Each of these focalizers is also internally divided. The one who eats the madeleine is both the explorer and the 'dark region' through which he must search; both consciousness, and the unconscious memories that 'overtake' it (61). The other Marcel is not just double, but *multiple*. As we discover in the opening pages of *Swann's Way*, he fell asleep in many different beds during his childhood, and when he awoke the next morning, he often didn't know which one he was lying in. Until he was able to determine *where* he was, he did not know *who* he was, because each bed contained a different Marcel (4). This phenomenon is not limited to the moment of awakening. The first few time he encounters the band of girls, he registers their features, but is unable to determine to whom they belong. 'Except for one, whose straight nose and dark complexion singled her out from the rest', he confides, '[...] they were known to me only by a pair of hard, obstinate and mocking eyes, for instance, or by cheeks whose pinkness had a coppery tint reminiscent of geraniums, and even these features I had not indissolubly attached to any one of these girls rather than another.'[18]

Later Marcel 'deals' these features into little 'heaps' (508), attaches names to them, identifies Albertine as the object of his desire, and sequesters her in his house in Paris, but she proves as elusive in isolation as she was in the group. Sometimes she is 'thin, with a grey complexion, a sullen air, and a violet transparency slanting across her eyes'. On other occasions, 'happiness bathes [her] cheeks with a radiance so mobile that the skin, grown fluid and vague, [gives] passage to a sort of subcutaneous glaze', or her face draws his desires 'onto its varnished surface', but prevents them from 'going further' (718–19). And these changes have a destabilizing effect upon Marcel; he becomes a 'different person, according to the particular Albertine to whom [his] thoughts [turn]: a jealous, an indifferent, a voluptuous, a melancholy, a frenzied person' (720). So heterogeneous are 'the selves who [think] about Albertine', he adds near the end of this passage, that each ought really to have a 'different name' (721).

The activities which precipitate this proliferation of competing Marcels are those which fill Descartes with the greatest doubt: dreaming and sensory perception.[19] However, whereas the philosopher excludes them from his definition of himself, Proust gives them absolute pride of place. In the final volume of the novel, he not only emphasizes the multiple identities of the Marcel who used to go to bed early, but also suggests that each of these selves was stranded from, and ignorant of, the others. The only thing capable of bridging the distance between them, and of allowing the post-madeleine Marcel to reflect upon them, is a material object. 'Like the dress which a woman was wearing when we saw her for the first time,' the narrator explains, '[re-reading] the novels of my childhood in the same editions permitted me to rediscover the love that I then had [...] even though I am no longer the "I" who first beheld it, even though I must make way for the "I" that I then was if that "I" summons the thing that it once knew and that the "I" of today does not know.'[20]

Proust associates each of these focalizers with a different kind of photographic practice. The first 'freezes' or 'arrests' movement. The second activates a contrary impulse: development. Proust introduces the distinction between these two ways of looking in the madeleine episode. Before tasting the morsel of cake dipped in tea, the narrator is only able to visualize one 'luminous panel' of his childhood house, 'detached and solitary against a vague and shadowy background', and it is always 7 pm.[21] Afterwards, he sees 'all the flowers in [his family's] garden and in M. Swann's park, and the water-lilies on the Vivonne and the good folk of the village and their little dwellings and the parish church and the whole of Combray and its surrounding', from 'morning to night and in all weathers' (64).

We have grown used to thinking of the camera as a controlling and even aggressive device: as a mechanism for 'shooting' and 'capturing' the world. And since most cameras require an operator, and it is usually a human hand that picks up the apparatus, points it in a particular direction, makes certain technical adjustments, and clicks the camera button, we often extend or transfer this power to our look. It might therefore be hard to see what is photographic about the madeleine episode. However, it was not until 1858, when Thomas Skaife created his Pistolgraph, that the camera was equated with a gun,[22] and the first recorded use of the verb 'to shoot' as a synonym for the verb 'to photograph' occurred in 1890.[23]

What permitted Skaife to think of his camera as a pistol was its instantaneity; unlike earlier photographers, he did not have to wait for the gradual development of an image on a sensitive surface exposed to light.[24] The generalization of the ballistic metaphor was made possible by the occlusion of another important part of the development process. When George Eastman produced the first Kodak camera, in 1888, he marketed it under the slogan 'you press the button, and we do the rest.'[25] The word 'rest' covered a lot of things; the Kodak arrived 'loaded' with paper, and was sent back to Eastman with the paper still in it so that the negatives could be processed and printed.[26] The ostensible purpose of these innovations was to make the camera a more democratic apparatus – one available to amateur as well as professional photographers. However, by separating the 'wet' components of photography from its 'dry' ones, Eastman promoted the illusion that the prints that arrived in the mail were the exact positive equivalents of the negatives earlier shipped off.

I take the distinction between the 'wet' and 'dry' components of photography from Jeff Wall, who argues that the medium has two kinds of 'intelligence' – one 'optical' and the other 'liquid'. He associates the first with the 'glass (lenses) and machinery (calibrators and shutters)' of the photographic apparatus, which augment the 'projectile or ballistic nature of vision', and are based upon calculation.[27] Wall associates photography's 'liquid intelligence' with the development process, which depends upon water. The 'archaism of water' links the medium to 'very ancient production processes', like 'washing', 'bleaching' and 'dissolving', and prevents it from ever being fully calculable.

Wall concludes his essay with a brief discussion of Andrei Tarkovsky's *Solaris* (1972), which he uses to illustrate the distinction between photography's optical intelligence and its liquid intelligence (93). In this film, a group of scientists study an oceanic planet – but the ocean also studies them. It 'experiments on the experimenters by returning their own memories to them in the form of hallucinations in which people from their pasts appear in the present and must be related to once again, maybe in a new way' (93). We are obviously in Proustian territory here – not only because of the central role played by memory in *In Search of Lost Time*, and the fact that the narrator is both the 'seeker' and the 'dark region where it must seek and where all its equipment will avail it nothing',[28] but also because the memories out of which the novel grows develop in a cup of tea.[29] But if we want to understand all the photographic dimensions of the madeleine episode, we must search for another lost time: the time when photography was a graphic rather than an ocular practice.

Photography's inventors and early practitioners associated it more with drawing than with seeing. Both Louis Daguerre and Henry Fox Talbot use this metaphor,[30] and although Nicéphore Niepce links the medium to vision in a letter of 1816,[31] elsewhere he equates this 'eye' with light, and links it to the slow appearance of an image.[32] We find a similar account of photographic vision in a much later text – Elizabeth Eastlake's essay 'Photography' of 1857. 'When the "great luminary concentrates his gaze for a few earnest minutes" on the "prepared plate of Daguerre and on the sensitive paper of Fox Talbot"', she writes, he 'traces', with a 'detail and precision beyond all human power, the glory of the heavens, and the wonders of the deep'.[33]

Photography's inventors and early practitioners also knew that they were not the source of its images. Niepce called his photographic process 'heliography'; Daguerre referred to the images that resulted from his as 'the imprint[s] of nature';[34] and Fox Talbot called his book of photographs *The Pencil of Nature* (1844–46). Fox Talbot also emphasizes the disparity between 'Nature's drawings', and his own. He began experimenting with photography because he was a poor draughtsman, and hoped to get better results by tracing the pictures that appeared inside the camera obscura. The resulting images looked beautiful as long as he viewed them through its 'prism', but when he removed his eye from this device, he found the 'traces' left by his 'faithless pencil' so inferior to 'the pictures of nature's painting which the glass lens of the Camera [Obscura] throws upon the paper in its focus' that they were 'melancholy to behold'. Fox Talbot therefore abandoned his quest to become a better draughtsman, and began searching for a way of preserving these 'fairy pictures, creations of a moment, and destined as rapidly to fade away'.[35]

Fox Talbot attributed his turn to photographic experimentation to the following thought: 'How charming it would be if it were possible to cause these natural images *to imprint themselves* durably, and remain fixed upon paper' [author's emphasis].[36] This exclamation imputes a new power to the pencil of nature: the power to 'fix' the pictures it draws. The photographer is only a supporting player. In 1834 Fox Talbot thought that he had found a way of facilitating this preservation, but even this modest goal proved too much for him. The technique he used produced a negative rather than a positive image, and its 'shadows' darkened over time.[37] Until early 1835 all his photogenic drawings were negatives, and had to be sheltered from light, in order to prevent fading.

In February 1835 Fox Talbot realized that if the paper used to produce the first photogenic drawing were transparent, 'the first drawing [could] serve as an object to produce a second drawing, in which the lights and shadows would be reversed' – that is, that the negative could be used to generate numerous positive prints.[38] He implemented this idea in the summer through a series of experimental cameras. These cameras had a box-like structure, and required less exposure time, but they did not have a viewfinder or ground-glass focusing screen, so the operator could only look at the pictures they produced when they were 'done'.

Not surprisingly, then, Fox Talbot still perceived these pictures as nature's handiwork, instead of his own. 'You set the instrument in action, the allotted time elapses, and you find the picture finished, in every part, and in every minute particular,' he wrote in the *Literary Gazette*, 'There is something in this rapidity and perfection of execution which is very wonderful. But what is Nature, but one great field of wonders past our comprehension.'[39]

The next few years constituted a relatively fallow period in Fox Talbot's photographic career, but after Daguerre announced the discovery of his process in 1839, the British inventor exhibited some of his photogenic drawings at the Royal Institution in London. One popular reviewer maintained that 'even a shadow, the emblem of all that is most fleeting in this world, [was] fettered by the spell of the invention', and quoted Fox Talbot himself as saying that 'the picture is "ended as soon as begun."'[40] Another reviewer was more equivocal; he wrote that Fox Talbot's method 'promises to be valuable for obtaining exact representations of *fixed* and *still* objects, although at present they seem only to possess the correct elements for a finished painting.'[41]

But although he bitterly contested Daguerre's claim to be the inventor of photography, and spent much of his life battling others over patents, Fox Talbot imputed less agency to himself at this juncture, not more. 'It is not the artist who makes the picture, but [rather] the picture which makes ITSELF,' he wrote in a contemporaneous letter to the *Literary Gazette*[42] – and once again, his modesty was well founded. In order to produce multiple positive prints from a single negative, Fox Talbot had to develop the negative, and this introduced a new kind of incalculability into photography. Initially this incalculability made itself felt primarily through the unknowability of what transpired inside the box-like camera. 'All that the artist does is to dispose the apparatus before the object whose image he requires,' Fox Talbot confided in the same letter. 'He then leaves it for a certain time, greater or less, according to the circumstances. At the end of the time he returns, takes out his picture, and finds it finished.' Before long, though, it bled over into the next stage of the photographic process.

In 1840 Fox Talbot invented a technique called the 'calotype', which further shortened the exposure time, but only produced a 'latent picture'. The operator was unable to see what was in it until the development process was complete.[43] He also played as minor a part in this process as he did in the production of the negative, his only intervention being to halt the development process when it reached what was 'in his judgment the most perfect state'.[44] The wonder that Fox Talbot and his contemporaries felt when looking at images drawn by the pencil of nature was renewed and strengthened by the autonomy of the development process. 'I know of few things in the range of science more surprising than the gradual appearance of the picture on the blank sheet,' he wrote in a letter of 1841 to the *Literary Gazette*.[45]

It is also difficult to understand how the second of the reviewers quoted above could have seen even the 'promise' of 'exact representations of fixed and still objects' in the work shown in Fox Talbot's exhibition of 1839, because many of his early camera photographs still seem to be developing. As Gail Buckland puts it, 'all share a sense of becoming – of becoming pictures. Their most notable characteristic is their dynamism [. . .] They appear to be in a state of evolution, of being slowly created by dancing rays of light.' (33) But as Fox Talbot helps us to see, the same is true of every photograph. Even the digital images we 'shoot' with our most technically advanced cameras continue to develop long after we have finished tinkering with them, because what we see in them is constantly changing. 'It frequently happens [...] that the operator himself discovers on examination, perhaps long afterwards, that he has depicted many things that he had no notion of at the time,' Fox Talbot confides in *The Pencil of Nature*. 'Sometimes inscriptions and dates are found upon the buildings, or printed placards, most irrelevant, are discovered upon their walls: sometimes a distant dial-plate is seen, and upon it – unconsciously recorded – the hour of the day at which the view was taken.'[46]

Walter Benjamin expands upon many of these claims in his essay of 1931: 'Little History of Photography'. There is a blind spot in every photograph, a detail that links it to one time and place but becomes intelligible in another. Photographs also have a second kind of opacity: they show us a 'space' which is not 'informed' by our consciousness, because 'another nature [...] speaks to the camera than the eye.' Photographs do not deliver this 'nature' to us, nor can we ourselves stake a claim to it. It will forever escape us, because it is part of the 'optical unconscious'. The optical unconscious is as resistant to our attempts to know it as the one discovered by Sigmund Freud, but it lies outside us, rather than within us, and it can in no way be said to 'belong' to us.[47]

The invention of photography was as epochal an event as the Copernican revolution. It showed its early practitioners and viewers that there really is a world, and that this world reveals different aspects of itself to the camera than the eye. This gave rise to an even more disturbing thought – the thought that the world may also open itself differently to other looks. If this is the case, then we must only be able to see what we are given to see. And as we are not only seers, but also part of the spectacle of the world, those who look at us must perceive dimensions of our being that are invisible to us. We cannot neutralize the threat which these differences pose to our unity and autonomy by underscoring the subjectivity of human vision, because perspective is not something we bring to visual phenomena. It is internal to their Being, and it dramatically restricts what we can know about ourselves and the world.[48]

Although Jean-Paul Sartre, Maurice Merleau-Ponty and Jacques Lacan are all obsessed with the issues I have just raised, neither of the first two writers traces them back to photography.[49] Lacan invokes the still camera in a famous passage from *Four Fundamental Concepts of Psychoanalysis*, but only as a metaphor for an omnipresent but unlocalizable Gaze.[50] Proust, however, dots every one of these 'i's, and crosses every one of these 't's. In the passage with which I began my reading of *In Search of Lost Time*, Marcel realizes that his grandmother is not a simple extension of his look – that St Loup also sees her, and that he does so from a vantage point that is inaccessible to him. The camera forces this realization upon him, because it testifies to the fact that his grandmother has other faces than the one she turns towards him. He attempts to recover his egoic footing by producing a counter-photograph. In the scene in which Marcel finds his grandmother sitting alone, absorbed in thoughts that she has not allowed him to 'see', he realizes that she also looks at the world from a perspective that is unavailable to him. Marcel punishes her for this by mobilizing a different kind of camera.

Albertine's look denotes an even more radical alterity – and one which includes Marcel, thereby making him a stranger to himself. 'If she had seen me, what could I have represented to her?' he asks himself later in the same volume,

> From the depths of what universe did she discern me? [...] If we thought that the eyes of such a girl were merely two glittering sequins of mica, we should not be athirst to know her and to unite her life to ours. But we sense that what shines in those reflecting discs is the dark shadows, unknown to us, of the ideas that the person cherishes about the people and places she knows.'[51]

Although there are no explicit references to photography in this passage, Marcel expresses his desire to plumb the depths of this 'universe' (511), and he later attempts to satisfy this desire by kissing her. When he approaches Albertine for this purpose, she turns not just into a grainy photograph, but one that can be viewed from a potentially infinite number of angles, only one of which can be occupied at a time. 'At first, as my mouth began to approach the cheeks which my eyes had recommended it to kiss', Marcel writes, 'my eyes, in changing position, saw a different pair of cheeks; the neck, observed at closer range and as though through a magnifying-glass, showed in its coarser grain a robustness which modified the character of the face.'[52]

As Bal points out, this passage is in dialogue with a later one.[53] In this later passage, the narrator describes photographs into which multiple viewpoints have been crammed, presumably so as to overcome the limits of human vision. He emphasizes the absurdity of this project by comparing it to his own attempt to get behind Albertine's eyes by kissing her, and by suggesting that the photographic image has a directly contrary effect upon the human eye. 'I can think of nothing that can to so great a degree as a kiss evoke out of what we believed to be one thing with one definite aspect, the hundred other things which it may equally well be', he wryly observes, 'since each is related to a no less legitimate perspective.'[54]

But Proust does more than document the crises precipitated within Western subjectivity by photography. He also helps us to see that this medium really is the pencil of nature, and he provides an analogous account of human perception, and of literary production. The psyche is a receptive surface, like a photographic negative, on which sensory 'impressions' are traced, he writes in *Le Temps retrouvé* (*Time Regained*). The 'essential feature' of this 'magical scrawl, complex and elaborate', is that we do not control the pen with which it is written; it is, rather, 'dictated to us by reality [itself]' (274–5). The 'hieroglyphs' inscribed on our psyche by the pencil of nature are also invisible to us until they have been developed, since they are negative rather than positive prints. Not until 'we are back at home, and have once again found at our disposal that inner darkroom the entrance to which is barred to us as long as we are with other people' (616–17), do we begin processing them, and many remain undeveloped, because this operation requires a sensory catalyst. The same principle holds within the domain of art. Writers and painters are translators, not creators (291); they decipher and make intelligible to others the '"impression" [...] printed in [them] by reality' (275).

There are striking parallels between Proust's account of perception and the one that Henri Bergson presents in *Creative Evolution*. For both writers, there are no forms, because everything is in a state of 'radical becoming', but this movement escapes us, because perception transforms 'the fluid continuity of the real' into a series of photographs.[55] However, there are also important differences. For Bergson, this segmentation is an ontological violation, because time is an uninterrupted continuum (306). We cover the tracks of this crime by assembling the images we produce with our perceptual camera into a strip of 'film', and running them quickly through our mental 'projector', so that we do not see the divisions between them. Proust describes our everyday perception in terms that resemble more closely a slide projector than a film projection; he compares it to a shop 'in the window of which is exposed now one, now another photograph of the person'.[56] He also attributes photographic fixation to the ego, rather than to any of the technical properties of the medium.

As Proust repeatedly shows, the ego cannot tolerate any kind of movement – even that produced by the perceptual apparatus. It attempts to stabilize itself and its objects in two ways: by immobilizing them conceptually (that is, by pushing the 'pause' button on the mental slide projector);[57] and by impeding or even reversing the development process (that is, by returning every print to the negative from which it was struck, or reducing a multiplicity of negatives to a single prototype). The 'detached and solitary' panel of Marcel's childhood home dramatizes the first kind of arrestation. Proust describes the second in an equally famous passage from *À l'ombre des jeunes filles en fleurs* (*Within a Budding Grove*):

> If in this craze for amusement Albertine might be said to echo something of the old original Gilberte, that is because a certain similarity exists, although the type evolves, between all the women we successively love, a similarity that is due to the fixity of *our* temperament [...] They are, these women, a product of our temperament, an image, an inverted projection, a negative of our sensibility. (647)

Proust also valorizes what Bergson most dislikes about the photographic image: its stillness and its delimitation. This is because the fluid in which a perceptual negative develops is analogy; we dip it in that fluid when we recognize the similarities linking it to another perceptual negative from a different time and place. These similarities are always there, but they are not visible until we have removed the perceptual negative from the sequence in which it is embedded. Syntagmatic relationships prevent us from seeing figural ones, and it is within the latter, rather than the former, that truth resides. '[A writer] can describe a scene by describing one after another the innumerable objects which at a given moment were present at a particular place,' Proust writes in *Time Regained*, 'but truth will be attained only when he takes two different objects, [and] states the connection between them' (289–90).[58]

Still photography is also a powerful mechanism for halting the forward march of time, and mobilizing another kind of temporality – one with the capacity to redeem or resurrect the past. This 'stoppage' is also the first step in a process that will allow us to experience the mobility of the world, because when the perceptual negative is developed, its frame-lines fall away. Like the 'little pieces of paper' that are 'without color and form' when they are dry, but which 'stretch and twist and take on color and distinctive shape' as soon as they are immersed in a bowl of water (64), it starts to expand. If it is not impeded, this process will continue far into the future.

Although there is a dizzying assortment of 'I's in *In Search of Lost Time*, there are not many 'you's. Proust attempts to make room for others in the last volume of his novel by abstracting away from sensory experience to universal laws, but this leads to a generalization of the first-person pronoun, rather than a greater accommodation of the second.[59] A new Marcel also emerges in some passages in *Time Regained:* one whose perceptual coordinates are closer to 'radiography' than to photography. As the narrator points out in *Within a Budding Grove*, this is a mortifying optic; it peels away the 'tiny particles of epidermis whose varied combinations form the florid originality of human flesh' to reveal the 'joyless universality of a skeleton' (648). But although Marcel recoils from this kind of looking in the second volume of *In Search of Lost Time*, he later justifies it as the necessary condition for art-making. A book is 'a huge cemetery in which on the majority of the tombs the names are effaced,' he writes in *Time Regained* (310). Fortunately, though, the perceptual negatives that Proust develops in the earlier volumes of his novel have continued to develop – not only in the psyches of his readers, but also in the work of later artists and critics. Bal's *The Mottled Screen* is one such work, and Chantal Akerman's *The Captive* another.

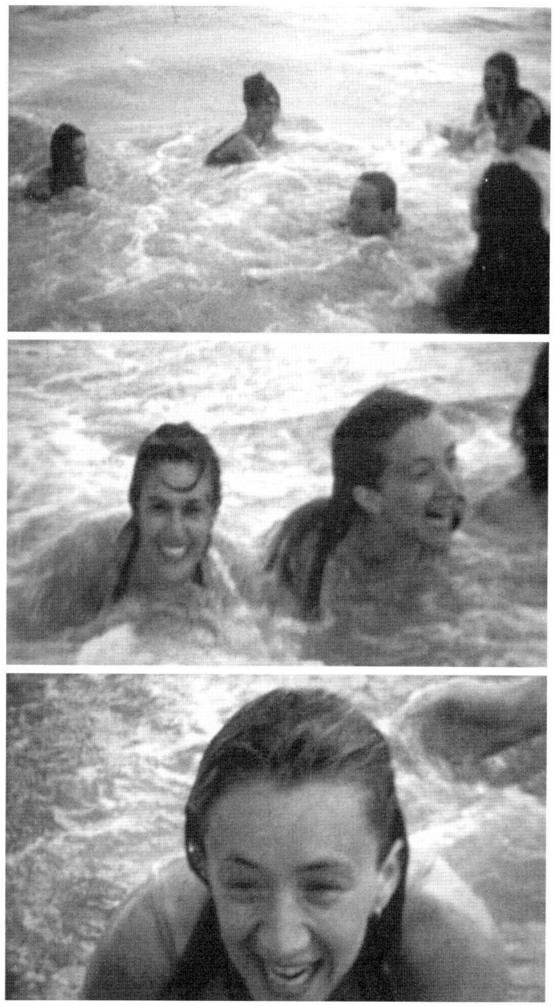

10.1–10.3 Stills from Chantal Akerman, *The Captive*, France, 2000. Images reproduced with the permission of Chantal Akerman, and courtesy of Artificial Eye Film Company, London.

Like *In Search of Lost Time*, which it 'renovates', *The Captive* has two focalizers.[60] However, instead of different versions of a single person, both of whom have the same name, and rely upon the first-person pronoun, these focalizers are Simon, the male protagonist, and the film-maker herself, and they mobilize both the 'I' and the 'you'. Akerman foregrounds both of these innovations in the first scene of the film. *The Captive* opens with credits over a 35mm nocturnal shot of the sea. This shot – which comes slowly and moodily into focus – is accompanied by the sound of crashing waves. The transition from it to the film 'proper' is unusually smooth, because the first scene also begins with a frontal shot of a seascape, accompanied by the sound of waves. Now, though, the sun is high in the sky, and a group of girls are playing in the water. This shot is also grainier than the one that precedes it, and it is followed by a series of hand-held and equally grainy shots of the girls and the water. The sound of a film projector competes with – and eventually replaces – the sound of waves, and from time to time we hear the 'click' of a still camera.

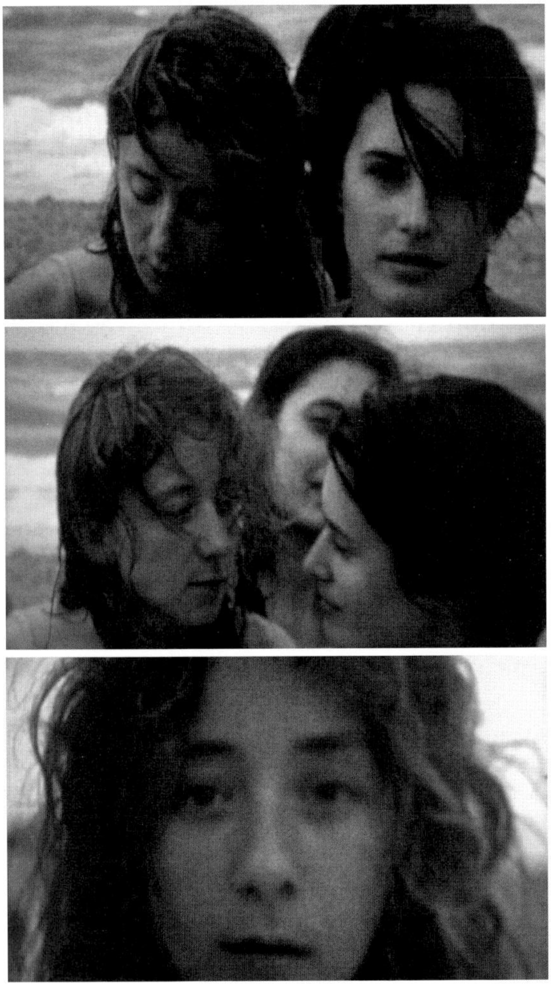

10.4–10.6 Stills from Chantal Akerman, *The Captive*, France, 2000. Images reproduced with the permission of Chantal Akerman, and courtesy of Artificial Eye Film Company, London.

Two girls leave the water, and approach the camera: Ariane and Andrée, Akerman's 'updated' versions of Albertine and Andrée. They pause briefly in front of the camera, allowing the photographer to study their faces, and their friends gather around them. Then the girls begin playing with a football on the beach, and the image loses its clarity. The photographer attempts to follow their movements, but the jerkiness of his hand-held camera renders them even less intelligible. Eventually he manages to isolate Ariane from the others, and moves in to an extreme close-up of her face. Akerman cuts from this close-up to a 35mm shot of Simon, her version of Proust's narrator. He stands beside a projector, which he is using to screen a film. It is a home movie, presumably shot by him, and the source of the grainy images at which we have been looking.

The projector permits us to identify the mechanical 'whirr' that competes with, and eventually drowns out, the crashing waves. At first, it also seems responsible for the mysterious 'click', because Simon repeatedly stops the projector and rewinds a bit of film, and each time he does so, we hear this sound. Before long, though, it becomes evident that this 'click' is the auditory exteriorization of a mental camera. Akerman also treats the amateur camera and the film projector as perceptual metaphors. She uses the blur that results when unpredictable movements are filmed with a hand-held camera and then re-photographed with a higher-resolution camera to depict the 'spectacle of forms undergoing an incessant process of change';[61] the clicking sound to dramatize Simon's perception, which transforms this mobile beauty into a series of still photographs; and the stopping and starting of the projector to suggest another sort of arrestation – that through which the ego attempts to stabilize itself and the world.[62]

As the camera holds on Simon, he says 'je . . . je . . . je . . . vous.' Since he looks at Ariane as he utters these words, she is clearly the referent for one of them, but it is impossible to determine which, since he could be speaking either for her, or for himself. These pronouns become even shiftier when the camera cuts back to the home movie. Ariane and Andrée stand together on the beach, against the backdrop of the sea. They are wrapped in towels, and lean into each other like lovers, but – because they stand with their backs to the sun – their faces are difficult to make out. As we look at this ambiguous shot, we hear Simon utter the following words, from an off-screen position: 'je . . . je vous . . . je vous . . . je vous aime bien.' Since 'vous' is the plural as well as the formal version of the second-person pronoun in French, its field of possible referents now expands to include Andrée. Initially, this expansion seems to secure Simon in the position of the 'je', but before long another possibility emerges: the possibility that the first- and second-person pronouns are the reversible designators of another intersubjectivity: Ariane's and Andrée's.

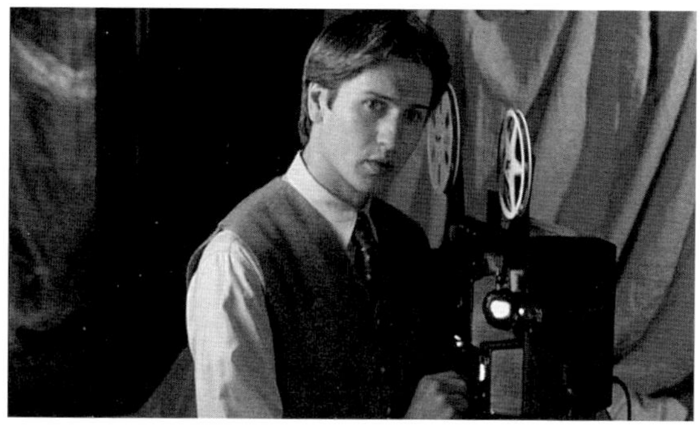

10.7 Still from Chantal Akerman, *The Captive*, France, 2000. Images reproduced with the permission of Chantal Akerman, and courtesy of Artificial Eye Film Company, London.

The camera returns to Simon, who repeats these words, but this time he smiles as he speaks, and there is a lilt to his voice. It then cuts back to the home movie, and remains facing in this direction until the end of the scene. Simon approaches the screen, sits down in front of it, and presses his face against Ariane's image. His head forms an over-sized shadow in the lower left frame. From this strange position, which is simultaneously inside and outside the home movie, Simon again says 'je vous aime bien.' The emphasis now falls as much upon the last two words as upon the first two. In this iteration, 'aimer bien' means not only 'to love a lot', but also 'to love well'.

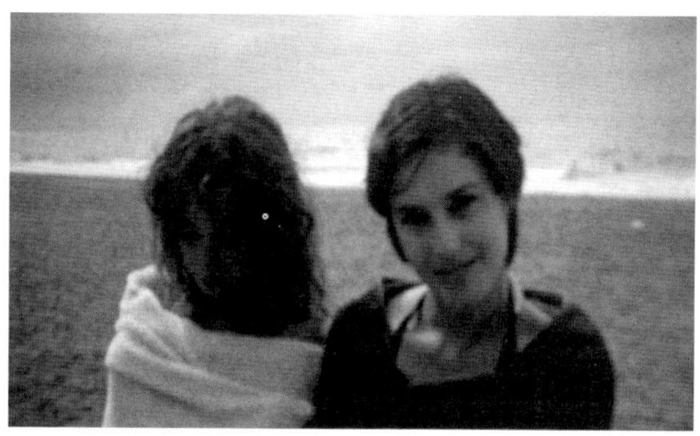

10.8 Still from Chantal Akerman, *The Captive*, France, 2000. Images reproduced with the permission of Chantal Akerman, and courtesy of Artificial Eye Film Company, London.

In *The Captive*, as in the novel it analogizes, the central male character derives erotic gratification from pressing against the female body.

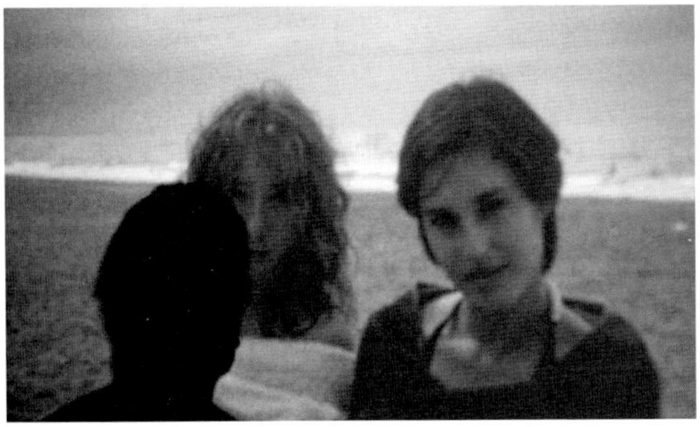

10.9 Still from Chantal Akerman, *The Captive*, France, 2000. Images reproduced with the permission of Chantal Akerman, and courtesy of Artificial Eye Film Company, London.

Proust represents this as a masturbatory sexuality, but Bal gives it a lesbian inflection by tracing it back to Albertine's breast-to-breast dance with Andrée, and focusing on the 'swellings' that emerge when Marcel moves his imaginary magnifying-glass across the surface of his mental photographs. Akerman carries this project further: she links Simon's erotic to his perceptual practices, and attributes both to his obsession with lesbian desire, but she also makes room within this libidinal economy for her female characters. There are two scenes in *The Captive* in which Simon climaxes while pressing against Ariane's body, and both times she also manifests extreme sexual pleasure. She enjoys this activity, she later tells him, because it is non-invasive – because it does not encroach upon her physical or (even more importantly) her psychic interiority. She is therefore free to think about Andrée while she is experiencing the pressure of his body, that is to be with both of them at the same time.[63] The second time Simon says 'je vous aime bien', he acknowledges that his own pleasure derives from the same source – that he loves Ariane because she and Andrée love each other. The third time, he goes even further: he affirms their right to address these words to each other. And since by doing this, he loves them well, he also finds his own way back to the 'je'.

This scene relies heavily upon the shot/reverse-shot formation. Because this device is often used within normative cinema to construct sexual difference and conceal the presence of the camera, Akerman ostentatiously avoids it both in *Jeanne Dielman* (France, 1975) and *News from Home* (France, 1976). However, because the basis of this construction is reversibility, it has the potential to be the visual equivalent of the 'I' and the 'you', and she actualizes this potential here. Ariane and Andrée are separated from Simon by the fourth wall, which means that they should not be able to return his look, but they miraculously *do*; after he acknowledges the interdependence of his desire for Ariane, and hers for Andrée, and affirms the girls' right to say 'je vous aime bien' to each other, they respond by smiling first at each other, and then at him. And when Simon walks over to the screen, and presses his head against Ariane's image, he responds to their response.

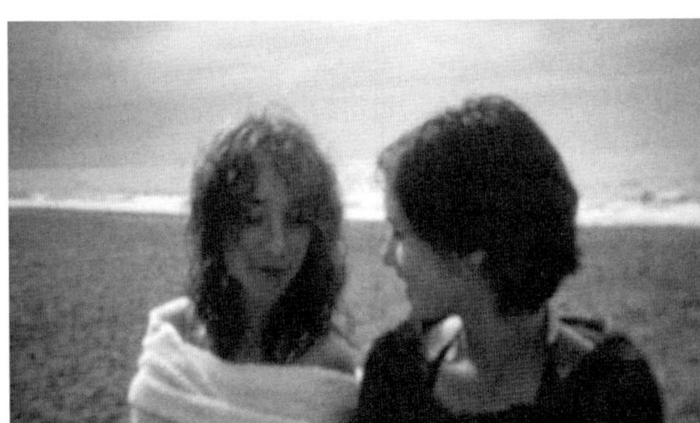

10.10 Still from Chantal Akerman, *The Captive*, France, 2000. Images reproduced with the permission of Chantal Akerman, and courtesy of Artificial Eye Film Company, London.

Akerman often signals her authorial presence by correlating the height of the camera to her own look – by positioning it lower than usual.[64] She follows this practice when filming Simon, but because these shots establish him as the source of the home movie, this is easy to miss. However, in the last shot of this scene, Akerman alerts us to her presence in a number of additional ways: by not moving her camera when Simon does; by continuing to film the screen from a standing position after he sits down; by dramatizing the lateral distance separating him from the camera by situating his head in the left corner of the image; and by showing Ariane and Andrée looking away from him, towards another viewer.

We recognize this viewer from other Akerman films – not just as a formally rigorous eye, but also as a person named 'Chantal', who is Belgian, part-Jewish and a lesbian. The parallels between *The Captive* and *Je tu il elle* (France, 1974) are particularly striking. In the latter film Akerman plays a lesbian who seduces a former girlfriend, and during their love-making the two women press their bodies passionately together. The title of the film also consists entirely of pronouns. Chantal is the only character who appears in every scene, which might seem to entitle her to the 'je', but there are also two other claimants to this position, and there are times when she seems more closely aligned with one of the other pronouns. In the second part of the film, she is picked up on the side of a road by a truck-driver. He commandeers the first-person pronoun by doing most of the talking, thereby assigning the second-person pronoun to her. Chantal later gives him a 'hand-job', at which point she could be a 'you', a 'she', or an 'I', and he a 'you', 'he', or 'I'. In the scene in which she visits her former girlfriend, each exercises power, and then has it wrested away from her by the other. The 'I' and 'you' shift positions at a dizzying rate, both literally and metaphorically, and the surprisingly frank way in which Akerman films their lovemaking marks both of them as a 'she'. As Ivone Margulies so elegantly puts it, the four pronouns in the title of the film 'seem to be on call, performing rituals of abeyance.'[65]

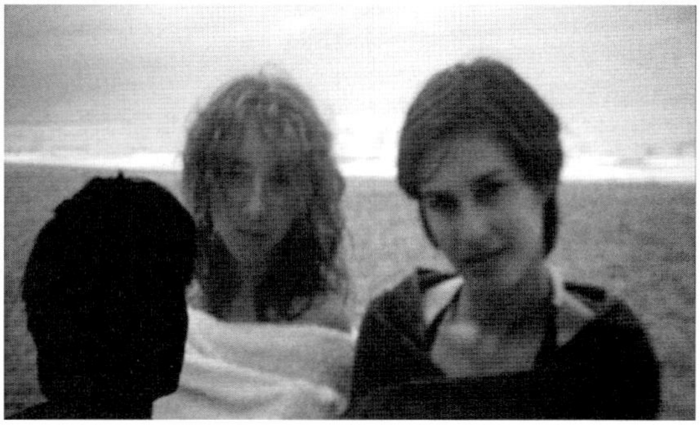

10.11 Still from Chantal Akerman, *The Captive*, France, 2000. Images reproduced with the permission of Chantal Akerman, and courtesy of Artificial Eye Film Company, London.

Things are every bit as labile in *The Captive*, both within the fiction, and at the level of the enunciation. Here, though, Akerman is less contestatory. She emphasizes the impossibility of replacing Simon's look with hers by depicting it as a blind spot within her own field of vision. She also presents her look as a second vantage point from which to observe and desire the band of girls, rather than as an alternative to it. Last, but not least, Akerman shows these two looks meeting at the site of Ariane's body. If we were to translate this meeting into language, it would read: 'je . . . vous . . . je vous.' This essay is the site of a similar exchange. In it, two old friends come together through a book they both love, and give and receive the 'you'.

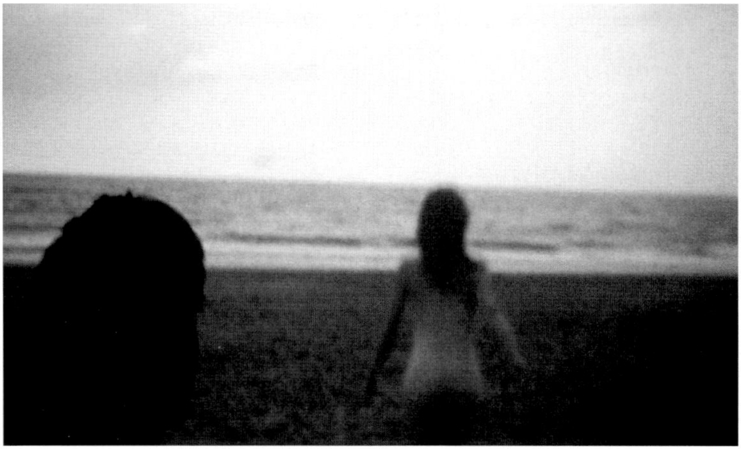

10.12 Still from Chantal Akerman, *The Captive*, France, 2000. Images reproduced with the permission of Chantal Akerman, and courtesy of Artificial Eye Film Company, London.

## Notes

1 Mieke Bal, 'First Person, Second Person, Same Person: Narrative as Epistemology', *New Literary History*, 24:2, 1993, 302–303.

2 Johannes Fabian, *Power and Performance: Ethnographic Explorations Through Proverbial Wisdom and Theater in Shaba, Zaire*, Madison, 1990.

3 Hubert Damisch, *The Origin of Perspective*, trans. John Goodman, Cambridge, 1995.

4 Mieke Bal, *Reading 'Rembrandt': Beyond the Word–Image Opposition*, Cambridge, 1991.

5 Mieke Bal, *The Mottled Screen: Reading Proust Visually*, trans. Anna-Louise Milne, Stanford, 1997, 201.

6 Marcel Proust, *À la recherche du temps perdu*, 7 vols, Paris, 1913–27. All references to this text hereafter refer to Marcel Proust, *In Search of Lost Time*, trans. C.K. Scott Moncrieff, Terence Kilmartin and D. J. Enright, New York, 2003.

7 This is a word coined by the Dutch novelist Willem Brakman, and discussed by Ernst van Alphen in 'Reading Visually', *Style*, 22, 1988, 219–29.

8 Bal, *The Mottled Screen*, 195–7.

9 Proust, *Within A Budding Grove*, 500.

10 Bal, *The Mottled Screen*, 196.

11 Proust, *Sodom and Gomorrah*, 237.

12 Proust, *Within A Budding Grove*, 335. For an excellent discussion of the exorbitance of Marcel's desire for his grandmother, see Serge Doubrovsky, *Writing and Fantasy in Proust: La Place de la Madeleine*, trans. Carol Mastrangelo Bové, Lincoln, 1986, 18–23.

13 Bal, *The Mottled Screen*, 198. Bal also provides a detailed analysis of this passage (198–200).

14 Proust, *The Guermantes Way*, 183–4.

15 This inelegant neologism is mine, not Bal's.

16 Proust, *Sodom and Gomorrah*, 264.

17 Proust, *Swann's Way*, 64.

18 Proust, *Within A Budding Grove*, 505.

19 See René Descartes, 'Discourse on Method', in *Discourse on Method and the Meditations*, trans. F.E. Sutcliffe, London, 1968, 53–60.

20 Proust, *Time Regained*, 287–8. This passage forms a striking contrast with Descartes's 'I think, therefore I am', but it could be read as an amplification of the doubts expressed by the philosopher in the famous passage from the *Meditations* that begins: 'But what, then, am I? A thing that thinks. What is a thing that thinks? That is to say, a thing that doubts, perceives, affirms, denies, wills, does not will, that imagines also, and that feels.' (*Discourse on Method and the Meditations*, 106–107).

21 Proust, *Swann's Way*, 58.

22 Robert Hirsch, *Seizing the Light: A History of Photography*, Boston, 2000, 89. The lethal implications of Skaife's Pistolgraph were immediately apparent to his contemporaries; he was 'almost arrested' when he directed this device at Queen Victoria (89). In 1878, when Etienne-Jules Marey was having difficulty recording movement photographically, he expressed his desire for a 'kind of *photographic* gun' (Mart Braun, *Picturing Time: The Work of Etienne-Jules Marey [1830–1904]*, Chicago, 1992, 47). However, what made him think of a gun as a model for his camera was its revolving barrel, rather than its ballistic force. By copying this aspect of its design, he hoped to devise a way of exposing one section of a light-sensitive plate while shielding the rest of it, then doing the same with the next section, until the entire plate had been exposed (57). In 1888, when he was in possession of such a camera, he wrote to his mother that there was 'nothing murderous about it.'

23 *The Compact Oxford English Dictionary*, 2nd edn, Oxford, 1991, 1749.
24 Hirsch, *Seizing the Light*, 173.
25 Jean-Luc Daval, *Photography: History of an Art*, New York, 1982, 103.
26 Hirsch, *Seizing the Light*, 172–3.
27 Jeff Wall, 'Photography and Liquid Intelligence', in *Jeff Wall*, London, 2002, 90.
28 Proust, *Swann's Way*, 61.
29 Brassai also notes that Proust's famous cup of tea serves as a 'developing bath'. See his wonderful book: *Proust: In the Power of Photography*, trans. Richard Howard, Chicago, 2001, 136.
30 Louis Jacques Mandé Daguerre, 'Daguerrotype', in *Classic Essays on Photography*, ed. Alan Trachtenberg, New Haven, 1980, 13; and Henry Fox Talbot, 'Introductory Remarks', in *The Pencil of Nature*, ed. Beaumont Newhall, New York, 1969.
31 Geoffrey Batchen, *Burning with Desire: The Conception of Photography*, Cambridge, 1997, 81. Batchen also emphasizes the long tradition of associating the camera obscura with vision (82).
32 Joseph Nicéphore Niepce, 'Memoire on the Heliograph', in *Classic Essays on Photography*, 6.
33 Lady Elizabeth Eastlake, 'Photography', in *Classic Essays on Photography*, 52.
34 Daguerre, 'Daguerrotype', 12.
35 Fox Talbot, 'Brief Historical Sketch of the Invention of the Art', in *The Pencil of Nature*, n.p.
36 Fox Talbot, 'Brief Historical Sketch', n.p.
37 Gail Buckland, *Fox Talbot and the Invention of Photography*, Boston, 1980, 28.
38 Buckland, *Fox Talbot*, 29–30.
39 Buckland, *Fox Talbot*, 30–1.
40 Buckland, *Fox Talbot*, 42.
41 Buckland, *Fox Talbot*, 42.
42 Buckland, *Fox Talbot*, 43.
43 Buckland, *Fox Talbot*, 62.
44 Buckland, *Fox Talbot*, 68.
45 Buckland, *Fox Talbot*, 62.
46 This passage accompanies Plate XIII in *The Pencil of Nature*.
47 Walter Benjamin, 'Little History of Photography', in *Selected Writings, Volume 2: 1927–1934*, ed. Michael W. Jennings, Howard Eiland and Gary Smith, Cambridge, 1999, 510–12.
48 I am, of course, echoing Merleau-Ponty here. See his posthumously published book, *The Visible and the Invisible*, ed. Claude Lefort, trans. Alfonso Lingis, Evanston, 1968; and 'Eye and Mind', in *The Merleau-Ponty Aesthetics Reader: Philosophy and Painting*, ed. Galen A. Johnson, Evanston, 1993, 121–49.
49 See Merleau-Ponty, *The Visible and the Invisible*, 130–55; Jean-Paul Sartre, 'The Look', in *Being and Nothingness*, trans. Hazel E. Barnes, New York, 1958, 340–400; and Jacques Lacan, 'Of the Gaze as *objet petit a*', in *Four Fundamental Concepts of Psychoanalysis*, trans. Alan Sheridan, New York, 1978, 67–119, esp. 106.
50 I offer detailed readings of this passage in *Male Subjectivity at the Margins*, New York, 1992, 125–56; and *The Threshold of the Visible World*, New York, 1996.
51 Proust, *Within a Budding Grove*, 510–11.
52 Proust, *Within a Budding* Grove, 202.
53 Bal, *The Mottled Screen*, 221.
54 Proust, *The Guermantes Way*, 498–9.
55 Henri Bergson, *Creative Evolution*, trans. Arthur Mitchell, New York, 1998 (1911), 302 and 273.
56 Proust, *Within A Budding Grove*, 642.
57 Proust, *Swann's Way*, 4.
58 As Eduardo Cadava shows in his book *Words of Light* (Princeton, 1977) there are many important parallels between Proust's account of analogy and Benjamin's account of history. Analogy also occupies a prominent place in my own thought. In my forthcoming book, *Flesh of My Flesh*, I argue that analogy is a relationship of greater or lesser similarity between two ontologically equal terms, and that it is the basis of Being. In the last chapter of *Flesh of My Flesh*, I also argue that photographs analogize their referents, rather than representing them. I expand upon this claim – as well as many of the claims I have made in this essay – in *The Miracle of Analogy*, a book that I am currently writing about photography.
59 In a chilling passage in *Time Regained* Proust maintains that 'matter is indifferent', and that 'anything can be grafted upon it by thought.' (320–1). He invokes this axiom as proof of his 'idealism'.
60 I take this metaphor from Akerman, who encourages us to think of *The Captive* as a 'renovation' of Proust's novel by showing us workmen inexplicably replastering and repainting Simon's apartment.
61 Proust, *Within a Budding Grove*, 661.
62 Proust maintains in *Time Regained* that 'nothing is further from what we have really perceived than the vision that the cinematograph presents' (279), but it is difficult to place much credence in this assertion, since associational montage works in a comparable way to Proustian analogy; both privilege resemblance over temporal contiguity. As Bal argues in *The Mottled Screen*, *In Search of Lost Time* also evokes a certain kind of avant-garde film: the kind where the diegesis is based on vision rather than narrative (213). *The Captive* provides both an instantiation of, and a reflection upon, this last sort of cinema.
63 Simon is later overcome by the desire to know what Ariane is thinking about, and this desire proves fatal for her.
64 Akerman reflects upon this practice in an interview with the editors of *Camera Obscura*: 'Delphine [Seyrig] said "Why do you use such a low angle?" I said, "That's my size." She said "It's better from a little higher up." And I said, "No, I don't want to do that. That's not how I see the world." [*Jeanne Dielman*] was never shot from the point of view of the son or anyone else. It's always me.' *Camera Obscura*, 2, 1977, 119.
65 Ivone Margulies, *Nothing Happens: Chantal Akerman's Hyperrealist Everyday*, Durham, 1996, 116.

# SELECTED BIBLIOGRAPHY

## BOOKS


In press *Sleeping Beauty*. Chicago, IL: University of Chicago Press, 2008 (with John Sparagana).

*Loving Yusuf: Conceptual Travels from Present to Past*. Chicago, IL: University of Chicago Press, 2008.

*Balthus: Works and Interview*. Barcelona: Ediciones Polígrafa, 2008.

*A Mieke Bal Reader*. Chicago, IL: University of Chicago Press, 2006.

*Travelling Concepts in the Humanities: A Rough Guide*. Toronto, ON: University of Toronto Press, 2002.

*Mieke Bal Kulturanalyse*, trans. Joachim Schulte, with an Afterword by Thomas Fechner-Smarsly and Sonja Neef (eds.). Frankfurt am Main: Suhrkamp, 2002.

*Louise Bourgeois' Spider: The Architecture of Art-Writing*. Chicago, IL: University of Chicago Press, 2001.

*Ann Veronica Janssens: Lichtspiel*, trans. Karen Lauer. Munich: Kunstverein München/ Berliner Künstlerprogramm/DAAD, 2001.

*Looking In: The Art of Viewing*, with an introduction by Norman Bryson (ed.). Amsterdam: G & B Arts International, 2001.

*Quoting Caravaggio: Contemporary Art, Preposterous History*. Chicago, IL: University of Chicago Press, 1999.

*Jeannette Christensen's Time*. Bergen: Center for the Study of European Civilization, 1998.

*Hovering between Thing and Event: Encounters with Lili Dujourie*. München: Kunstverein München/Brussels: Xavier Hufkens/London: Lisson Gallery, 1998.

*The Mottled Screen: Reading Proust Visually*, trans. Anna-Louise Milne. Stanford, CA: Stanford University Press, 1997.

*Double Exposures: The Subject of Cultural Analysis*. New York: Routledge, 1996.

*On Meaning-Making: Essays in Semiotics*. Sonoma, CA: Polebridge Press, 1994.

*Reading 'Rembrandt': Beyond the Word–Image Opposition*. New York and Cambridge: Cambridge University Press, 1991.

*On Story-Telling: Essays in Narratology*. Sonoma, CA: Polebridge Press, 1991.

*Verkrachting verbeeld: Seksueel geweld in cultuur gebracht*. Utrecht: HES, 1988.

*Death and Dissymmetry: The Politics of Coherence in the Book of Judges*. Chicago: University of Chicago Press, 1988.

*Murder and Difference: Gender, Genre and Scholarship on Sisera's Death*, trans. Matthew Gumpert. Bloomington, IN: Indiana University Press, 1988.

*Lethal Love: Literary-Feminist Readings of Biblical Love Stories*. Bloomington, IN: Indiana University Press, 1987.

*Het Rembrandt effect: Visies op kijken*. Utrecht: HES, 1987.

*Over literatuur*. Muiderberg: Coutinho, 1987 (with Jan van Luxemburg and Willem Weststeijn).

*Femmes imaginaries: L'Ancien Testament au risque d'une narratologie critique*. Utrecht: HES/Montréal: HMH/Paris: Nizet, 1986.

*En Sara in haar tent lachte: Patriarchaat en verzet in bijbelverhalen*. Utrecht: HES, 1984 (with Fokkelien van Dijk and Grietje van Ginneken).

*Inleiding in de literatuurwetenschap*. Muiderberg: Coutinho, 1981 (with Jan van Luxemburg and Willem Weststeijn).

*Narratology: Introduction to the Theory of Narrative*, trans. Christine van Boheemen. Toronto: University of Toronto Press, 1985.

*Narratologie: Essais sur la signification narrative dans quatre romans modernes*. Paris: Klincksieck, 1977/Utrecht: HES, 1984 (reprint).

*Complexité d'un roman populaire*. Paris: La Pensée Universelle, 1974.

**Catalogue essays and essays in artist books**

'Double Movement', in *2MOVE: Video Art Migration*. Murcia: Cendeac, 2008, 13–82 (with Miguel Á. Hernández-Navarro).

'Re-: Killing Time', in *Stan Douglas: Past Imperfect Works 1986–2007*, eds. Hans D. Christ and Iris Dressler. Staatsgallerie Stuttgart and Würtembergischer Kunstverein Stuttgart, Stuttgart: Hatje Cantz, 2007, 64–93.

' "Anthropometamorphosis": Forking Paths and Crystals in Louise Bourgeois' Philosophy of Temporality', in *Louise Bourgeois: La Sage Femme*. Murcia: Murcia Cultural, 2007, 20–41.

'Earth Aches: The Aesthetics of the Cut', in *Doris Salcedo: Shibboleth*. London: Tate Modern Publishing, 2007, 40–63.

'Forms of Movement', in Stereo Jesús Segura, 2007, 9–16.

'Light Politics', in *Take Your Time Olafur Eliasson*, ed. Madeleine Grynsztejn, San Francisco Museum of Modern Art. New York & London: Thames and Hudson, 2007, 153–82.

'Inside the Polis', in *Ann Veronica Janssens: An den Frühling*, for Museum Morsbroich Leverkusen. Köln: DuMont Literatur und Kunst Verlag, 2007, 165–201.

'Water en los zand: drie vormen van beweging', in *Land of Water: Tijdschrift voor de toekomst*. Enkhuizen: Zuiderzeemuseum, 2007, 86–95.

'Invisible Art, Hypervisibility, and the Aesthetics of Everyday Life', in *Nichts/Nothing*, eds. Martina Weinhart and Max Hollein. Frankfurt: Schirn Kunsthalle Frankfurt, 2006, 81–104.

'Los Cuerpos Barrocos y la ética de la percepción', in *Andreas Serrano, El Dedo en La Llaga*. Madrid: ARTIUM de Alava, 2006, 17–44.

'De-Centering: The Fragility of Mastery', In *Pieter Friedl, Work 1964–2006*, ed. Bartomeu Marí. Barcelone: MACBA (Museu d'Art Contemporani de Barcelone), 2006, 79–110.

'A l'Est d'Eden'/'East of Eden'/'Ten Oosten van Eden', in *Marthe Wéry: Les couleurs du monochrome*, ed. B.P.S.2 Projects. Tournai: Musée des Beaux-Arts, 2005, 35–104 and 119–27.

'Setting the Stage: The Subject Mise-en-scène'/'Eine Bühne schaffen: das Thema Mise-en-scène', in *Videodreams: Zwischen Cinematischem und Theatralischem –*

*Between the Cinematic and the Theatrical*, ed. Peter Pakesch. Köln: Verlag der Buchhandlung Walter König, 2004, 28–49.

'Matter and Memory'/'Materie en geheugen', in *Seet van Hout: Rood draad – Red Thread*. Staphorst: Hein Elferink, 2004, 6–25.

'What if ... Exploring "Unnaturality"', in *World rush: _4 artists* (exhibition catalogue). Victoria, Australia: National Gallery of Victoria, 2004, 30–7.

'Antropometamorfoza: rozwidlające się ścieżki i kryształy filozofii czasowości Louise Bourgeois'/' "Anthropometamorphosis": Forking Paths and Crystals in Louise Bourgeois' Philosophy of Temporality', in *Louise Bourgeois: Geometria pożądania/Geometry of Desire*, trans. Dorota Kozińska, ed. Jolanta Pieńkos. Warsaw: Zachęta Państwowa Galeria Sztuki i Autorzy, 2003, 31–7 (Polish)/253–61 (English).

'Strings Attached', in *Devil-may-care: The Nordic Pavilion at the 50th Venice Biennial 2003*, eds. Anne Karin Jortveit and Andrea Kroksnes. Oslo: Office for Contemporary Art Norway, 2003, 116–25.

'Women as the Topic', in *Women Who Ruled: Queens, Goddesses, Amazons in Renaissance and Baroque Art*, ed. Annette Dixon. Published on the occasion of the exhibition *Women Who Rule: Queens, Goddesses, Amazons 1500–1650*. London: Merrell, in association with the University of Michigan Museum of Art, 2002, 61–96.

'The Dissolution of the World', in *Martijn Schuppers: Early Monograph*, 2002, 14–21.

'Companion Portraits: A Collaborative Project by Rembrandt van Rijn & Ken Aptekar', in exhibition brochure. New York: Pamela Auchincloss Project Space, May 2001, 1–4.

'George Deem and Peter Angelo Simon: Timely Conversation', in *George Deem and Peter Angelo Simon: Paintings and Photographs in Conversation*, with an introduction by John W. Streetman III. Evansville, IN: Evansville Museum of Arts and Science, 2001, 4–40.

'Beckoning Bernini', in *Louise Bourgeois: Memory and Architecture*. Madrid: Museo Nacional Reina Sofía, 2000, 75–85.

'Ann Veronica Janssens: Labo de Lumière/Light in Life's Lab', in *Ann Veronica Janssens: Une image différente dans chaque oeil/A Different Image in Each Eye*, ed. Laurent Jacob, French trans. by Daniel Vander Gucht. Liège: Espace 251 Nord, 1999, 73–102.

'Zwarte Piet's *Bal Masqué*', in *Zwarte Piet, Anna Fox*. London: Black Dog Publishing, 1999, 1–11.

'Points of Departure: Portraits of the Body's Cover-Up', in *Jeannette Christensen/Kim Soo-Ja* (exhibition catalogue). Feldbach, Austria: Kunsthalle Feldbach (Steirischer herbst), 1999, 4–23.

'David Reed's *275*: A Story of Erotic Vision', in *David Reed Paintings: Moving Pictures*. San Diego: Museum of Contemporary Art San Diego, 1998, 36–49.

'Looking at the Other Side with Lili Dujourie', in *The Fascinating Faces of Flanders: 58/98 Two Hours Wide or Two Hours Long*. Antwerp: City of Antwerp, 1998, 188–92.

'Larger than Life: Reading the Corcoran Collection', in *Ken Aptekar: Talking to Pictures*. Washington, DC: Corcoran Gallery of Art, 1997, 5–12.

'De verbeelding van vrouwen', in *Cahier Charlotte van Pallandt*. Scheveningen: Museum Beelden aan zee, September 1995, 39–56.

'Verbeelding: verschijningsvormen van narcisme'/'Imagination: Manifestations of Narcissism', in Edwin Janssen, *Narcissus en de poel des verderfs/Narcissus and the Pool of Corruption*. Rotterdam, Museum Boijmans Van Beuningen, 1994, 33–50.

## Books and special issues edited

*Journal of Visual Culture: Acts of Translation*, 6:1, April 2007 (ed. with Joanne Morra).

*Inge Boer: Uncertain Territories*. Boundaries in Cultural Analysis. Amsterdam: Rodopi, 2006 (ed. with Bregje van Eekelen and Patricia Spyer).

*The Artemisia Files: Artemisia Gentileschi for Feminists and Other Thinking People*. Chicago, IL: University of Chicago Press, 2005.

*Inge E. Boer: Disorienting Vision: Rereading Stereotypes in French Orientalist Texts and Images*. Amsterdam and New York: Rodopi, 2004.

*Narrative Theory: Critical Concepts in Literary and Cultural Studies*, vols I–IV. London and New York: Routledge, 2004.

*Cultural History: Straddling Borders. John Neubauer zum 70. Geburtstag*. Special issue of *arcadia (International Journal of Literary Studies)*, 38:2, 2003 (ed. with Jan van Luxemburg).

*The Practice of Cultural Analysis: Exposing Interdisciplinary Interpretation*. Stanford, CA: Stanford University Press, 1999.

*Acts of Memory: Cultural Recall in the Present*. Hanover, NH: University Press of New England, 1999 (with Jonathan Crewe and Leo Spitzer).

*ASCA Brief: Intellectual Traditions in Movement*. Amsterdam: ASCA Press, 1998 (ed. with Thomas Elsaesser, Burcht Pranger, Beate Roessler, Hent de Vries and Willem Weststeijn).

*ASCA Brief: Visions and Voices of Otherness*. Amsterdam: ASCA Press, 1997 (ed. with Thomas Elsaesser, Burcht Pranger, Hent de Vries and Willem Weststeijn).

*Passagen 2000: The City, Pace and Space. Parallax*, 12, July–September 1999 (ed. with David Vanderburgh).

*Territorialism and Desire. European Journal for Semiotic Studies*, 9:1, 1997 (ed. with Mario Caro).

*Dire l'indicible. Une écriture moderne de la vision. Etudes littéraires*, 28:3, 1996 (ed. with Monique Moser-Verrey).

*ASCA Brief: Issues in Cultural Analysis*. Kampen: Kok Pharos, 1996 (ed. with Thomas Elsaesser, Burcht Pranger, Patricia Spyer, Hent de Vries and Willem Weststeijn).

*The Point of Theory*. Amsterdam: Amsterdam University Press/New York: Continuum, 1994 (ed. with Inge Boer).

*Anti-Covenant: Counter-Reading Women's Lives in the Hebrew Bible*. Sheffield, UK: Sheffield Academic Press and the Almond Press, 1989.

*Visual Poetics. Style*, 22:2, 1988.

*Psychopoetics at Work. Style*, 18:3, 1984.

*Psychopoetics: Theory. Poetics*, 13:4/5, 1984.

*Literaire genres en hun gebruik*. Muiderberg: Coutinho, 1981.

*Mensen van papier. Over personages in de literatuur*. Assen: Van Gorcum, 1980.

## Book chapters and articles

'"You Do What You Have To Do": A Response To Joseph Frügtl', *Krisis, Journal for Contemporary Philosophy*, Issue 1, 2008, 59–69.

'Exhibition as Film', in *(Re)Visualizing National History: Museums and National Identities in Europe in the New Millennium*, ed. Robin Ostow. Toronto: University of Toronto Press, 2008, 15–47.

'Gemengde Gevoelens', in *Denkwerk: Cahier EAJ*. Uitgave in het kader van het Programma Een Ander Justitie, Den Haag: Ministerie van Justitie, 2008, 118–33.

'Phantom Sentences', in *Phantom Sentences: Essays in Linguistics and Literature Presented to Ann Banfield*, eds. Robert S. Kawashima, Gilles Philippe and Thelma Sowley. Bern: Peter Lang, 2008, 17–42.

'Loving Yusuf: A Story of Taboos', *Hecate: An Interdisciplinary Journal of Women's Liberation*, 33:2, 2007, 14–30.

'A Thousand and One Voices', *The Amsterdam International Electronic Journal for Cultural Narratology*, no. 4, Autumn 2007; http://cf.hum.uva.nl/narratology/a07_bal.htm

'Far Encounters: Looking Desire', in *Ways of Seeing, Ways of Speaking*, eds. Kristie S. Fleckenstein, Sue Hum and Linda T. Calendrillo. West Lafayette: Parlor Press, 2007, 179–202.

'What If? The Language of Affect', in *In(ter)discipline: New Languages for Criticism*, eds. Gillian Beer, Malcolm Bowie and Beate Perrey. London: Modern Humanities Research Association and Maney Publishing, 2007, 6–24.

'Lost in Space, Lost in the Library', in *Essays in Migratory Aesthetics*, eds. Sam Durrant and Catherine Lord. Thamyris Intersecting no. 17. Amsterdam: Rodopi, 2007, 23–36.

'From Cultural Studies to Cultural Analysis', *Kritische Berichte: Zeitschrift für Kunst- und Kulturwissenschaften*, 2, 2007, 33–44.

'Lost in Space: the Violence of Language', in *Interpretations: European Research Project for Poetics and Hermeneutics*, vol. 1: *Violence and Art*, ed. Kata Kulavkova. Skopje: Macedonian Academy of Sciences and Arts, 2007, 53–68.

'Exhibition as Film', in *Exhibition Experiments*, eds. Sharon MacDonald and Paul Basu. Oxford: Blackwell, 2007, 71–93.

'Translating Translations', *Journal of Visual Culture*, 6, April 2007, 5–11; 109–24.

'Migratory Aesthetics', in *Another Publication*. Rotterdam: Piet Zwart Institute, 2007, 13–19.

'Women's Rembrandt', in *Museums after Modernism: Strategies of Engagement*, eds. Griselda Pollock and Joyce Zemans. Oxford: Blackwell, 2007, 40–69.

'The Pain of Images', in *Beautiful Suffering: Photography and the Traffic in Pain*, eds. Mark Reinhardt, Holly Edwards and Erina Duganne. Chicago, IL: University of Chicago Press, 2007, 93–115.

'LOOPS & GAPS: Video as Entrance into the Unknown', *The Amsterdam International Electronic Journal for Cultural Narratology*, no. 3, Autumn 2006; http://cf.hum.uva.nl/narratology/a06_bal.html

'Facing Severance', in *Intermédialités*, ed. Johanne Villeneuve, no. 8, Autumn 2006, 189–210.

'Nothing is Missing', in *Intermédialités*, ed. Johanne Villeneuve, no. 8, Autumn 2006, 189–224.

'Lepljive podobe: krčenje časovne dimenzije v umetnosti trajana' ('Sticky Images: The Foreshortening of Time in an Art of Duration'), *Likovne Besede (Art Words)*, Summer 2006, 39–51. Ljubljana: Union of the Slovene Fine Artists Associations, 2006.

'Affekt als kulturelle Kraft', Einleitung in *Affekte. Analysen ästhetisch-medialer Prozesse*, eds. Antje Krause-Wahl, Heike Oehlschlägel and Serjoscha Wiemer. Bielefeld: transcript Verlag, 2006, 7–19.

'Metaphoring: Making a Niche of Negative Space', in *Metaphoricity and the Politics of Mobility*, eds. Maria Margaroni and Effie Yiannopoulou. Amsterdam and New York: Rodopi, 2006, 159–80.

‘Dreaming Art’, in *Psychoanalysis and the Image: Transdisciplinary Perspectives*, ed. Griselda Pollock. Oxford: Blackwell, 2006, 30–59.

‘Faithfully Submitted: The Logic of the Signature in Marcel Proust’s *A la recherche*’, in *Sign Here! Handwriting in the Age of New Media*, eds. Sonja Neef, José van Dijck and Eric Ketelaar. Amsterdam: Amsterdam University Press, 2006, 150–63.

‘Erste Person, zweite Person, dieselbe Person. Zum Verhältnis von Ausstellen und Beschreiben aus narratologischer Sicht’, in *Narration und Geschlecht. Texte – Medien – Episteme*, eds. Sigrid Nieberle and Elisabeth Strowick. Köln, Wiemar, Wien: Böhlau Verlag, 2006, 283–314.

‘Aestheticizing Catastrophe’, in *Reading Charlotte Salomon*, eds. Michael P. Steinberg and Monica Bohm-Duchen. Ithaca, NY, and London: Cornell University Press, 2006, 167–93.

‘What If … Exploring “Unnaturality”’, trans. into Norwegian, as: ‘Hva om? Å utforske det som ikke er naturlig’ (trans. by Harald Nortun), in *Estetiske teknologier 1700–2000*, vol. 2, eds. Anne Beate Maurseth and Erik Østerud. Oslo: Scandinavian Academic Press, 2005, 157–71.

‘Food, Form, and Visibility: *Glub* and the Aesthetics of Everyday Life’, *Postcolonial Studies,* 8:1, 2005, 51–77. Reprinted in *Enigma Objekta – Zbornik teorijskih tekstova*, eds. Gordan Karabogdan and Nikica Klobuèar. Zagreb: I.T.GRAF, 2005, 9–23.

‘Introduction’, in *The Artemisia Files: Artemisia Gentileschi for Feminists and Other Thinking People*, ed. Mieke Bal. Chicago, IL: University of Chicago Press, 2005, ix–xxv.

‘Grounds of Comparison’, in *The Artemisia Files: Artemisia Gentileschi for Feminists and Other Thinking People*, ed. Mieke Bal. Chicago, IL: University of Chicago Press, 2005, 129–68.

‘To Read a Picture’, in *The J. Hillis Miller Reader*, ed. Julian Wolfreys. Edinburgh: Edinburgh University Press, 2005, 82–8.

‘Interdisciplinary Approaches to Narrative’, in *Encyclopedia of Narrative Theory*, eds. David Herman, Manfred Jahn and Marie-Laure Ryan. London and New York: Routledge, 2005, 250–2.

‘Visual Narrativity’, in *Encyclopedia of Narrative Theory*, eds. David Herman, Manfred Jahn and Marie-Laure Ryan. London and New York: Routledge, 2005, 629–33.

‘The Violence of Gender’, in *A Companion to Gender Studies*, eds. Philomena Essed, David Theo Goldberg and Audrey Kobayashi. Oxford: Blackwell, 2005, 530–43.

‘Light Writing: Portraiture in a Post-Traumatic Age’, in *The Photograph*, ed. Dawne McCance. Special issue of *Mosaic* (*A Journal for the Interdisciplinary Study of Literature*), 27:4, December 2004, 1–19.

‘Figuration’, *PMLA (Publication of the Modern Language Association of America)*, 119:5, October 2004, 1289–92.

‘Akte des Schauens: Proust und die visuelle Kultur’ trans. Maria Imhof and Kirsten Kramer, in *Marcel Proust und die Kunste*, eds. Wolfram Nitsch and Riner Zaiser. Frankfurt am Main and Leipzig: Insel Verlag, 2004, 90–111.

‘Over-Writing as Un-Writing: Descriptions, World-Making, and Novelistic Time’, in *Narrative Theory: Critical Concepts in Literary and Cultural Studies*, vol. I, ed. Mieke Bal. London/New York: Routledge, 2004, 341–88.

‘Exposing the Public’, in *Die Spur durch den Spiegel: Der Film in der Kultur der Moderne*, eds. Malte Hagener, Johann N. Schmidt and Michael Wedel. Berlin: Bertz-Verlag, 2004, 51–64.

'Cultuur en traditie', in *Denken over cultuur*, ed. P. van Zilfhout. Heerlen: Open Universiteit Nederland, 2003, 225–55.
'Embracing the Horizon', in *Cultural History: Straddling Borders. John Neubauer zum 70. Geburtstag*', eds. Mieke Bal and Jan van Luxemburg. Special issue of *arcadia (International Journal of Literary Studies*, 38:2, 2003, 414–18.
'De droom als theater: De droomduiding in het licht van hedendaagse cultuurstudies', in *De droomduiding herdacht: Essays over cultuuronderzoek en psychoanalyse*, ed. Mieke Taat. Amsterdam: Uitgeverij Boom, 2003, 93–107.
'Mieke Bal's Reply to the Responses to Her Article "Visual Essentialism and the Object of Visual Culture" (*Journal of Visual Culture* 2, 1, 2003: 5–32)', *Journal of Visual Culture*, 2:2, 2003, 260–8.
'Allo-Portraits', in *Mirror or Mask: Self-Representation in the Modern Age*, eds. David Blostein and Pia Kleber. Berliner Theaterwissenschaft 11. Berlin: VISTAS Verlag, 2003, 11–43.
'Meanwhile: Literature in an Expanded Field', *AUMLA (Journal of the Australasian Universities Language & Literature Association)*, 99, May 2003, 1–22.
'Anthropometamorphose – Sich verzweigende Pfade und Kristalle in Louise Bourgeois' Philosophie der Temporalität'/' "Anthropometamorphosis": Forking Paths and Crystals in Louise Bourgeois' Philosophy of Temporality', in *Louise Bourgeois – Intime abstraktionene/Louise Bourgeois: Intimate Abstractions*, eds. Beatrice E. Stammer et al. Berlin: Akademie der Künste, 2003, 116–44.
'Antropometamorfoza: rozwidlające się ścieżki I kryształw filozofii czasu Louise Bourgeois' (trans. Dorota Kozińska), *Teksty Drugie*, 2/3, 2003, 314–29.
'Her Majesty's Masters', in *The Art Historian: National Traditions and Institutional Practices*, ed. Michael F. Zimmermann. Williamstown, MA: Sterling and Francine Clark Art Institute, 2003, 81–109.
'Critique of Voice: The Open Score of her Face', in *Travelling Concepts III: Memory, Narrative, Image*, ed. Nancy Pedri. Amsterdam: ASCA Press, 2003, 91–114.
'From Cultural Studies to Cultural Analysis: "A Controlled Reflection on the Formation of Method" ', in *Interrogating Cultural Studies: Theory, Politics and Practice*, ed. Paul Bowman. London: Pluto Press, 2003, 30–40.
'Norman Bryson, British Historian of Art and Visual Culture', in *Key Writers on Art: The Twentieth Century*, ed. Chris Murray. London and New York: Routledge, 2003, 62–8.
'Visual Essentialism and the Object of Visual Culture', *Journal of Visual Culture*, 2:1, 2003, 5–32.
'Autotopography: Louise Bourgeois as Builder', *Biography: An Interdisciplinary Quarterly* 25:1, Winter 2002, 180–202. Also in *Interfaces: Women, Autobiography, Image, Performance*, eds. Sidonie Smith and Julia Watson, 163–85. Ann Arbor: University of Michigan Press, 2003.
'Descrizioni, costruzione di mondi e tempo della narrazione', in *Il romanzo*, vol. II: *Le Forme*, ed. Franco Moretti. Milan: Einaudi, 2002, 189–224.
'The Genius of Rome: Putting Things Together', *Journal of Visual Culture*, 1:1, 2002, 25–45.
'Der Rembrandt der Frauen', in *Korrespondenzen: Visuelle Kulturen zwischen Früher Neuzeit und Gegenwart*, eds. Matthias Bickenbach and Axel Fliethmann. Köln: DuMont Literatur und Kunst Verlag, 2002, 27–54.
'Yesterday Isn't What It Used to Be', *Documents 21*, Fall 2001/Winter 2002, 11–23.

'Fragmented Bodies' (ch. 7 of *Louise Bourgeois' Spider: The Architecture of Art-Writing*, trans. Petr and Olga Serebriany), *Novy Mir Isskustva (The New World of Art)*, 23, 2001, 24–8 (St. Petersburg).

'Dreaming Art', *Umění/Art* (Journal of the Institute for Art History of the Academy of Sciences of the Czech Republic), 5:XLIX, 2001, 370–83.

'Prosthetic Poetics', in *Homo Orthopedicus: le corps et ses prothèses à l'époque (post)-moderniste*, eds. Nathalie Roelens and Wanda Strauven. Paris, Budapest and Turin: L'Harmattan, 2001, 139–66.

'*Mise en scène*: Zur Inszenierung von Subjektivität' (trans. from the English by Sonja Neef), in *Ästhetik der Inszenieurung. Dimensionen eines künstlerischen, kulturellen und gesellschaftlichen Phänomens*, eds. Josef Früchtl and Jörg Zimmermann. Frankfurt am Main: Suhrkamp Verlag, 2001, 198–221.

'Jeannette Christensen', *Likovne besede (Artwords)*, Winter 2001, 57/58, 98–102.

'Legal Lust: Literary Litigations', in *Writing against Legal Racism: Law and Literature Explorations*, eds. Judith Grbich and Peter Hutchings. Special issue of *The Australian Feminist Law Journal*, 15 December 2001, 1–22.

'Postmodern Theology as Cultural Analysis', in *The Blackwell Companion to Postmodern Theology*, ed. Graham Ward. Oxford: Blackwell, 2001, 33–23.

'Pour une histoire pervertie', in *Résurgences baroques: les trajectoires d'un processus transculturel*, eds. Nicolas Goyer and Walter Moser. Brussels: Éditions de la Lettre Volée, 2001, 61–88.

'La répétition, la tête dans les nuages'/'Rehearsal, Head in the Clouds', in *Action, on tourne/Action, We're Filming*, ed. Laurence Gateau. Nice: Villa Arson, 2001, 34–73.

'Voix/voie narrative: la voix métaphorée', in *La Voix Narrative: Cahier de Narratologie*, vol. 1, no. 10, ed. Jean-Louis Brau. Nice: Centre de Narratologie Appliquée, 2001, 9–36.

'Mission Impossible: Postcards, Pictures, and Parasites', in *Religion and Media*, eds. Hent de Vries and Samuel Weber. Stanford, CA: Stanford University Press, 2001, 241–68.

'Introduction: Travelling Concepts and Cultural Analysis', in *Travelling Concepts: Text, Subjectivity, Hybridity*, eds. Joyce Goggin and Sonja Neef. Amsterdam: ASCA Press, 2001, 7–25.

'Performance and Performativity', in *Exploding Aesthetics*, eds. Annette W. Balkema and Henk Slager. Special issue of *Lier en Boog*, 16, 2001, 108–24. Expanded version in: *Kultur – Analysen* (Interventionen 10), ed. Jörg Huber. Zurich: Instituts für Theorie der Gestaltung und Kunst an der Hochschule für Gestaltung und Kunst and Edition Voldemeer 2001, 197–241.

'Three-Way Misreading', *Diacritics*, 30:1, 2001, 2–24.

'Pour une interprétation intempestive', in *Où en est l'interprétation de l'oeuvre d'art?*, ed. Régis Michel. Paris: Musée du Louvre and École Nationale Supérieure des Beaux-Arts, 2000, 239–67.

'Heteroglossia', in *Encyclopedia of Feminist Theories*, ed. Lorraine Code. London: Routledge, 2000, 24–5.

'Narratology', in *Encyclopedia of Feminist Theories*, ed. Lorraine Code. London: Routledge, 2000, 357–9.

'Poetics, Today', in special issue 'Harshav Festschrift', *Poetics Today*, 21:3, 2000, 479–502.

'Enfolding Feminism', in *Feminist Consequences: Theory for the New Century*, eds. Elisabeth Bronfen and Misha Kavka. New York: Columbia University Press, 2001, 21–52.

'Auf die Haut/Unter die Haut: Barockes steigt an die Oberfläche', in *Barock: Neue Sichtweisen einer Epoche*, ed. Peter J. Burgard. Wien, Köln, Weimar: Böhlau Verlag, 2001, 17–51.

'Fantasy and the Mirror of Nature', in *Imagination und Wirklichkeit: Zum Verhältnis von mentalen und realen Bildern in der Kunst der frühen Neuzeit*, eds. Klaus Krüger and Alessandro Nova. Mainz: Verlag Philipp von Zabern, 2000, 183–94.

'Ecstatic Aesthetics: Metaphoring Bernini', in *Critical Issues*, monograph, series 4/2000 of Artspace Visual Art Centre, Sydney, 2000 (32 pp.).

'Religious Canon and Literary Identity', *European Electronic Journal for Feminist Exegesis*, 2/2000 (no page nos.).

'Visual Narrativity', in *The Visual-Narrative Matrix: Interdisciplinary Collisions and Collusions*, ed. Graham Coulter-Smith. Southampton: Southampton Institute, 2000, 7–16.

'Sticky Images: The Foreshortening of Time in an Art of Duration', in *Time and the Image*, ed. Carolyn Bailey Gill. Manchester: Manchester University Press, 2000, 79–99.

'Memory Acts: Performing Subjectivity', *Performance Research*, 5:3, 2000, 102–14.

'The Spirit as Parasite', in special issue 'Text and Spirit', from the Tanner Lectures on Human Values of Western Humanities, *Western Humanities Review*, LIII:4, Winter 1999–2000, 315–35.

'Crossroad Theory and Travelling Concepts: From Cultural Studies to Cultural Analysis', in *The Future of Cultural Studies: Essays in Honour of Joris Vlasselaers*, eds. Jan Baetens and José Lambert. Leuven: Leuven University Press, 2000, 3–21.

'Snow White in the Wrong Story: Cultural Analysis, Aesthetics, and Catastrophic Culture', in *Aesthetic Theory, Art and Popular Culture*, ed. Jostein Gripsrud. Kulturstudier no. 8. Kristiansand: Nordic Academic Press, 1999, 33–57.

'Selbstporträt in einem facettierten Spiegel', in *Schneewittchen: über den Mythos kalter Schönheit. Ein Eiskristallbuch*, eds. Gerda Buxbaum and Christina Lammer. Tübingen: Konkursbuchverlag Claudia Gehrke, 1999, 105–17.

'Narrative Inside Out: Louise Bourgeois' "Spider" as Theoretical Object', *Oxford Art Journal*, 22:2, 1999, 101–26.

'Basic Instincts and Their Discontents', in *Text and Visuality: Word and Image Interactions* 3, eds. M. Heusser et al. Amsterdam and Atlanta, GA: Rodopi, 1999, 13–32.

'Introduction', in *Acts of Memory: Cultural Recall in the Present*, eds. Mieke Bal, Jonathan Crewe and Leo Spitzer. Hanover, NH, and London: University Press of New England, 1999, vii–xvii.

'Memories in the Museum: Preposterous Histories', in *Acts of Memory: Cultural Recall in the Present*, eds. Mieke Bal, Jonathan Crewe and Leo Spitzer. Hanover, NH, and London: University Press of New England, 1999, 171–90.

'Geelzucht en Schone Letteren', *De Witte Raaf*, 77, January–February 1999, 1–3.

'All in the Family: Familiarity and Estrangement According to Marcel Proust', in *The Familial Gaze*, ed. Marianne Hirsch. Dartmouth, NH: University Press of New England, 1999, 223–47.

'Ruumiiseen sisällytetty Tila' ('Space, Incorporated'), in *Kuvasta tilaan*, ed. Kirsi Saarikangas. Tampere: Vastapaino, 1999, 299–333.
'Frame Her If You Can!' *Art Bulletin of Nationalmuseum Stockholm*, 5, 1998, 137–52.
'Quoting Caravaggio', in *Center 18: Record of Activities and Research Reports, June 1997–May 1998*. Washington, DC: National Gallery of Art, Center for Advanced Study in the Visual Arts, 1998, 45–8.
'Seeing Signs: The Use of Semiotics for the Understanding of Visual Art', in *The Subjects of Art History: Historical Objects in Contemporary Perspectives*, eds. Mark A. Cheetham, Michael Ann Holly and Keith Moxey. New York: Cambridge University Press, 1998, 74–93.
'Close Reading Today: From Narratology to Cultural Analysis', in *Grenzüberschreitungen: Narratologie im Kontext/Transcending Boundaries: Narratology in Context*, eds. Walter Grünzeig and Andreas Solbach. Tübingen: Gunter Narr Verlag, 1998, 19–40.
'A Meagre One Thousand Words for Stefan Germer', *Texte zur Kunst*, 8:31, 1998, 43–5.
'Reading Bathsheba: From Master Codes to Misfits', in *Rembrandt's 'Bathsheba Reading King David's Letter'*, ed. Ann Jensen Adams. New York and Cambridge: Cambridge University Press, 1998, 119–46.
'Semiotics as a Theory of Art', in *Encyclopedia of Aesthetics*, vol. 4, ed. Michael Kelly. New York and Oxford: Oxford University Press, 1998, 263–7 (with Norman Bryson).
'Narrative and the Visual and Literary Arts', in *Encyclopedia of Aesthetics*, vol. 3, ed. Michael Kelly. New York and Oxford: Oxford University Press, 1998, 328–31.
'Charles Sanders Peirce', in *Encyclopedia of Aesthetics*, vol. 3, ed. Michael Kelly. New York and Oxford: Oxford University Press, 1998, 448–51.
'Back to the Future: Art and Its History', *Semiotica*, 119:3/4, 1998, 287–308.
'Alter Ego: le regard hétéropathique dans *A la recherche du temps perdu*', in *Texte: Iconicité et Narrativité*, ed. J. Leblanc. Toronto: Trinity College, 1998, 107–25.
'Introduction to *Reading "Rembrandt": Beyond the Word-Image Opposition*', in *Interdisciplinarity: Essays from the Literature*, ed. William H. Newell. New York: The College Entrance Examination Board, 1998, 363–87.
'Space, Inc.', in *Signs & Space/Raum & Zeichen*, Proceedings of International Conference on the Semiotics of Space and Culture in Amsterdam, eds. E.W.B. Hess-Lüttich, Jürgen E. Müller and Aart van Zoest. Tübingen: Gunter Narr Verlag, 1998, 199–223.
'Semiotics and Art History: A Discussion of Context and Senders', in *The Art of Art History: A Critical Anthology*, ed. Donald Preziosi. Oxford: Oxford University Press, 1998, 242–56 (with Norman Bryson).
'Túl a szó-kép oppozíción (an adaptation of ch. 1 of *Reading "Rembrandt": Beyond the Word-Image Opposition*)', *Enigma*, 14–15, 1998, 132–64.
'Shifting Visions: History and the Contemporary Collection' (and discussion), in *The Curator, the Museum, the Collection*, International Committee of Museums of Modern Art (CIMAM) Annual Meeting, Barcelona, 1997. Barcelona: Fundación 'la Caixa', 1997, 27–37.
'Vers une narratologie visuelle: poétique du détail dans la narration. L'exemple de Proust', in *Los Géneros Literarios: Curso Superior de Narratología Narratividad-Dramaticida*, ed. María Concepción Pérez. Seville: University of Seville, 1997, 17–30.

'Documenta X: le parcours', *Omnibus* hors-série, October 1997, 8–40.

'Narratologie et dialogue', in *Le dialogique*, eds. Daniel Luzzati et al. Bern: Peter Lang, 1997, 259–68.

'Looking at Love: An Ethics of Vision', *Diacritics*, 27:1, 1997, 59–72.

'Narcissus' Vision and Semiotic Space', *European Journal for Semiotic Studies*, 9:1, 1997, 139–57.

'Een jongetje van zes en een plaatje van een moeder', in *Liber amicarum. Over kunst, literatuur en filosofie*, eds. J.J. Pott, V. Vasteling, R. van de Vall and K. Vintges. Meppel: Boom, 1997, 96–107.

'In het museum: hedendaags exhibitionisme', in *Teken en betekenis*, eds. Jan C.A. van de Lubbe and Aart J.A. van Zoest. Haarlem: Aramith, 1997, 126–40.

'Focalization', in *Narratology: An Introduction*, ed. and with an introduction by Susana Onega and José Angel García Landa. London and New York: Longman, 1996, 115–28.

'Reading Art?' in *Generations and Geographies in the Visual Arts: Feminist Reading*, ed. Griselda Pollock. London: Routledge, 1996, 25–41.

'Proust et l'image primitive', *Gradiva, Revue Européenne d'anthropologie littéraire*, 1:1, 1996, 59–70.

'Un objet d'obsession: la photo d'outre-tombe', *Vives lettres*, 1:2, 1996, 75–91.

'Lacan in dialoog: Kaja Silverman en film', in *In dialoog met Lacan*, eds. Nathalie Kok and Kees Nuijten. Meppel: Boom, 1996, 195–216.

'Le verre grossissant', *Etudes littéraires*, 28:3, 1996, 13–28.

'Second-Person Narrative', in *Painting and Narrative*, ed. Michael Worton. Special issue of *Paragraph*, 19:3, 1996, 179–204.

'Semiotic Elements in Academic Practices (Critical Response)', *Critical Inquiry*, 22, Spring 1996, 569–85.

'The Discourse of the Museum', in *Thinking About Exhibitions*, eds. Reesa Greenberg, Bruce Ferguson and Sandy Nairne. New York: Routledge, 1996, 201–18.

'Signs in Painting', *The Art Bulletin*, LXXVIII:1, 1996, 6–9.

'The Gaze in the Closet', in *Vision in Context: Historical and Contemporary Perspectives on Sight*, ed. Teresa Brennan and Martin Jay. London: Routledge, 1996, 139–54.

'Franco Adami', *Tableau. Fine Arts Magazine*, 19:1, 1996, 106–11.

'Cultural Studies and Philosophy', *Parallax*, 1:1, 1995, 110–13.

'Reading the Gaze: The Construction of Gender in "Rembrandt"', in *Vision & Textuality*, eds. Stephen Melville and Bill Readings. London: Macmillan, 1995, 147–73.

'Bird Watching: Visuality and Lesbian Desire in Marcel Proust's *A la recherche du temps perdu*', *Thamyris*, 2:1, 1995, 45–66.

'Lire l'un avec l'autre: Chardin et Proust', in *Rhétorique et image. Textes en hommage à A. Kibédi Varga*, eds. Leo Hoek and Kees Meerhoff. Amsterdam and Atlanta, GA: Rodopi, 1995, 179–97.

'Plaidoyer pour un personnage plat: à propos d'une page de Proust', in *Le personnage romanesque. Cahiers de narratologie*, ed. Gérard Lavergne. Nice: Association des Publications de la Faculté des Lettres de Nice, 1995, 11–28.

'Zichtbaar ont-zettend: Proust en het fotografisch oog', in *Marcel Proust Vereniging Jaarboek*, eds. J. Plessen et al. Amsterdam: Marcel Proustvereniging and Bosbespers, 1993–4, 77–93.

'De Turner-turn. Over de ritueelgekte in de literatuurwetenschap in de jaren tachtig', *Antropologische verkenningen*, 13:4, 1994, 56–68.

Four chapters – 'Verhalende teksten', 237–62; 'De vertelsituatie', 263–90; 'Effecten', 319–42; and 'Interpretatie', 343–64 – in *Inleiding Letterkunde*, part 1: *Literatuuranalyse*, ed. Lizette Duyvendak. Heerlen: Open Universiteit, 1994.

'Instantanés', in *Proust contemporain*, ed. Sophie Bertho. Special issue of *C.R.I.N.*, 28, 1994, 117–30.

'The Rape of Lucrece and The Story of W', in *Reclamations of Shakespeare*, ed. A.J. Hoenselaars. Amsterdam: Rodopi, 1994, 75–104.

'Een gebruiksaanwijzing in gebruik: narratologie van onderzoek naar onderwijs', *De Nieuwe Taalgids*, 87:4, 1994, 352–5.

'Head Hunting: "Judith" on the Cutting Edge of Knowledge', *Journal for Studies on the Old Testament*, 63, 1994, 3–34.

'Kiekjes', in *Virtute e canoscenza*, eds. Rob de Jong, David Rijser and Jan de Ruijter. Amsterdam: Barlaeus Gymnasium, 1994, 63–72.

'Identification et apprentissage de la compassion: Proust et la photographie', in *(En)jeux de la communication romanesque. Hommage à Françoise van Rossum-Guyon*, eds. Suzanne van Dijk and Christa Stevens. Amsterdam and Philadelphia: Rodopi, 1994, 241–56.

'Dead Flesh, or the Smell of Painting', in *Visual Culture: Images and Interpretations*, eds. Norman Bryson, Michael Holly and Keith Moxey. Hanover, NH, and London: Wesleyan University Press, 1994, 365–83.

'Telling Objects: A Narrative Perspective on Collecting', in *The Cultures of Collecting*, eds. John Elsner and Roger Cardinal. London: Reaktion Books, 1994, 97–115.

'Weliswaar, maar: de binaire oppositie voorbij', *Simulacrum*, 3:1, 1994, 9–12.

'Scared to Death', in *The Point of Theory*, eds. Mieke Bal and Inge E. Boer. Amsterdam: Amsterdam University Press/New York: Continuum, 1994, 32–47.

'A Body of Writing: Judges 19', in *A Feminist Companion to Judges*, ed. Athalya Brenner. Sheffield, UK: Sheffield Academic Press, 1993, 208–30.

'Light in Painting: De-Seminating Art History', in *Deconstruction and the Visual Arts: Art, Media, Architecture*, eds. Peter Brunette and David Wills. New York: Cambridge University Press, 1993, 49–64.

'Vitsen med narratologi', *Tidskrift för litteraturvetenskap*, 2–3, 1993, 3–25.

'Heroism and Proper Names, or the Fruits of Analogy', in *A Feminist Companion to Ruth*, ed. Athalya Brenner. Sheffield, UK: Sheffield Academic Press, 1993, 42–70.

'Letteren, vrouwenstudies, psychoanalyse: een driehoeksverhouding met relatieproblemen', *Allure*, 1, 1993, 89–106.

'The Elders and Susanna', *Biblical Interpretation*, 1:1, 1993, 1–19.

'Metaphors He Lives By', *Semeia*, 61, 1993, 185–207.

'His Master's Eye', in *Modernity and the Hegemony of Vision*, ed. David M. Levin. Berkeley: University of California Press, 1993, 379–404.

'Give and Take', in *Gender, Race, Identity*, eds. Craig Barrow, Katherine Frank, John Phillips and Reed Sanderlin. Chattanooga, TN: Southern Humanities Press, 1993, 3–9.

'First Person, Second Person, Same Person: Narrative as Epistemology', *New Literary History*, 24:2, 1993, 293–320.

'Cultuur en macht, leereenheid 12', in *Denken over cultuur: gebruik en misbruik van een concept*, eds. Auke van Breemen and Johannes Fabian. Heerlen: Open Universiteit, 1993, 327–47.
'Als de dood: theorie, metaforen en het avontuur van wetenschap', inaugural address, monograph, Universiteit van Amsterdam, 1993 (22 pp.).
'Avec son regard de maître', *Protée*, Autumn 1992, 54–68.
'Prema kritickoj naratologiji', in *Suvremena teorija pripovijedanja*, ed. Vladimir Biti. Zagreb: Globus, 1992, 54–68, 313–40.
'Telling, Showing, Showing Off: A Walking Tour', *Critical Inquiry*, Spring 1992, 18, 556–94.
'Over Her Dead Body', in *Literature and Gender*, ed. Iqbal Kaur. New Delhi: D.K. Publishers Ltd, 1992, 3–24.
'Narratology and the Rhetoric of Trashing', *Comparative Literature*, 44:3, 1992, 293–306.
'The Predicament of Semiotics', *Poetics Today*, 13:3, 1992, 543–52.
'Rape: Problems of Intention', in *Feminism and Psychoanalysis*, ed. Elizabeth Wright. Oxford: Blackwell, 1992, 367–71.
'De hang naar houvast', *Opzij*, 20:2, 1992, 51–9.
'Who Cares? Where Stories Come From and What They Do', in *Information in a Healthy Society/Health in the Information Society*, eds. Ad van Berlo and Yvonne Kiwitz-De Ruijter. Knegsel: Akontes Publishing, 1992, 276–81.
'De grenzen van wetenschappelijkheid', *Forum der Letteren*, 33:4, 1992, 275–83.
'The Point of Narratology', *Poetics Today*, 11:4, 1991, 727–53.
'A Body of Writing', *Crossroads/Continuum*, 1:2, 1991, 110–26.
'Semiotics and Art History', *The Art Bulletin*, LXXIII:2, 1991, 174–208 (with Norman Bryson).
'The Politics of Citation', *Diacritics*, Spring 1991, 21:1, 25–45.
'Mooie boel: een driehoeksverhouding in lagen', in *Visies op cultuur en literatuur: opstellen naar aanleiding van het werk van J.J.A. Mooi*, ed. Rien T. Segers. Amsterdam and Atlanta, GA: Rodopi, 1991, 157–62.
'Murder and Difference: Uncanny Sites in an Uncanny World', *Journal of Literature and Theology*, 5:1, 1991, 11–19.
'"Door zuiverheid gedreven": het troebele water van Het land van herkomst van E. du Perron', in *De canon onder vuur. Nederlandse literatuur tegendraads gelezen*, eds. Ernst van Alphen and Maaike Meijer. Amsterdam: Van Gennep, 1991, 122–42.
'Une ou deux choses . . .', *Protée*, 19:1, 1991, 51–60.
'Lots of Writing', *Semeia*, 54, 1991, 77–102; also in *Poetics Today*, 15:1, 1994, 89–114.
'Experiencing Murder: Ritualistic Interpretation of Ancient Texts', in *Victor Turner and the Construction of Cultural Criticism: Between Literature and Anthropology*, ed. Kathleen M. Ashley. Bloomington: Indiana University Press, 1990, 3–20.
'Dealing/With/Women: Daughters in the Book of Judges', in *The Bible and Critical Theory*, ed. Regina Schwartz. Oxford: Blackwell, 1990, 16–39.
'The Rape of Narrative and the Narrative of Rape: Speech Acts and Body Language in Judges', in *Selected Papers from the English Institute*, ed. Elaine Scarry. Baltimore, MD: Johns Hopkins University Press, 1988, 1–32.
'Dis-Semination: "Rembrandt" and the Navel of the Text', *Literature, Interpretation, Theory*, 2, 1990, 145–66.
'De-Disciplining the Eye', *Critical Inquiry*, 16:3, 1990, 506–31.

'Showcase', in *Natuur en cultuur*, eds. Raymond Corbey and Paul van der Grijp. Baarn: Ambo, 1990, 209–19.
'Over haar lijk: waarheid, wetenschap en cultuurverschil', Amsterdam: An Dekker, monograph, 1990.
'Visual Poetics: Reading with the Other Art', in *Theory between the Disciplines: Authority, Vision, Politics*, eds. Martin Kreiswirth and Mark A. Cheetham. Ann Arbor: University of Michigan Press, 1990, 135–50.
'Reading as Empowerment. Teaching the Bible from a Feminist Perspective', in *Teaching the Bible as Literature in Translation*, eds. Barry N. Ohlsen and Yael S. Feldman. New York: The Modern Language Association of America, 1989, 87–92.
'Visual Readers and Textual Viewers', *V/S Versus*, 52/53, 1989, 133–50.
'On Looking and Reading. Word and Image, Visual Poetics, and Comparative Arts', *Semiotica*, 76:3/4, 1989, 283–320.
'Language and Its Motivations', in *Three Cultures: Fifteen Lectures on the Confrontation of Academic Cultures*, a publication of the Stichting Praemium Erasmianum. Rotterdam: Universitaire Pers Rotterdam, 1989, 31–42.
'The Effects of Language', in *Three Cultures: Fifteen Lectures on the Confrontation of Academic Cultures*, a publication of the Stichting Praemium Erasmianum. Rotterdam: Universitaire Pers Rotterdam, 1989, 57–70.
'Literature and its Insistent Other', *Journal of the American Academy of Religion*, LVII:2, 1989, 373–83.
'Geheimpjes uit het rovershol. Een reactie op Evelyn Kellers analyse van wetenschappelijke taal', *Tijdschrift voor vrouwenstudies*, 38, 10, 2, 1989, 271–86.
'Macht, mythe en misverstand of het recht om verkeerd te lezen. Over Richteren 19 en het interpretatieprobleem', monograph, Katholieke Theologische Universiteit Amsterdam, 1989 (40 pp.).
'Beste mensen', in *En zij lachte en het lichtte: scepsis als grondslag voor het zien van vrouwen*, eds. Hanna van Dorsen et al. Voorburg: Protestantse Stichting tot Bevordering van het Bibliotheekwezen en de Lectuurvoorziening in Nederland, 1989, 13–18.
'Eine Notlüge', in *Feministisch gelesen*, vol. 2, eds. Renate Jost, Mieke Korenhof and Eva Renate Schmidt. Stuttgart: Kreuz Verlag, 1988, 47–54.
'Communicatie of eenzijdige macht: Susanna en de ouderlingen in de bijbel en bij Rembrandt', in *Communicatie*, eds. L. Feenstra, R.O. Fock and N.H.H. Beyer. Meppel and Amsterdam: Boom, 1989, 58–87.
'Literatuurwetenschap interdisciplinair', *Spektator*, 18:5, 1988–9, 336–9.
'Rivalität zwischen Männer – Grund der Unterdrückung von Frauen', in *Feministisch gelesen*, vol. 1, eds. Renate Jost, Mieke Korenhof and Eva Renate Schmidt. Stuttgart: Kreuz Verlag, 1988, 60–6.
'Tricky Thematics', *Semeia: An Experimental Journal for Biblical Criticism*, 42, 1988, 133–55.
'Introduction: Visual Poetics', *Style*, 22:2, 1988, 177–82.
'Speech, Murder, Tricks and Gender: Judges 4 and 5', *Recherches sémiotiques/Semiotic Inquiry*, 7:2, 1987, 127–51.
'Myth à la lettre: Freud, Mann, Genesis and Rembrandt, and the Story of the Son', in *Discourse in Psychoanalysis and Literatur*, ed. Shlomith Rimmon-Kenan. London: Methuen, 1987, 57–89.

'Force and Meaning: Rembrandt and the Interdisciplinary Struggle of Psychoanalysis, Semiotics and Aesthetics', *Semiotica*, 63:3/4, 1987, 244–317.

'Virginity: Toward a Feminist Philology', *Dispositio: Revista Hispanica de Semiotica Literaria*, XII, 1987, 30–2, 65–82.

'Naar zijn beeld en gelijkenis, of de identiteit van en tussen vertelinstanties', *Forum der Letteren*, 28:1, 1987, 43–52.

'Tekst en geschiedenis. Reflecties over de sociale kleur van literatuur', in *Verbeelden. Themaboek 10*, eds. Lida Coumou et al. Groningen: Z.U.V., 1987, 9–24.

'Tuer sur parole. Pour une narratologie dynamique', in *Sémiotique et analyse textuelle: description, paraphrase, métalangage*, ed. Maryse Souchard. Winnipeg: Collège Saint Boniface, 1987, 234–77.

'The Language of Subjectivity', in *Linguistics and the Study of Literature*, ed. Th. D'haen. Amsterdam: Rodopi, 1986, 201–17.

'Tell-Tale Theories', *Poetics Today*, 7:3, 1986, 555–64.

'Quelle est la faute de l'abbé Mouret? Pour une narratologie diachronique et polémique', *Australian Journal of French Studies*, 23:2, 1986, 149–68.

'De tekenen des tijds en de tijd als teken', in *De macht van de tekens. Opstellen over maatschappij, tekst en literatuur*, ed. Aart van Zoest. Utrecht: HES, 1986, 71–84

'De Bijbel als volksliteratuur', in *Ik zing mijn lied voor al wie met mij gaat. Vrouwen in de volksliteratuur*, ed. Ria Lemaire. Utrecht: HES, 1986, 45–71. Also in *Eu canto a quen comigo camiña*, ed. Ria Lemaire. Santiago de Compostela: Edicións Laiovento, 1998, 43–70.

'The Bible as Literature: A Critical Escape', *Diacritics*, Winter 1986, 71–9.

'Inconsciences de Chéri; Chéri existe-t'il?', in *Colette, nouvelles approches critiques*, ed. Bernard Bray. Paris: Nizet, 1986, 15–25.

'Sexuality, Sin and Sorrow: The Emergence of the Female Character. A Reading of Genesis 1–3', in special issue 'The Female Body in Western Culture: Semiotic Perspectives', *Poetics Today*, 1985, 6:1–2, 21–42.

'Ruth o come ammettere l'amore. Preliminari a proposito d'un particolare', in *Le donne e i segni. Scrittura, linguaggio, identità nel segno della differenza femminile*, ed. Partizi Magli. Ancona: il lavoro editoriale, 1985, 131–51.

'Semiotiek in de literatuur. Communiceren, vertellen, liegen: de narratieve semiotiek van Bernstein', in *Semiotiek*, ed. Suzette Haakma. Utrecht: Studium Generale, 1985, 40–54.

'Why I? Discussing the Subject in/of Semiotics', *Poetics Today*, 5:4, 1984, 857–965.

'The Rhetoric of Subjectivity', *Poetics Today*, 5:2, 1984, 337–76.

'Pour une théorie critique de la subjectivité narrative', *Lalies*, IV, 1984, 107–48.

'Réfléchir la réflexion: du nom propre à la mise en abyme', *Annali dell'Istituto Universitario Orientale*, Naples, 1984, 7–48.

Preface and Introduction to special issue 'Psychopoetics – Theory', *Poetics*, 13:4/5, 1984, i–ii; 279–98. Also in special issue 'Psychopoetics at Work', *Style*, 18:3, 1984, 239–60.

'Mise en abyme and Metatextuality: Sexual Politics in the Book of Ruth', in *Pragmatics and Stylistics*, eds. W. van Peer and J. Renkema. Leuven and Amersfoort: Acco, 1984, 71–94.

'Verteltheorie', in *Moderne encyclopedie van de wereldliteratuur*, vol. 10, eds. A.G.H. Bachrach et al. Haarlem: De Haan, 1984, 106–8.

'Sexuality, Semiosis and Binarism: A Narratological Comment on Bergren and Arthur', in special issue 'Semiotics and Classical Studies', *Arethusa*, 16:1–2, 1983, 117–35.
'The Semiotics of Symmetry, or the Use of Hermeneutic Models', *V/S Versus*, 35–6, 1983, 7–36.
'Hoe eng is de poort? Het boek Ruth vanuit een feministische visie', *Schrift*, 85, 1983, 30–9.
'Over interpretatie', *Tijdschrift voor vrouwenstudies* 4:13, 1983, 121–34.
'Naar een kritisch gebruik van genre-begrippen', *Schrift*, 90, 1983, 234–40.
'The Narrating and the Focalizing: A Theory of the Agents in Narrative', *Style*, 17:2, 1983, 234–69.
'Verteltheorie als instrument voor ideologiekritiek', in *Feministische theologie*, ed. C. Halkes. Nijmegen: Studium Generale, 1982, 266–80. Revised version: *Spektator*, 13:4, 1983.
'Théorie de la description. L'exemple de Madame Bovary', in *Flaubert. La dimension du texte*, ed. P.M. Wetherhill. Manchester: Manchester University Press, 1982, 175–236.
'Mimesis and Genre Theory in Aristotle's Poetics', *Poetics Today*, 3:1, 1982, 171–80.
'Delila's onschuld. Narratologie, psychoanalyse en ideologiekritiek', *Tijdschrift voor vrouwenstudies*, 3:9, 1982, 34–73.
'Wilde dieren, of de verscheurde eenheid. Over "De Sirenen" van Maria Dermoût', in *Over verhalen gesproken*, eds. J. Hoogteijling and F.C. de Rover. Groningen: Wolters-Noordhoff, 1982, 97–124 (with Ernst van Alphen).
'Structuralism, History and the Semiotics of the Subject: Recent Developments in French Literary Theory', in special issue 'Schwerpunkte der Literaturwissenschaft ausserhalb des deutschen Sprachraums', *Amsterdämmer Beiträge zur neueren Germanistik*, 15, 1982, 55–78.
'On Meanings and Descriptions', in special issue 'The Semiotics of Literary Signification', *Studies in 20th Century Literature*, 6:1&2, 1981–2, 100–48.
'The Laughing Mice, or On Focalization', *Poetics Today*, 2:2, 1981, 203–12
'Notes on Narrative Embedding', *Poetics Today*, 2:2, 1981, 41–59.
'Aristoteles semioticus. Een aantekening bij een voetnoot bij 47a', *Spektator*, 10:6, 1981, 490–5.
'Methoden in de literatuurwetenschap', *Tijdschrift voor vrouwenstudies*, 2:7, 1981, 394–417.
'Logica en realisme. Kanttekeningen bij J.A. Dautzenberg: "De logische opbouw van de verhaaltheorie"', *Forum der Letteren*, 22:2, 1981, 204–6.
'Teksttypen en taalhoudingen', in *Literaire genres en hun gebruik*, ed. Mieke Bal. Muiderberg: Coutinho, 1981, 7–31.
'Narrativité et manipulation', in special issue 'Texte et Idéologie', *Degrés*, 8:24–5, 1980–1, c-1–c-24.
'Descriptions. Etude du discours descriptif dans le texte narratif', *Lalies*, 1, 1980, 99–129.
'L'iconicité narrative', *Zagadnienia Rodzajôw Literackich*, 23:1, 1980, 11–18.
'Tradition et renouvellement. Enseigner la littérature, à quoi bon?' *Le Français dans le monde*, 20:154, 1980, 59–64.
'Huisje, boompje, beestje. Over beschrijvingen in verhalende teksten', *Spektator*, 9:4, 1980, 304–34.

'Structure narrative et signification. Le cas de *Wuthering Heights*', *Neophilologus*, 1980, 333–46 (with Aart van Zoest).

'Flaubert', in *Moderne encyclopedie van de wereldliteratuur*, vol. 3, eds. A.G.H. Bachrach et al. Haarlem: De Haan, 1980, 243–6.

'Wat zijn personages en wat doen we ermee?', in *Mensen van papier. Over personages in de literatuur*, ed. Mieke Bal. Assen: Van Gorcum, 1979, 1–13.

'De homo semioticus en zijn interpretatie van de werkelijkheid', *Hollands Maandblad*, 375, 1979.

'Over lachende muizen en naïve zieners', *Forum der Letteren*, 20:4, 1979, 471–6.

'Mise en abyme et iconicité', *Littérature*, 29, 1978, 116–28.

'Over narratologie, narrativiteit en narratieve tekens', *Spektator*, 7:9, 1978, 528–48.

'Gebruiksaanwijzing bij het bestuderen van de verhaaltheorie van Greimas', internal publication, Instituut voor Algemene literatuurwetenschap, Rijksuniversiteit Utrecht, 1978.

'De grote afstand tussen leerling en literatuur', *NRC Handelsblad*, Cultureel Supplement, 7 April 1978.

'Wanbegrip is nog sterieler' (discussion), *Forum der Letteren*, 18:4, 1977, 301–4.

'Strukturalistische verhaalanalyse: een poging tot sytematisering', *Forum der Letteren*, 18:2, 1977, 105–19 (reprinted in *Romaneske*, 1978).

'L'analyse structurale du récit', *Le Français dans le monde*, 17 July 1977, 6–14.

'Narration et focalisation; pour une théorie des instances du récit', *Poétique*, 29, 1977, 107–27.

'L'enseignement de la narratologie', *Rapports*, 47:2, 1977, 59–64.

'Du nouveau sur Colette', *Rapports*, XLI:4, 1974, 12–23.

'Un roman dans le roman: encadrement ou enchâssement?' *Neophiologus*, LVII:1, 1974, 2–21.

'Fonction de la description romanesque', *Revue des Langues Vivantes*, XL:2, 1974, 132–49.

'Fonction narrative de la description', in *Actes de la journée de travail sur Madame Bovary*, Paris: E.N.S., February 1973, 7–14.

'Colette devant la critique', *Rapports*, XLI:2, 1971, 56–63.

# Index

Note: page numbers in *italics* refer to illustrations.